HITLER STRIKES POLAND

HITLER STRIKES POLAND

Blitzkrieg, Ideology, and Atrocity

Alexander B. Rossino

University Press of Kansas

Published by the University Press of Kansas (Lawrence, Kansas 66049), which was organized by the Kansas Board of Regents and is operated and funded by Emporia State University, Fort Hays State University, Kansas State University, Pittsburg State University, the University of Kansas, and Wichita State University

Library of Congress Cataloging-in-Publication Data

Rossino, Alexander B., 1966–
Hitler strikes Poland : Blitzkrieg, ideology, and
atrocity / Alexander B. Rossino.
p. cm. — (Modern war studies)
Includes bibliographical references and index.
ISBN 0-7006-1234-3 (alk. paper)
1. World War, 1939–1945—Campaigns—Poland.
2. Lightning war. 3. National socialism—Germany.
4. World War, 1939–1945—Atrocities—Poland.
5. World War, 1939–1945—Atrocities—Germany.
I. Title. II. Series.
D765 .R596 2003
940.54'05'09438—DC21   2002151894

British Library Cataloguing in Publication Data is available.

Printed in the United States of America
10 9 8 7 6 5 4 3 2 1

The paper used in this publication meets the minimum requirements of the American National Standard for Permanence of Paper for Printed Library Materials Z39.48-1984.

FOR MY PARENTS

CONTENTS

List of Illustrations   *ix*

Acknowledgments   *xi*

Introduction   *xiii*

1 The Ideological Dimensions of War with Poland   *1*

2 Nazi Radicals and SS Killers   *29*

3 The German Army and the Opening Phase
of Operation TANNENBERG   *58*

4 Nazi Anti-Jewish Policy during the Polish Campaign   *88*

5 Institutional Brutality and German Army Reprisal Policy   *121*

6 From Retaliation to Atrocity:
Wehrmacht Soldiers and Irregular Warfare   *153*

7 Explaining German Brutality   *191*

Conclusion   *227*

Notes   *237*

Glossary   *303*

Bibliography   *305*

Index   *337*

ILLUSTRATIONS

Polish hostages taken by German troops in Bydgoszcz await execution   65

A member of *Einsatzgruppe* IV questions hostages on the Old Market Square in Bydgoszcz   68

Polish hostages collected on the Old Market Square in Bydgoszcz   69

The men of *Einsatzgruppe* IV and the 6th Motorized Order Police Battalion sort prisoners arrested in Bydgoszcz   70

Order policemen from the 6th Motorized Order Police Battalion at work during the *Aktion Schwedenhöhe*   71

An SD officer works with Wehrmacht troops during the search of a building in a Polish city   74

SD officers interrogate a Polish cleric on the street in Sosnowiec   80

SD officers interrogate Polish prisoners arrested in Sosnowiec   81

Demolition of the ruins of the synagogue in Będzin   91

German police publicly humiliate a Jewish man in Sosnowiec   93

A Wehrmacht firing squad executes two hostages in the town of Konin   127

A German soldier stands guard over Jewish men arrested in Aleksandrów Kujawski   131

Wehrmacht guards look on as two ethnic German civilians question Poles arrested for the alleged murder of a fellow ethnic German in Cyców   134

A Reprisal in Częstochowa, 4 September 1939

German troops occupy defensive positions in a park across Strazacka Street, opposite the building from which they took sniper fire   145

German troops guard men pulled from the apartment building on Strazacka Street   146

The terrified captives await German orders   *147*

Two groups of prisoners wait to be "processed"   *148*

Set aflame by German soldiers, smoke rises from the apartment building
out of which the gunshots were allegedly fired   *149*

A view down Strazacka Street toward the marketplace where German
troops led the captives   *150*

German soldiers guard the prisoners on the marketplace   *151*

The execution of prisoners in the park adjacent to Strazacka Street   *152*

Thousands of Polish prisoners of war wait at an open-air holding
center to be processed by German army authorities and sent to other
POW camps   *180*

The commander of the 15th Motorized Infantry Regiment gives the order
for Polish prisoners of war to be executed near Ciepielów   *182*

Troops with the 15th Motorized Infantry Regiment lead Polish POWs to
their execution near Ciepielów   *183*

Soldiers with the 15th Motorized Infantry Regiment survey the bodies of
Polish POWs they have just executed   *184*

An Atrocity in Konskie

German troops order Jewish men into a park in Konskie where they
will be forced to dig a grave for the bodies of German soldiers found
in the area   *187*

German military personnel look on as Jewish men dig a grave for the
four German soldiers   *188*

Jewish men in Konskie wait their turn to dig the grave   *189*

Flanked by a member of her film crew, a distraught Leni Riefenstahl
looks on during the murder of Jews in Konskie   *190*

German troops in Kielce cut the hair of a Jewish man   *211*

German soldiers and civilians look on as a Jewish man is forced to cut
the beard of another Jewish man   *213*

Map: Advance of the XIII Corps, September 1–17, 1939   *155*

ACKNOWLEDGMENTS

The list of people to whom I owe a debt of gratitude for their help during the many years of researching and writing this study is extensive. My thanks go above all to my mentor and friend, Frederick Marquardt, at Syracuse University, whose high standards of professional training and unflagging support for my work helped make me the historian I am today. I would like to extend my appreciation as well to professors David Bennett, Michael Miller, and Daniel Field, also at Syracuse University, for their excellent instruction, careful reading of my work, and helpful comments. My colleague Geoffrey Megargee at the Center for Advanced Holocaust Studies, U.S. Holocaust Memorial Museum (USHMM), generously took the time to read the manuscript and to suggest ways it could be improved. Thanks go as well to my other colleagues at the center, Wendy Lower, Jürgen Matthäus, Martin Dean, Peter Black, Robert Ehrenreich, and Paul Shapiro, for their moral and intellectual support.

Hans Mommsen and Hilary Earl also devoted considerable attention to reading this manuscript while they were in Washington on research fellowships. I appreciate their efforts more than I can express here. Special mention must also be made of the help given to me by Aaron Kornblum, formerly the USHMM reference archivist, as well as the support given to me by Genya Markon, Sharon Muller, and Leslie Swift in the museum's photo archive. In addition, a significant section of this book could not have been written without Eve Kristine Belfoure, a volunteer at the USHMM, who translated literally hundreds of Polish documents for me.

The Visiting Scholars Program of the Center for Advanced Holocaust Studies, U.S. Holocaust Memorial Museum, provided invaluable financial support for this book. I would also like to thank the German Academic Exchange Service (DAAD) for a 1996 fellowship that facilitated my research in Germany. Special thanks goes to the helpful archivists and lawyers at the Bundesarchiv/Militärarchiv in Freiburg, Germany; the U.S. National Archives and Records Administration in College Park, Maryland; the Zentrale Stelle für Landesjustizverwaltungen in Ludwigsburg, Germany; the Bibliothek für Zeitgeschichte in Stuttgart, Germany; the Bundesarchiv-Zentralnachweisstelle in Aachen-Kornelimünster, Germany;

and the Staatsanwaltschaften in Landau/Pfalz, Osnabrück, Stuttgart, and Würzburg. I am also grateful to David A. Kohlbrenner for his help in drawing up the map on page 155.

Last, but certainly not least, others in my life helped in ways that were critical to the completion of this book. These people include my friend Melissa Baker, whose support I greatly appreciated, and my late grandfather, Clifford Mersereau, who instilled in me a love of history. Pride of place, however, must go to my parents, Allen and Dale Rossino, whose love and faith in my work sustained me throughout the years. It is to them that this book is dedicated.

The views, opinions, and conclusions expressed in this book are those of the author alone. They do not represent the position of the U.S. Holocaust Memorial Museum.

INTRODUCTION

In contrast to its protracted conflict with the Soviet Union, the Third Reich's war against Poland in 1939 was a short-lived affair, lasting only five weeks from beginning to end. And yet despite its brevity, the historical importance of the Polish campaign cannot be overestimated. The German Army High Command planned the offensive as a quick and localized assault. But in attacking Poland, Germany instead precipitated a new, general European conflict several times more devastating than the war that had ravaged the Continent one generation earlier. German innovations in tactics and military technology developed between the wars and introduced during the Polish campaign also ensured that the devastation of this new conflict would not be limited to the battlefield. Beginning with the attack on Poland, urban centers became the target of German aerial attacks that were intended to terrorize the enemy as much as to destroy his capacity to make war. Similarly, the advent of blitzkrieg tactics and the mass armored assault destroyed the physical and psychological distance between the fighting front and the rear. Areas deep behind the lines were transformed into battlefields, and in this broader geographical context of war, civilians often became indistinguishable from actual combatants.

Each of these developments dramatically brutalized European warfare in the mid–twentieth century. But while they are significant in this regard, perhaps the most decisive change that occurred in the German method of waging war was the morally corrosive influence of National Socialism. This influence manifested itself in the deadly racial-political policies that the SS, police, and German army implemented against Poland's civilian population, both Christian and Jewish. In the weeks and months prior to the attack, the leaders of the Nazi regime, including Adolf Hitler, Hermann Göring, SS chief Heinrich Himmler, and his ruthless subordinate, Reinhard Heydrich, decided to eliminate entire segments of Polish society. Educators, intellectuals, political figures, noble families, Catholic clergy, leaders in the medical and legal professions, and many others were all slated for "liquidation" as part of an overall program to decapitate Polish society and deter resistance to German rule. The SS directed its terror campaign against Polish Jews as well, utilizing mass executions and the destruction of Jewish property to force Jews out of German-occupied territory, all as part of the broader effort to "cleanse" the new German East of peoples the Nazis defined as racially, ethnically, and culturally inferior. In effect, the Third Reich's invasion of Poland was not an ordinary war, but a new kind of conflict, a *Volkstumskampf,* or ethnic struggle, that conflated the unique ideological goals of National Socialism with the traditional military-political objective of establishing a German empire in Eastern Europe.

The military operations of the German army and combat between German and Polish forces provide the context within which Nazi policies were implemented in September 1939, but they are not the primary focus of this book. Instead, this study provides a detailed examination of the ideological dimensions of the Polish campaign, including SS plans to murder Polish political and intellectual leaders, Nazi anti-Jewish policy, cooperation between the SS and the Wehrmacht, German army reprisal policy, the treatment of Polish civilians by German troops, and a survey of German attitudes toward Poland and its inhabitants at the outset of the war. Taking into account the ideological elements of the Polish campaign will provide significant insight into issues that are central to the connection between the outbreak of World War II and the radicalization of National Socialist racial-political policies. Among these issues is the extent to which the German invasion can be considered an "ordinary" operation, the objectives of which were purely military and diplomatic in nature. Phrased differently, did the Polish campaign bear a closer resemblance to the relatively "clean" war Germany fought in France and the Low Countries in 1940, or was the conflict with Poland more like the Third Reich's barbaric assault on the Soviet Union in June 1941, during which the slaughter of noncombatants was a common occurrence? It is my contention that Germany's wars in Poland and the Soviet Union bore striking similarities. Therefore, reexamining the ideological dimensions of the Polish campaign can also help us understand the origins of the Wehrmacht's *Vernichtungskrieg,* or War of Annihilation, against the USSR.

Related to these larger historical issues are several narrower questions, beginning with the fact that the invasion of Poland ushered in the first of several large-scale killing programs that Nazi Germany undertook during the war. In this case, the murder campaign that was initiated entailed systematically liquidating the leading and educated elements of Polish society. From where did the impetus for murdering Polish intellectuals and others arise? How was the killing campaign organized? What resources, human and otherwise, were allotted for its implementation? What problems did the SS encounter when killing Polish civilians? Lastly, was the murder of

Poles connected in any way to the evolution of the so-called Final Solution to the Jewish Question?

Concerning German policy against Jews, the eruption of war brought on a dramatic escalation in the persecution of Jews, both in Germany and in German-occupied territories. However, the reasons for the increasing use of violence against Polish Jews by the Germans during the Polish campaign remain poorly understood. Consequently, the murder of Jews and the destruction of Jewish property by the SS are often characterized as a spontaneous outburst of anti-Semitic violence that foreshadowed the later genocide of the Jews during the Russian campaign in summer 1941. Was this really the case? Did the Nazi regime, and by extension the SS, already intend in September 1939 to eradicate Polish Jewry? Precisely what were the goals of the SS on the eve of the invasion, and can links be identified between anti-Jewish acts during the war in Poland and the evolution of Nazi anti-Jewish policy in the year prior to the beginning of the invasion? Furthermore, what role, if any, did the regular German army play in the implementation of policies against Jews?

The detailed examination of the violence employed by the Wehrmacht against civilians, Poles and Jews alike, is a particularly important aspect of this work. Specialists in German military history have long recognized the Janus-faced nature of the Wehrmacht's war in Poland. Specifically, the conduct of German troops during the Polish campaign was reminiscent of the imperial German army's march across Belgium in August 1914, during which the kaiser's men shot thousands of civilians and leveled scores of communities. On the other hand, the scale and extent of German violence against civilians during the Polish campaign was far greater than in Belgium during World War I. Many readers will also note that the widespread use of shootings and the obliteration of villages by the Wehrmacht in 1939 were common practices during Germany's attack on the Soviet Union and its war in the Balkans.

Germany's war in Poland represented in this sense a transitional conflict between the limited violence against civilians utilized by the *Kaiserheer* in the First World War and the unlimited, almost nihilistic violence of the Wehrmacht in the Second World War. The invasion of Poland thus occupies a critical place in the history of Nazi Germany's descent into mass murder and genocide. The evolution of German military practice to include the eradication of political and ideological enemies, as defined in racial-biological terms by National Socialism, did not begin in 1941 as has commonly been argued; it began in Poland in 1939 and escalated in 1941 with the outbreak of the *Vernichtungskrieg* against the Soviet Union and the beginning of brutal antipartisan warfare in the Balkans.

ONE

THE IDEOLOGICAL
DIMENSIONS OF WAR
WITH POLAND

In late March 1939, Adolf Hitler instructed General Walther von Brauchitsch, the commander in chief of the German army, to begin planning an invasion of Poland. The attack, Hitler insisted, should devastate Poland so thoroughly that it could not "be taken into account as a political factor for the next few decades."[1] Although Hitler tended toward hyperbole when speaking about military operations, the level of violence he demanded in this case was not exaggeration. Rather, it was a genuine expression of the brutality with which he wanted his armed forces and SS to wage war against the Poles. And as the five-week war in Poland took its course, it became clear that Hitler's wish had been granted. The German army and SS conducted the Polish campaign with a viciousness that was unprecedented in the annals of European conflict up to that point. The outright massacre of civilians and prisoners of war by German troops frequently attended combat operations, as did widespread looting and the destruction of property. German artillery mercilessly shelled cities like Warsaw without regard for civilian casualties, while Luftwaffe pilots brazenly attacked Red Cross aid stations and strafed columns of refugees.[2]

The shocking level of violence that attended the brief Polish campaign set it apart from the battles of World War I and the invasion of France and the Low Countries in May 1940. On the other hand, certain aspects of the war in Poland, such as the ideologically motivated killing of specific groups among the indigenous population, bore a striking resemblance to Nazi Germany's later invasion of the Soviet Union. During and after the military campaign, the SS and police, frequently with the cooperation of the Wehrmacht, targeted categories of people that the regime defined as "racial-political opponents." Polish political leaders, socialists, intellectuals, members of the nobility, the Catholic clergy, and Jews fell by the tens of thousands to marauding SS units charged with "cleansing" the newly conquered territory of so-called "dangerous elements." In its combination of military and ideological dimensions, therefore, the invasion of Poland heralded a fundamental shift in the way that Germany waged war in Eastern Europe. Both the civilian population and the Polish army were enemies in this new war, and mass murder was employed on the battlefield as an instrument of German state policy.

Hitler set the ideological tone for the German offensive in spring 1939. From the moment that he authorized his Army High Command to prepare an invasion plan, he spoke of the attack in increasingly radical terms, many of which were remarkably consistent with pronouncements on the "Polish Question" that he had made in the past. Hitler claimed publicly that Germany's dispute with Poland centered on the return of Danzig to the Reich and the safety of the sizable ethnic German minority then living in Poland.[3] In private, however, he assured his subordinates that "Danzig is not the subject of the dispute at all."[4] Rather, Hitler explained that the war against the Poles was the first step toward securing Lebensraum (living space) for the German people. To a certain extent, Hitler's designs echoed the traditional notion of a German "push to the east" *(Drang nach Osten),* but in fact the Nazi leader's goals in 1939 were far more extreme.[5] Gaining Lebensraum in Poland was to Hitler a necessary antecedent to preparing the territory for German use. The second step entailed cleansing the land of what National Socialism defined as inferior ethnic and racial contaminants—Poles and Jews—in order to make it habitable for Germans.

Between 1934 and 1939, Hitler had allowed practical considerations to dominate his Polish policy. Nazi Germany and Poland concluded a nonaggression pact on 26 January 1934, but the agreement was far from a genuine gesture of peace on Adolf Hitler's part.[6] The pact instead served several purposes. In the first place, it stabilized the Reich's eastern frontier and allowed the Nazi Party time to consolidate its rule.[7] This result was particularly significant to Hitler because the Poles had felt threatened by the Nazis' rise to power. In response, Poland's leader, Marshal Józef Pilsudski, had explored the idea of a joint French-Polish invasion of Germany in 1933 to prevent the prospect of future German expansion in Central Europe.[8] Germany could not have withstood such an invasion and thus the pact with Poland gave Hitler and his generals the time they needed to rearm and enlarge the Reich's armed forces. Critical in this regard was what Hitler referred to in February 1934 as his plan for securing Germany's hegemony in Europe and acquiring Lebensraum in the east. As Klaus Hildebrand notes, in a speech Hitler delivered to senior army officers shortly after signing the nonaggression pact, his arrangement with the Poles was intended to weaken Poland's ties with France and open the possibility of a future joint Polish-German offensive against the Soviet Union.[9] With Germany's eastern frontier no longer a concern, the German military could concentrate on striking blows against the Western Powers, especially France, before turning to attack the USSR.

As of early 1934, therefore, Poland's place in Hitler's plans remained ambiguous. Clearly, his long-term goal was to move against the Soviet Union. But because Poland was located in the path of Germany's invasion route in the east, Hitler either had to convince the Poles to join the Nazi crusade against Bolshevism, or Poland would have to be destroyed. According to Hildebrand, Hitler remained open to the idea of waging war "first against Poland and then Russia" from 1934 on.[10] However, which nation Germany attacked first was largely a political detail. In ideological terms, it mattered little if Poland or the Soviet Union was the initial target of German armed aggression in Eastern Europe because the Third Reich would eventually have to confront and eliminate both states in its pursuit of Lebensraum. Only after Poland and the USSR had been destroyed could the conquered territory be "Germanized."

Concerning Germanization policy, Hitler concurred with ideas that Richard Walter Darré, a Nazi Party "blood and soil" agricultural expert, had espoused even before the Nazis' rise to power in January 1933.[11] According to a secret proposal Darré had submitted to Hitler in 1930, one of the Nazi Party's primary aims should be enlisting farmers to settle lands that Germany would conquer from the Slavs in the east.[12] Darré's proposal echoed, in systematic fashion, the general ideas that Hitler had already outlined in speeches and in his 1926 political manifesto, *Mein Kampf*. Convinced that the survival of a nation depended upon the racial purity of its populace and the size of the geographic area it occupied, Hitler believed the superior German race was perfectly within its rights to seize territory from the racially and culturally "inferior" Slavs and Jews that already inhabited Poland.[13]

In contrast to traditional Prussian imperialism, however, the lands Germany acquired by war would not be Germanized through what Hitler considered the misguided policy of "linguistic integration."[14] Rather, Hitler argued, "what has been profitably Germanised in history is the soil which our ancestors acquired by the sword and settled with German peasants."[15] Germany "must under no circumstances annex Poles with the intention of wanting to one day make Germans out of them. On the contrary, it must be determined either to seal off these racially foreign elements, so as not to let the blood of our people once again be polluted, or it must without further ado remove them and hand over the liberated soil to its own racial comrades."[16] According to this doctrine, then, the social, political, economic, and ethnic landscape of occupied Poland was to be transformed through an extensive resettlement program that displaced the indigenous Polish and Jewish population in favor of German settlers.

Although Hitler often spoke vaguely about the policy of conquest and aggression that he would embark upon when the time was right, his statements defining the next war as a struggle for German living space became progressively more common in the 1930s. As early as 3 February 1933, Hitler informed an assembly of military officers that he intended to rearm the Reich and then use Germany's armed forces for the "conquest of *Lebensraum* in the East, and its ruthless germanization."[17] The German foreign minister, Joachim von Ribbentrop, was more circumspect, but he also hinted that Hitler's policy toward Poland in the early years of his reign concerned altering "the position of Danzig and the Polish Corridor" in order to "restore agricultural areas to Germany and to improve her food situation" rather than to correct the injustice of Versailles.[18] Four years later, Hitler continued to speak about the importance he attached to winning and exploiting new territory for German settlement. At a conference in the newly constructed Reich Chancellery on 5 November 1937, Hitler told an audience of military and political leaders his plans for solving Germany's space problem in the near future. Stating during a long monologue that 85 million Germans faced a critical shortage of geographic space, Hitler argued that a "solution to the German Question" could only be solved through military force.[19] However, even though the current pace of rearmament meant that Germany would probably be prepared to fight a large-scale war by 1943, Hitler refused to let circumstances dictate when and where he would decide to go to war.[20]

The opportunity arrived less than one year later, as Hitler steered Germany toward a military confrontation with Czechoslovakia and the Western Powers over the Sudetenland. War was narrowly avoided by the last-minute agreement reached at Munich in early October 1938. But, as the chief of the army General Staff, General Franz Halder, assured the American diplomat Raymond Geist in November 1938, Western appeasement of Hitler's demands would only temporarily halt the dictator's quest to subjugate Eastern Europe and turn against France and Great Britain.[21] For his part, Hitler still had not drawn an explicit connection between an invasion of Poland and the acquisition of living space. He continued to speak in general terms of the next war in Europe, assuring his senior military officers only that the conflict would be "ideological and racial" in nature.[22] The turning point came in early 1939 when Hitler decided that the attack on Poland would be the first step in establishing Germany's hegemony in the east.

Several factors informed Hitler's decision to go to war in 1939. Although invading Poland also brought the risk of war with Great Britain and France, Gerhard Weinberg suggests that as early as summer 1938 Hitler was gravely concerned about the possibility that the Western Powers and the Soviet Union would quickly surpass Germany once those nations began to rearm.[23] Second, according to Weinberg, there was an intangible factor to consider: Hitler's fear that he would die or be assassinated before his plans were complete. As Weinberg notes, the Nazi leader firmly believed that "Germany's fate and future [coincided] with his personal life and his role in its history," and it was therefore imperative that Germany fight the war Hitler wanted sooner rather than later.[24] Then, too, relations between Poland and Germany had deteriorated considerably by late March 1939.

Since the end of the preceding year, Hitler had attempted to drive a wedge between Poland and its western allies by inviting the Polish government to join Germany and Italy in the anti–Comintern Pact against the Soviet Union. But even though the Poles certainly disliked and feared the Soviets, the Polish political leadership balked at the prospect of joining the pact because it would have effectively subordinated Poland to Germany. As Weinberg makes clear concerning Hitler's intentions, "it was the end of Poland's independence that Germany was insisting upon; the demand that the anti-Communist government of Poland join the anti-Comintern Pact was the most obvious sign of a demand for ritual submission to Berlin."[25] The failure of his efforts on this front was therefore an important turning point for Hitler, who decided shortly afterward to attack Poland.[26] Hitler's disappointment concerning Polish involvement in the anti–Comintern Pact also came at roughly the same time that the resolve of the Western Allies was stiffening in response to the Wehrmacht's surprise occupation of Bohemia and Moravia on 15 March 1939. Faced with Polish intransigence and his increasing concern about the willingness of Great Britain and France to go to war, Hitler finally authorized General Brauchitsch to begin planning an invasion of Poland on 23 March. If Hitler was going to have his war and keep it a localized affair, it was necessary to destroy Poland before turning against Great Britain and France.[27]

The support of German officers was another factor that likely influenced Hitler's decision. In contrast to the desire of many in the army to avoid another war with Great Britain and France, an overwhelming majority in the officer corps favored launching an assault on Poland. The source of this bitterness lay in the history of conflict between the two nations. Fighting between German army units and Polish insurgents bent on creating a Polish homeland had raged in the Poznan district and East Upper Silesia from November 1918 to spring 1921 and was attended by numerous atrocities perpetrated by both sides.[28] After the victorious Entente powers recognized independent Poland at Versailles in 1919, the revision of Germany's eastern frontier became a primary goal of the German officer corps. As the commanding officer of the *Truppenamt* (Troops Office) in the Army Directorate of the Defense Ministry, General Hans von Seeckt declared that Poland's fall would bring with it the collapse of the "strongest pillar of the Versailles Treaty. . . . [therefore] Poland must be destroyed."[29] Seeckt repeated his firm conviction in 1920 that Poland was Germany's "mortal enemy," and German military exercises conducted in 1925 were premised on the likelihood of a future conflict with Poland.[30] One year later, in March 1926, another *Truppenamt* document made it abundantly clear that "the return of the Polish Corridor and [East] Upper Silesia" were principal goals of the German military establishment.[31]

These sentiments remained strong into the late 1930s, and although many German officers feared the possibility of war against the Western Powers, they were fully prepared to see their dream of obliterating Poland fulfilled by Adolf Hitler. One of these officers was General Halder. Despite his extensive connections with the military opposition to Hitler, Halder delivered a speech to the assembled officers of the Armed Forces Academy in spring 1939 that clearly expressed his concept of goals shared by the regime and the army:

> As I speak to you today on the subject of the "coming war," I want to point out in advance that political considerations, etc. will be left aside. The German Armed Forces are charged with using the sword, but it is not up to them to decide if and how it will be used. I am fully aware there are those among us who think differently than the political leadership on matters of foreign policy, and even ideology. Nevertheless, I will not miss this opportunity to warn them that members of the officer corps should not become unnecessarily involved in issues that lay far from the tasks with which the armed forces of the State have been charged.[32]

Halder afterward clarified the fact that he was referring to Germany's deteriorating relations with Poland: "I believe many of you would agree from the bottom of your souls that with the end of our 'friendly relationship' with Poland, which, incidentally, neither side took fully to heart, we feel a sense of relief."[33] Germany's preparations for the coming conflict must therefore be made with every consideration for speed, Halder continued, so that the complete destruction of Poland would result in "record time." As for Poland's sizable military, Halder explained that although it was the fifth largest army on the European Continent, everyone knew the Polish soldier was "[the] stupidest in all of Europe *(der polnische Soldat ist wohl der dümmste in Europa)*," and need not be feared despite his number.[34] In short, Halder concluded, "Poland must not only be struck down, but liquidated as quickly as possible. . . . we must be finished with Poland in no more than three weeks, and if possible, even within fourteen days."[35]

Several of Halder's contemporaries expressed similar sentiments, including two officers who later went on to distinguish themselves in the war against the Soviet Union. One of these officers was General Erich Hoepner, who agreed that "the Polish Question must be solved once and for all."[36] The other was the highly gifted tank commander and leading proponent of the mass armored assault, General Erich von Manstein, who recorded in his postwar memoirs:

Poland was bound to be a source of bitterness to us after she used the dictated peace of Versailles to annex German territories to which neither historical justice nor the right of self-determination gave her any claim. For us soldiers she had been a constant cause of distress in the years of Germany's weakness. Every time we looked at the map we were reminded of our precarious situation. That irrational demarcation of the frontier! That mutilation of our Fatherland![37]

General Johannes Blaskowitz, whose later criticism of the SS would mark him as an implacable opponent of Nazi occupation policies, also voiced support for the German attack. Admitting on the stand at Nuremberg that a solution to the "Polish Question" appealed to the Army High Command in 1939, Blaskowitz stated:

From 1919, and particularly from 1924, three critical territorial questions occupied attention in Germany. These were the questions of the Polish Corridor, the Saar and Ruhr, and Memel. I myself, as well as the whole group of German staff and front officers, believed that these three questions, outstanding among which was the question of the Polish Corridor, would have to be settled some day, if necessary by force of arms. About ninety percent of the German people were of the same mind as the officers on the Polish Question. A war to wipe out

the political and economic loss resulting from the creation of the Polish Corridor, and to lessen the threat to East Prussia [which was] surrounded by Poland and Lithuania was regarded as a sacred duty
though a sad necessity.[38]

Blaskowitz's opinion echoed that expressed by General Werner von
Blomberg during postwar trial testimony he gave at Nuremberg. Claiming
that German resentment over the Polish Corridor was one of the most pressing foreign policy issues of the interwar period, Blomberg considered a war
to "eradicate the disgrace" *(Schmach auszumerzen)* of Poland's existence an
unfortunate necessity. Unfortunate or not, Blomberg reminded the court
that destroying Poland remained the primary objective behind Germany's
clandestine rearmament, even before Hitler assumed power in 1933.[39] Lieutenant Colonel Helmuth Groscurth also straddled the fine line between concern about Hitler's reckless foreign policy and agreement with Hitler that
Poland had to be eliminated as an independent state. As Groscurth confided
to his diary following Hitler's denunciation of the German-Polish nonaggression treaty in April 1939, "That is good; it was high time."[40] Groscurth
wrote this despite the fact that he was a leading conspirator against Hitler
in the *Abwehr,* the German military's Counterintelligence Office. Finally, on
the day before Germany opened its offensive against Poland (31 August
1939), Colonel Eduard Wagner, the chief of section 6, the quartermaster's
section of the army General Staff, admitted in a letter to his wife that he and
his colleagues were "looking forward to it gladly."[41]

Thus, while many in the German officer corps may have differed with
Hitler on the timing of a military reckoning with the Poles, these misgivings did not arise from a general unwillingness to fight a war against
Poland. Anti-Polish sentiment in this sense provided a basis for coordinating short-term war aims between the Nazi regime and the German army.
The immediate objective was to destroy Poland, and this became the military leadership's focus, their fears about the outbreak of a new general European war notwithstanding. It was against this backdrop that on 3 April
1939, *Oberkommando der Wehrmacht* (OKW; Armed Forces High Command) submitted to Hitler the "Directive for the Unified Preparation of the
Wehrmacht for War 1939/40," which included a section on military operations against Poland. Hitler approved and signed the document, stipulating that the army be ready to execute the invasion plan, code-named CASE
WHITE, by 1 September 1939 at the very latest.[42]

The ideological dimensions of Hitler's thinking did not take a backseat
to diplomatic and foreign policy considerations for long. Late in the spring

of 1939, Hitler at last drew an explicit connection between a military assault on Poland and the onset of a war to gain Lebensraum. At a meeting in the Reich Chancellery on 23 May 1939, Hitler stated to an audience of senior army, air force, and naval commanders that Germany faced a "choice [between] advancement or decline," repeating as he had in the past that the solution to Germany's problems could be found in "expanding our living space in the east."[43] He then specified that Poland was the intended opponent, asserting, "The Pole is not a secondary enemy [*zusätzlicher Feind*]. Poland will always stand by the side of our adversaries and despite our treaty intended to exploit every opportunity to do us harm."[44] Realistically, therefore, traditional Polish hostility and the threat posed to Germany by Poland's ties with the Western Powers led Hitler to conclude, "There is no question of sparing Poland, we are left with the decision to attack at the first suitable opportunity."[45] Following the Poles' defeat, Hitler assured his audience, conquered territory would be subjected to "thoroughgoing German exploitation," including the use of native populations as a source of labor.[46]

This was the most unambiguous statement to date of Hitler's intentions for the coming occupation of Poland. Following the elimination of Poland as a political entity, Germany would install a harsh regime to resolve once and for all the ethnic conflict between Germans and Poles. The question remains if the men in Hitler's audience, who were responsible for executing the German battle plan, understood the level of brutality their Führer demanded of them. Hitler clarified this during a conference in late August at the Berghof, his mountain retreat in Bavaria. Assembling on the morning of 22 August 1939, the commanders of Germany's military endured a long monologue during which Hitler referred to the Reich's rapidly deteriorating relations with Poland.[47] He informed his audience that the Polish situation had become "unbearable" and that leaders in Britain and France did not want war with Germany. As for the Soviet Union, Hitler surprised the assembled military commanders by revealing that negotiations with Stalin were under way. These would soon lead to the conclusion of a non-aggression pact between Germany and the USSR, an event that he said would place Poland in the isolated position he desired.[48] Hitler then commented on the conduct of the coming invasion and exhorted the officers to avoid viewing the military campaign in traditional terms. They should instead concentrate on the "elimination of living forces, not the arrival at a certain line."[49] "Have no pity," Hitler demanded; the campaign was to be carried out with "the greatest brutality and without mercy."[50]

According to some accounts, Hitler also stated that one of the invasion's goals was the physical elimination of at least some of Poland's inhabitants.

Following an afternoon break the audience reconvened. At this time Hitler reportedly informed his listeners that "SS Death's Head units stand ready under orders to mercilessly send to death men, women, and children of Polish descent."[51] General Halder was sitting in the audience that day, and he later recorded a similar statement in his diary, writing that Hitler had called for the "physical annihilation of the Polish population."[52] Field Marshal Fedor von Bock, the commander of Army Group North, provides further evidence. Recalling in his memoir that Hitler "did not wish to burden the army with the necessary liquidation [of] the Polish upper class, especially the Polish clergy," the Führer had stated that he was designating the task to the SS instead.[53] Hitler concluded his monologue by declaring that occupied Poland would be "depopulated and settled by Germans."[54] Given this comment, it appears certain that Hitler had decided mass murder and the extensive resettlement of Poles and Jews would be the twin elements of his plans for the Germanization of Poland.

Most Wehrmacht officers had never heard of plans for the physical elimination of the educated and leading segments of Polish society before 22 August 1939. However, negotiations had been under way for several months between Gestapo headquarters, *Oberkommando des Heeres* (OKH; Army High Command), and the *Abwehr* for the deployment of SS and police forces behind German lines during the invasion.[55] Called *Einsatzgruppen* (Operational Groups), these units would be composed primarily of men from the Gestapo, *Sicherheitspolizei* (Sipo; Security Police), *Sicherheitsdienst* (SD; Security Service), and *Kriminalpolizei* (Kripo; Criminal Police). The *Einsatzgruppen* would be responsible for security in areas of Poland conquered by the German army, but they were also charged with carrying out the liquidation of the Polish intelligentsia, clergy, nobility, and political leadership. One of the military officers intimately involved in arranging the use of *Einsatzgruppen* by the army was General Halder. Already in late April 1939, just weeks after Hitler informed Army High Command of his intention to attack the Poles, Halder notified his colleagues on the General Staff that "paramilitary [Nazi] Party formations" would undertake the occupation of Poland alongside the army.[56]

Meanwhile, SS and police preparations for the coming campaign began to take shape in early May. Overall responsibility for collecting personnel for the *Einsatzgruppen* fell to Reinhard Heydrich, chief of the Security Police, who received his instructions directly from Hitler.[57] Pursuant to these orders, Heydrich established a new office in Security Service Headquarters called *Zentralstelle* II P (Central Office II P [Poland]) and placed it under the authority of Franz Six.[58] As its head, Six was charged with collecting intelligence on all events "of an ideological-political, cultural, propagandistic, [or] economic nature" concerning ethnic Germans in Poland.[59] Part of this task apparently also included enlisting members of pro-Nazi ethnic German political organizations in Poland to compile "comprehensive data on Polish Jewry."[60] Additionally, Six's office received authorization to create a personnel card file organized on a local, regional, and individual name basis. This file was intended to provide a comprehensive list of SS and police personnel who could be called upon to form a special command for action in Poland.[61] Heydrich ordered Six to provide him with summaries of his office's activities every two days as well as in weekly reports.

The fruits of Six's intelligence activities eventually appeared in a report entitled "The German-Polish Ethnic Conflict," which was completed at the beginning of July 1939.[62] Dr. Helmut Knochen, Six's chief of staff, presented the report to Heydrich and other senior Security Police and Gestapo officers during a meeting convened on 8 July at Heydrich's residence in Berlin.[63] Following this conference, Heydrich transferred the responsibility for organizing the *Einsatzgruppen* from Six's *Zentralstelle* II P to Dr. Werner Best. An SS-*Brigadeführer* and trained lawyer, Best was Heydrich's deputy in *Hauptamt Sicherheitspolizei* (HA-Sipo; Security Police Headquarters). Following the reorganization of the Security Police and Gestapo on 1 July 1939, Best also occupied a central place in the hierarchy of both institutions. In Sipo Headquarters, he was chief of *Amt* V, the Office of Administration and Law, while in Gestapo Headquarters, he headed *Abteilung* I, the Department of Organization, Personnel, Administration, and Law, as well as *Abteilung* III, the Department of Counterintelligence.[64] From a bureaucratic standpoint, therefore, Best was the logical choice to supervise the formation of Operational Groups for service in Poland.

Best's assignment initially required that he find at least 2,000 men to fill the ranks of four *Einsatzgruppen*. These groups were to be composed of 500 men each, which then would be further broken down into five subcommands, called *Einsatzkommandos*, of 100 men apiece. Manpower for the *Einsatzgruppen* came from the Gestapo, Sipo, Kripo, and SD, although given its small size, the SD could only be expected to commit between 350 and 450 men. Above all, the Gestapo would be called upon to provide the bulk of the manpower for operations in Poland. Best set the selection process in motion by assigning the initial choice of *Einsatzgruppen* personnel to Hans Tesmer, the head of Section V 3 (Personnel) in Sipo Headquarters and chief of Department I E (Senior Level Personnel) in Gestapo Headquarters.[65] It was in Security Police Section V 3 and Gestapo Department I E that the lists of Sipo and other SS and police staff throughout Germany, including the

Kripo, Gestapo, and SD, were stored. Even though Best charged Tesmer with making the initial choice of *Einsatzgruppen* personnel, he retained for himself the authority to veto Tesmer's recommendations. Heydrich, in turn, ultimately approved Best's selections. As a general guideline for choosing the appropriate personnel, Best made it abundantly clear to Tesmer that he should select SS officers who would work "ruthlessly and harshly to achieve National Socialist aims," meaning the implementation of severe racial-political policies in Poland.[66]

Notes from Best's daily calendar indicate that he first reported his progress to Heydrich on 14 July.[67] Eight days later, on 22 July, Heydrich ordered the assembly of *Einsatzgruppen* personnel to begin.[68] By this time the number of groups anticipated for action in Poland had been increased to five, with their size ranging from two to four *Einsatzkommandos* of 120 to 150 men apiece. In the first phase of their creation, the name of each *Einsatzgruppe* was derived from the location where it was formed. Following this, numerical designations were assigned to the groups in late August. Thus, the *Einsatzgruppe* Vienna, commanded by SS-*Brigadeführer* Bruno Streckenbach, became EG I. Similarly, the EG Oppeln, under SS-*Obersturmbannführer* Emanuel Schaefer, became EG II; the EG Breslau, headed by SS-*Obersturmbannführer* Hans Fischer,[69] was redesignated EG III; the EG Krössinsee under SS-*Brigadeführer* Lothar Beutel became EG IV; and the EG Allenstein, under SS-*Standartenführer* Ernst Damzog, became EG V.

New units and commands in addition to the five original Operational Groups were also formed in the days immediately prior to and after the beginning of the campaign. For example, at the very beginning of September an Operational Group designated the *Einsatzgruppe zur besonderen Verwendung* (EG z.b.V.; Special Purpose *Einsatzgruppe*) was created and placed under the command of SS-*Obergruppenführer* Udo von Woyrsch for action in East Upper Silesia and Western Galicia. The formation of new groups eventually raised the total number of *Einsatzgruppen* deployed in Poland during the war to seven, and the manpower involved from the SD and Sipo, but especially the Gestapo and Criminal Police, to around 2,000.[70] In addition, 2,250 *Ordnungspolizei* (Orpo; Order Police), or regular uniformed police, were attached to von Woyrsch's unit, raising the full number of *Einsatzgruppe* personnel deployed in Poland to 4,250.[71] Most EG personnel were outfitted with the field gray uniform of the *Waffen-SS* despite the fact that some were not actually members of the SS. Special marks on the uniforms also differentiated EG members from "regular" SS troops, in particular a small diamond-shaped patch embroidered with the initials "SD" and a thin, black, silver-lined band, both of which were worn on the left forearm.

For their part, military authorities took care to coordinate the deployment and operation of SS and police units during the upcoming offensive. The first instructions came from the army General Staff when Colonel Eduard Wagner, the quartermaster general, handed down the "Special Regulations for CASE WHITE" on 24 July 1939.[72] Wagner's orders outlined security measures that military units were to implement during the fighting. According to these orders, German troops were authorized to take hostages and to execute them in the event that irregulars *(Freischärler)* attacked Wehrmacht personnel. Armed civilians were to be captured when possible and brought before an army court martial. Other measures intended to secure entire regions called for German troops to summarily arrest all Polish and Jewish men between the ages of seventeen and forty-five and hold them as prisoners of war.[73] However, Wagner's specifications concerning the authority of the police were ambiguous, noting, "Police powers belong solely to the institution that possesses executive authority (i.e., to make arrests and executions). Just as the exercise of police power in Germany is the domain of the established [police] institutions, its exercise in enemy territory is entrusted to the representatives of those institutions. All police forces are therefore to operate according to the instructions of the institution that possesses executive authority and its responsible representatives."[74] Wagner's orders closed with the stipulation that orders for the supply and deployment of all German police units, including Sipo *Einsatzkommandos,* would be issued separately.[75]

Five days later, on 29 July, Wagner met with Heydrich to hammer out an agreement between the army and the Sipo on the security responsibilities of the *Einsatzgruppen.* Werner Best wrote up the "Guidelines for the Foreign Operations of the Sipo and SD" that resulted from this meeting, and Heydrich signed them on 31 July.[76] As the guidelines noted, "By agreement with Army High Command . . . the task of the Security Police *Einsatzkommandos* is combating all elements in foreign territory and behind the fighting troops that are hostile to the Reich and German people."[77] Best's guidelines further detailed command relations between the army and *Einsatzgruppen,* as well as Security Police responsibilities, for the invasion. According to these, Security Police commanders were required to maintain close working relationships with all local military commanders, *Chefs der Zivilverwaltung* (CdZs; chiefs of civil administration), and the Order Police. A liaison officer *(Verbindungsoffizier)* from each *Einsatzgruppe* was to be named to ensure "frictionless communications" *(reibungslosen Verkehr)* with the relevant military and police officials.[78] The Security Police were also authorized to request assistance from the army and Order Police, as well as provide aid to other German formations in a given area.

While in the field, Security Police commanders were required to file daily reports with Heydrich at Gestapo Headquarters. These reports summarized the locations of units, the number of arrests made, and the names of important political or military figures who had been apprehended. Prisoners were to be placed in provisional holding centers until they could be transported to the nearest Gestapo office or concentration camp.[79] Best's guidelines further outlined the specific duties of each type of police official within the *Einsatzgruppen*. Gestapo and Sipo officers would be responsible for checking the names of arrested political and racial opponents against the so-called *Sonderfahndungslisten,* or Wanted Persons Lists, that each Operational Group carried with it into Poland. These men were also charged with seizing archives, important government documents, and the records of groups that were deemed dangerous; among them Polish underground organizations, Jews, Freemasons, the Catholic Church, and Marxists.[80] For their part, members of the Criminal Police were responsible for securing all Polish police records having to do with so-called "normal" crimes (e.g., robbery, theft, extortion), as well as with arresting the persons who committed such transgressions. Last, the officers of the SD were charged with establishing a network of informants in the occupied territory, gathering intelligence on enemy political organizations, and with ensuring the safe transport of seized materials to Berlin for analysis.[81]

Despite the detail into which Best's guidelines went, they did not mention the responsibility of *Einsatzgruppen* personnel to eliminate the Polish intelligentsia, clergy, nobility, military elite, and certain leading elements of Polish-Jewish society. These killings were to be conducted as part of an effort to neutralize centers of potential resistance in occupied Poland and to destroy the classes of society thought to be carriers of Polish nationalism. This operation received the code name TANNENBERG in honor of the German victory over Russian armies in the Battle of Tannenberg in August 1914, and it was conceived at the highest governmental levels.[82] Heydrich later revealed the genesis of Operation TANNENBERG in a letter he wrote to SS-*Obergruppenführer* Kurt Daluege, the chief of the Order Police, on 2 July 1940. After complaining to Daluege about senior military commanders, many of whom had been strongly critical of SS shootings in Poland, Heydrich noted that Hitler had given him an "extraordinarily radical . . . order for the liquidation of various circles of the Polish leadership, [killings] that ran into the thousands."[83]

From the limited evidence that exists, it appears that Heydrich and Best informed the *Einsatzgruppen* and *Einsatzkommando* chiefs of this killing order during a series of conferences at Gestapo Headquarters in mid-August 1939. Notes in Best's daily calendar specify that he held separate meetings on 14 August with Fischer (EG III), Beutel (EG IV), and SS-*Oberführer* Emil Otto Rasch, head of the Sipo contingent of the EG z.b.V.[84] A conference that Heydrich and Best held with several *Einsatzgruppe* and *Einsatzkommando* commanders followed these meetings on 18 August. It is difficult to determine precisely which of the heads of the EGs and EKs were actually present at the 18 August conference. In his postwar trial testimony, Lothar Beutel stated that all of the *Einsatzgruppen* leaders were in attendance as well as all of the heads of the smaller *Einsatzkommandos*.[85] At this point, however, it is only possible to conclude that the participants included Beutel; his aide, Dr. Ernst Gerke; SS-*Sturmbannführer* Otto Sens, the commander of EK 1/II; SS-*Sturmbannführer* Karl-Heinz Rux, the head of EK 2/II; and SS-*Standartenführer* Walter Huppenkothen of EG I.[86]

According to Beutel, Heydrich opened the 18 August meeting by informing the men about the atrocities being perpetrated by Poles against *Volksdeutsche* (ethnic Germans) in Poland.[87] In this connection, Heydrich specified that Polish secret organizations like the *Westmark Verband* (Western Association) and the members of certain Polish political parties were expected to put up heavy resistance. It was the responsibility of the *Einsatzgruppen* to neutralize these threats in areas overrun by German troops. This meant punishing individuals who committed crimes against Poland's ethnic German inhabitants as well as fighting saboteurs, partisans, Jews, and the Polish intelligentsia.[88] In reference to the latter group, Beutel recalled that Heydrich did not issue a clear killing order per se but instead hinted that "the driving force of the resistance movement could be found in the Polish intelligentsia." Heydrich further alluded to the extreme measures EG personnel were authorized to take, stating, "Within the context of combating [Polish] resistance movements and groups, everything was allowed, including shootings and arrests."[89] Gerke corroborated the guarded language Heydrich used when discussing the elimination of Polish intellectuals, commenting, "At that time it was not the method to speak of such things (i.e., mass shootings) so clearly."[90]

However, Heydrich did not rely solely on innuendo to convey his orders. In addition to obtaining their instructions on 18 August, EG and EK leaders also received copies of the *Sonderfahndungslisten*. Containing the names of 61,000 Polish Christians and Jews classified by the Security Police as "anti-German elements," the lists had been compiled in Section V 8, the Armed Forces and Reich Defense desk in Sipo Headquarters, under the direction of SS-*Oberführer* Heinz Jost.[91] Names for the *Sonderfahndungslisten* came from records the SD had collected since 1936.[92] Among those individuals under SD surveillance were important political figures, clergymen, political activists, Communists, and the members of clandestine political groups in Poland. The names of these people were held in a file called the *A-Kartei*, or Catalog of State Enemies, that was maintained at Security Police Headquarters in Berlin.[93] Regional Gestapo offices, such as those along the German-Polish border, kept similar lists, and names were also pulled from these records for the Wanted Persons Lists. Finally, the *Sonderfahndungslisten* incorporated names submitted by a variety of German state institutions, including the Reich Interior Ministry and Armed Forces High Command.[94]

The German military played a pivotal role in identifying individuals and groups to be targeted by the *Einsatzgruppen* during the invasion. After the war, Werner Best pointed to cooperation between the military Counterintelligence Office and the Gestapo and Security Police as being particularly important to the overall success of Operation TANNENBERG. Recalling that "the *Abwehr* took the initiative in drawing up an *A-Kartei* for arrests that were to take place in the event of mobilization," Best noted that "of the categories of persons to be arrested, saboteurs and [individuals suspected] of espionage, stood in the foreground."[95] After the war Walter Huppenkothen, the liaison officer of *Einsatzgruppe* I to Fourteenth Army headquarters during the campaign in Poland, confirmed Best's recollections. As Huppenkothen testified, "In order to carry out their security tasks, the units *[Einsatzgruppen]* were supplied with lists of names compiled by a collaborative effort between the Sipo and the Counterintelligence Office of Armed Forces High Command."[96] A document dated 26 August 1939 indicates that the Gestapo and *Abwehr* continued to share information up to the eve of the German attack. On that day officials in *Abwehr* acknowledged receiving from the Gestapo ten ledgers filled with names. Included with these ledgers were ten additional lists of names that had been "compiled by *Abwehr*-Section III [and] integrated into the *Sonderfahndungslisten*."[97]

The involvement of *Abwehr* in preparing lists of Poles to be targeted by the Security Police and Gestapo illustrates both the depth of the German military's concern for the safety of its personnel and its desire to neutralize the threat posed by Polish insurgent groups. To a certain extent, the unease of Wehrmacht officers about rear area security also reflected changes in German military offensive doctrine as it had evolved between the wars. As Robert Citino makes clear in his recent study of German blitzkrieg tactics, by 1939 the German army sought to achieve victory by concentrating troops and resources at narrow points on the front.[98] This "front-loaded" approach limited the ability of field commanders to dedicate units to security behind the lines.[99] Consequently, Wehrmacht officers made extensive efforts to integrate SS and police units into military security operations. Contact between the *Einsatzgruppen* and the army during the fighting would be coordinated on three levels. In the combat area, army intelligence officers (Ic/AO) and quartermasters (O.Qu.) assigned to the staffs of divisional, corps, and army level commands were to provide the first line of communication. Detailed orders distributed throughout August 1939 authorized the Ic/AO and quartermasters to deploy *Einsatzgruppen* and *Einsatzkommandos* as needed in the areas occupied by their formations. For example, in Army Group North, Colonel Werner Richter, the quartermaster of the Fourth Army, notified his subordinates that "behind the fighting troops in enemy territory *Einsatzgruppe der Sipo* IV will be used to combat all elements hostile to Germans and the Reich. The members of this *Einsatzgruppe* are responsible for reporting all of their activities to local military commanders."[100] The Eighth Army, part of Army Group South, issued similar instructions on 16 August: "It can be assumed that only weak police forces will be available in enemy territory [therefore] Sipo *Einsatzgruppen* will be employed in rear areas fighting all anti-German elements. The Quartermaster of the Eighth Army will oversee the deployment of *Einsatzgruppe* III."[101]

Another directive handed down by the army General Staff on 21 August soon followed the instructions issued by field commanders. According to this directive, intelligence officers could oversee the activities of the *Einsatzgruppen* "in order to ensure that unified military direction of counter-insurgency actions remains in effect." As this order concluded, "The closest cooperation between the *Einsatzgruppen* and the Ic/AO [must be] assured. . . . [therefore] the assignment of liaison officers from the *Einsatzgruppen* to the Intelligence Officers is to be expected."[102] Just days before the attack, intelligence officers issued marching orders to the *Einsatzgruppen* and their subcommands. As Lieutenant Colonel Eppendorf, the Ic/AO of the Fourteenth Army noted in his war diary, "The activities of the Gestapo-*Einsatzgruppen* are arranged. One *Einsatzkommando* is assigned to the XVIII Corps; its task is security. Marching orders have also been established: *Einsatzkommando* 1/I will operate near Gleiwitz; tasks are security in enemy territory."[103] Finally, five days prior to the offensive, German troops themselves received notification of their responsibility to pass information to the *Einsatzgruppen*. Orders from General Blaskowitz, the commander of the Eighth Army, were typical in this respect, requiring that the men were to report "all cases of activities that could be construed as hostile to the *Volk* or the State" to the Military Police or *Einsatzgruppe der Sipo* III.[104]

Once hostilities commenced, the army's own police forces, the *Feldgendarmerie* (regular Military Police) and particularly the *Geheime Feldpolizei* (GFP; Secret Field Police), provided a second line of contact with the SS. Originally organized in autumn 1938 in *Abwehr*-Section III, the GFP was responsible for counterespionage, information gathering, and the policing of German troops. Because of the terroristic methods employed by GFP officers in pursuit of this latter duty, Klaus Gessner has aptly referred to the GFP as the "Gestapo of the Wehrmacht."[105] Yet, as was outlined in army regulations on 24 July 1939, the GFP was slated to perform other crucial functions, including "surveillance of the civilian population" in occupied areas.[106] During the invasion of Poland, this "surveillance" duty also came to include executions in close cooperation with the *Einsatzgruppen*.

GFP personnel mobilized in stages for the invasion, beginning on 2 August 1939. By 26 August a total of fifteen GFP Groups had been formed, each having a numerical strength of fifty men.[107] These groups were composed of a unit commander, thirty-two *Feldpolizeibeamten* (Field Police Officers), and seventeen army clerical support personnel, bringing the number of GFP men deployed in Poland to 600.[108] Collaboration between the GFP, Security Police, and Gestapo was facilitated by the fact that the *Feldpolizeibeamten* in each GFP detachment were exclusively Gestapo and Kripo personnel. In addition, the overall commander of the *Geheime Feldpolizei* was SS-*Standartenführer* Wilhelm Krichbaum. A member of the Gestapo since 1933, Krichbaum came to the GFP from the ranks of the SS Border Police. He had been appointed SS border inspector II for the Southeast (*Grenzinspekteur* II *Südost*) in 1937 and was stationed in Silesia.[109] Krichbaum was a close friend of Werner Best and allegedly also on friendly terms with Reinhard Heydrich.[110] His appointment as head of the GFP by *Abwehr* chief Wilhelm Canaris on 20 August 1939 ensured that cooperation in the field between the *Einsatzgruppen* and GFP would be close.[111]

During the campaign, the GFP provided an important link between civilian and military authorities that facilitated the exchange of information and prisoners. This purpose was clear in instructions the General Staff issued on 21 August, stipulating that "sections of the Security Police *Einsatzgruppen* are to render assistance" if the GFP was not able to sufficiently carry out its duties.[112] The tasks of the GFP were also defined similarly to those of the *Einsatzgruppen*. Members of the GFP were specifically ordered to "seek out and combat all activities in the operational area that present a danger to the

Volk and the State."[113] Instructions issued to the Eighth Army on 28 August 1939 also required the *Feldgendarmerie* and GFP to immediately report all civilian activities in Poland that could be construed as anti-German *(Deutschfeindlich)*.[114] Given these orders, it is clear that the GFP and *Einsatzgruppen* were practically interchangeable for certain duties.

Far behind the battlefront, officials called chiefs of civil administration (CdZs) formed the third point of contact between SS and police units and army rear area formations. Initially responsible to the regional military commander, the CdZs were administrators charged with coordinating activities during the transition from military rule to the establishment of a fully operational civilian government. A measure of the importance placed on the role of the CdZs was expressed in a report completed by the Reich War Ministry in 1936. As the report's author, Dr. Danckwerts, stressed, "The CdZ is the instrument, confidant, and advisor to the Commander-in-Chief of the army. He is also the instrument and confidant of the Reich administrative offices or, if necessary, of the local state government. *The aim* [of creating a CdZ] *is to provide a fully operational apparatus that will facilitate frictionless cooperation between the Wehrmacht and civilian administration.*"[115]

Yet the installation of CdZs in Poland would also have an unforeseen and in some cases adverse impact on the Wehrmacht's control over security operations. The difficulty originated with orders issued by Hitler on 26 August granting the army complete executive authority *(vollziehende Gewalt)* over arrests and executions during the coming campaign.[116] CdZs could act autonomously once installed, and they therefore possessed the authority to initiate security operations in rear army areas.[117] This independence, notes Klaus-Jürgen Müller, translated into a potential hindrance to the Wehrmacht's exercise of full executive authority.[118] Furthermore, although Army High Command was formally responsible for naming CdZs, Hitler also held this power as the overall commander of Germany's armed forces.[119] For his part, Hitler was determined to name as chiefs of civil administration only those individuals he trusted to implement the brutal Germanization program he envisioned in the months before the attack.

This intention was likely what Hitler had in mind on 5 September 1939 when he ordered General Brauchitsch to appoint SS-*Brigadeführer* Albert Forster as the CdZ to the Fourth Army in Danzig and West Prussia.[120] Already the *Gauleiter* of Danzig, Forster had been the CdZ to the Third Army since 1 September. Brauchitsch was well aware of Forster's brutal reputation, and he initially denied Forster's request for an extension of his authority from Danzig into the entire province of West Prussia. Following

Forster's direct appeal to Hitler, however, Brauchitsch was forced to concede. Forster then immediately set to work "Germanizing" his new area of control, a murderous process that eventually implicated him in the deaths of nearly 60,000 people.[121] In short, the army's executive authority during and immediately after the war in Poland was to a certain extent illusory even before the first shot had been fired. Nevertheless, the attempt by many officers to exercise this authority would generate serious conflicts between the army and German civilian administrators.

The potentially problematic relationship between army rear area officers and ideologically motivated CdZs was further complicated by the lack of clarity in the command relationship between the military and the SS and police. Despite the agreement worked out by Heydrich and Wagner at the end of July authorizing the SS and police to combat enemies of the Reich behind German lines, details about the actual chain of command remained murky. On the surface, Hitler's orders at the end of August granting the army executive authority meant that all SS and police activities would have to be approved or endorsed by the local commanding Wehrmacht officer. However, this arrangement appeared to contradict the statement outlined in the "Special Regulations for CASE WHITE" issued by Colonel Wagner on 24 July 1939 that "just as the exercise of police power in Germany is the domain of the established [police] institutions, its exercise in enemy territory is entrusted to the representatives of those institutions." Further muddying the waters was the fact that CdZs were installed to facilitate combined security operations between the SS and police and the military. Although CdZs were theoretically required to undertake operations with the cooperation of local military commanders, they retained the authority to initiate security actions independent of those commanders. The confusion in the structure of command between the army, the CdZs, and the SS and police would prove all but impossible to sort out during the war in Poland. Final resolution of the problem would only come with the complete removal of the SS (at Himmler's request) from Wehrmacht jurisdiction in October 1939.[122]

With the granting of full executive authority to the army, it once again became necessary for Colonel Wagner to clarify arrangements with Heydrich. Growing concerns about the intended role of SS units in the coming campaign also may have motivated Wagner's consultation with Heydrich. These concerns seem to have first been raised by Wilhelm Canaris during a meeting he had with Halder on 25 August. At the time, Canaris took the opportunity to convey to Halder the misgivings he had about the planned activities of the SS *Totenkopfverbände* (SSTV; SS Death's Head units), which, like the *Einsatzgruppen,* were to be deployed behind German lines for security purposes.[123] Composed of specially selected SS personnel trained to administer the concentration camp system, the SS Death's Head units were under the authority of SS-*Gruppenführer* Theodor Eicke, a coarse man known for his ruthlessness and ideological conviction as well as his bitter rivalry with Reinhard Heydrich.[124] By the beginning of the war in September 1939, Eicke had nearly 24,000 men in the SSTV at his disposal, and from these he mobilized three battalions, named *Oberbayern,* *Brandenburg,* and *Thuringen,* for action in Poland.[125]

The fears Canaris voiced on 25 August appear to have been well founded. According to some accounts of the conference at the Berghof three days earlier, Hitler had specifically referred to killings that he was ordering the *Totenkopfverbände* to undertake in Poland. Moreover, Eicke was fully prepared to have his SS troops carry out so extreme an order, as demonstrated by comments he made to an assembly of SS officers in the Oranienburg concentration camp only days after the outbreak of the war.[126] Stating that "the harsh laws of war . . . required that [the SS] must consider all orders sacrosanct," Eicke asserted it was the duty of every SS man to "carry out even the severest and harshest [orders] without hesitation."[127] He continued: "It was the most important task of the SS to protect the State. . . . every enemy [of National Socialism] would have to be incarcerated or annihilated."[128] Given the predilection of SS commanders to speak euphemistically when referring to killing programs, it is likely that Eicke's comment was more than simply bluster intended to whip up the battlefield élan of his men; it was an indication of the wave of murder that was about to break over Poland.

Following Canaris's discussion with Halder on 25 August and Hitler's granting of executive authority to the army on 26 August, Wagner and Halder met on 26 and 27 August to confer about the army's upcoming cooperation with the SS.[129] What was discussed at this meeting has been lost to history, but two days later, on 29 August, Wagner arranged an additional meeting with Heydrich and Werner Best at Gestapo Headquarters.[130] According to Wagner's diary notes, the point of this conference was to discuss plans for "the deployment of Gestapo groups in the [military] operational area."[131] Wagner recorded in his diary that the demeanor of Best and Heydrich was "impenetrable" *(undurchdringlich)* throughout the conference, and that Heydrich in particular was "cold" *(unsympathisch)* to him. Despite Heydrich's and Best's standoffishness, Wagner noted that they "came quickly to an agreement" on plans for the *Einsatzgruppen* to arrest 30,000 people in Poland.[132] Wagner reported the results of the meeting to

Halder, who noted in his diary that the arrests were to be made on the basis of names collected by the Security Police in the *A-Kartei*, or Catalog of State Enemies, the very source of lists used for the *Sonderfahndungsbücher* carried into Poland by the *Einsatzgruppen*.[133] The arrests were to be conducted in two stages, with 10,000 persons incarcerated in the first sweep and another 20,000 in the second.[134] All of those arrested would be interned in concentration camps. This information provided by Wagner apparently raised concerns for Halder, who confided to his diary the doubts he had "about the measures intended by Himmler."[135] In contrast, Heydrich and Best thought the agreement "an extremely favorable result of cooperation with the Wehrmacht."[136]

Therefore, by the beginning of the invasion, the conditions had been set for conflicts to erupt between the army and the SS over executive authority and the harsh police measures Heydrich had ordered his men to execute. Although the *Einsatzgruppen* were technically subordinate to army field commanders, the Operational Groups were also under the direct command of Heydrich and Himmler, who had charged them with implementing Operation TANNENBERG.[137] The threat of a massive number of arrests revealed by Heydrich on 29 August indicated the scale of the "security" program planned by the SS. Nevertheless, Halder did not deem it necessary to warn the field commanders whose responsibility it would be to work with the SS. To be certain, Heydrich and Best had stated only that Poles and Jews suspected of anti-German activity would be arrested, not liquidated. This arrangement seems to have largely satisfied officers like Halder, who entered the campaign confident that the Security Police and Gestapo units deployed in Poland would provide a measure of security behind German lines.

Halder's apparent lack of concern over the coming operations of SS and police units in Poland is comprehensible when viewed within the overall context of the German army's preparations for the invasion. As extant *Abwehr* documents and the postwar testimony of several *Einsatzgruppe* officers show, the German army agreed to deploy SS and police units because it intended to use them to search out and destroy Polish political and insurgent groups. Many in the Wehrmacht anticipated that activist elements among the Polish populace would join the fighting and attempt to operate in rear areas as saboteurs and partisans. Faced with this threat to German personnel and ethnic Germans in Poland, the army was fully prepared to help the SS neutralize suspected enemies. German worries about the potential for popular insurgency were well founded given Polish history, but elements of ethnic and cultural prejudice also informed the military's security plans. The intense anti-Polish feeling that existed in German society since at least the end of World War I deepened dramatically between 1933 and 1939 due to the polarizing influence of National Socialism. This disdain for Poles and Polish Jews alike led German officers to expect that enemy civilians would take up arms against German forces and commit atrocities against ethnic German civilians. SS personnel also shared this outlook, and it was largely because of this common security concern that the way was paved for cooperation between the otherwise rival institutions.

Even before Hitler and the Nazis came to power in 1933, anti-Polish prejudice was evident in reports prepared by officers in the *Reichswehr*. One such report published in August 1927 by the Army Statistical Section of the Reich War Ministry and entitled "The Polish Army" contained commentary on Polish culture. Not surprisingly, the report's authors concluded that "Poles living in former German areas stood at the highest cultural level, [while] Congress Poles occupied the lowest," thus suggesting that Poles who had been exposed to German culture were better off for it compared with their backward neighbors inhabiting Poland's interior.[138] Of present Polish army recruits, the report continued, "about 50 percent are illiterate," and while Poles from the western provinces adjoining Germany fought well during the Russo-Polish war in the early 1920s (hinting that they fought well because of German cultural influence), those from the Polish heartland (Congress Poland) did not acquit themselves well in either the czar's armies or in fully Polish armies after 1919.[139] As for "the Jewish element," which was strongly represented in Poland, the worth of these men as fighters was "well below average" in either their "willingness" or "suitability" to bear arms.[140]

Similar studies on Poland prepared by the Wehrmacht just prior to the invasion reveal a corresponding tendency to judge Poles and Jews based upon stereotypes of their ethnic character. In a pocket manual entitled "The Polish Army" that was distributed throughout the 10th Infantry Division in Regensburg in July 1939, Polish ethnic character was defined as "sanguine, temperamental, passionate, and hospitable, but also very foolish and erratic."[141] In addition, Poles were described as having "highly developed nationalist sentiment, [and] strong chauvinism [that] can be found in all levels of society, manifesting itself against other ethnic groups as contempt, [in efforts to] polonize, and in repression."[142] Culture in the former German provinces was "created by Germans" rather than by the Poles themselves, leading to the overall conclusion that "the educational and cultural level [of the populace] in Poland is not high."[143] Regarding the Jews, the manual explained that they primarily occupied Polish cities and exercised a "strong influence over the press and radio in Warsaw and Łódź [beson-

ders Sender Warschau und Lodz stark verjudet]."[144] Altogether, the Jews "live in tightly packed urban ghettos, are friendly to the Bolsheviks, and hate the Germans *[sind bolschewistenfreundlich und deutschenhasser]."*[145]

A report produced by the Wehrmacht Propaganda Office on 25 August 1939 also offered a consideration of the "minority problem" in Poland. The report was prepared to clarify the ethnic tensions that army commanders should be aware of as well as potential hotspots of ethnic conflict that they could use to their advantage. Ethnic groups listed as inhabitants of Poland (excluding Poles themselves) included Czechs, Hungarians, Germans, Lithuanians, Ukrainians, White Russians, and Jews. Of these groups, those said to pose the greatest concern to Polish authorities were the Ukrainians, Germans, and Jews. Logically to the authors, therefore, evidence of the *Volkskampf,* or ethnic struggle, in Poland was most abundant around Poznań (Posen) and in East Upper Silesia, where large numbers of *Volksdeutsche* lived.[146] Ethnic Germans in these areas were assumed to be in particular danger from the Polish population, which was being incited against them by a Polish nationalist group called the *Westmark Verband,* or Western Association. Concerning the "Jewish Question," the report concluded that it remained largely unsolved given that the overwhelming percentage of Poland's capital could still be found in Jewish hands. This situation fostered widespread anti-Semitism "among the rural population in particular because the younger Jews above all are anti-Polish and communist."[147]

The educational level of the Polish population was generally limited, the report continued. Poles were described as "volatile, disorganized, and illogical," their thought processes governed largely by emotion. Care was advised when dealing with Poles in the countryside because they were "arbitrary and merciless. . . . cruelty, brutality, treachery, and lies are [their] methods of fighting." Educated Poles, such as civil officials and certain city dwellers, were "adroit at their jobs, nimble-minded, and occupied by varied interests," though they were also "shallow and foolish."[148] Finally, the national idea was said to be very strong in all Poles and inseparably bound to Catholicism.

In planning the offensive, German officers also went out of their way to specifically determine the percentage of ethnic Germans in given locations. This was done to minimize the possibility that these towns would be destroyed and to locate sympathetic *Volksdeutsche* who could be utilized as a fifth column and provide information about local Poles who were known for their anti-German attitudes.[149] Wehrmacht officers foresaw that many of these same people could also be used as auxiliary police and security personnel.[150] As one set of instructions to the troops noted, "German and other ethnic groups want to be free of the Polish yoke and will support the Wehrmacht during the fight."[151] Furthermore, estimations of expected civilian resistance were based on the number of *Volksdeutsche* in certain areas. A high percentage of ethnic Germans in a given locality led to the conclusion that armed opposition from civilians would be minimal. An example of one such study was a report on "Ethnic Germans in Poland" completed in the last days of August by the staff of Eighth Army headquarters. In it, the district of Tarnowitz (Tarnowiec) was described as an "area of sharpest ethnic conflict" in which 45 percent of the population was of Germanic descent. Areas of similarly high ethnic German composition included the Lublinitz (Lubliniec) district with a 50 percent *Volksdeutsch* population, the Leszno district, the Turek district, and the Kalisz district.[152] Those districts with predominantly Polish and Jewish populations were also noted, including Kepno, Częstochowa, Sieradz, and Krotoszyn.

Preparing the troops for the coming conflict entailed informing them of what they could expect to find in Poland. For this purpose, personnel from the Wehrmacht Propaganda Office used "data" accumulated from studies on Poland's ethnic composition and culture for orientation sessions. One such report to the rank and file dealt specifically with "ethnic policy." In it, German soldiers were told that Poles were acting mercilessly against minority groups in an effort to "polonize" them. Ukrainians were also being targeted, but "repressive measures and terror have taken on their crassest form against ethnic Germans,"[153] which led to a considerable rise in ethnic tensions and the formation of opposition groups by ethnic Germans who were actively resisting Polish efforts. Polish anti-German activities were supposedly aided by the Jews, who incited hate between ethnic groups and who "with the beginning of German-Polish [diplomatic] tensions formed a common front against National Socialism."[154]

Sentiments like these were not limited to official propaganda material, but also found their way into orders given to German formations in the months and days before the offensive. As early as 1 July 1939, the army General Staff issued a bulletin describing the Poles as "fanatically stirred-up *[fanatisch verhetzt]* and capable of sabotage and other attacks."[155] With small successes, the bulletin continued, "the Pole will become arrogant *[Überheblich]* and aggressive *[Angriffslüstig]*, while defeat quickly makes him pessimistic." In terms of what to expect for the coming campaign, German troops were informed that

> courteous treatment [of Poles] will be seen as weakness, [and] the Catholic clergy is generally responsible for nationalist rabble-rousing.

Ethnic Germans, many Poles in former German areas, and above all
the Ukrainians are all against the Polish State. The numerous Jews see
in Germans their personal enemies. [Lastly] the extensive evacuation
and destruction of all valuable industrial and transportation centers in
the western areas of Poland is to be anticipated. The destruction and
poisoning of food supplies is also to be expected.[156]

Other instructions given to German military personnel before the invasion drew a clear connection between the so-called Polish ethnic character,
which was described as "cruel and sly," and the crimes that Poles were allegedly committing against *Volksdeutsche*.[157] As natural enemies of the
Reich, neither Christian Poles nor Polish Jews were to be trusted; instead
they were to be considered hostile and treated as such. For their part, German troops could expect that "acts of terror" would be perpetrated behind
the front. All German columns, occupied locations, and encampments were
to remain constantly on guard against "terrorists."[158] For example, a report drawn up in the Third Army on 14 June 1939 noted that Polish border units would be reinforced by elements of a paramilitary resistance force
called the *Obrana Narodowa* (National Defense).[159] And on 17 August,
Halder reiterated his concern about the guerrilla war (*Kleinkrieg*) he expected the Poles to wage behind German lines.[160]

As a precautionary measure, security instructions similar to those drawn
up by Colonel Wagner in July 1939 were reissued to the troops in the days
before the invasion. These once again called for the summary internment
of all Polish and Jewish male youth and men between the ages of seventeen
and forty-five. Prisoners taken in accordance with these orders were to be
assembled in camps but separated from regular Polish prisoners of war.[161]
Any person of non-Polish ethnic background was to be separated from
those of "pure Polish nationality" and placed in a special camp behind the
front.[162] Additional reissued security measures included provisions for the
taking of hostages by German troops and full instructions on the authority
and responsibilities of the GFP and *Einsatzgruppen*. The troops received information that military and SS police units were charged with combating
all elements hostile to the German people and state. Accordingly, military
personnel were required to immediately report any such activities to the
nearest police official.[163]

From the evidence cited above, it becomes quite clear that anti-Polish
and anti-Semitic stereotypes formed the basis of views that many German
officers held about Poles and Polish Jews. According to these notions, Polish civilians were treacherous, underhanded opponents who would shoot

at German columns as they passed, poison water supplies, and fall upon unwitting German troops as they slept. Above all, it was the dangerous and deceitful Jews of Poland who were said to be exhorting the Poles into a fanatical, anti-German frenzy. The fears of German officers regarding the Poles were not entirely irrational. They were based in part on lingering memories of the Polish uprisings along the German-Polish frontier in the wake of World War I. However, the widespread anti-Polish and anti-Semitic prejudice predominant in Nazified German society significantly reinforced these suspicions. Given these attitudes and the army's desire to destroy Polish underground groups, it is little wonder that the army readily agreed to deploy Heydrich's Operational Groups behind German lines and took measures to coordinate the Sipo's and SD's work with that of its own security apparatus.

German officers told their troops that this was a war "against Polish impudence" and in defense of ethnic Germans who wished to be "liberated from the Polish yoke."[164] Thus led and oriented, the troops massed around western Poland on three sides prepared to embark on Nazi Germany's first military venture. Their mission was to wipe away the shame of Versailles and come to the aid of their ethnic German comrades who were the victims of systematic Polish repression incited by anti-German and anti-Nazi Jews. Such was the gist of a speech given by the commanding officer of the 21st Infantry Division, Lieutenant General Kuno-Hans von Both, on the night of the attack:

> Soldiers of the Twenty-First Division! This is for the honor and existence of the Fatherland! Prove to your fathers that you are worthy! East Prussia is in danger. . . . we will be marching into ancient German land that was ripped away by the treason of 1919. In these former areas of the Reich our blood brothers have suffered frightful persecution! This is the living space of the German people. Our struggle and our lives belong to this people and its leader, our supreme commander —Adolf Hitler![165]

Viewpoints like von Both's were common among German commanders, and their open expression by these men would prove critical in influencing the behavior of subordinate officers and troops during the coming campaign. Regularly issued instructions informed rank-and-file soldiers that any measure they instituted against civilians was justified because Poles and Jews were always hostile and always suspect. But shared attitudes did not always provide the firmest foundation upon which to base institutional collaboration in wartime. It was for this reason, therefore, that Reinhard Heydrich attempted to shore up cooperation between his Operational Groups and the army by ordering Werner Best to select SS and police commanders who had military training. Clearly, Heydrich wanted committed National Socialists who would work to carry out Operation TANNENBERG. However, given the potential for conflict with the Wehrmacht, these men would also have to be experienced enough to deal with regular German officers. The extent to which Werner Best was successful in finding these men, as well as the impact that the selection of such personnel may have had on combined army-SS security operations, is the subject of my next discussion.

NAZI RADICALS AND SS KILLERS

Twenty-one SS and police officers served as the commanders of *Einsatz-gruppen* I through V, the Special Purpose *Einsatzgruppe,* and their *Ein-satzkommandos* during the German-Polish conflict. These men represented the vanguard of SS and police presence in Poland, and as such their back-grounds differed radically from the "ordinary men" examined by Christo-pher R. Browning and Daniel Jonah Goldhagen in their respective studies of Reserve Police Battalion 101.[1] The leaders of the *Einsatzgruppen* and *Einsatzkommandos* constituted instead an elite group of highly trained and well-educated police professionals specifically chosen from the ranks of the Gestapo, Security Police, Criminal Police, and Security Service for duty in Poland. Little is known, however, about the men selected to command the *Einsatzgruppen* and *Einsatzkommandos,* despite the central role that they played in implementing Nazi Germany's first large-scale killing operation on foreign soil. Given the importance of the racial-political tasks they were assigned, it is therefore worth examining the criteria that were employed when central figures in the SS and police hierarchy chose these individuals.

Investigating the personnel who made up the leadership corps of the Op-erational Groups in Poland can provide insight into several important is-sues. Above all, discerning who these men were and the paths that they took to the killing fields in Poland offers greater understanding of the process by which professional police and SS officers were integrated into the increasingly radical policies of the Third Reich. This process began with Hitler, who ordered Security Police chief Reinhard Heydrich in summer 1939 to form *Einsatzgruppen* and *Einsatzkommandos* for the campaign.[2] Heydrich's subordinates in Sipo Headquarters, Werner Best and Hans Tes-mer, then chose the appropriate personnel based upon the extent to which each man had proven himself a committed National Socialist. The signifi-cance of this chain of events rests in the fact that the responsible figures in the SS hierarchy methodically allotted the human resources that were nec-essary to carry out Operation TANNENBERG, the slaughter of Poland's lead-ing social and political classes. At the very least, the systematic nature of the selection and mobilization process demonstrates that the radicalization of Nazi racial and occupation policies did not come about capriciously as a result of the outbreak of war. Rather, the escalation of violence against so-called racial-political opponents was an intended result of decisions that were consciously made by Heydrich, Best, and Tesmer in response to direct orders from Hitler.

Equally worth considering is the extent to which the selection of Operational Group commanders was based on concern about relations between the SS and the German army on the eve of the invasion. Army Quartermaster General Eduard Wagner, Reinhard Heydrich, and others in the military, Security Police, and Gestapo coordinated their efforts well before the invasion to construct a system of mutual assistance and support in matters of security behind German lines. The question remains, however, if this cooperation extended to the selection of appropriate SS and police personnel to command the *Einsatzgruppen*. According to a document from July 1939, authored by the SD foreign intelligence expert Walter Schellenberg, Heydrich emphasized putting into place individuals who possessed the "relevant [level of] experience *[entsprechende Lebenserfahrung]* and faultless military bearing *[einwandfreie soldatische Haltung]*."[3] How successful were Best and Tesmer in meeting these general guidelines? Considering the massive scale and unprecedented violence of the ideological program the SS was called upon to implement in Poland, what prior experience qualified as relevant? Furthermore, did the possession of proper soldierly bearing necessarily mean that a given individual had to receive formal training in the German army? And after finding the appropriate men for the job, did Best and Heydrich take the German army's plans into account when bringing the *Einsatzgruppen* together? In effect, did the selection of personnel and the method of their deployment help secure cooperation between the *Einsatzgruppen* and the respective German military formations to which each was assigned?

The Selection of Personnel and Assembly of the Operational Groups

Reinhard Heydrich officially authorized Operation TANNENBERG on 25 August 1939 with the creation of a *Sonderrefferat*, or special administrative section, in Security Police headquarters, which he placed under the command of Werner Best.[4] It was in this section that all administrative and communications questions pertaining to *Einsatzgruppen* operations in

Poland were to be handled. The staff of the special section totaled ten men, who had been reassigned from various offices in Security Police headquarters.[5] German plans had called for the invasion to begin the following day (26 August), but due to a last minute flurry of diplomatic activity Hitler ordered a temporary halt to the Wehrmacht's preparations. Two days later, on 28 August 1939, Hitler settled on the first of September as the new date for the attack.[6] The disruption of the German army's mobilization timetable came at a fortuitous time for Werner Best and the men of the *Sonderreferat,* as even by the late date of 25 August the Operational Groups were still coming together.

The largest Operational Group was *Einsatzgruppe* I, which assembled in Vienna and was placed under the command of SS-*Brigadeführer* Bruno Streckenbach. Born the son of a customs official in Hamburg on 7 February 1902, Streckenbach grew up in a middle-class household until the First World War and Germany's subsequent political upheavals intruded on his life.[7] By February 1919, Streckenbach was enrolled at the Johanneum *Gymnasium* in Hamburg, but he dropped out of school to join a newly formed right-wing paramilitary group called the *Freikorps* Hermann.[8] Soon thereafter he left this group to join the Volunteer Guard Section Bahrenfeld *Freikorps,* which was eventually absorbed into the 6th Rifle Regiment of the *Reichswehr.*[9] After nearly a year fighting left-wing opponents in the streets of Hamburg, Streckenbach left the *Reichswehr* to start a new life. He did not return to school, instead beginning an apprenticeship in an importing firm. This and other positions occupied Streckenbach until 1925, when he took a new job with the German Automobile Club, which he held until 1928.

Working an ordinary job did not keep Streckenbach out of right-wing politics. In 1920 he still belonged to the all-volunteer Greater Hamburg *Freikorps,* and he participated in the Kapp putsch.[10] Streckenbach also belonged to a *völkisch,* or nationalist club, called the North German Home Association *(Norddeutsche Heimatbund),* and a group known as the *Wehrwolf.*[11] It was the Nazi Party, though, that truly attracted Streckenbach's attention. He became a member in October 1930 and joined the *Sturmabteilung* (SA; storm troops) for a brief period. Less than a year later, in August 1931, he became a member of the SS, and then in November 1933 he joined the SD.[12] As in the *Freikorps,* Streckenbach proved his mettle as an SS fighter against communists, socialists, and trade unionists. Consequently, he rose quickly through the ranks of the SS and SD; only an SS-*Sturmbannführer* in September 1933, by the beginning of the war six years later Streckenbach was an SS-*Brigadeführer.*[13]

With his star rising in the SS, Streckenbach also steadily accumulated police power. Following the reorganization of the police and Gestapo in mid-1936, he was named head of the newly formed State Police Main Office *(Staatspolizeileitstelle)* in Hamburg and a year and a half later, in February 1938, became inspector of the Sipo and SD for the Tenth Military District *(Wehrkreis X)*.[14] In this capacity, he coordinated the activities of the Gestapo, Sipo, SD, and Kripo in parts of Lower Saxony. Other professional and personal developments in Streckenbach's life in the mid-1930s included military training with the 20th Anti-Tank Regiment from November 1934 to early 1935, and his decision in December 1936 to adhere to SD policy by renouncing his affiliation with Lutheranism and declaring himself agnostic *(gottgläubig)*.[15] By 1939, Bruno Streckenbach had developed a reputation for efficiency and ruthlessness, qualities he would put to good use during the campaign in Poland.

Toward the end of August 1939, it became apparent that the *Einsatzgruppe* under Streckenbach's command would be smaller than Best and Heydrich had originally envisioned. Instead of five *Einsatzkommandos* (EKs), *Einsatzgruppe* I would be composed of four, each of which was made up of roughly 100 men. The personnel selected for the *Einsatzkommandos* assembled at the *Waffen*-SS "Der Führer" barracks in Vienna in mid-August 1939. *Einsatzkommando* 1/I was placed under the command of SS-*Sturmbannführer* Dr. Ludwig Hahn, the chief of the Gestapo office in Weimar.[16] Born on 23 January 1908 into a lower middle-class farming family in Eitzen, near Lüneburg, Germany, Hahn felt drawn to nationalist politics in his early twenties.[17] He became a member of the Nazi Party at the beginning of February 1930 and joined the SA in June of that same year. Surprisingly, given his firm Nazi connections and the fact that he had not seen military service, Hahn also joined the right-wing *Stahlhelm* organization in June 1930 and remained a member until the end of July 1931.[18] At that point, he left both the *Stahlhelm* and the SA to concentrate on his university studies.

Hahn attended the university in Göttingen in 1931 and then in Jena, where he earned a law degree in 1935. While pursuing his studies, however, Hahn also applied to and was accepted by the SS in April 1933.[19] Because of his university training, he received an immediate assignment to the Security Police, and in June 1935 he transferred to the SD with the rank of SS-*Rottenführer*.[20] After joining the SD, Hahn adhered to official policy by declaring himself an agnostic despite his Lutheran background.[21] Over the next few years, between June 1934 and August 1938, he received five promotions and occupied several posts. These included a brief stint at SD headquarters in Berlin, a period in early 1937 as deputy chief of the Gestapo office in Hamm, and eventually head of the Gestapo office in Weimar in December 1937. Along the way, Hahn also served eight weeks in the army reserves, training with the 3rd Antitank Section in Frankfurt/Oder.[22] In all, he had risen to the rank of SS-*Sturmbannführer* by the time he was called for service in Poland in 1939. Comments in Hahn's SS personnel file indicate that the basis for his rapid rise through the ranks lay not only in his competence as a Sipo and SD officer, but also in the fact that he was an "old, reliable National Socialist and energetic SS leader," possessed of "no particular weaknesses."[23]

SS-*Sturmbannführer* Dr. Bruno Müller led Streckenbach's second *Einsatzkommando* (EK 2/I). Born in Strasburg on 13 September 1905, Müller was Alsatian in origin.[24] However, following the end of World War I, his family relocated to the German city of Oldenburg after the Weimar government ceded the provinces of Alsace and Lorraine to France. Müller completed his schooling in Oldenburg, and in summer 1925 he found employment with a local firm. The onset of economic depression in Germany disrupted Müller's life, and in 1930 he chose to study law at the university in Oldenburg. He also became decidedly more active in politics and joined the Nazi Party in December 1931.[25] Müller simultaneously applied for membership in the SS, was accepted in February 1932, and after receiving the rank of SS-*Mann*, was assigned to the 24th SS-*Standarte* as a driver with the unit's motor pool.[26]

It was not until he completed his law degree in June 1934 that Müller's career with the SS truly advanced. As was the case with many in the SS who possessed advanced degrees, he was recruited into the SD and entered both the Security Service and Sipo in April 1936.[27] He declared himself agnostic shortly thereafter, was promoted to SS-*Untersturmführer* in June of that same year, and was named chief of the Gestapo office in Oldenburg.[28] While chief of the Oldenburg Gestapo, Müller also served two months in the army reserves (August to October 1937), training with the 32d Flak Section.[29] Less than one year later, he came to the attention of Bruno Streckenbach, who had him transferred to Wilhelmshaven to assume command of the local Gestapo office. A document remaining in Müller's SS personnel file indicates that Streckenbach selected him for the Wilhelmshaven post because of the confidence he had in "[Müller's] character and ideological outlook."[30] Other documents in Müller's file echo Streckenbach's judgment, such as a profile submitted by SS-*Untersturmführer* Eckardt on 23 April 1936 that stated Müller was "known to be an upright and steadfast National Socialist . . . [whose] political and ideological outlook is unconditionally reliable."[31]

Given his demonstrated ability, it is clear why Streckenbach chose Müller to accompany him to Poland.

SS-*Sturmbannführer* Dr. Alfred Hasselberg was Müller's colleague at the head of *Einsatzkommando* 3/I. The son of a businessman, Hasselberg was born into a middle-class household on 30 August 1908 in the industrial city of Essen.[32] He completed *Gymnasium* in Essen and then attempted to embark on a career in the military, but he was denied entry due to limitations on the size of the army officer corps imposed by the Versailles settlement after World War I. Therefore, in 1927, Hasselberg decided to pursue a career as a jurist, and over the next four years he studied law at the universities of Munich and Cologne.[33] By November 1931, Hasselberg had completed the first in a series of legal examinations and began acquiring practical experience working for the State Court and State Prosecutor's Office in Essen. Hasselberg finally acquired his law degree in May 1935 and began exploring his professional options.[34]

It was at this point that Hasselberg decided to link his future with that of the Nazi Party (NSDAP). Although he had been a member of the party since May 1933, by his own admission he was not active before 1935.[35] Beginning in that year, however, Hasselberg energetically pursued a career with the NSDAP by joining the SA on 20 May 1935.[36] He remained in the SA only briefly until he discovered in July 1935 that real opportunity for an ambitious young lawyer lay with the SS and Gestapo. After being accepted into the SS, Hasselberg transferred to the Security Service in October 1935.[37] It was at this point that the young jurist began to rise rapidly through the ranks. He went to work in Gestapo headquarters in Berlin in September 1936 and two months later was promoted to SS-*Scharführer*.[38] Less than three weeks later, Hasselberg transferred to Schneidemühl, in Pomerania, where he headed the local Gestapo office.[39]

Over the next two years Hasselberg received three promotions: in April 1937 he was made an SS-*Untersturmführer,* in August 1938 an SS-*Hauptsturmführer,* and in September 1938 an SS-*Sturmbannführer*.[40] Along the way, he trained for two months with the 22d Flak Regiment while also carrying out his duty as chief of Gestapo in Schneidemühl. Several months later, in early 1939, he completed a second series of training exercises with the 24th Flak Regiment in Iserlohn.[41] There is little in Hasselberg's SS personnel file to indicate the level of his commitment to National Socialism. His career clearly benefited from service in the SS and Gestapo, but beyond this it is difficult to determine the vigor with which he carried out his duties. As was common among SD officers, Hasselberg declared himself an agnostic, but the only clue that he indeed believed in the regime he served was a comment written in his file by a superior noting that he possessed a "firm" *(gefestigt)* National Socialist disposition.[42]

The last *Einsatzkommando* leader in EG I was SS-*Obersturmbannführer* Dr. Karl Brunner, who led EK 4/I. The son of a regional civil servant, Brunner was born on 26 July 1900 in Passau, Bavaria.[43] Service in the Imperial German Army seems to have fired Brunner's imagination early in life, and in September 1917 he volunteered to fight in the First World War.[44] He served nineteen months altogether with the 16th Bavarian Infantry, during which he won the Iron Cross Second Class. Following his demobilization in April 1919, Brunner returned to Passau and reentered the school he had attended before the war. His education was interrupted, however, by the formation of a leftist revolutionary council government in Passau. In reaction, Brunner and several of his comrades formed a small unit, the *Freikorps* Miemgau, and later joined the larger *Freikorps* Passau to fight the city's new left-wing government.[45] By November 1919 the struggle for political power in Passau had run its course, and Brunner began to look elsewhere for adventure. Political unrest soon led him back to the *Freikorps* and the suppression of left-wing movements in the Ruhr region. At the end of 1922 he joined the notorious Erhard Brigade and participated in the Kapp putsch. His eventual break with Hermann Erhard, Brunner later explained, came after Erhard's failure to support the putsch in Munich led by Adolf Hitler on 9 November 1923.[46]

Now unemployed, Brunner spent three semesters in a trade school in Munich before deciding to enter the university there. He completed his studies in 1927, graduated with a law degree, and worked in the Bavarian state civil service until the Nazi seizure of power in 1933.[47] Although he remained politically active as a member of the *Stahlhelm* from 1929 to 1933, Brunner professed to have been a supporter of the Nazi cause throughout the 1920s. However, because he was afraid that the conservative Bavarian government would fire him from his job, he kept his political beliefs quiet.[48] Therefore, it was not until shortly after Hitler became chancellor that Brunner formally joined both the NSDAP and the SA. Brunner's membership in the SA was short-lived. In June 1934 he became a member of the SS and was recruited into the Bavarian Political Police until the Gestapo absorbed that organization later in the year.[49] Upon joining the SS, Brunner received the rank of *Untersturmführer* and was assigned to the SD. As was required upon joining the SD, Brunner officially broke with Catholicism and declared himself agnostic.[50] Over the next four years he received regular promotions. In April 1937 he was made an SS-*Sturmbannführer* and chief of the Munich Gestapo.[51] By the following April, he had become an

SS-*Obersturmbannführer,* the rank he held at the outbreak of the war. Finally, while in the Munich Gestapo, Brunner earned a reputation for being a diligent taskmaster, a highly competent officer, and a dedicated National Socialist.[52]

Streckenbach exercised control over *Einsatzgruppe* I through a *Gruppenstab* (command staff) of some twenty-five to thirty men. In addition to his adjutants, radio operators, translators, drivers, and other administrative personnel, Streckenbach's *Gruppenstab* consisted of individuals from several branches of the SS police apparatus.[53] The duties of these officers were assigned in accordance with each individual's institutional affiliation.[54] In addition, two members of the *Gruppenstab* were assigned to act as liaisons between the local military commander and the chief of civil administration (CdZ). Despite the formal distribution of duties, however, the limited number of police deployed in the field necessitated that every member of the *Einsatzgruppe* participate in all security activities. The command structure of the *Einsatzkommandos* is less clear, but it apparently mirrored that of the *Gruppenstab.* EK commanders had at their disposal at least one adjutant, who also served as a driver. Translators, radio operators, and technical support personnel, such as weapons specialists and auto mechanics, also belonged to each EK.[55] The structure of the *Einsatzkommandos* was flexible. When necessary, an EK could be split into smaller formations, called *Teilkommandos* (TKs). *Teilkommandos* could be of varying size and operate independently. Subordinate officers included the heads of *Teilkommandos,* who were usually members of the Gestapo or Sipo but not the SD or Kripo. As for the overall number of personnel in each EK, according to Streckenbach, a typical *Einsatzkommando* included around sixty Gestapo and Kripo officers, fifteen SD officers, and fifteen administrative personnel.[56]

The police personnel who filled the ranks of *Einsatzgruppe* I came from Gestapo and Kripo offices all over Germany. In the first place, several officers from Streckenbach's Sipo and SD Inspectorate in Hamburg as well as the Hamburg Gestapo headquarters accompanied their commander to Vienna. Among them were SS-*Standartenführer* Walter Huppenkothen and Streckenbach's personal secretary, Heinrich Johann zum Broock.[57] Others arrived in Vienna from Gestapo offices in Koblenz, Troppau, Augsburg, Dortmund, and Kiel. Records indicate that the three largest groups of personnel came from the Gestapo headquarters in Oppeln, Weimar, and Munich. The latter group included a detachment of some thirty Gestapo men led by *Kriminalkommissar* Johann Schmer.

Schmer was a veteran of the First World War, in which he fought as a member of the 11th Bavarian Field Artillery Regiment. He was born on 30

January 1891 and grew up in Weissenberg, Bavaria.[58] Initially, Schmer sought a lifelong career in the army, but he found opportunities in the military limited after the end of the war. Disaffected and alienated from Germany's new socialist government, he briefly joined the *Freikorps* as a member of the Probstmeyer detachment, and after this unit was absorbed into the *Reichswehr,* he remained in the army until October 1923.[59] Following his discharge, Schmer decided to become a career policeman. He took a position with the Bavarian State Police *(Landespolizei)* and eventually joined the Bavarian Political Police, which was then integrated into the Gestapo in 1934.[60]

Schmer maintained his connections with the new German army by participating as an artillery training expert in five separate military exercises throughout the 1930s.[61] His superiors in the Gestapo also made full use of his experience by selecting him for the *Einsatzgruppen* that moved into Austria and Bohemia/Moravia in 1938. Given his extensive background in the process of establishing police presence in newly occupied territories, Schmer thus proved to be an obvious choice for service in Poland.[62] Upon reporting to Vienna for duty on 12 August 1939, his group was designated an independent command. Two weeks later, the *Gruppe Schmer,* as it was now known, was placed at the disposal of the XVIII Corps and transferred to Zipser-Neudorf near the Slovakian-Polish border, where the local military Secret Field Police commander deployed it to guard an airfield. Here Schmer's men remained until they were ordered into Poland in mid-September.[63]

On 20 August, with less than two weeks remaining before the attack, Streckenbach's *Gruppenstab* gathered in Neu-Titschein (Novy Jicin), along the Slovak-Polish border, to work out operational plans for the coming invasion. Streckenbach explained in postwar trial testimony that beginning the campaign in Neu-Titschein was necessary in order to coordinate his unit's activities with General Wilhelm List, whose Fourteenth Army headquarters was located nearby.[64] Following their initial assembly in Vienna, the *Einsatzkommandos* of EG I also traveled to Neu-Titschein. From there they were deployed in strategic places along the Polish frontier where the four corps of the Fourteenth Army were also stationed. EK 1/I was ordered to the headquarters of the VIII Corps in Gleiwitz (Gliwice), EK 2/I to the XVII Corps in Mährisch-Ostrau (Ostrava), EK 4/I to the XXII Corps in Sillein (Žilina), and EK 3/I to the XVIII Corps in Ungarisch-Hradisch (Uherskè Hradištĕ).[65] As Streckenbach made clear, "it was anticipated that each *Einsatzkommando* should work [directly] with the four corps in List's [Fourteenth] Army and that the EG staff would maintain contact with the [Fourteenth] Army staff itself."[66] The Fourteenth Army's objective for the invasion was to advance from the southwest into East Upper Silesia, take Kraków, and then move east into Western Galicia. Streckenbach's *Einsatzgruppe* would follow along in its wake.

Just to the north, meanwhile, a second *Einsatzgruppe* was assembling in Upper Silesia under the command of SS-*Obersturmbannführer* Dr. Emanuel Schaefer. Designated *Einsatzgruppe* II, very little is known about the composition of Schaefer's unit, but the limited evidence that is available suggests its creation was hurried.[67] After the war a former member of *Einsatzgruppe* II, *Kriminalrat* Dr. Richard Schulze, testified before West German investigators that the unit was created at Gestapo headquarters in the Silesian city of Oppeln (Opole) during the third week of August.[68] SS-*Obersturmführer* Hellmut Rottler, another former member of EG II, corroborated the date, stating that on 21 August 1939 he and an unspecified number of his comrades received orders to leave the personnel office of SD headquarters in Berlin and report to Oppeln.[69] Upon reaching their destination, the SD men from Berlin were integrated into *Einsatzgruppe* II along with most of the SS police personnel, including the criminal police, from the Gestapo headquarters in Oppeln. The assembled police were organized into two *Einsatzkommandos*, each of which incorporated roughly 90 police personnel, bringing the total number of men in EG II to about 200.

Einsatzgruppe II's commander, Emanuel Schaefer, was Silesian by birth and an ideal candidate for police service in Poland. At the time he was born in the small town of Hültschin on 20 April 1900, his parents owned and operated a hotel.[70] Schaefer attended school in the nearby city of Rybnik until June 1918 when he was called up for military service and detailed to the 3d Guard Artillery Regiment.[71] He never saw combat, however, and in early 1919 his family was forced to flee Hültschin after receiving threats from Polish insurgents during the uprising in East Upper Silesia. In response to these events, Schaefer joined the German nationalist movement. He volunteered for the border patrol *(Grenzschutz)* in early 1919 and served in the Von Eycken *Freikorps,* which fought against the third Polish uprising in East Upper Silesia in May 1921.[72] Schaefer afterward joined the nationalist *Stahlhelm* organization, in which he remained until 1928.[73]

In 1926 Schaefer earned a law degree in Breslau and began a career in the Criminal Police beginning in May of that year. He demonstrated an early affinity for Nazism by becoming a member of the SS in 1931, but he did not join the Nazi Party until after the seizure of power because of regulations that prevented Weimar police from belonging to the NSDAP.[74] Because of his formal police training, Schaefer rose rapidly in the Gestapo. In March 1933 he was named the political police chief in Breslau, and the next year he transferred to Oppeln to head the Gestapo there. Two years later, in September 1936, Schaefer entered the SD, shortly after which a superior praised him as "an old fighter with the ethnic German militia *[alter Selbstschutzkämpfer]* and a long-standing nationalist. He actively participated in the post–World War I struggle for East Upper Silesia and left the Catholic Church around 1926 for nationalistic *[völkischen]* reasons."[75] Additional evaluations consistently described Schaefer as having a "solid National Socialist world-view."[76]

At one time or another, historian Eric Johnson notes, Emanuel Schaefer "would become a member of almost every single Nazi and proto-Nazi strong-arm organization."[77] This was in many ways indicative of what Johnson terms Schaefer's "insatiable appetite for violence and adventure." Both the pace of his advancement and the nefarious nature of the tasks with which he was charged demonstrated the high esteem in which he was held by members of the SS hierarchy.[78] For example, in May 1934, after becoming the head of the Gestapo office in Oppeln, a position he held until the beginning of the war, Schaefer was actively involved in conducting surveillance on fellow members of the Nazi Party. And it was Schaefer who Heydrich charged with staging the attack on the German radio station in Gleiwitz that Hitler used as a pretext to justify the invasion of Poland.[79]

Two *Einsatzkommando* chiefs served under Schaefer: SS-*Sturmbannführer* Otto Sens and SS-*Sturmbannführer* Karl-Heinz Rux. As the deputy head of the Gestapo office in Dessau, Sens was well suited to command *Einsatzkommando* I/II. Born on 14 April 1898 in Dessau, Sens was only seventeen years old when he volunteered to fight in the Imperial German Navy during the First World War.[80] At the war's end, he was discharged and joined the III Marine Brigade, also known as the Von Loewenfeld Brigade, a *Freikorps* formation composed of former sailors who held right-wing political sympathies.[81] As a member of the *Freikorps*, Sens participated in the Kapp putsch in 1919 and fought Polish nationalists in East Upper Silesia. Following his military service he finally returned home to Dessau in August 1920, where he worked as a salesman until February 1934.[82] Three years earlier Sens had become politically active once again by joining the SS in November 1931. This move proved to be the beginning of a new career for Sens, and in March 1934 he was accepted into the Sipo and SD at the rank of SS-*Untersturmbannführer*.[83] Sens received an assignment to the Political Police in the state of Anhalt and remained at the headquarters in Dessau even after the Anhalt Political Police were integrated into the Gestapo. From 1934 to 1939, he proved to be a reliable Sipo operative and rose rapidly through the ranks. Altogether, Sens was promoted three times in less than five years, and he received regular praise from his superiors, one of whom considered him a "proven National Socialist."[84]

Karl-Heinz Rux was Sens's equivalent at the head of *Einsatzkommando* 2/II. Born on 3 September 1907 in Bromberg, West Prussia (Bydgoszcz, Poland), Rux was unique among *Einsatzkommando* leaders in that he was originally from a part of Germany that had been ceded to Poland after the Versailles Treaty was signed in 1919.[85] While he was still a teenager, Rux's family moved from Poland to Schneidemühl, Germany, and it was there that he finished his schooling. The details about the location and duration of his subsequent university training have been lost, but it is certain that he studied for a law degree and never took his final examination.[86] What is perfectly clear, however, is that Rux leaned increasingly toward right-wing politics in the early 1930s and eventually decided to pursue a career in the SS. He became a member of the National Socialist Civil Servants Association in 1932 and formally joined the NSDAP on 1 February 1933, the day after Adolf Hitler was named chancellor.[87] By 1936, Rux had joined the SS, attained the rank of SS-*Hauptscharführer*, and renounced Catholicism, noting in his SS file that he was now agnostic.[88] He began to make his way through the ranks of the Security Police as well. He was assigned to SD headquarters and promoted three times in 1938 alone, from SS-*Untersturmführer* in April to SS-*Sturmbannführer* in November.[89] Finally, by the time he was called for duty in *Einsatzgruppe* II, Rux headed the Gestapo office in Salzburg, Austria.

In the week before the German attack, *Einsatzgruppe* II was assigned to the Tenth Army, under the command of General Walter von Reichenau. And as was the case with *Einsatzgruppe* I, Schaefer's *Gruppenstab* stationed itself in the same location as Reichenau's Tenth Army headquarters. From the available documentation it is possible to conclude that Sens's EK 1/II began the campaign attached to the IV Corps of General Schwedler.[90] Rux's EK 2/II was stationed farther to the north, but it has proven impossible to determine the corps with which he coordinated his deployment. This difficulty notwithstanding, it is clear that the movements of Schaefer's *Einsatzgruppe* in the coming campaign were to be linked with those of the Tenth Army.[91]

Also assembling in Silesia toward the end of August was *Einsatzgruppe* III under the direction of SS-*Obersturmbannführer* Dr. Hans Fischer.[92] Fischer was born in Rottenburg, Thuringia, on 21 August 1906.[93] His father, Willy Fischer, had been a civil servant in the city administration. After completing his preparatory schooling, Fischer decided to study law and entered the University of Jena in 1926. He received his degree in 1933 and began his career with the SS, to which he had belonged since February 1932.[94] From 1933 to 1935, SS-*Untersturmführer* Fischer worked as the chief political officer and as a member of the district court in Erfurt. Then, in March 1935, he received command of the second company of the 67th SS-*Standarte*. Despite his relatively low rank, Fischer was also tapped to head the Erfurt Gestapo.[95] Six months later, he transferred to Münster to head the Gestapo office there, and in December 1935 he became a member of the SD.[96] Upon joining the SD, Fischer took the required step of declaring himself an agnostic.[97] He was promoted twice more in 1936 and 1937 and finally attained the rank of SS-*Obersturmbannführer* in August 1938. In addition, Fischer trained two times with the 11th Flak Regiment in 1936 and 1937. Reports in his SS personnel record indicate that his abilities and ideological commitment impressed his superiors, one of whom described him in 1936 as a "steadfast" Nazi. A subsequent report further characterized Fischer as an "old SS man and member of the Party, whose bearing is in every way perfectly representative of a Gestapo chief. Fischer works tirelessly for the interests of the NSDAP and the SS."[98]

Like Schaefer's group, *Einsatzgruppe* III was split into two *Einsatzkommandos,* with SS-*Hauptsturmführer* Dr. Wilhelm Scharpwinkel commanding EK 1/III and SS-*Sturmbannführer* Dr. Fritz Liphardt leading EK 2/III. Each of these EKs was made up of between 80 and 100 men, who assembled in Breslau throughout the third week of August. *Kriminalsekretär* Leo Stanek recalled after the war that he and a large number of his comrades at Kripo headquarters in Berlin received orders to report to Breslau on 21 August 1939.[99] The other men who made up EG III came from a variety of locations. For example, SS-*Hauptsturmführer* Alois Globisch reported to Breslau, along with several of his colleagues, from the Liegnitz Gestapo office. Arriving in late August, Globisch, who spoke Polish fluently, was assigned to EK 1/III to work as a translator for Scharpwinkel.[100] Small detachments of men from the Munich SD were also assigned to EG III, as were officers from SS Border Police stations along the German-Polish frontier.[101]

The largest group of men came from the Kripo and Gestapo offices of Breslau itself, including Scharpwinkel, the head of the Breslau Gestapo.[102] Born to a middle-class family on 4 July 1904 in Wanne-Eickel, Westphalia, Scharpwinkel attended school in Westphalia before acquiring his law degree in Berlin in March 1933.[103] There are few documents detailing Scharpwinkel's life before the early 1930s, but it is known that on 1 April 1932 he joined the NSDAP, and one year later, in August 1933, he became a member of the SA. Once he was a member of the Nazi Party, Scharpwinkel's professional life underwent a series of changes. From April 1934 until June 1936, he was the party district press chief for Bottrop, and in December 1936 he left the Lutheran Church, declaring himself an agnostic.[104] Scharpwinkel then built a career for himself in the Gestapo, which he entered on 1 October 1936 after working for three years as an insurance fraud investigator for the Reich Institute for Labor Investigation and Unemployment Insurance.[105]

Assigned to the Berlin Gestapo office on 1 October 1936, Scharpwinkel stayed put until 1 September 1938 when he became head of the Gestapo in Breslau. In May 1938 he joined the SS and the SD, and in November 1938 he was promoted to SS-*Hauptsturmführer*. Scharpwinkel's time in Breslau was brief, however, as he transferred to Liegnitz less than a year later to head the Gestapo office there.[106] Although he did not have prior police experience, he rose rapidly through the ranks of the Gestapo, a fact that likely attests to his competence and ideological commitment. Evidence of this commitment is provided by a comment that one of Scharpwinkel's superiors entered in his SS personnel file. The evaluation stated that as a member of the Gestapo, Scharpwinkel "possessed comprehensive knowledge of his profession, based without any reservations whatsoever on National Socialist ideology."[107]

Fritz Liphardt, the head of *Einsatzkommando* 2/III, was only slightly younger than Scharpwinkel. Born on 3 May 1905, he was the youngest son of Robert Liphardt, a district court judge in Stettin.[108] Fritz Liphardt originally aspired to a military career and joined the army in April 1924. Within two years he had attained the rank of *Unteroffizier,* but he was abruptly released from the *Reichswehr* in March 1926. His military career at a premature end, the twenty-one-year-old Liphardt sought to improve his lot by becoming a university student. He studied law for ten semesters but never completed his degree. By the early 1930s Liphardt had also become active in right-wing politics, and he joined the *Stahlhelm* in July 1933. After the Nazis dissolved that organization in November 1933, he became a member of the SA in Stettin, where he remained until November 1936.[109] Liphardt joined the Nazi Party on 1 May 1933. In contrast to his fellow EG and EK leaders, he was a latecomer to the SS, only applying for and gaining membership in November 1936. Afterward he was detailed to the Sipo and stationed at the Gestapo office in Frankfurt/Oder as a *Staffel-Scharführer*.[110] Increased responsibility and other changes came rapidly for Liphardt in 1938, and in August he declared himself agnostic.[111] Moreover, by September 1938 he headed the Gestapo in Frankfurt/Oder and had risen to the rank of SS-*Obersturmführer*. He became an SS-*Hauptsturmführer* in November 1938 and held this rank until after the Polish campaign. Immediately following his promotion, Liphardt transferred to SD headquarters in Berlin to work on the intelligence materials gathered by the Security Service. It was from Berlin that he came to Fischer's *Einsatzgruppe*. One of Liphardt's superiors described his character as "lively" and "determined." Furthermore, this same officer noted that as an SD officer entrusted with the "intellectual property" of the Third Reich, Liphardt's ideological outlook was "faultless" *(einwandfrei)*.[112]

Once Scharpwinkel's and Liphardt's *Einsatzkommandos* had been assembled, Fischer's Operational Group was subordinated to the Eighth Army under General Johannes Blaskowitz. *Einsatzgruppe* III began the campaign stationed close to Eighth Army headquarters in Breslau. Scharpwinkel's EK 1/III deployed itself behind the X Corps of General von Ulex, which began the assault headquartered west of Schildberg. Meanwhile, just to the south, Liphardt's EK 2/III positioned itself in Gross-Wartenburg to move into Poland behind the advance of General von Weichs's XIII Corps.[113] The Eighth Army's objective for the invasion was to penetrate Polish defenses below Poznań and drive northeast toward Łódź. Fischer's force would follow in the Eighth Army's wake.

In addition to the three *Einsatzgruppen* deployed with Army Group South, two Operational Groups were formed in the area of Army Group North. The first of these was *Einsatzgruppe* IV, which was created in Pomerania at the *Ordensburg*, or SS training facility, in Krössinsee and led by SS-*Brigadeführer* Dr. Lothar Beutel.[114] A well-educated man, Beutel's background was somewhat unusual in comparison to those of his fellow *Einsatzgruppen* commanders. He was born in Leipzig on 6 May 1902, making him too young to have fought in the First World War. In spring 1920, however, Beutel demonstrated his support for anti-Weimar forces by joining the *Organisation Escherich,* or *Orgesch,* one of the largest right-wing paramilitary associations in Germany at that time.[115] He then served in the *Reichswehr* with the 11th and 38th Infantry Regiments from 1921 to 1923.[116]

Following his military service, Beutel attended university to study economics, art history, and pharmaceutics.[117] After completing his doctorate in this last subject in 1926, Beutel found employment as an apothecary. For the next seven years he excelled in his field, attaining positions as both deputy Reich apothecary and district apothecary for Saxony by 1933. Politically, Beutel became an active Nazi before the seizure of power, joining the NSDAP in May 1930 and the SA in Braunschweig in 1931. Membership in the working-class SA apparently did not suit him, however, and in June 1931 he entered the *Allgemeine*-SS.[118] One year later, in October

1932, Beutel transferred to the SD and renounced Lutheranism. Becoming an SS-*Untersturmführer* in 1933, he rose quickly through the SS ranks in the years thereafter. In 1937, two years after being promoted to head of the SD Higher Administrative Section for Saxony (SD *Oberabschnitt Sachsen*), Beutel, now an SS-*Oberführer,* became the inspector of the Sipo and SD *(Inspekteur der Sipo und des SD)* for Munich.[119] He was then promoted to SS-*Brigadeführer* in April 1939 and held this rank when he was named head of *Einsatzgruppe* IV.[120]

For all intents and purposes, *Einsatzgruppe* IV was identical to *Einsatzgruppen* II and III. Beutel exercised command through a *Gruppenstab,* which coordinated the activities of two smaller *Einsatzkommandos.* The command staff consisted of Sipo, SD, Gestapo, and Kripo officers in addition to a complement of drivers, radio operators, and translators. Included among the members of the *Gruppenstab* were the deputy commander of *Einsatzgruppe* IV, SS-*Sturmbannführer* Josef Meisinger; the liaison officer to the Fourth Army, Ernst Gerke; and Heinrich Himmler's brother-in-law, Hans von Kalckstein, who belonged to the SD staff.

As for the *Einsatzkommandos,* command of the first, EK 1/IV, fell to thirty-one-year-old SS-*Sturmbannführer* Helmut Bischoff. Despite his youth, Bischoff was an accomplished Gestapo operative and chief of the Gestapo office in Köslin (Koszalin) at the time of his appointment.[121] A native of Glogau, Silesia, Bischoff was born on 1 March 1908 and raised very close to the German-Polish frontier.[122] Although he came from a lower-middle-class family (his father was a butcher), he attended *Gymnasium* and university. He acquired his law degree in June 1934 and worked for the civil administration *(Landratsamt)* in the Silesian towns of Schweidnitz and Strehlau until October 1935, when he began his career with the Gestapo. Bischoff's connections with the Nazi Party actually dated back to October 1929 when he was a member of the Hitler Youth. He formally joined the NSDAP in March 1930 and belonged to the SA from November 1933 to November 1935.[123] Upon finding work with the Secret State Police, Bischoff joined the SS and in December 1935 was named chief of the Gestapo in Liegnitz. One year later, in autumn 1936, Bischoff was recruited into the SD, declared himself agnostic, and was reassigned to the Gestapo office in Harburg-Wilhelmsburg, near Hamburg, where he was once again made chief.[124] His transfer to the Köslin Gestapo office came in October 1937. By that time, he had been promoted to the rank of SS-*Untersturmführer* and was a sergeant in the army reserves after having completed four months of training, first with the 51st and then the 69th Infantry Regiments.[125] Finally, in August 1938, Bischoff was promoted to

SS-*Sturmbannführer* and held this rank when called to serve in the *Einsatzgruppen* in late summer 1939.

Bischoff's counterpart as head of *Einsatzkommando* 2/IV was the equally youthful SS-*Sturmbannführer* Dr. Walter Hammer. Born in the Westphalian city of Hagen on 30 June 1907, Hammer was the son of a local judge.[126] He attended *Volksschule* and the *Gymnasium* before attending the university in Freiburg where he acquired his law degree in July 1931. Over the next two years, Hammer gravitated toward the Nazi Party. He joined the NSDAP and SA in May 1933 while working for the State Court in Hagen. In July 1935, Hammer decided to pursue his livelihood in the Gestapo, explaining to West German investigators after the war that the Gestapo offered a young policeman "better opportunities" for a long-term career.[127] He indeed rose quickly through the ranks. By March 1937, two years after his initial assignment to Gestapo headquarters in Berlin, Hammer was appointed head of the Gestapo office in Erfurt. He was then promoted to chief of the Gestapo border post at Schneidemühl (Pila) in 1938 and held this position when he received the call to command EK 2/IV in Poland.[128]

As for the police personnel in *Einsatzgruppe* IV, these numbered 250 altogether, with each *Einsatzkommando* receiving roughly half of the total manpower available.[129] Included were two large groups of men that Bischoff and Hammer brought with them from their Gestapo offices in Köslin and Schneidemühl.[130] According to the postwar testimony of SS-*Hauptscharführer* Fritz Kruttke, a former member of the Köslin Gestapo, he and a significant number of his comrades received orders to report to Krössinsee on 20 August.[131] SS-*Scharführer* Erich Müller similarly recounted traveling to Krössinsee in mid- to late August, along with about 75 percent of his comrades from the Schneidemühl Gestapo office.[132] In addition, several smaller groups of men from SS Border Police outposts (SS *Grenzpolizeikommissariäte*) along the Polish Corridor, such as that at Lauenberg (Lebork), also reported to Krössinsee. Bischoff later explained that he valued the participation of these men in particular because "their many years of service on the border [had] accustomed them to the methods and character of the Poles."[133] Last, close to fifty men from the Gestapo office in Frankfurt/Oder also reached Krössinsee on 22 August.[134]

Hammer and Bischoff personally greeted the men as they arrived at the *Ordensburg*. Afterward, the two commanders assigned each new group to its respective *Einsatzkommando*. The personnel of *Einsatzgruppe* IV were quartered in the SS barracks at Krössinsee for several days, during which they received weapons, equipment, and uniforms. Shortly before the beginning of the German offensive, the members of the Operational Group were divided into *Teilkommandos* and issued vehicles. On the eve of the attack, Beutel's *Gruppenstab* and EK 2/IV moved into position behind the 20th Motorized Infantry Division, a part of General Heinz Guderian's XIX Corps. Hammer's *Einsatzkommando* 1/IV took up positions in areas behind General Adolf Strauss's II Corps. *Einsatzgruppe* IV was now poised to follow General Günther von Kluge's Fourth Army into the Polish Corridor as it drove east toward the city of Bydgoszcz.[135]

At roughly the same time, *Einsatzgruppe* V was assembling in East Prussia in the city of Allenstein (Olsztyn). Command of *Einsatzgruppe* V fell to SS-*Standartenführer* Ernst Paul Damzog, the oldest Operational Group leader in Poland.[136] A professional police officer, Damzog was born in Strasbourg, Alsace, on 30 October 1882 to the family of a senior customs official.[137] In 1912, at the age of thirty, he joined the criminal police in Königsberg and was promoted to criminal commissar two years later in April 1914. In 1915, Damzog joined the kaiser's army and served with the military's Secret Field Police while also fighting in an artillery regiment on the Western Front. Following the war he became an officer in the *Schutzpolizei,* or uniformed police, and took an early interest in the Nazi Party. He was promoted to director of the criminal police office in Breslau and joined the SS in June 1933.[138] Six months later, in August 1934, SS-*Untersturmführer* Damzog transferred to Berlin and entered the SD. He held a number of posts over the next six years, including chief of Gestapo headquarters, Section III *(Abteilung Abwehrpolizei),* in charge of police counterintelligence, head of the Frankfurt/Oder Gestapo office, and Border Inspector I East *(Grenz-Inspekteur I Ost).*[139] Throughout his SS career, Damzog proved himself a "convinced" *(gefestigt)* National Socialist and obedient officer known for diligence in carrying out his orders.[140]

According to postwar West German legal authorities, Damzog had two *Einsatzkommandos* at his disposal.[141] However, practically nothing is known about these EKs except for the names of their commanding officers. SS-*Sturmbannführer* Dr. Heinz Graefe led the first, EK 1/V, while SS-*Hauptsturmführer* Dr. Robert Schefe commanded EK 2/V. A native of Leipzig, Heinz Graefe was born on 15 July 1908.[142] His father fell at the front in 1914, leaving his widowed mother to raise him by herself. Until 1928, the young Heinz attended *Gymnasium* in Leipzig. After completing his studies, Graefe enrolled at Heidelberg University to study law.[143] He spent the next few years attending classes at Heidelberg before transferring to the university in Leipzig. Graefe finished his law studies in 1932 and began acquiring practical experience working in various state law offices in

Saxony. At the same time, he started writing his doctoral dissertation and completed the work in 1937.[144]

Concerning his involvement with the Nazi Party and police, Graefe joined the SA in June 1933.[145] He then transferred to the SS in December that same year. Although the details are unclear, it appears that during his legal apprenticeship in Saxony in 1935, Graefe decided to pursue a career in the Security Service (SD). In July 1935, he received an assignment with the SD Higher Section Elbe and was stationed in Leipzig.[146] One year later, in January 1936, he transferred to Kiel, where he assumed command of the local Gestapo office. It was at this time that Graefe renounced Lutheranism and declared himself agnostic.[147] He remained in Kiel until September 1937, when he was reassigned to head the Gestapo office in Tilsit, East Prussia. One month after arriving in Tilsit, Graefe also assumed command of the SD subsection in Gumbinnen.

On the eve of the Polish campaign, Graefe was an SS-*Sturmbannführer*. He had also been reassigned to Security Police headquarters in Berlin in September 1938, and it was here that he received orders to head *Einsatzkommando* 1/V. Rounding out his qualifications for EK command was a typical three-month stint of training with a flak unit of the German army. After completing this training, Graefe received the rank of corporal in the army reserves.[148] Reviews of his character described him as "capable," but in the opinion of his superior, Jakob Sporrenberg, head of the SD Higher Section Northeast, Graefe was primarily a careerist whose commitment to National Socialism remained shaky. To remedy the problem, Sporrenberg recommended that Graefe receive further ideological instruction, although he did not specify what training Graefe needed.[149]

Graefe's fellow *Einsatzkommando* leader in *Einsatzgruppe* V was Dr. Robert Schefe. Born in Schwerin, Mecklenburg, on 23 August 1909, he was only thirty years old in September 1939, yet he had already forged a successful career in the SD.[150] Schefe joined the NSDAP in April 1932, and his application to the SS was accepted in February 1934. He entered the SD later that same year and appears to have taken a professional interest in law, studying for his degree in Schwerin while simultaneously pursuing his career in the SS. After acquiring his doctorate in May 1936, Schefe was reassigned to SD headquarters in Berlin in 1937 and then made head of the SD and Gestapo office in Allenstein on 1 September 1938.[151] Earlier that same year, he also attended two months of training in an army flak unit. Comments by superiors recorded in his SS file indicate that Schefe was "energetic" and assertive in carrying out his orders, a man who enjoyed exercising authority and "a single-minded SS leader

. . . ideologically *[weltanschaulich]* National Socialist and well suited for the SS *[SS-Mässig]*."[152]

Damzog's group was attached to the Third Army of General Georg von Küchler. Curiously, however, no effort seems to have been made to coordinate the activities of EG V with the command staff of the Third Army. The *Gruppenstab* of EG V gathered in Allenstein, some distance from von Küchler's Third Army headquarters in Mohrungen (Morag). The same did not hold true for the two *Einsatzkommandos*. After initially assembling in Allenstein, Graefe's EK 1/V moved into position near Major General Nikolaus von Falkenhorst's XXI Corps in the vicinity of Marienwerder (Kwidzyń). Similarly, Schefe's EK 2/V went forward to Neidenburg (Nidzica), where it began the campaign close behind Major General Walter Petzel's I Corps.[153] German plans called for the Third Army to strike southward out of East Prussia in two directions.[154] The XXI Corps would advance southwest toward Graudenz (Grudziądz), while the I Corps would launch its attack due south against the Polish defensive stronghold at Mława. Damzog's Operational Group was to move in behind the Third Army once Polish lines had been penetrated.

The final *Einsatzgruppe* to receive attention here is that commanded by SS-*Obergruppenführer* Udo von Woyrsch. Formed at the very beginning of September, von Woyrsch's Operational Group was unusual in several ways. To begin with, the unit differed from its counterparts in that it did not receive a numeric designation. Von Woyrsch's command was instead officially named the *Einsatzgruppe zur besonderen Verwendung* (EG z.b.V.), or Special Purpose Operational Group, implying that it was to serve a particular function in the coming campaign. Second, although the Special Purpose Operational Group included the same SS police personnel found in the other *Einsatzgruppen*, it also contained a sizable contingent of Order Police. Of the two groups within von Woyrsch's unit, the Sipo, SD, Kripo, and Gestapo personnel formed the core. Contingents of these officers arrived from Gestapo posts in Stuttgart, Nuremberg, Magdeburg, Hildesheim, Oppeln, and Wesermünde. They were then joined at the end of August by detachments from two Security Police training facilities.[155] SS-*Brigadeführer* Otto Hellwig commanded the first, a group of fifty to eighty cadets from the Sipo Leadership School *(Führerschule der Sipo)* in Berlin-Charlottenburg.[156] The second group included between forty and fifty men from the Sipo Border Police School (Sipo *Grenzpolizeischule*) at Pretzsch, under the leadership of SS-*Standartenführer* Dr. Hans Trummler.[157] In total, the combined strength of Sipo, Kripo, SD, and Gestapo personnel was 350 men. These officers assembled at the police headquarters in Oppeln and were placed under the command of von Woyrsch's deputy, SS-*Oberführer* Dr. Otto Rasch.[158]

The second, larger part of von Woyrsch's group comprised five battalions of Order Police led by Orpo Colonel Dr. Friedrich Wolfstieg. The units involved included Police Battalions 62 and 63 from Münster, Police Battalion 81 from Breslau, and Police Battalion 92 from Kassel.[159] In addition, Police Battalion 171 from Vienna arrived separately in East Upper Silesia to begin the invasion stationed directly on the German-Polish frontier. Each battalion was made up of roughly 450 men, bringing the total number of deployed Order Police personnel to around 2,250.[160] In the very last days of August and early September, the four battalions of von Woyrsch's group, excluding Police Battalion 171, assembled in Gleiwitz on the German-Polish border and were incorporated into *Polizeigruppe* 1 (Police Group 1) for the campaign.[161] Unfortunately, the command structure of EG z.b.V. is impossible to reconstruct. Postwar investigations into the activities of von Woyrsch's police shed little light on the organization of either the *Gruppenstab* of the Special Purpose Operational Group or the command apparatus of the subordinate Order Police units. However, detailed information exists on some of the ranking officers in the EG z.b.V., beginning with its commander.

A member of the Silesian nobility, Udo von Woyrsch was born on 24 July 1895 on his family's estate in Schanowitz bei Brieg, which was located near Breslau.[162] His grandfather, General Karl Remus von Woyrsch, had commanded a corps of Silesian militia *(Landwehr)* during the First World War and Udo himself served in the 4th Hussar Regiment.[163] Immediately after the war, in February 1919, von Woyrsch joined the Silesian Frontier Defense *Freikorps (Grenzschutz Schlesien Freikorps)* and participated in the failed Kapp putsch against the Weimar government in March 1920. Von Woyrsch's disaffection with the Weimar system remained strong throughout the 1920s, motivating him to become a member of the Nazi Party in October 1929. One year later, in November 1930, he joined the *Allgemeine*-SS and began to rise quickly through the ranks.[164] In September 1932, Heinrich Himmler promoted von Woyrsch to SS-*Oberführer* and charged him with the task of expanding the SS in Silesia.[165] Two years later, in December 1934, he received another promotion, this time to SS-*Obergruppenführer,* and was given command of the SS Higher Administrative Section Southeast (SS *Oberabschnitt Südost*) in Breslau.[166] Von Woyrsch remained in this post until April 1936, when he was called to Berlin to serve as a member of Himmler's personal staff.[167] His police training did not cease upon moving to Berlin. In October 1938, Himmler offered von Woyrsch the unique opportunity to complete four weeks of training with the Order Police. The reason, Himmler explained in a letter to Orpo chief Kurt Daluege, was to give von Woyrsch a thorough understanding of the "technical and practical" aspects of Order Police service.[168] Less than a year later, this experience would serve von Woyrsch well when he commanded mixed Sipo-Orpo police units in Poland.

Von Woyrsch's deputy and the commander of the Security Police contingent of the *Einsatzgruppe z.b.V.* was SS-*Oberführer* Dr. Emil Otto Rasch. The son of a finance officer for a local firm, Rasch was born in Friedrichsruh, East Prussia, on 7 December 1891.[169] He served on a torpedo boat during the First World War and after the armistice joined the 12th Border Guard Regiment *(Grenzschutzregiment)*. As a member of the 12th Border Guards, Rasch spent two years on the German-Polish frontier, participating in the fight against Polish nationalist groups.[170] He rounded out his combat experience against the Poles as a member of the Von Loewenfeld *Freikorps,* which he joined in January 1920 and remained a part of until the unit disbanded in March 1920.[171] Following Germany's political stabilization, Rasch devoted himself full-time to studying law, philosophy, and political science. He eventually acquired a law degree and worked as an attorney in Dresden.

The upsurge in the influence of the Nazi Party in the early 1930s apparently attracted Rasch, and he joined the NSDAP in 1931. Rasch subsequently joined the SS in 1933 and became the mayor of Radeberg that same year.[172] In 1936 he became a member of the Security Service (SD) and began to work full-time under Werner Best in Department I (Personnel and Administration) of Gestapo and Security Police headquarters in Berlin. The years thereafter saw Rasch occupy a variety of important positions, including chief of the Gestapo in Frankfurt/Main in 1937, inspector of the Security Police for Upper Austria in 1938, and, following several months employed in the newly established SD office in Prague, chief of the Higher SS Section Fulda-Werra.[173] Like many of his fellow EG and EK commanders, Rasch received promotions with dizzying speed throughout his career in the SD. Over the brief span from 1936 to 1939, he rose from the rank of *Untersturmführer* to *Oberführer,* a successful career path undoubtedly linked to his growing reputation as a "steadfast" National Socialist.[174]

Rasch's subordinate officers in the Sipo section of the *Einsatzgruppe z.b.V.* were SS-*Obersturmbannführer* Otto Hellwig and SS-*Standartenführer* Dr. Hans Trummler. Hellwig commanded the Sipo Leadership School in Berlin-Charlottenburg and led a unit of fifty to eighty Security Police cadets from his school into Poland. Hellwig's own background was as a veteran of the First World War and career police officer. Born in Nordhausen on 24 February 1898, he was the son of a businessman and thus came from the German middle class.[175] When he was just seventeen, Hellwig enlisted in the Imperial German Army in 1915 and fought for three years in France and Russia.[176] Following his discharge in 1918, he joined the Rossbach *Sturmabteilung,* a notorious right-wing *Freikorps* unit that fought in the Baltic States in 1919.[177] He left the Rossbach Storm Section in January 1920 and began his postwar career in the Prussian Political Police as an expert in counterespionage. Therefore, by the time he was twenty-two years old, Hellwig had seen five years of bloody combat, had firmly aligned himself with the radical right-wing political movement in Weimar Germany, and had become a member of the secret police apparatus.

When Hitler came to power in 1933, Hellwig was made chief of the Prussian Political Police office in Minden.[178] He then transferred to Hannover and became a member of the Nazi Party when the Gestapo absorbed the Prussian Political Police in October 1933. By July 1935 Hellwig had joined the SS and SD at the rank of *Hauptsturmführer.* He declared himself an agnostic and was reassigned to command the Gestapo office in Breslau.[179] Hellwig remained at this post until March 1937, when he was promoted to SS-*Obersturmbannführer* and given command of the Sipo Leadership School in Berlin-Charlottenburg, a position he retained until 1941.[180] His superiors regularly praised him throughout his career in the SS and SD. For example, a report filed in 1937 by the chief of staff for Security Police headquarters described Hellwig's character as "impeccable." Moreover, his peers universally respected him for his measured and professional behavior. And regarding his ideological commitment, Hellwig was described as "solidly" Nazi *(durchaus gefestigt).*[181]

Hellwig's opposite in the Special Purpose Operational Group was Dr. Hans Trummler. Born in Friedrichsroda, Thuringia, on 24 October 1900, Trummler was the son of a businessman *(Kaufmann).* He was also three years younger than Hellwig by the outbreak of the war in September 1939.[182] Like Hellwig, Trummler had enlisted in the Imperial German Army (at the age of seventeen) and fought in the 104th and 106th Infantry Regiments.[183] For nearly two years after the end of the war, he also served in *Freikorps* units, including the 5th Saxon Rifle Battalion and the Leipzig Volunteer Regiment, participating in, as he put it, "the struggle against internal unrest, particularly during the Kapp Putsch."[184] Following the *Freikorps*'s dissolution, Trummler attended the university in Leipzig, earned his doctorate in economics, and began a career as a banker. However, he never strayed far from the political right, joining the Nazi Party and the SA in 1928. Within a few years he had assumed responsible positions in the SA hierarchy and was named head of the SA training school in Leipzig in April 1934.[185]

Trummler was then swept up in the turmoil following the purge of the SA that Hitler ordered in June 1934. He was arrested by the SS in Leipzig on 30 June and interned in Berlin for several weeks.[186] After his release in July, Trummler realized that his days in the SA were numbered, and he applied to join the SS. He was accepted into the SS in July 1935 and given the rank of *Standartenführer*, which he retained until the outbreak of the war.[187] Trummler's failure to receive promotions was undoubtedly linked to his erratic behavior in the various locations to which he was assigned between 1935 and 1936. Assigned first to the Higher SS Section Northwest in 1935, where he headed the SS sports training facility, and then to the SS Border Police office in Munich in spring 1936, Trummler left a trail of complaints against him wherever he went. These complaints are instructive in that they contain commentary on his disposition by SS and Nazi Party officers.

The regional Nazi Party agricultural office in Braunschweig lodged one such complaint in September 1935. After condemning Trummler's behavior in the strongest terms, the reporting official described him as "brutal and ruthless." Ironically, though, the report also noted that Trummler fully commanded the obedience *(Kadavergehorsam)* of his students and that he carried himself like a "Prussian officer."[188] His bad conduct ultimately led to a systematic investigation by the Criminal Police in Leipzig. In February 1936, this investigation concluded that Trummler's behavior was "shameful" to the Nazi Party.[189] He was notorious for his excessive drinking and for brawling with local members of the Nazi Party. Possessing a "raw and brutal character," one report concluded that he was prone to childish outbursts, the author stating categorically that Trummler was a "psychopath."[190] But while these and other complaints likely kept him from receiving promotions in rank, they did not have any tangible effect on the responsibilities he was given. He was assigned to SD headquarters in May 1938, declared himself agnostic, and was eventually chosen to head the SS Border Police School at Pretzsch. By mid-1939, Trummler was also the chief of Department III H in Gestapo headquarters, which made him responsible for the establishment of SS Border Police posts.[191] Comments from his file indicate that despite his reputation for brutality and violent behavior, Trummler excelled at training Security Police officers to be dedicated National Socialists. It was apparently this talent that saved him from prosecution by an SS honor court and that recommended him for service with the *Einsatzgruppen* in Poland.

Conclusions

Upon reflection it becomes clear that the backgrounds of the *Einsatzgruppe* and *Einsatzkommando* leaders examined above shared certain fundamental characteristics that appealed to Heydrich, Werner Best, and Hans Tesmer. In general, these men fit the basic profile outlined by Jens Banach for members of what he calls the Security Police and Security Service leadership corps. Most of the leaders of Operational Groups I-V, as well as many of the *Einsatzkommando* chiefs, were in their mid- to late thirties by the beginning of the Polish campaign. Fifty-six-year-old Ernst Damzog, forty-four-year-old Udo von Woyrsch, forty-eight-year-old Johann Schmer, forty-one-year-old Otto Sens, forty-eight-year-old Otto Rasch, and forty-one-year-old Otto Hellwig were the exceptions. Moreover, practically all of the Operational Group and *Einsatzkommando* commanders, once again with the exception of noble-born von Woyrsch, came from the middle-class, a segment of German society that Banach finds was overrepresented in the Gestapo, SD, and Criminal Police.[192]

According to Banach, these older Sipo and SD officers saw their world destroyed with the collapse of the German empire and the birth of the socialist Weimar republic in late 1918.[193] Raised in a time of political upheaval, street violence, and revolution, they reacted to the instability around them by turning to authoritarian groups on the political right. In the years immediately after the war, those who were of military service age, including Streckenbach, Schaefer, Beutel, von Woyrsch, Brunner, Schmer, Sens, Rasch, Hellwig, and Trummler, joined *Freikorps* (nationalist and anti-Weimar paramilitary units). These units were filled with men bent on destroying the republic, fighting communism, and defending German interests in Eastern Europe, particularly against the territorial claims of the Poles. Following the establishment of an uneasy status quo in Germany between 1921 and 1923, many of these men remained affiliated with various right-wing political parties or *völkisch* movements that were hostile to the republic, and they eagerly joined the Nazi Party as it rose in popularity in the late 1920s and early 1930s. In this sense, service with the *Freikorps* proved to be an important ideological and experiential platform for later affiliation with the NSDAP.[194]

It is important, however, to draw some distinctions at this point between older (those born before 1899) and younger EG and EK commanders. Based on Banach's detailed analysis, the outlines of two clearly definable groups within the *Einsatzgruppen* become clear: the older group described above and a younger group of men who led the *Einsatzkommandos*. Banach concludes that many of the younger members of the Sipo, SD, and Gestapo attended *Gymnasia* and universities in the 1920s that had been radicalized by the recent changes in German society. Nationalistically inclined teachers and professors exposed their students to the ideology of "heroic realism," which drew certain lessons from the violence of the First World War. Heroic realists portrayed the postwar generation as a new elite brought up in a world of constant struggle. These views included anti-Semitism and Social Darwinism as core concepts that allegedly revealed the "biological causes of social conflict" and that echoed *völkisch* calls for "cleansing" the German race of contaminants.[195] Alongside racism and anti-Semitism was a sense of social activism, a fascination with technology, and careerism, which explains to Banach why so many in the leadership corps of the Sipo, Gestapo, and SD held advanced degrees.[196]

Twelve of the younger commanders of the *Einsatzkommandos* examined above (those born after 1899) certainly fit this profile. Rux attended but did not complete university, while Hahn, Müller, Hasselberg, Brunner, Scharpwinkel, Liphardt, Bischoff, Hammer, Graefe, Schefe, and Trummler all held law degrees, which recommended them for positions in the Security Police, and particularly the SD. The early involvement of these younger men with the Nazi Party and SS similarly bears out Banach's argument. Of the twelve EK and detachment commanders discussed above, six were members of the NSDAP before 1933, while the other six joined in 1933.[197] Regarding the SS, seven of twelve already belonged to the SS by 1933, while the other five had joined the SS by 1936. In short, the younger heads of the *Einsatzkommandos* and other subordinate detachments were well educated, of middle-class backgrounds, and attracted to Nazism early on. As Banach contends, these men brought intelligence and ambition to the Sipo, SD, and Gestapo as well as a revolutionary activism that suited the professional esprit de corps of Himmler's SS.[198] And while their paths to the SS did not run directly from the *Freikorps* to the NSDAP, as did those of some of the older EG and EK commanders, the Nazi Party provided a political movement flexible enough to suit senior and junior officers alike.

Clearly, the common elements in the backgrounds of younger and older *Einsatzgruppen* and *Einsatzkommando* chiefs help explain how these men came to the Nazi Party and the SS. Yet they do not directly answer the questions posed at the beginning of this investigation. Specifically, is it possible to glean from the backgrounds of these men what experience they had by the summer of 1939 that Heydrich, Best, and Tesmer would have considered "relevant" to upcoming operations in Poland? Furthermore, Heydrich had demanded that EG and EK commanders have a proper military bearing, but did this necessarily mean that the men chosen by Tesmer and Best had to have formal military training? Based on the detailed biographies discussed above, it is possible to construct a threefold answer to these questions. In the first place, knowledge of conditions in the east seems to have been a significant factor in the selection of at least some of these individuals. Whether this meant having experience fighting the Poles at the end of World War I, being a native of eastern Germany, or being assigned to a Gestapo office near the border, personal familiarity with the political tensions along the German-Polish frontier and the history of German-Polish ethnic conflict apparently recommended certain men for command positions in the *Einsatzgruppen*. In this sense, for example, Emanuel Schaefer, Udo von Woyrsch, Otto Sens, Otto Rasch, and Otto Hellwig had all fought against the Poles as members of paramilitary or border units during the 1919–1921 uprisings in East Upper Silesia. Moreover, Rasch was raised in East Prussia, while Schaefer and von Woyrsch were natives of Silesia. The commander of EK 1/IV, Helmut Bischoff, was also born and raised in Glogau, Silesia, and the family of *Einsatzkommando* 2/II chief Karl-Heinz Rux had lost its home in Bromberg (Bydgoszcz) after Germany ceded territory to Poland in 1919.

In other cases, individuals given command positions already had considerable experience policing the German-Polish frontier. Included among these men were Alfred Hasselberg, the chief of the Gestapo in the border town of Schneidemühl; Ernst Damzog, chief of the Border Inspectorate East *(Grenzinspekteur I: Ost)*; Wilhelm Scharpwinkel, head of the Breslau Gestapo; Fritz Liphardt, head of the Gestapo in Frankfurt/Oder; Robert Schefe, chief of the Gestapo in Allenstein, East Prussia; Heinz Graefe, leader of the Gestapo office in Tilsit; and Hans Trummler, head of the SS Border Police School in Pretzsch. Altogether, three of the six *Einsatzgruppen* commanders and ten of the fifteen commanders of the *Einsatzkommandos* and smaller detachments shared experience of some kind along Germany's frontier with Poland. Therefore, given the vagueness of Heydrich's instructions about the selection of *Einsatzgruppen* personnel, Best and Tesmer likely considered familiarity dealing with the Poles and other issues pertaining to Germany's eastern border relevant to the task at hand.

A second criterion in the selection of suitable SS and police personnel by Best and Tesmer was professional achievement in the Sipo, SD, Gestapo, or Kripo as well as what this illustrated about the character of the individual officer. According to the testimony of Hans Tesmer during the 1968 trial of Werner Best, he had been ordered by Best to find "SS leaders who would work ruthlessly and callously to achieve National Socialist aims."[199] Looking back at the extant comments on the character and ideological conviction of the men examined above, it would be difficult to conclude that these individuals were not committed National Socialists. With the exception of the reputed "psychopath" Hans Trummler, all of the men whose biographies are reconstructed here rose rapidly through the ranks of the SS and Gestapo. Yet even Trummler, because of his devotion to National Socialism, continued to acquire important responsibilities training young Sipo and SD officers.

It is perhaps no surprise, then, that to a man, the heads of *Einsatzgruppen* I–V as well as Udo von Woyrsch were reputed to be competent and dedicated SS officers who had assumed ever more responsibility as their careers in the Gestapo progressed. Officers like Schaefer, Fischer, and Beutel had held multiple commands by 1939, while Streckenbach and Damzog had risen in the ranks of the SS Inspectorate, making them, in the words of George Browder, "direct agents for Heydrich and Himmler in the field."[200] And for his part, von Woyrsch was a member of Himmler's personal staff. The situation was no different with the *Einsatzkommando* leaders, every one of whom headed a Gestapo office. These men had risen to positions of responsibility because of their ideological commitment and willingness to vigorously carry out orders. As one witness commented during Best's trial, a man like Streckenbach was well known for being a "radical" *(Scharfmacher)* when it came to completing his tasks.[201] Heydrich, Best, and Tesmer sought out these men among the SS ranks and installed them at the head of the *Einsatzgruppen* and *Einsatzkommandos* precisely because of their reliability and willingness to implement a radical program like Operation TANNENBERG.

This result raises the issue of Heydrich's demand for men who possessed a proper military bearing. It appears that Best and Tesmer took Heydrich's instructions literally, because practically all of the officers they selected either had direct combat experience in World War I or had trained as members of the army reserve.[202] EG commanders Schaefer, Damzog, and von Woyrsch all saw combat in the First World War, as did EK commanders Schmer, Brunner, Sens, Rasch, Hellwig, and Trummler. Lothar Beutel, the head of *Einsatzgruppe* IV, served two years in the *Reichswehr* immediately after the war. The remaining men, Streckenbach, Fischer, Hahn, Müller, Hasselberg, Liphardt, Bischoff, Hammer, Graefe, and Schefe, received their military training in various units of the army reserve. And of all the individuals named here, Damzog, Beutel, Hasselberg, and Liphardt had actually aspired to careers in the German army but had their ambitions thwarted by political developments in the 1920s. The fact that 99 percent of the *Einsatzgruppen* and *Einsatzkommando* chiefs deployed in Poland had military training is surely not coincidental. Rather, it is evidence of the efforts made by Heydrich, Best, and Tesmer to find men who could work most effectively with German military officers.[203] The Operational Groups were, after all, paramilitary SS and police units deployed in wartime and expected to cooperate closely with a variety of Wehrmacht security forces.[204] As Streckenbach made perfectly clear after the war, and as the deployment locations of many of the *Einsatzkommandos* further demonstrate, Best and Heydrich tried hard to coordinate the work of their forces with the military. They took the army's operational plans well into account when selecting locations to start the campaign, and the army reciprocated by using units like the *Gruppe Schmer* to guard important installations.

In the final analysis, the men who commanded the *Einsatzgruppen* and *Einsatzkommandos* were selected on the basis of their experience and accomplishments in the SS and police. More important, however, is what the backgrounds of these men suggest about the way in which the SS implemented its murderous policies. In the case of Operation TANNENBERG, Adolf Hitler set the overall ideological parameters for the Germanization of Poland and then ordered Heydrich to go about organizing the appropriate forces for the job. Heydrich responded by issuing general guidelines to Werner Best, who in turn sought the assistance of Hans Tesmer in finding the necessary manpower. Thus, the Third Reich's first steps toward mass murder, in this instance the annihilation of a segment of Polish society, were not driven by capricious historical circumstances but by orders, and it was pursuant to these orders that the commanders of the *Einsatzgruppen* and *Einsatzkommandos* were deployed in Poland. Heydrich and his subordinates did their best to put into place appropriate personnel to facilitate cooperation with the military. Anti-Polish and anti-Semitic sentiment also smoothed the progress of arrangements worked out by the SS and army before the invasion. Generally speaking, these sentiments continued to have a beneficial impact on combined SS-army security operations in the field. The same would not prove true of cooperation between Wehrmacht and SS leaders back in Berlin. For although Canaris, Wagner, and Halder had hints before the campaign about the scale and ferocity of the killing program the SS intended to implement in Poland, once detailed information about the intended extermination of the Polish upper class came to light and the murderous activities of the *Einsatzgruppen* were fully revealed, hate for and fear of Poles and Jews would not prove strong enough to ultimately prevent a marked deterioration of relations between Army High Command and SS authorities.

THREE

THE GERMAN ARMY AND THE OPENING PHASE OF OPERATION TANNENBERG

Within hours after Nazi Germany opened its offensive against Poland on 1 September, armed civilians and paramilitary groups fighting alongside regular Polish troops began inflicting casualties on advancing Wehrmacht units. Armed resistance by the civilian population confirmed German fears and validated the army's agreement to work with the *Einsatzgruppen* and other police formations. But while preinvasion negotiations and the exchange of information between the Wehrmacht and the Gestapo demonstrated the former's readiness to target Polish political opponents and insurgent groups, the potential for conflicts to arise between the army and the SS during the campaign remained very real. The intended liquidations mentioned by Hitler on 22 August, as well as Heydrich's and Best's admission to Colonel Wagner on 29 August about the extensive arrests that were planned, fueled the suspicions of officers like Franz Halder that the Security Police and SS Death's Head units had been charged with a more nefarious task than simply providing security behind the lines.

These reservations posed a quandary for Wehrmacht commanders who were fully prepared to support the arrest and imprisonment of the Reich's enemies, but not the murder of entire segments of Polish society. Consequently, some officers, particularly Admiral Canaris and General Brauchitsch, grew increasingly critical of the SS during the campaign. Their condemnation of SS killings was significant, but the extent to which it represented opinion throughout the German officer corps is questionable. Indeed, a close examination of the rapport between the SS and the army during the Polish campaign reveals a variety of responses by German officers to SS operations. Those who objected to SS killings did not necessarily do so because they found such actions morally repugnant. They often protested out of concern for the potentially negative impact that those actions could have on military discipline as well as in jealous defense of the army's executive authority. By the same token, many officers remained completely silent on the issue of SS killings, and still others worked quite successfully with the SS. Combined SS-army actions bore fruit especially in the suppression of civilian resistance and the arrest of political opponents. When all was said and done, it would be the army's collaboration with the SS in destroying Polish "irregulars" that proved critical to the initial success of SS efforts to liquidate the leading and educated elements of Polish society.

The Suppression of Polish Resistance in the Polish Corridor

Military intelligence reports compiled in the months before the German attack indicated that civilians living in areas of western Poland would probably pose the greatest threat to Wehrmacht troops. In particular, German military planners expected opposition to be strongest in the so-called Polish Corridor, which was a narrow stretch of territory that lay between Pomerania and East Prussia. According to Włodzimierz Jastrzębski, this region was home to no fewer than twelve paramilitary organizations established during the interwar period, and by 1939 their combined membership totaled nearly 12,000 men.[1] To German commanders, these irregular formations posed a grave danger to military personnel and the thousands of ethnic Germans who lived in the region. Therefore, the army and SS focused considerable energy and resources on destroying these guerrilla groups, both while formal hostilities were under way and even after Polish forces in the Corridor had been destroyed.

General Günter von Kluge's Fourth Army was assigned the task of cutting through the Corridor from the west. The Fourth Army was one of two that made up Field Marshal Fedor von Bock's Army Group North, with the other being the Third Army under the command of General Georg von Küchler. Facing the Fourth Army was the Polish *Pomorze* Army, which had been assigned the difficult task of defending the Corridor from both the east and the west. The *Pomorze* Army absorbed the initial shock of the Fourth Army's assault on 1 September, but by the following day its defensive positions had already begun to crumble. Confronted with the Third Army's attack near Grudziądz (Graudenz), the *Pomorze* Army increasingly found itself squeezed between Kluge and Küchler's armies. On 4 September, Major General Bortnowski, the commander of the *Pomorze* Army, recognized the precarious position his forces were in and ordered a general retreat toward Łódź and Warsaw. The Third and Fourth Armies then linked up north of Grudziądz and quickly destroyed Polish units that remained in the Corridor.[2]

Behind General Kluge's front, SS-*Brigadeführer* Lothar Beutel and the men of *Einsatzgruppe* IV waited at the SS *Ordensburg* (training facility) in Krössinsee for orders to move east. On 1 September Josef Meisinger, a Gestapo officer and the deputy commander of *Einsatzgruppe* IV, stood before the Operational Group's assembled personnel in the courtyard of the *Ordensburg*. Meisinger announced first that as of 4:45 A.M. a state of war existed between Poland and Germany.[3] He then declared that in the coming days events were likely to take place that might make many of the men uncomfortable. Regardless of these difficulties, Meisinger reminded them, the outbreak of war meant that every man was now under military law. Accordingly, all SS personnel were expected to show "unconditional obedience" in carrying out their orders. Disobedience due to cowardice or for any other reason, Meisinger threatened, would not be tolerated, and he hinted that discipline in the unit would be strictly enforced.[4] Early the next day the men of SS-*Sturmbannführer* Helmut Bischoff's *Einsatzkommando* 1/IV loaded into their vehicles and drove into Poland past the smoking wreckage of the *Pomorze* Army's defensive fortifications. Lothar Beutel remained behind in Krössinsee with his command staff, intending to accompany SS-*Sturmbannführer* Walter Hammer and *Einsatzkommando* 2/IV into the Corridor several days later.

Upon departing from the *Ordensburg* barracks, Bischoff split his men into two *Teilkommandos,* or sections, which separated and moved east in the wake of the 50th and 3d Infantry Divisions. Bischoff and his staff traveled with the larger of these *Teilkommandos,* that of SS-*Untersturmführer* Edmund Schoene. The second *Teilkommando,* under SS-*Untersturmführer* Kurt Vogel, remained stationed along the frontier southwest of Chojnice (Konitz). Both *Teilkommandos* had instructions from the outset of the invasion to "free army rear areas from saboteurs, enemy agents, and partisans." But as Bischoff later admitted to West German prosecutors, he also entered Poland on the lookout for political opponents listed in the *Sonderfahndungsbuch*. It was for this reason, Bischoff stated, that he elected to have Edmund Schoene's men operate as a unified *Teilkommando*.[5] Because of their long years of service at the Gestapo border post of Koszalin (Köslin), Bischoff had complete trust in the anti-Polish attitudes of Schoene's men, and he valued their intimate knowledge of the "methods and character traits of the Poles."[6]

After passing through Łobżenica (Lobsens), Schoene's *Teilkommando* headed southeast toward Nakło (Nakel), where heavy fighting continued to take place between General Bortnowski's troops and the 50th Infantry Division. Outside of Nakło, soldiers with the 50th Infantry turned over their first prisoners to the *Teilkommando*. One of these was an unfortunate farmer on whose property the *Pomorze* Army had planted land mines. German soldiers detained the man after he failed to warn them about the danger and one of the explosives mortally wounded a Wehrmacht sergeant.[7] The second prisoner was the owner of a mill on whose property Polish troops had set up a machine-gun nest. German troops took the man into custody after destroying the stronghold and then transferred him to Schoene's *Teilkommando*. Bischoff ordered Schoene's men to shoot both of the prisoners without the benefit of a formal court-martial.

Shortly thereafter, Bischoff personally executed a Pole in Nakło for plundering. He claimed to have detained the man for carrying an armload of goods, and he shot the Pole on the spot to demonstrate to civilian onlookers the penalty for looting. Upon later reading of this shooting in a letter Bischoff had written in 1943, Walter Hammer dismissed Bischoff's version of the incident, commenting that killing the Pole was likely "all the same" to an unusually brutal man like Bischoff.[8] Schoene's *Teilkommando* was delayed in Nakło for the next two days as the Polish 15th Infantry Division of General Przyjałkowski stiffened its resistance around the nearby city of Bydgoszcz (Bromberg). This delay gave Schoene's men additional time to scour the area for Poles named in the Wanted Persons List. As it turned out, Schoene's men arrested a priest named Geppert and executed between eight and ten other Poles. Father Geppert was not killed straightaway but was transferred to the Gestapo office in Schneidemühl for questioning and later sent to the Dachau concentration camp, where he perished in July 1942.[9]

Meanwhile, the other half of Bischoff's command, the *Teilkommando* Vogel, had begun conducting security operations just to the north of Nakło. Arriving in Wiecbork (Vandsburg) on 2 September, Vogel reported to the local military commander for orders. This officer informed Vogel that Wehrmacht troops had already assembled all Polish men in the vicinity between the ages of seventeen and forty-five and interned them in the local prison.[10] Vogel was instructed to interrogate the detainees and discover which of them worked at the local rail station. Those who had experience were to be put to work immediately repairing the important rail junction. The army commander also informed Vogel that the perpetrators of crimes against local ethnic Germans could probably be found among the prisoners. After receiving his orders, Vogel and his men spent the next two days searching for railroad workers and interrogating prisoners. He also took the opportunity to check the names of the prisoners against those listed in the *Sonderfahndungsbuch*.[11] All in all, Bischoff later recalled, his *Teilkommandos* cooperated quite closely with the Wehrmacht in these first days of the war.[12]

By 4 September a steady flow of reports from German units in the region indicated that the mistreatment of *Volksdeutsche* in Wiecbork was not an isolated incident. According to one such report, filed by the III Corps, "the Polish military [had] searched the dwellings of ethnic Germans" in several locations and savagely abused the inhabitants.[13] This news prompted the Fourth Army General Staff to coordinate reprisals against Polish civilians, and a conference was called at Fourth Army headquarters in the village of Kosowo.[14] Responding to the summons, Lothar Beutel arrived in Kosowo with his command staff on the evening of 4 September, just as the Fourth Army placed Major General Walter Braemer, the commander of the 580th Rear Army Area (*Korück* 580), in charge of security for the region.[15] Braemer's appointment came as Fourth Army troops were preparing to assault Bydgoszcz the following day. Consequently, and in preparation for the pacification of the city, Beutel's Operational Group and the military units in the area as well as the 6th Motorized Police Battalion from Berlin under Police General Mülverstedt were put at Braemer's disposal. *Einsatzkommando* 2/IV had only just entered the region on 5 September, however, and Walter Hammer's men had their hands full combing Chojnice (Konitz) for political opponents.[16] Beutel reported to Berlin on 6 September that the area in and around Chojnice was "swimming with Polish troops detached from their units, and with irregulars," which forced him to leave Hammer's command in its place.[17] In an effort to bring *Einsatzkommando* 2/IV to Bydgoszcz, Beutel sent a request to Berlin for the deployment of additional Order Police in Chojnice to continue the pacification of the town.

Conditions in Bydgoszcz itself had steadily deteriorated in the days immediately after the beginning of the German invasion. Situated squarely between Pomerania and East Prussia, Bydgoszcz was home to a considerable number of ethnic Germans, many of whom belonged to underground political groups organized by Nazi sympathizers.[18] Armed clashes between Polish troops and members of the *Volksdeutsche* underground broke out in the days between the beginning of the German offensive and the Wehrmacht's occupation on 5 September. This fighting resulted in a significant number of ethnic German casualties, the exact number of which has never been determined. The best estimate of one Polish scholar is that Polish troops killed around 1,000 *Volksdeutsche* in Bydgoszcz and shot 100 others during a forced march to Kutno.[19] Soon after the news of these casualties broke in Germany, however, Joseph Goebbels's Propaganda Ministry launched a press campaign to inflame public opinion against the Poles. Reports in the press soon inflated the total number of ethnic Germans killed to over 5,400, thus giving birth to the legend of the so-called "Bromberg Bloody Sunday."[20]

The last Polish troops pulled out of Bydgoszcz on the night of 4–5 September, leaving defense of the city to the civilian militia, which the Bydgoszcz Civil Defense Committee mobilized on 2 September. Konrad Fiedler, the editor of the *Bydgoszcz Gazette* and chair of the city council, headed the nine-man Civil Defense Committee, while the other members included Reserve Lieutenant Stanisław Pałaszewski; Dr. Mieczysław Nawrowski, the vice president of the city government; Józef Szulc, the dean of the city cathedral; and the head of a local electronics firm named Marian Miczuga.[21] Word of the militia's formation spread rapidly, resulting in the mobilization of roughly 2,200 railway workers, artisans, laborers, civil servants, postal workers, boy scouts, and students. Arms were distributed from army arsenals, and two strongholds were established. The first of these was in the center of Bydgoszcz, where the Civil Defense Committee established its headquarters in the city hall. Defending the Civil Defense Committee headquarters were 200 members of the *Obrana Narodowa* (Polish National Defense), a paramilitary force organized throughout Poland's western provinces. Two thousand members of the militia erected a second line of defense in the southern half of the city centered on the neighborhood of Schwedenhöhe.[22] Streets were hastily barricaded, and the militia members took up positions in the apartment blocks to await the German assault.

The first troops from Lieutenant General Konrad Sorsche's 50th Infantry Division entered Bydgoszcz from two directions early on 5 September. The 121st and 122d Infantry Regiments advanced from the north, while the 123d Infantry Regiment, under the command of Major General von Block, entered the city from the west. After bypassing the city center, the 123d Regiment moved south toward Schwedenhöhe, where its reconnaissance detachments suddenly came under concentrated rifle fire. Consistent with standard army policy at the time, Block ordered his men to respond by razing any building from which shots had come. Fighting then broke out in earnest between the 123d Regiment and the Polish militia.[23] At roughly the same time, the 122d Regiment also encountered gunfire as it advanced along Danzig Street toward city hall. The *Teilkommando* Schoene joined in the fighting at this time, and the Poles fell back under German pressure until they reached the market square outside city hall.[24] Cut off from their comrades in Schwedenhöhe, the militiamen in city hall surrendered a short time later. According to Bischoff's version of the incident, the roughly 190 Poles gave themselves up after the Security Police killed ten of their countrymen in the firefight.[25] However, several Polish witnesses stated after the war that the Civil Defense Committee ordered the surrender after two German army officers under a white flag promised safe conduct home to those who threw down their weapons.[26] Whatever the conditions of their capitulation, the defenders of Bydgoszcz city hall were immediately arrested after stacking their weapons. As they left the building, witnesses recalled, "the militia members were beaten by German soldiers who kicked and struck them with rifle-butts."[27]

Soon after German troops secured the city hall, the new *Stadtkommandant* (military commander) of Bydgoszcz, Brigadier General Eccard Freiherr von Gablenz, established his headquarters in the former offices of the Civil Defense Committee. Military officers and the Security Police then interrogated several members of the committee and eventually compelled them to sign an order calling for the surrender of the remaining militia units in the city.[28] Within an hour, German troops escorted a messenger from the militia forces still fighting in Schwedenhöhe to city hall where he received a copy of the order.[29] This courier then returned to Schwedenhöhe, and the militia forces there gave themselves up shortly thereafter.

The formal end of combat in Bydgoszcz on 5 September did not bring an end to shooting in the city. Reports of attacks on German personnel continued to arrive at General Gablenz's headquarters throughout the night of 5–6 September, prompting him to order the city's full-scale pacification.[30] This operation began early the next morning as Wehrmacht troops, Order Police, and Bischoff's Security Police searched housing blocks for weapons and snipers. The definition of a weapon even included flintlock rifles and antique bayonets, and the unfortunate owners of such "weapons" were shot on the spot.[31] *Volksdeutsche* informants also supplied the Security Police with the names of Poles who were considered "suspicious." As a result, General Gablenz recorded in his war diary, German troops and police arrested "several thousand" Poles and incarcerated them in the Polish military facilities that were scattered throughout the city.[32] Of these prisoners, at least 500 were imprisoned in the former barracks of the Polish 15th Light Artillery Regiment, located on Danzig Street. These barracks served as the central internment center in Bydgoszcz, although makeshift prisons were also created in the barracks of the 10th and 16th Cavalry Regiments.[33]

Walther Nethe, a member of Schoene's *Teilkommando,* later testified that during these sweeps "the city of Bromberg and the surrounding area were also combed for members of the Polish intelligentsia," leading to the capture of hundreds of teachers, civil servants, lawyers, and other prominent persons in the community.[34] Among the captives was Franciszek Derezinski, who later described to Polish prosecutors what had transpired after his arrest: "I was picked up on the street by German police and led to the artillery barracks, along with around five hundred other Poles. Ethnic Germans were

Polish hostages taken by German troops during the "pacification" of Bydgoszcz await execution, 6–13 September 1939. (Institute of National Remembrance, Commission for the Prosecution of Crimes against the Polish Nation; courtesy of the U.S. Holocaust Memorial Museum, Photo Reference Collection: WS 50832)

there identifying people who had allegedly murdered *Volksdeutsche*. These persons were immediately shot and local Jews were forced to dig a grave for them in the courtyard of the barracks."[35] The executions were carried out by "uniformed men [armed with] machine pistols," a weapon favored by Sipo and Gestapo officers.[36] Two other witnesses recounted that Security Police stood at the entrance to the barracks screening new prisoners according to their religion. Catholics (generally Poles) were held indefinitely, while Lutherans (typically Germans) were released quickly. According to Nethe, it was during these actions that all of the prisoners who could be classified as members of the intelligentsia were identified and "liquidated."[37]

The summary execution of prisoners in the artillery barracks and the shooting of persons in the streets of Bydgoszcz were fully in line with instructions that Himmler had secretly issued to the *Einsatzgruppen* on 3 September. Calling for "insurgents" to be "shot on the spot" if they surrendered or if a civilian was discovered to be in possession of a weapon, Himmler's 3 September directive stipulated that in cases where large groups of Polish irregulars were captured, the Security Police were to consult him immediately to decide the prisoners' fate. The directive further stated:

Insurgents are defined as all persons who individually or communally attack members of the German occupation forces, or *Volksdeutsche,* or who threaten institutions and properties critical to protecting the lives of these persons in the occupied territories. In every area where insurgents are encountered, leading figures from the local Polish political administration are to be taken as hostages. If it becomes necessary to shoot hostages in order to prevent attacks by insurgents, it is to be reported to me immediately so that I may render a decision.[38]

Scholars have made much of the fact that Himmler's directive was technically illegal due to Hitler's granting of executive authority *(vollziehende Gewalt)* in Poland to the Wehrmacht and not the SS.[39] Yet the use of leading civilians as hostages and the immediate execution of irregulars were consistent with orders that military authorities issued at roughly the same time as Himmler's directive. Instructions handed down by Army High Command before the invasion required that civilians arrested for attacks on Germans were to be tried by court-martial, and it was for this purpose that on 6 September the III Corps established a temporary Special Court *(Sondergericht)* in Bydgoszcz city hall.[40] However, an activity report produced by the court reveals that it was overwhelmed by its task. Court officers were required to investigate anti-German acts "for which atonement was demanded," but pacification actions in the city had already netted "hundreds of suspicious elements *[verdächtigen Elementen].*"[41]

What was more, reports coming in over the next several days noted that Polish snipers were still regularly inflicting casualties on German units in the city. These reports also made their way to Berlin, as illustrated by an entry on 7–8 September in the war diary of Gestapo headquarters, which mentioned that during the night in Bydgoszcz "troop transports had been fired on, [as well as] soldiers quartered in private houses, official German offices, individuals and military patrols." This gunfire had already claimed the lives of two men, and after 8:00 P.M. sniping began on German offices in Bydgoszcz city hall and continued sporadically until the early morning hours.[42] The III Corps's court-martial had neither the time nor the staff to investigate these incidents, and consequently its members concluded that in order to properly try those persons responsible for the murder of ethnic Germans it would be necessary to establish a permanent court-martial.[43]

In the interim, the pressing need to respond to civilian attacks led military authorities to implement draconian measures that essentially bypassed the Special Court and allowed German troops and the Security Police to take matters into their own hands. Beginning on 7 September, the Fourth

Army ordered that all military and police units in Bydgoszcz were to take and summarily execute hostages in response to civilian attacks.[44] Accordingly, after the spate of new attacks on German troops and ethnic German civilians during the night of 7–8 September, Werner Kampe, the new German lord mayor of Bydgoszcz, and Major General Braemer issued a public warning: "Anyone shooting at German soldiers or civilians, or found with a weapon, will be shot. Similarly, anyone found plundering or otherwise pillaging will be shot. The large number of hostages arrested on 8 September will be executed if any Germans are shot or other attacks against Germans are undertaken. The hostages will be displayed to the populace on the Old Market Square [in front of city hall]."[45] Heedless of the warning, a Polish civilian shot and severely wounded a soldier with the 218th Antitank Section during the night. On the following morning (9 September), the 6th Motorized Police Battalion, the Security Police, and regular German troops, particularly men from the 1st Signal Regiment, carried out executions on the Old Market Square. Werner Kampe estimated that nearly 400 Polish hostages lost their lives in these and other reprisal shootings, but he was unable to arrive at an exact total.[46]

The execution of hostages was not the most radical measure instituted by Wehrmacht authorities in Bydgoszcz. Also on 8 September, General von Haase, commander of the III Corps, ordered that Polish civilians found with firearms or any other kind of weapon *(Angriffswerkzeug)* were to be "shot on the spot."[47] General Haase's instructions further stated that the same harsh treatment was to be meted out to plunderers and Polish soldiers guilty of "raiding" shops and private homes. It was only through "the ruthless and rapid deployment of all available forces *[Machtmittel]*," Haase concluded, that "units in army rear areas, the [German] civil administration, and the German populace" could be protected. Four hours later, Major General Braemer ordered placards posted throughout the city warning Poles that "whoever shoots at German soldiers or civilians, or in whose possession weapons are found, will be shot."[48]

Comments about the measures being implemented in Bydgoszcz by the army eventually found their way into reports the Security Police sent back to Berlin. On the morning of 7 September, Beutel reported to Gestapo headquarters that German forces in Bydgoszcz had taken casualties due to civilian gunfire. He added that countermeasures were being instituted. Beutel completed his report by noting that he and his staff would arrive shortly to participate in the pacification of the city.[49] Reaching Bydgoszcz late the next day (8 September), Beutel's staff joined the now reunified *Einsatzkommando* 1/IV (Vogel's *Teilkommando* had entered the town a day

A member of *Einsatzgruppe* IV questions hostages on the Old Market Square
in Bydgoszcz, 9–11 September 1939. (Institute of National Remembrance,
Commission for the Prosecution of Crimes against the Polish Nation; courtesy of
the U.S. Holocaust Memorial Museum, Photo Reference Collection: WS 50845)

earlier) and set up headquarters in city hall alongside the offices of the
Stadtkommandant. The Security Police imposed an evening curfew of 6:00
P.M. and strictly forbade Polish civilians from consuming alcohol. Inhabitants of the city were also required to carry identification, and placards
were hung warning that any person caught plundering would be punished
with death.[50]

Concerning the killing of *Volksdeutsche* in Bydgoszcz, Beutel reported to
Berlin that the "terrorist measures" undertaken by the Polish army against
ethnic Germans had left those who remained behind "very intimidated"
(sehr eingeschüchtert).[51] Moreover, many of Bydgoszcz's ethnic German inhabitants could no longer be found, leading Beutel to speculate that a
"large number of them had been murdered."[52] His reports to Berlin soon
found their way to Hitler, who flew into a rage upon hearing that Polish
troops had killed ethnic Germans. In response, he instructed Himmler to
have Beutel's men carry out a large-scale reprisal action in Bydgoszcz on 9
September. *Einsatzgruppe* IV and Mülverstedt's 6th Motorized Police Battalion subsequently shot 500 known Polish communists and members of
the Polish intelligentsia. Army High Command instructed local commanders "not to stand in the way" of the Security Police as they conducted these

Polish hostages collected on the Old Market Square in Bydgoszcz, 9–11 September 1939. The police guarding the men are members of *Einsatzgruppe* IV. (Institute of National Remembrance, Commission for the Prosecution of Crimes against the Polish Nation; courtesy of the U.S. Holocaust Memorial Museum, Photo Reference Collection: WS 50837)

executions.[53] The evidence indicates, however, that Major General Braemer actually aided the Security Police by turning over for execution 500 prisoners held in the artillery barracks on Danzig Street.[54] The following day (10 September), a civilian sniper wounded yet another German soldier, and Braemer again responded by ordering "for the last time that [the inhabitants] immediately turn over all weapons to the local commander in Bromberg City Hall. Anyone caught carrying a weapon, or found with one in his residence, will be executed."[55] In addition, he authorized the execution of twenty more Poles on the Old Market Square as punishment for the shooting of the German soldier.[56]

The activities of Beutel's men in Bydgoszcz during the period of military command in the city reached a murderous crescendo on 10 September. To this point, the sweeps conducted by German troops and the Security Police had generally targeted the city center, but now the focus shifted to Schwedenhöhe, where the local Polish militia had made its last stand on 5 September.[57] Beutel assigned command over the so-called *Aktion Schwedenhöhe* to Helmut Bischoff and requested the assistance of General Mülverstedt's

The men of *Einsatzgruppe* IV and the 6th Motorized Order Police Battalion sort prisoners arrested during the *Aktion Schwedenhöhe*, Bydgoszcz, 19 September 1939. (Gertrude Adams; courtesy of the U.S. Holocaust Memorial Museum, Photo Reference Collection: ws 15753)

6th Motorized Order Police Battalion for the operation. After gathering the men of *Einsatzgruppe* IV early in the morning on 10 September, Bischoff made a speech in preparation for the raid. Holding in his hand several German newspapers containing stories of Polish atrocities against the ethnic Germans of Bydgoszcz, Bischoff told his men that the moment had arrived to avenge those members of the German *Volk* who had been butchered by the Poles on "Bloody Sunday."[58] He exhorted the assembled police to be "tough" and "harsh" with the Polish "bandits" *(Banditen)* and told them that the opportunity had arrived for those who doubted themselves to prove that they were men.[59] The search would be carried out in cooperation with the Order Police, and the objectives were to identify Poles who had perpetrated crimes against the *Volksdeutsche* and find weapons that were allegedly hidden in homes throughout the neighborhood. Only a thorough sweep of the Schwedenhöhe "criminal district" *(Verbrecherviertel)*, Bischoff promised, would atone for the crimes committed by the Poles.[60] All weapons were to be seized, and Polish men were to be arrested regardless of whether or not they were actually armed. Finally, as some of the former Security Police present for the speech later recalled, Bischoff stated that it was fine with him if they shot unarmed Poles who even looked "suspicious" *(polnische Personen die sich irgendwie verdächtig machten)*.[61]

The raid began when Bischoff deployed Mülverstedt's Order Police in a

Order policemen from the 6th Motorized Order Police Battalion at work during the *Aktion Schwedenhöhe*, 10 September 1939. The man in the right foreground is likely an ethnic German informant, while the prisoners against the fence have been marked to facilitate their recapture in case of escape. (Gertrude Adams; courtesy of the U.S. Holocaust Memorial Museum, Photo Reference Collection: WS 15752)

ring around the neighborhood and squads of Security Police started to enter the houses. Gunshots and screams soon could be heard throughout Schwedenhöhe as families were chased into the street and Polish men were killed. By midafternoon the Security Police had shot between fifty and sixty men where they were found, and the operation had yielded another 900 prisoners.[62] These survivors were collected in a field, and Order Police guards using *Volksdeutsche* informants began to search through the prisoners looking for Poles suspected of killing ethnic Germans on "Bloody Sunday." For his part, General Braemer recorded in his war diary that the 900 prisoners arrested by the Security Police looked to him like an "evil mob" *(übler Mob)*.[63] Braemer's war diary also noted that 120 Poles were shot. This was indeed true, but what Braemer neglected to mention was a brief conference he held with Lothar Beutel and EK 2/IV chief Walter Hammer following the police action to discuss what was to be done with the 120–150 prisoners who either had been identified by ethnic German informants or whose names had been found in the *Sonderfahndungsbuch*. Braemer agreed with Beutel's suggestion that these people be liquidated. Beutel then passed the order to Hammer, and over the next two days small groups of prisoners were taken into the forest outside Bydgoszcz and shot into antitank ditches until all were dead.[64]

Sporadic civilian attacks on German troops continued to occur during the final two days that Braemer was in Bydgoszcz, leading military and police authorities to respond with still more arrests and executions. The persistence of Polish civilian opposition was reflected in a telegram sent by General Adolf Strauss, the commander of the II Corps, to Army High Command requesting increased police manpower to aid German forces already in the city. As Strauss described the situation on 11 September, "The army was provided too late with entirely insufficient police forces. . . . ruthless measures are therefore being implemented by the Fourth Army."[65] However, it would not be the Wehrmacht that oversaw the final stages of the city's pacification. On 11 September, General Braemer received orders to move into East Prussia, and he turned over authority in the city to Police Colonel Gösch, the commander of a regimental police unit.[66] The departure of Beutel's men from Bydgoszcz followed soon thereafter, and by 13–14 September the entire *Einsatzgruppe* had relocated to Allenstein in East Prussia. Overall control of the city was eventually transferred to the new CdZ and soon-to-be *Gauleiter* of Danzig–West Prussia, Albert Forster.[67] Security Police units from Danzig and ethnic German shooting squads carried out additional killing actions in Bydgoszcz and the surrounding area throughout October and November 1939. These actions resulted in the deaths of as many as 5,000 people, at least 1,200 of whom were killed in Bydgoszcz alone, including the city's entire Jewish population and most of its intelligentsia.[68]

As was true elsewhere in Poland, members of the leading and educated classes in Bydgoszcz suffered the most during the initial days and weeks of the German occupation. In one particularly cruel instance, Schoene's *Einsatzkommando* executed fifty students from the Copernicus *Gymnasium* in reprisal for a shot fired from their school that hit a German army officer. The executions were carried out despite the fact that the individual student who fired the shot had given himself up.[69] Also on 8 September "priests, teachers, civil servants, rail operators, postal officers, and small business owners" made up a group of the nearly fifty hostages chosen by the army for execution that day.[70] These and the other events described above suggest that we modify our understanding of the reasons why the Security Police and army cooperated so closely in Bydgoszcz.

Clearly, the conclusion that the military and Security Police slaughtered at least 1,000 Polish civilians between 5 and 13 September 1939 in retaliation for "Bloody Sunday" is only partially correct.[71] The murder of ethnic Germans was the background against which the violence in Bydgoszcz after 5 September played out. These killings infuriated rank-and-file German troops as well as General Brauchitsch, who issued an announcement on 17 September stating that "German troops are to be informed of the transgressions of the Polish armed forces against defenseless ethnic Germans. Such an opponent is capable of any lowly act and deserves no mercy."[72] The search for specific perpetrators of the "Bloody Sunday" killings also proceeded apace. Nevertheless, of the numerous actions conducted by German military and police forces over eight days in Bydgoszcz, only the execution of 500 people ordered by Hitler and the 150 Poles killed after the *Aktion Schwedenhöhe* were explicitly rationalized as retaliation for "Bloody Sunday." In contrast, the other shootings conducted in the city, resulting in the deaths of nearly 400 people, were direct responses to ongoing civilian resistance and therefore were an integral part of the army's pacification policy.

Although there is no evidence to directly indicate that military commanders were aware of Operation TANNENBERG, the cooperation offered by General Braemer in Bydgoszcz and other officers in the Polish Corridor undoubtedly facilitated the SS killing program. German troops transferred prisoners to the Security Police for execution, and military commanders allowed Operational Group personnel to sort prisoners, conduct raids, and kill large numbers of civilians during reprisals. Retaliatory actions ordered by the army also targeted the Polish intelligentsia as part of an overall effort to break the resistance of clandestine Polish paramilitary organizations. Furthermore, the brutality of the measures implemented for the pacification of the city demonstrated the willingness of Wehrmacht commanders to lay aside their own regulations concerning the treatment of the civilian population. The inability of the III Corps's Special Court in Bydgoszcz to cope with the opposition offered by Polish irregulars is a case in point, as it led the army to resort to increasingly harsh measures to pacify the city. Certainly the shooting of Poles by the Security Police did not elicit complaints from the army. In fact, a report authored by Captain Heyer, a member of General Gablenz's staff, the night before the clearance of Schwedenhöhe suggests that just the opposite was true. To Heyer, Schwedenhöhe was "a criminal district inhabited by extremely radical elements," and the local military authorities fully agreed with the use of Beutel's men in order to destroy these opponents.[73] Wehrmacht commanders, in short,

An SD officer (in the foreground) works with Wehrmacht troops during the search of a building in a Polish city. September–October 1939. (Bundesarchiv, Koblenz; courtesy of the U.S. Holocaust Memorial Museum, Photo Reference Collection: WS 13186)

welcomed the actions of the Security Police and decisively contributed to their success in Nakło, Wiecbork, Bydgoszcz, and elsewhere in the Polish Corridor.

SS-Army Collaboration in East Upper Silesia: The Convergence of Pragmatic Violence and Ideologically Motivated Brutality

Circumstances similar to those in the Polish Corridor also held sway in East Upper Silesia, a region in southwestern Poland that had often been the focus of disputes between Germans and Poles in the decades before 1939.[74] East Upper Silesia belonged to the German second empire until after the First World War, and between 1919 and 1921 it was the scene of three Polish uprisings against German rule. A bitterly contested plebiscite took place in the region in 1921, after which Poland formally annexed the territory, leaving the Germans resentful and determined to exact revenge. East Upper Silesia's importance lay in the region's high concentration of heavy industries. With factories spread throughout the cities of Katowice, Będzin, Sosnowiec, Dabrowa, and Oświęcim (Auschwitz), East Upper Silesia constituted the largest manufacturing center in Poland. It was because of the region's strategic and economic importance, therefore, that throughout the summer of 1939 officers in both the SD Higher Administrative Section Southeast (SD-*Oberabschnitt Südost*) and the *Abwehr* office in Breslau compiled detailed reports on Polish saboteurs and paramilitary groups using information supplied by ethnic German informants.[75] Of the many Polish militia groups active in the area, the Polish National Defense and the Association of Silesian Insurgents were the largest.[76] In addition, the so-called Korfanty Brigades, which had been trained in demolition and industrial sabotage, were of considerable concern to the Germans as well.[77]

Wehrmacht invasion plans called for General Wilhelm List's Fourteenth Army to enter East Upper Silesia from two directions. General Ernst Busch's VIII Corps was to advance from the west, with its assault spearheaded by the 5th Panzer Division. The 5th Panzer was to sweep south around Katowice and then east toward Kraków while the 8th and 28th Infantry Divisions supported its left flank and rear. Farther to the northeast, meanwhile, General Ferdinand Neuling's 239th Infantry Division was to pin down Polish forces in the fortifications around Katowice. The forces of General Werner Kienitz's XVII Corps, including the 44th and 45th Infantry Divisions, were located to the south and ordered to operate on the right flank of the 5th Panzer Division. Kienitz's objective was to capture the cities of Bielitz and Wadowice before continuing to the east.[78] Responsibility for security behind the front fell to the 239th Infantry Division and the 3d Frontier Guards of Lieutenant General Georg Brandt, which belonged to Busch's VIII Corps. Other units slated for deployment in East Upper Silesia included the Waffen SS-*Standarte* "Germania," Bruno Streckenbach's *Einsatzgruppe* I, and the *Freikorps* Ebbinghaus, a paramilitary unit created by the army in July and August 1939 out of *Volksdeutsche* who had fled the region between the wars.

Polish militia groups went on heightened alert in the last days of August and entered the fray immediately after the German attack began. According to a report filed on 1 September by Lieutenant General Brandt, Polish militia and regular troops inflicted heavy casualties on the *Freikorps* Ebbinghaus near Nowy Bytom, indicating the tenacity with which Polish irregulars intended to defend their homeland.[79] Further reports to the VIII Corps filed on the following day agreed that the rear echelons of the 8th Infantry Division also encountered considerable resistance from Polish irregulars and snipers *(Freischärler)*.[80] An entry in the war diary of the 45th Infantry Division noted that the enemy "did not present a defensive front, but rather was using hedgerows and underbrush to fight isolated actions *(Kleinkrieg)*, against which advance battalions are foundering. Sniper fire is making the troops very uncomfortable and insecure."[81]

The ferocity of Polish resistance soon made it clear that the available military security forces could not deal with the problem. On 2 September, therefore, General Busch instituted measures to counter the danger posed by Polish irregulars. Assigning the SS-*Standarte* "Germania" to guard artillery positions, Busch alerted his subordinates that "special *Einsatzkommandos*" were being deployed the next day "to prevent attacks on rear area troops, their communications, and command posts."[82] He then issued an order to the entire VIII Corps, demanding that "any guerilla activity *[Freischärlerunwesen]* be dealt with severely using the harshest means available." In addition, Busch ordered General Neuling to shift his 239th Infantry Division from west of Katowice to the south behind the 8th Infantry Division. By late in the day on 2 September, Neuling's troops had moved into place near VIII Corps headquarters in Orzesze and initiated pacification actions. These resulted in the first executions of civilians by the army in East Upper Silesia as troops with the 239th Infantry Division shot thirty-seven Poles in Łaziska Gorne, seventeen in Łaziska Dolne, thirteen in Gostyń, and eleven in Łaziska Srednie.[83]

Like General Busch, Lieutenant Colonel Eppendorf, the intelligence officer of the Fourteenth Army, responded to the problem of civilian resistance on 2 September by calling in the Security Police. Reporting to Major Rudolf Langhäuser, the intelligence officer of Army Group South, that the demands on the Secret Field Police detachments assigned to him were too great, Eppendorf decided to assign the GFP "purely defensive military tasks."[84] Tasks that fell outside of this area of responsibility, he continued, "were to be given over to the *Einsatzkommandos* of the Gestapo, whose cooperation in these matters has been guaranteed." Eppendorf concluded by writing that, thus far, "collaboration with the *Einsatzkorps* is good."[85] For his part, Bruno Streckenbach had already split his Operational Group into *Einsatzkommandos,* which he deployed in four areas. SS-*Sturmbannführer* Ludwig Hahn's *Einsatzkommando* 1/I positioned itself on the German border in Gliwice (Gleiwitz), just opposite Katowice, while Bruno Müller's *Einsatzkommando* 2/I prepared to enter Cieszyn (Teschen). *Einsatzkommando* 3/I, under Alfred Hasselberg, was also stationed in the south near the city of Zakopane. Last, Streckenbach and his *Gruppenstab* stood ready near Rybnik along with Karl Brunner's *Einsatzkommando 4/I*.

On 3 September, the 5th Panzer Division finally broke through Polish defenses near Oświęcim, and the VIII Corps reported that regular Polish forces were evacuating Katowice. General Busch reacted by informing General Brandt that the 239th Infantry Division was now at his disposal, as well as *Einsatzkommando 1/I*, the *Freikorps* Ebbinghaus, and the SS-*Standarte* "Germania."[86] Busch charged these units with the task of reducing Polish resistance in Katowice and the surrounding area, as well as with securing the important industrial facilities that were located there.[87] The available evidence suggests that the severity of the methods to be employed by Brandt and the Security Police was of little concern to the army given the intensity of Polish resistance. As the war diary of Colonel Wagner indicated, "a difficult battle with [Polish] bands has erupted in [East] Upper Silesia, which can only be broken through the use of draconian measures."[88]

SS chief Heinrich Himmler apparently agreed with Wagner's assessment of the situation and took the opportunity to issue a directive on 3 September calling for "insurgents" to be "shot on the spot."[89] At the same time, Hitler instructed General Brauchitsch to warn "the population of Upper Silesia that mayors and city councilors, as well as all other community leaders, would guarantee with their lives that no sabotage of any kind, nor attacks by snipers will occur in their hometowns."[90] The following day, Major General Otto von Knobelsdorff, the chief of staff for the 3d Frontier Guards, suspended standing regulations for the troops to capture snipers when possible for trial before a court-martial. Ordering instead that "the troops can only spare themselves bloody losses if irregulars are fought using the most ruthless and severe measures," Knobelsdorff demanded that "civilians found bearing arms be shot immediately!"[91] His orders also stated, however, that German soldiers were only to return fire "when the target is clear," perhaps revealing concern that such an order could have a detrimental effect on the behavior of his men.

In contrast, Ludwig Hahn was under no such illusion. Gathering together *Einsatzkommando 1/I* outside of Katowice, Hahn announced that the Sipo and SD were being called upon to help the Wehrmacht destroy Poland. He made it clear that the men were to kill any Pole possessing a weapon, including civilians. Furthermore, no distinction was to be drawn between the civilian population and Polish soldiers separated from their units. The latter, Hahn continued, "were not to be treated like prisoners of war, but rather liquidated as insurgents [*Widerstandskräfte*]"; even the slightest resistance was to be answered by shootings and arrests.[92] The men of *Einsatzkommando* 1/I then separated into five *Teilkommandos* and entered Katowice on 3 September amid ongoing fighting between German troops, Polish army units, and paramilitary groups. Hahn's TKs immediately fanned out and began searching buildings for weapons and persons listed in the *Sonderfahndungsbuch*. To aid their search for anti-German activists and guerrillas, the Security Police also employed *Volksdeutsche* informants and members of the *Freikorps* Ebbinghaus to identify their targets. It was in this way that Nikodem R., a participant in the Silesian insurgency of 1921 and an elderly man in 1939, was arrested. According to Nikodem's daughter Maria, local *Freikorps* men were well aware that her father was a former insurgent, and at around 4:00 A.M. on 4 September, eight members of the *Freikorps* Ebbinghaus and a "German soldier" burst into their home to seize Nikodem and Maria's brother Józef.[93] The Germans led the two prisoners away and executed them in a courtyard on Zamkowa Street along with thirty-five others, including a teacher who "did not belong to the Association of [Silesian] Insurgents."[94]

Although executions took place all over Katowice on 4 September, a particularly large number of shootings occurred in the Zamkowa Street courtyard as the Security Police and German soldiers liquidated opponents in the city. The story of Rafal K. is illustrative of the measures implemented by the Security Police and Wehrmacht at the time. A member of the Polish boy scouts, Rafal became entangled in running street battles between the Germans and his comrades. Rafal testified before a postwar Polish tribunal investigating German crimes in Katowice that he and his comrades fell back into the center of the city under the pressure of the German attack.[95] As the fighting turned desperate, Rafal ducked into a house and acquired clothing from the inhabitant. He stripped out of his scout uniform and quickly donned the civilian clothes he was given. Rafal then exited the house and attempted to pose as a noncombatant, but he was detained by a pair of rifle-bearing *Volksdeutsche* and taken to the walled courtyard of a bottling plant on Gliwicka Street.[96] Upon entering the courtyard, Rafal saw German soldiers guarding a group of civilians, among whom were several women and teenage girls. The number of prisoners grew over the next several hours as more people were brought into the courtyard at gunpoint. Finally, Rafal stated, he and perhaps forty others were separated from the rest of the prisoners and marched by German troops to a nearby government building.[97] The prisoners were beaten by the guards and forced to sing "Deutschland über alles" during the march. German guards kicked those who did not know the lyrics or struck them with rifle butts.

When the column reached its destination, Rafal and the others had to face a German officer who demanded to see their papers. The Germans separated Polish soldiers who could produce military identification from the group. All the rest, including Rafal, found themselves placed in a group of "insurgents" and "terrorists" *(Heckenschützen)* and forced to march to the entrance of a walled courtyard on Zamkowa Street, where a small group of riflemen from the *Freikorps* Ebbinghaus awaited them.[98] Rafal noticed during the march that as he and the others were repeatedly subjected to blows, insults, and spittle, the people around him included several uniformed Polish soldiers, uniformed members of the Silesian Insurgents, ordinary civilians, and women. The German troops guarding the group pushed Rafal and the others through the entrance to the courtyard and closed the gates behind them, at which point the *Freikorps* men opened fire. Hitting the ground and feigning death as the bodies fell on and around him, Rafal lay as still as possible while the gunmen searched for survivors and delivered the coup de grâce to those who still lived. After a short time, Rafal heard another group of prisoners arrive, and the shooting began once again. At this point, he lost his nerve and began to shake. Several riflemen noticed Rafal moving and opened fire, hitting him in the back, chest, and right forearm. He then lost consciousness. Coming to some time later, Rafal pulled himself out from under the corpses and surveyed the horror around him. The courtyard was now quiet and it was growing dark. He was surrounded by what he estimated to be the bodies of 100 people, almost half of whom were women, including a young girl Rafal guessed to be about fourteen years old. He also noticed the bodies of several old men, the members of paramilitary groups, and nearly thirty Polish soldiers.[99]

Altogether, on 4 September, Ludwig Hahn's Security Police and ethnic German riflemen, with the assistance of regular German troops, killed 250 Polish men, women, and youths in the courtyard on Zamkowa Street.[100] The Security Police liquidated another thirty-five people in the Sacher Restaurant on that day, including boy scouts and prisoners of war.[101] These numbers were dwarfed, however, by the execution of as many as 500 Polish militia members and civilians whom German troops captured and shot into mass graves on the grounds of the Kosciusko Municipal Garden.[102]

There unfortunately is little evidence of the activities of Streckenbach's other *Einsatzkommandos* elsewhere in East Upper Silesia at this time. According to the Polish historian Andrzej Szefer, the Security Police conducted an action against the intelligentsia in the town of Orzesze, located several miles to the southwest of Katowice. On 3 September the Security Police and *Freikorps* men collected all of the Poles they could find on the local market square. An officer then read from a long list of names, calling out

SD officers interrogate a Polish cleric on the street in Sosnowiec, September 1939. It is unclear if these SD men belonged to the *Einsatzgruppe* I or *Einsatzgruppe* von Woyrsch. (Jacob Igra; courtesy of the U.S. Holocaust Memorial Museum, Photo Reference Collection: ws 19364)

of the assembled detainees members of the Association of Silesian Insurgents, prominent social and political leaders, and individuals denounced by *Volksdeutsche* informants. Twenty men were identified by name while the rest were released. The prisoners were then tortured and interrogated in a nearby cellar and shot the next day.[103]

As for events in Katowice, the violence employed by the army, the Security Police, and the *Freikorps* effectively broke organized Polish resistance by 5 September. Polish snipers continued to attack German personnel for the next week, but the focus of German security operations after 5 September shifted to the cities of Będzin, Sosnowiec, and Oświęcim, as well as to the forests in the region. At this point the demand for rear area troops elsewhere also forced the army to begin pulling units out of the region. General Busch ordered the 239th Infantry Division east on 5 September and requested the deployment of Udo von Woyrsch's Special Purpose *Einsatzgruppe* in the region.[104] Von Woyrsch had been preparing his men for action since his arrival in Gliwice two days earlier on 3 September. At the

SD officers interrogate Polish prisoners arrested in Sosnowiec, September 1939. Note the boy at center left. (Jacob Igra; courtesy of the U.S. Holocaust Memorial Museum, Photo Reference Collection: WS 19363)

Police Presidium in Gliwice, von Woyrsch found orders from Himmler naming him special commander of police *(Sonderbefehlshaber der Polizei)* and charging him with the ruthless suppression *(radikale Niederwerfung)* of the "Polish uprising" in East Upper Silesia.[105] According to Himmler's instructions, von Woyrsch was to report to General Busch for duty and use "every means available" to wipe out Polish insurgents. The Special Purpose *Einsatzgruppe* included a detachment of 350 Security Police under the command of von Woyrsch's deputy Emil Otto Rasch and three battalions of Order Police led by Orpo colonel Friedrich Wolfstieg. These units arrived in Katowice on 6 September and were placed under the overall command of General Brandt, the commander of the 3d Frontier Guards. The executions carried out by *Einsatzkommando* 1/I and the German army during the previous two days had already destroyed the so-called "Polish uprising," however, and by 7 September Rasch reported to Berlin that "an insurgency movement of any significance no longer existed in Kattowitz or the surrounding area."[106] Von Woyrsch's men then redirected their attention on "the forests east of [the town of] Nikolai" to search for Polish irregulars suspected of hiding there.[107] Detachments of Security Police and Order Police also fanned out in Będzin, Dabrowa, and Sosnowiec where

General Brandt ordered them to secure businesses and guard important industrial sites.[108] Over the next five days, von Woyrsch's men carried out searches for Polish guerrillas and weapons. The reports filed with Security Police headquarters in Berlin mentioned only that three Poles were executed during this period.[109]

The Polish historian Czesław Madajczyk concludes that in the first two weeks of September 1939, regular German soldiers, the men of *Einsatzgruppe* I, and Udo von Woyrsch's Special Purpose *Einsatzgruppe* carried out a total of fifty-eight executions and shot upward of 1,500 Poles in East Upper Silesia.[110] Few detailed accounts of these shooting actions exist, but most of the victims were undoubtedly killed during SS and Wehrmacht efforts to suppress civilian resistance in the region. Polish and German sources alike indicate that the participation of Polish civilians in combat during the first two weeks of the war in Poland was extensive. In this sense, large-scale executions were to be anticipated. As Madajczyk writes, "Particularly in Katowice, where military units and Nazi formations came under machine gun fire [from irregulars], one expected the Fascists to exact fearful retribution."[111]

Certain aspects of the suppression of civilian resistance in East Upper Silesia are nonetheless disturbing for what they imply about the brutality of the German army. The available evidence suggests that the army and the Security Police worked jointly to identify and target specific groups of Poles for execution. In addition to the *Sonderfahndungslisten* created at Security Police Headquarters in Berlin, Streckenbach's *Einsatzkommandos* also carried into East Upper Silesia lists prepared by the *Abwehr* and the SD in Breslau naming old men who had participated in the Polish uprisings twenty years earlier. Again citing Madajczyk, these lists contained the names of 2,500 Poles in East Upper Silesia who were to be arrested.[112] The Security Police and men of the *Freikorps* Ebbinghaus then sought out and murdered Poles who had neither the foresight nor the opportunity to flee. Among those targeted and killed in Katowice were old men, boys, women, and Polish prisoners of war as well as members of the intelligentsia located by Ludwig Hahn's *Teilkommandos*. Therefore, it is quite evident that just as it had in Bydgoszcz, the military consciously allowed the Security Police and ethnic German militia to destroy political opponents in East Upper Silesia. It was while on this mission that *Einsatzgruppe* I also began to implement Operation TANNENBERG in the region. The cases of Rafal K. and Nikodem R. demonstrate as well that the army did not leave the Security Police entirely to their own devices, as German troops actively participated in the identification, arrest, guarding, and execution of political opponents, insurgents, and Polish prisoners of war.[113]

Cooperation between the military and *Einsatzgruppen* in the Polish Corridor and East Upper Silesia was thus without problems when it came to suppressing Polish resistance. However, the same cannot be said of circumstances everywhere during the invasion. Specifically, friction over the summary execution of Polish civilians developed between the command staff of Army Group South and Dr. Emanuel Schaefer, the chief of *Einsatzgruppe* II, in the second week of the campaign. The incident that sparked the dispute occurred in the city of Lubliniec (Lublinitz) following a counterinsurgency operation conducted by the army's 520th Secret Field Police Group, the 652d Military Police Section, and a *Teilkommando* from SS-*Sturmbannführer* Otto Sens's *Einsatzkommando* I/II. The target of the operation in Lubliniec was the local branch of the Association of Silesian Insurgents, the entire regional membership of which was identified on 8 September after the Security Police discovered a copy of the group's membership list.[114] Four days later, on 12 September, army security units and *Einsatzgruppe* II carried out an operation in Lubliniec that resulted in the arrest of 102 "members of the Insurgent Association."[115] The 520th Secret Field Police Group left these prisoners in Security Police custody when it moved on to Kielce, along with another eighty civilian prisoners. As the GFP officer in command noted in his after-action report, "the prisoners were shot, or are to be shot, in accordance with instructions from the RFSS [Himmler]. The commander of Army Group South [General Gerd von Rundstedt] has personally ordered that attempts to confirm this be initiated."[116]

Upon receiving word of the impending execution, Major Rudolf Langhäuser, the intelligence officer of Army Group South, immediately ordered that the prisoners be handed over to the local military commander in nearby Częstochowa. The following day (13 September), he returned to Lubliniec and had a sharp argument with an SS officer who refused to turn the prisoners over to the army. This forced Langhäuser to speak with Emanuel Schaefer himself, who explained that "he had received orders from the RFSS to shoot all members of Polish insurgent bands."[117] Besides, Schaefer stated, "[similar] executions had already been carried out in Tarnów and Katowice." Major Langhäuser demanded that Schaefer transfer the prisoners to the army for protective custody *(Schutzhaft)* until he could get a final decision from General Rundstedt. After returning to Army Group South headquarters, Langhäuser confirmed that Rundstedt had no knowledge of Himmler's order. Rundstedt then ordered him to contact Army High Command for instructions, which he attempted to do from 14 September to 16 September in an effort to verify Himmler's directive.[118]

Finally making contact with Army High Command late in the day on 16 September, Langhäuser did not learn until the following day that Werner Best in Gestapo headquarters also claimed not to know about the 3 September order. Best commented that the orders were consistent with Hitler's instructions for combating insurgents, but he promised to look into the matter further.[119] Several hours later, two "high-ranking police officers" informed OKH "that the order to immediately shoot all Polish insurgents without a prior court-martial had been given to the *Einsatzkommandos* and commanders of the Order Police directly from the Führer's train."[120] Although this reply did not make it clear if it was Hitler, rather than Himmler, who had actually given the order, neither General Rundstedt nor Major Langhäuser pursued the matter after receiving this information from Army High Command.

It is difficult to determine precisely what lay behind the disagreement between Army Group South and *Einsatzgruppe* II. Was it simply the fact that Schaefer refused to obey Major Langhäuser's orders, or that Langhäuser and Rundstedt found the shooting of civilians by the SS objectionable? The records suggest that there were two issues central to the dispute, beginning with the challenge to the army's executive authority presented by Himmler's directive. Major Langhäuser and General Rundstedt sought only to establish the basis for Schaefer's claimed authority and the authenticity of Himmler's 3 September order. Once this matter had been clarified and OKH confirmed that the directive originated from the Führer's command train, Rundstedt and Langhäuser dropped the issue altogether. Furthermore, Rundstedt never brought charges of insubordination against Schaefer, Schaefer was never relieved of his command, and *Einsatzgruppe* II was never ordered to leave the area. More important, however, seems to be a personal reason that Major Langhäuser had for his concern about the shooting of the prisoners. Specifically, he had guaranteed the safety of the eighty civilian prisoners that the Secret Field Police had transferred to the Security Police along with the 102 captured insurgents.

According to testimony Langhäuser gave during the postwar trial of *Einsatzgruppe* I commander Bruno Streckenbach, the Polish mayor of Lubliniec turned over the eighty young men to the army on 10 or 11 September in an effort to "prevent breaches of public security and especially acts of violence against German troops."[121] Langhäuser explained that the prisoners were reservists and others who had retreated to Lubliniec after the collapse of Polish forces on the frontier. The mayor was concerned that any acts of resistance on their part would prompt the Germans to respond with the shooting of local citizens, and he wanted to prevent this possibility.

Considering this an act of "loyalty" on the part of the Polish mayor, Langhäuser held the "prisoners" in a school and promised that they would remain safe while Army Group South headquarters was in the area.[122] After General Rundstedt and his command moved on, the detainees were to be set free. But it was only after this shift that the conflict developed. As Langhäuser stated:

> After the headquarters moved forward to its next location, a military policeman came to me with a report that an SS *Einsatzkommando* had entered Lubliniec. The chief of this unit requested that the officer in command of the military police company transfer the prisoners to him for execution. The commander of the military police company denied this request until he could receive orders from me. I then immediately returned to Lubliniec . . . and sought out the SS officer. This SS officer also demanded of me that I turn over the prisoners so they could be shot as insurgents. He referred me to instructions that his unit had received from either "the Führer" or the "*Reichsführer* SS." I responded that neither the army nor I had received such an order [and] I refused to transfer the detainees. . . . they were to remain in protective custody as long as the headquarters of Army Group South remained in the area. I requested he allow the prisoners to be transferred to the next military unit that moved into the area so they could be sent to the rear and in this way their lives would be saved.[123]

It appears from this description of the events that the dispute with the SS in Lubliniec centered on the safety of the eighty men whose lives the mayor of the city had entrusted to Langhäuser. In contrast, Langhäuser never mentioned the other 102 prisoners who were captured during the joint army-SS anti-insurgency operation on 12 September, giving the impression that the fate of these prisoners mattered little to him. Whatever his motivation, Langhäuser's efforts to save the Poles failed, and Schaefer's men shot both groups of prisoners, 182 men in all.[124]

The conflict in Lubliniec illustrates the complicated and often contradictory nature of the relationship between the army and the Security Police during the invasion. Despite the fact that field commanders frequently ordered German troops to shoot Polish irregulars without a prior court-martial, the revelation that Himmler had independently issued the same instructions to SS personnel was taken as a serious challenge to the military's executive authority. For his part, Major Langhäuser was obviously concerned about this development in addition to having doubts about allowing the Security Police to liquidate innocent civilians. Both Langhäuser and General Rundstedt felt that the procedures established at the outset of the war gave the army exclusive control over the operations of the *Einsatzgruppen* and other SS units deployed in Poland. The killing of targeted groups and individuals by the Security Police in the heat of battle or as part of reprisals ordered by the army posed little problem, therefore, because these actions could be camouflaged. But while Langhäuser was willing to work with Schaefer's men to root out Polish insurgents, he balked when it came to murdering innocent people. The revelation of Himmler's 3 September "shoot to kill" directive clearly caused friction between Langhäuser and Rundstedt, who jealously guarded their military authority, and the SS personnel who were determined to carry out the directive.

On the other hand, the fact that the SS and military cooperated so closely to suppress resistance in the Polish Corridor and East Upper Silesia is not surprising given the tendency of officers like General Busch, General Braemer, and General Brandt to resort to draconian measures and actively support the operations of the *Einsatzkommandos* against the civilian population. The conduct of these officers on the battlefield was characteristic of what Michael Geyer refers to as the new military technocracy that developed in Germany during the interwar years.[125] As described by Geyer, and also Klaus-Jürgen Müller, the ranks of the German officer corps became diluted by the army's tremendous growth in the 1930s. Consequently, many officers abdicated their traditional role as a small, self-contained military-political elite in favor of becoming a professional, "functional" elite that organized and applied violence within a context of modern industrialized warfare.[126] The impact of this development became apparent after the outbreak of the war as many of these so-called "managers of force" jettisoned their moral considerations in favor of efficiency and achieving results. In effect, the ends on the battlefield came to justify the means used to achieve them.[127] This subscription by German officers to what might be called "pragmatic violence" was not necessarily a Nazi viewpoint, but it was sufficiently close to the ideologically motivated brutality of National Socialism to form a partial identity of interests between some German field officers and their counterparts in the SS.[128]

Altogether, it is clear that the willingness of many German officers to quell civilian resistance using any means available created circumstances that were conducive to the implementation of Operation TANNENBERG by the SS. Indeed, the brutality employed by German officers to stamp out paramilitary groups and spontaneous civilian opposition was so extreme that Wehrmacht firing squads had executed no fewer than 16,000 Poles by the time the Polish campaign drew to a close in early October.[129] As events in the Polish Corridor and East Upper Silesia also suggest, the German army often targeted members of the intelligentsia, politicians, and other prominent local personalities in its reprisals, thereby obviating the need for Heydrich's *Einsatzgruppen* to liquidate these individuals. Last, the army actively cooperated with the Security Police in seeking out and destroying Polish insurgent groups. These activities underscore the point that a fully laid-out series of criminal orders, such as those promulgated prior to the invasion of the Soviet Union, was not necessary in order for Wehrmacht officers and troops to conduct themselves in an extremely barbaric manner toward the Polish civilian population. A common perception, operative within a context of irregular warfare, of Poles as inferior and dangerous was more than enough to facilitate cooperation between the SS and the army and unleash a brutal campaign of repression and mass murder.

FOUR

NAZI ANTI-JEWISH POLICY DURING THE POLISH CAMPAIGN

The acrimony that occasionally characterized army and SS efforts to suppress Polish resistance also typified the military's reaction to SS operations against Polish Jews. German officers held no sympathy for Polish Jews, but at the same time the frequently excessive violence with which the Security Police and personnel in other SS formations terrorized Poland's Jewish community often shocked and offended army commanders who demanded order behind the front line. Added to this reaction was considerable concern in the army officer corps about the potentially detrimental impact that SS anti-Jewish violence could have on the conduct and discipline of regular army troops. It was primarily for these reasons, and not out of sympathy for Polish Jews, that several German field commanders tried to rein in rampaging SS units by selectively arresting and court-martialing SS personnel. The small number of Wehrmacht officers who challenged the SS faced significant obstacles. Hitler opposed any attempt to restrain the SS, and support from General Brauchitsch and the rest of Army High Command for curtailing SS operations remained half-hearted, both during and after the invasion. Brauchitsch, in particular, believed that the most prudent course of action was not to actively prevent SS atrocities, but rather to order German troops and officers to stay out of SS operations. Perhaps most disheartening, however, was the fact that many German officers actually agreed with the overall goal of removing Jews from newly occupied Polish territory; even though they would not tolerate the chaos caused behind the lines by SS terror, they cooperated with the SS on this basis.

The origins of SS violence against Jews during the invasion of Poland can be found in trends in Nazi anti-Jewish policy that had been developing since the latter half of 1938. Here a distinction must be drawn between SS policies directed against German Jews and those against so-called *Ostjuden* (Eastern European Jews) who lived in the Reich and incorporated territories. The Nazis subjected both communities to violence, but measures instituted against German Jews in the 1930s remained mild in comparison to the force employed against *Ostjuden*. As early as March 1933, Nazi *Sturmabteilung* (SA) had directed an inordinate level of violence against *Ostjuden* living in the Scheunenviertel section of Berlin. Saul Friedländer also points out that *Ostjuden* were the first Jews to be sent off to concentration camps.[1] Before 1938, though, this aggression remained sporadic and largely disorganized. The first centralized escalation of policy against *Ostjuden* came as early as 11 October 1938, when Hitler issued general instructions for the "appropriate government agency" (eventually the Gestapo and Security Police) to examine the possibility of expelling 27,000 Czech Jews from Vienna.[2] A little more than two weeks later, Heinrich Himmler and Reinhard Heydrich ordered the arrest and deportation from the Reich of all Jews holding Polish citizenship.

The presence of Polish Jews in Germany had been a source of increasing aggravation for the SS and police authorities since March 1938, when the Polish government nullified the citizenship of anyone who had lived abroad for more than five years. Suddenly faced with the possibility that nearly 70,000 Polish Jews residing in Germany and Austria would be rendered stateless, the German government demanded in April that Jews holding Polish passports leave the Reich.[3] However, the authorities in Warsaw refused to allow these Jews back into Poland, and by late October Himmler and Heydrich chose to act unilaterally. Using the Polish government's earlier move as a pretext, the Gestapo and Security Police detained and forcibly expelled nearly 17,000 Polish Jews across the German border.[4] These actions continued eight months later when German police and SS removed another 2,000 Polish Jews on 8 June 1939.[5] When taken into account alongside Hitler's earlier call for the expulsion of Czech Jews, the deportation of Polish Jews signaled a marked escalation in the terror that the Gestapo and Security Police were willing to use against "eastern Jews" in the Reich.[6]

The Polish historian Karol Jonca identifies this escalation as a decisive move by the SS toward a "violent solution" to the Jewish question in Germany.[7] It was only with the outbreak of the war in September 1939, however, that the "violent solution" initiated in 1938 became an integral part of exploiting the Lebensraum that German forces conquered in Poland. Hitler had hinted since the 1920s that a future German occupation of Poland would be attended by a comprehensive redrawing of the map and the resettlement of large numbers of Poles and Jews. Not surprisingly, though, given his frequent silence on such issues, it was not Hitler who made the most concrete statement on the subject of resettling Jews, but the

Nazi Party ideologue, Alfred Rosenberg, who stated during a speech in Detmold on 15 January 1939 that the Reich was examining the possibility of creating a "Jewish reservation."[8] Several weeks later, Rosenberg referred to the possibility that such a territory could be created in either Guyana or Madagascar.

Dr. Emil Schumburg, a diplomat in the *Referat Deutschland* of the German Foreign Office, which was responsible for handling Jewish affairs as they pertained to foreign relations, also confirmed that the search for a proper place to locate such a reservation was indeed "Germany's foreign political program regarding the Jewish question."[9] Rosenberg's and Schumburg's references to a reservation for the Jews clearly indicated that Reich authorities were casting about in early 1939 for a so-called "territorial solution" to the Jewish question. An attempt to impose this solution would be made in occupied Poland, but before that could happen the SS intensified the "violent solution" that it had initiated in 1938, and it is within this context that the anti-Jewish operations of the *Einsatzgruppen* and SS Death's Head units during the Polish campaign should be properly understood.

Of the seven Operational Groups deployed in Poland, four, including the Special Purpose *Einsatzgruppe* of Udo von Woyrsch, Bruno Streckenbach's *Einsatzgruppe* I, Lothar Beutel's *Einsatzgruppe* IV, and Ernst Damzog's *Einsatzgruppe* V, were the most active in carrying out measures against Polish Jews. And of these, the operations of von Woyrsch's Order Police and Security Police detachments against Jews were far and away the most violent. The role of von Woyrsch's police in suppressing Polish resistance in East Upper Silesia has been noted already. However, in addition to ordering him to destroy the Polish "uprising" in the region, Himmler also gave von Woyrsch instructions to spread "fear and terror in the population" in order to force Jews to flee from East Upper Silesia.[10] Pursuant to these orders, the Special Purpose *Einsatzgruppe* drove into East Upper Silesia on 6 September and over the next five days perpetrated a series of atrocities against Jews in the cities of Katowice, Będzin, and Sosnowiec.

Jewish shops were attacked, religious Jewish men were beaten and humiliated in the streets, and Jews were shot for allegedly possessing weapons.[11] The worst crimes were committed in Będzin on 8 September, where von Woyrsch's Order Police murdered Jewish children and razed the synagogue.[12] Set alight by flamethrowers, the blazing synagogue quickly burned out of control, destroying a large number of neighboring buildings in the city's Jewish residential district. At the same time, the rampaging police shot nearly 100 civilians in the streets, eighty of whom were Jews.[13] The synagogue in Katowice burned down two days later, and killings in

Demolition of the ruins of the synagogue in Będzin. The ruins were left behind after the men of Udo von Woyrsch's Special Purpose *Einsatzgruppe* burned the synagogue to the ground on 10 September 1939. (YIVO Institute; courtesy of the U.S. Holocaust Memorial Museum, Photo Reference Collection: WS 19621)

Będzin continued for the next forty-eight hours, resulting in the deaths of as many as 500 Jews altogether.[14] Before leaving East Upper Silesia entirely, von Woyrsch's personnel also killed an additional forty-three Jews in Krzeszowice, Dulowa, and Trzebnia while en route to Kraków.[15]

The first friction with military authorities in East Upper Silesia arose on the day that the Special Purpose *Einsatzgruppe* departed from the region. On 11 September, General Brandt cabled Army Group South commander General Rundstedt with a call for von Woyrsch's court-martial.[16] Brandt's request was undoubtedly related to violations of recent orders issued by military authorities. On 7 September, Colonel Emil Zellner, the Fourteenth Army quartermaster, informed General Busch of General List's request for the VIII Corps to delay measures against the Jews until the local chief of civil administration (CdZ) was in place. Zellner's communiqué added that "excesses [against the Jews] in Kraków are to be prevented by any means necessary."[17] Furthermore, on 9 September, Himmler had personally guaranteed the safety of the synagogues in Warsaw, Łódź, and Kraków in response to a demand from the army.[18] However, Brandt's request for the court-martial of von Woyrsch fell on deaf ears, apparently because some officers placed considerable importance on the security measures implemented by the Special Purpose *Einsatzgruppe*. Far from punishing von Woyrsch, Colonel Zellner informed Brandt and other commanders in East Upper Silesia on 12 September that the EG z.b.V. was being reassigned and von Woyrsch designated by Himmler as special commander of police *(Sonderbefehlshaber der Polizei)*. In essence, the Fourteenth Army confirmed to Brandt its acceptance of von Woyrsch's authority to conduct antiguerrilla operations, including "the suppression and disarming of Polish bands, executions, and arrests in cooperation with the CdZ in Kraków and the Commander of the Army Rear Area."[19]

In the meantime, von Woyrsch arrived in Kraków on 11 September and met with his counterpart in *Einsatzgruppe* I, Bruno Streckenbach. Reinhard Heydrich was also in the city at the time as part of an inspection tour through southwestern Poland. Heydrich probably spoke with both von Woyrsch and Streckenbach, but the evidence is unclear on this point.[20] Whatever the circumstances of the conference, it is certain that Heydrich met with Streckenbach, who later recalled that on or about 11 September the Security Police chief told him to explore "the possibility of expelling Jews to the east" over the San River where the demarcation line between German- and Soviet-held Poland was to be established.[21] According to Streckenbach, these instructions came directly from Himmler and were transmitted by Heydrich orally to all of the *Einsatzgruppe* and *Einsatzkommando* leaders in southern Poland. As Streckenbach stated to German investigators after the war, "The aim [of Himmler's orders] was to force as great a number of Jews as possible to flee east over the demarcation line using the harshest measures."[22]

Heydrich's presence in Kraków was not coincidental given the direction in which SS policies against Polish Jews were moving. Several days earlier in Berlin, on 7 September, Heydrich had informed his subordinates in Gestapo headquarters that SS Jewish policy in Poland would proceed along two lines, including forced expulsion and the concentration of Jews within a specially established district. He stated that the territorial administration in Poland would not be like that in the Protectorate of Bohemia and Moravia, but he offered no further details at the time. Heydrich made it clear, though, that "the expulsion of the Polish Jews from Germany must be carried out, including those Jews who had immigrated [before 1933] and had received German citizenship."[23] Also on 7 September, Heydrich ordered Gestapo and Security Police offices throughout the Reich to arrest Polish Jews still in Germany and to confiscate their property. These orders noted that "in as far as it is possible, detained Jews who formerly held Polish citizenship will at some point be pushed into regions of Poland that are not to be occupied

German police publicly humiliate a Jewish man in Sosnowiec. Although this image was taken after the end of the Polish campaign, the uniforms (Reich Labor Service tunics and collar markings) worn by these men strongly suggest that they belonged to the *Einsatzgruppe* von Woyrsch. This unit was redeployed in the vicinity of Sosnowiec after its recall from duty in Przemysl and elsewhere along the San River, 1939. (Eva Better-Heitner Sak; courtesy of the U.S. Holocaust Memorial Museum, Photo Reference Collection: WS 04745)

[festgenommenen Juden mit polnischer Staatsangehörigkeit . . . in Gebiete des nicht zu besetzende übrigen Polen abzuschieben]," indicating that the expulsion of Jews into the Soviet sphere of eastern Poland was to continue for as long as possible.[24] Incidentally, Franz Stahlecker, the head of the Security Police in Vienna, and Adolf Eichmann, the chief of the Central Office for Jewish Emigration in Prague, also received these instructions. Stahlecker and Eichmann met in Vienna three days later to discuss what eventually became the first plan to deport Jews from Vienna and the protectorate to Nisko, which lay on the eastern side of the San River.[25]

In shaping anti-Jewish policy during the Polish campaign, Heydrich had to take into account a variety of factors. The most important was securing the military's assistance, which fortunately was not difficult. As Streckenbach explained after the war, one day after his meeting with Heydrich in Kraków, orders arrived from Colonel Wagner in Armed Forces High Command stating that military units were to secure the San River line and prevent all Jews from crossing west into German-held territory.[26] Given von Woyrsch's efforts to force Jews to the east and Heydrich's orders to Streckenbach on 11 September, it seems entirely possible that Wagner was working with Heydrich against the Jews in southern Poland. Put another way, the Security Police would compel Polish Jews to leave their homes, and the army would ensure that they stayed out. As for the connection between the expulsion of Polish Jews and the formative stage of the territorial solution to the Jewish question, the steps outlined above suggest that Himmler and Heydrich had decided by 11 September, if not earlier, to establish a Jewish "reservation" in western Galicia. The problem remained the location of the demarcation line, as indicated by a meeting between Himmler and Hitler on 14 September. During their discussion, Himmler presented Hitler with various options for solving the "Jewish Problem" in Poland. According to Heydrich's report on the 14 September meeting, only Hitler could make the final decision regarding Jewish policy given the considerable impact this decision could have on Germany's foreign relations.[27]

Heydrich's mention of foreign policy most likely referred to Germany's relationship with the Soviet Union. A clause in the 23 August German-Soviet Pact placed the demarcation line between the two powers along the Pisa, Narew, Vistula, and San Rivers. However, until the third week of September, Stalin seems to have entertained the idea of creating a puppet state in eastern Poland that would be under Soviet influence.[28] Moreover, for reasons that remain unclear, Army High Command never received notification about the exact course of the demarcation line. Consequently, by the third week of the campaign German forces had advanced as far as 125 miles into

territory that would eventually fall to the Soviets. On 16 September, according to General Walter Warlimont, the chief of the operations branch of
Armed Forces High Command, Stalin telephoned Foreign Minister Ribbentrop to express concern that the Russian military attaché in Berlin had
learned of Germany's intention to annex the oil fields near Drohobycz, east
of the San River.[29] Stalin was referring to a map the Russian attaché had
seen in Berlin that showed the future eastern border of the Reich running
"along the Vistula River and through Warsaw, but then plotted so as to
leave Lwów (Lviv) on the German side."[30] The Soviet government could
not accept this arrangement and complained that it was a clear violation of
the 23 August agreement. Accordingly, Stalin continued to insist that the
original four-river arrangement remain the final demarcation line.

Further complicating matters was Germany's support for Lithuanian territorial claims to the city of Wilno (Vilna) and the surrounding hinterlands.
This situation placed Hitler in a difficult position because of the Soviet government's refusal to acknowledge Lithuania's claims and the fact that Red
Army troops had already occupied Wilno on 20 September. These developments had a decisive impact on anti-Jewish policy. Faced with an increasingly sticky diplomatic situation, Hitler was forced to authorize the
creation of a Jewish district in western Galicia or, in other words, in territory that unquestionably belonged to the Reich. Confirmation of this decision came on 21 September at another conference in Gestapo headquarters
during which Heydrich explained to his listeners that the options presented
to and authorized by Hitler included the formation near Kraków of a special district for Jews and Poles as well as the continued expulsion *(Ab-
schiebung)* of Jews over the German-Soviet demarcation line.[31] In all
likelihood, it was this combination of expulsion and resettlement that constituted what Heydrich referred to at the time as the "final aim" *(Endziel)*
of SS anti-Jewish policy.[32]

However, these plans would be altered one last time by the continuing
clash over Lithuanian claims in northern Poland. Stalin sought a way out
of the impasse by proposing on 25 September that Germany incorporate
the area between the Vistula and Bug Rivers (the Lublin province) if the
Reich nullified its arrangement with Lithuania concerning Wilno. Hitler
agreed to this proposal, and within days the arrangement was formally rat-
ified by the two nations in the German-Soviet Boundary and Friendship
Treaty signed on 28 September.[33] One day later, on 29 September, Heydrich
informed his subordinates in the newly formed *Reichssicherheitshauptamt*
(RSHA; Reich Security Main Office) that plans for a Jewish district in Galicia were being scrapped in favor of forming a new "Reich ghetto" near

Lublin. His remarks were apparently based on an earlier discussion with Hitler during which the Führer speculated about dividing occupied Poland into three sections, including a Jewish district in the Lublin province, an area of German colonization in western Poland, and an as yet undefined Polish "state."[34] It is unlikely that Hitler ever seriously considered creating a residual Polish state. Still, plans for the formation of the *Generalgouvernement* would not come to fruition until late October 1939, when responsibility for the administration of occupied Poland was transferred from the army to German civilian authorities.

During these negotiations, advancing German forces solidified their hold on territory adjacent to the demarcation line, a development that did not bode well for the Jews living in those areas. German troops reached the San River on 14–15 September and captured the city of Przemyśl before pursuing Polish forces east to Lwów. Streckenbach's and von Woyrsch's units entered Przemyśl the next day (16 September), and squads of Security and Order Police dispersed to the north and south along the western bank of the San. Ludwig Hahn's *Einsatzkommando* 1/I and men from the Special Purpose *Einsatzgruppe* also continued on toward Lwów, at which point a series of conflicts developed between the police and the army.[35] The first of these incidents involved the execution by the SS of four Jews for war profiteering and three Polish farmers for insurgent activity.[36] According to Major General Hingnoz, the officer who reported the incident to the XVIII Corps, the shootings had been unauthorized despite the fact that they were carried out during an officially sanctioned counterinsurgency action. The action was apparently motivated by an earlier army investigation of resistance activity in the vicinity of Przemyśl that turned up the names of several individuals in contact with insurgent groups. Hingnoz had therefore detailed 100 men from the 1st Battalion of the 3d Police Regiment to arrest the insurgents.

The operation was carried out on 18 September, but it led to the arrest of only two people, who were eventually released due to a lack of incriminating evidence. Police Major Willing, an officer with the 3d Police Regiment, then reported to Hingnoz that the execution of the seven men had been carried out for reasons unrelated to the original operation. Hingnoz immediately demanded an explanation from the SS-*Hauptsturmführer* responsible for ordering the killings. The SS officer told Hingnoz it was his understanding that the army's orders applied only to those persons specifically named as members of the insurgent band. His men had carried out the other executions on his authority alone and with what the SS officer had considered to be good reason. Von Woyrsch readily agreed with his subordinate after reviewing the case.[37] This matter was followed by another incident three days later in Sądowa Wisniza when German troops were allegedly fired upon from a house, and in reprisal the SS pulled eighteen Jews out of the house and shot them on the spot as "the probable assailants."[38] Hingnoz suspected that the killings were illegal but reported that he had been unable to investigate them due to the movement of the 1st Battalion from his area of command.

Soon after their arrival in the region, the Security Police and army formations received a series of directives concerning security along the demarcation line. Instructions such as those given to the 7th Infantry Division on 21 September stipulated that "the flow of Poles and Jews to the west is to be prevented." Orders issued by the XXII Corps the following day called for the *Feldgendarmerie* (Military Police) to "prevent refugees of Polish ethnicity and the Jewish race from crossing the demarcation line to the west."[39] And specifically concerning Streckenbach's men, Major General Rudolf Konrad, the XVIII Corps's chief of staff, ordered on 24 September that the two *Einsatzkommandos* from *Einsatzgruppe* I were to support the efforts of other German formations to "stop the flow of undesirable refugees, above all Jews and Poles."[40]

Military commanders went farther than simply using the Security Police to stop Jewish and Polish refugees from moving west by actually taking the initiative and working with the SS to push Jews over the demarcation line. For example, the Fourteenth Army directed the *Einsatzkommandos* to clear all unreliable elements *(unzuverlässigen Elementen)* from cities and locales adjacent to the demarcation line: "In the first place, the Jewish population of these border locales is—in as far as it is possible—to be pushed to the east, over the San."[41] A subsequent order from the XVII Corps on 28 September also made it clear that Wehrmacht formations on security duty were to coordinate their activities with the *Einsatzkommandos*:

The troops should arrest all people who cross the San River (*Volksdeutsche* are to be treated accordingly), and turn these over to *Einsatzkommando* 3, which is responsible for investigating civilians who come over the San. The *Einsatzkommando* has squads in the following areas: Nisko, Lezajsk, Jaroslaw, and Radymno. Contact with these *Einsatzgruppen* [sic] is to be established. Squads from the *Einsatzkommando* have also been set up along the western bank of the San [River].[42]

Rudolf Körner of *Einsatzkommando* 1/I recalled after the war that the army and Security Police worked together quite closely during operations on the demarcation line: "In Sanok at the time we transferred a large number of Jews to the army. The Jews were then pushed over the demarcation line toward the Russians."[43] Similarly, in Jaroslaw, the army and Alfred Hasselberg's EK 3/I forced hundreds of Jews to the east until the complaints of a Red Army officer brought these operations to a halt.[44]

Hasselberg's *Einsatzkommando* 3/I had entered Poland three weeks earlier via Zakopane, a popular resort town in the Tatra Mountains, and traveled through Nowy Sącz and Tarnów before reaching its base of operations in Jaroslaw.[45] Stationed along the San River between Jaroslaw and Sandomierz, Hasselberg's responsibilities included confiscating Jewish assets as well as expelling Jews to the east.[46] Soon after establishing his headquarters, Hasselberg received orders from Streckenbach to send a small unit called a *Rollkommando* into the Lublin district, where it was to search Jewish communities for valuables. Hasselberg placed the unit under the command of SS-*Hauptsturmführer* Hans Block and sent it to the city of Chełm.[47] From Chełm, Block's *Rollkommando* was to work its way west as the Red Army occupied the Lublin district. Although it was Heydrich who had told Streckenbach to create the *Rollkommando,* the instructions actually came from Hermann Göring, who was concerned that large numbers of Jews fleeing to the east were taking with them quantities of precious metals and currency that would fall into Soviet hands.[48] Göring's concerns reflected the fluidity of the diplomatic situation at the beginning of the third week of September, as the area between the San and Bug Rivers was still designated as the Soviet half of occupied Poland.

Sending an SS and police unit into the Lublin district to carry out organized looting was bound to cause friction with military commanders, many of whom considered plundering a serious criminal offense. But problems also arose because of the reckless behavior of Block's men. According to Block, Hasselberg had ordered him to "seize all things of value, including gold, silver items, and other valuables and to return with these items."[49] After arriving in Chełm, *Rollkommando* personnel located a local Pole willing to identify the wealthiest Jews in the community. These and other Jews were then called out into the street and forced at gunpoint to empty their pockets. Certain members of the Jewish community, women among them, were also strip-searched. As Block later explained before an SS Honor Court during the trial of Alfred Hasselberg in December 1939, women were forced to disrobe because "in nearly 99% of the cases" valuables were found hidden in their undergarments.[50] In addition, several members of the *Rollkommando* apparently broke into homes shouting "your gold or your life," including one in which the German military commander of Chełm was temporarily quartered. According to a complaint filed by this officer, a captain named Sommer, he witnessed *Rollkommando* personnel ripping rings off the hands of the female Jewish residents, in some cases breaking their fingers. Several of the women were then subjected to humiliating cavity searches that were conducted in an extremely rough manner.[51] The situation resulted in a heated exchange between Captain Sommer and Block, with Sommer threatening that he "would not tolerate [such activities] in the future."[52] Block's *Rollkommando* left Chełm soon thereafter with an undisclosed amount of Jewish valuables.

At the same time a far more severe conflict between Udo von Woyrsch and the military authorities responsible for security along the San River was developing because of widespread killings and the destruction of Jewish property by the Special Purpose *Einsatzgruppe*. In the small town of Dynów, for instance, squads of Order Police murdered a dozen Jews by burning them to death in the local synagogue.[53] The same perpetrators then collected another sixty Jewish men from the community, drove them into the nearby forest, and shot them into a pit.[54] Order Police personnel carried out similar shootings in Nienadowa, Krzywcza, and Dubiecko in addition to razing synagogues.[55] In Przemyśl regular German troops and personnel with the Special Purpose *Einsatzgruppe* looted and destroyed Jewish businesses and homes.[56] Rasch's Security Police also searched the city for rabbis, Jewish doctors, merchants, and lawyers whose names were listed in the *Sonderfahndungsbuch*.[57] These prisoners and other large groups of male Jews were then killed at several nearby sites in Nałipowice, Pratkowice, Pikulice, and Przekopana, where 102 Jewish men were murdered on 19 September.[58] As a result of these operations in and around Przemyśl, von Woyrsch's men killed at least 500, and perhaps as many as 600, Jewish men by 20 September.[59]

Murder and destruction on this scale soon brought complaints from locally stationed German officers. At issue was the chaos that the actions of von Woyrsch's police were causing along the demarcation line, but some officers also believed that the acts of von Woyrsch's men were unlawful. This concern was apparent in orders issued by General List on 19 September commanding subordinate officers to stop military and police personnel from perpetrating illegal acts.[60] List's directive came too late, however, as reports from the field had already begun to filter to the rear. The first telegram from the army command post in Rzeszów arrived at Fourteenth Army headquarters in Kraków while Wilhelm Canaris was visiting on 20 September.[61] This communiqué included information from Major Karl-Erich Schmidt-Richberg, who complained about the "partially illegal measures" *(die zum Teil unge-setzlichen Massnahmen)* implemented by von Woyrsch's men.[62] It appeared that the mass shooting of Jews was creating unrest among German military personnel who witnessed these acts. "Instead of fighting at the front," Schmidt-Richberg noted, "young [SS] men were demonstrating their courage against defenseless civilians."[63] These incidents led in one case to the outbreak of a brawl between SS and regular army personnel.[64]

The Fourteenth Army chief of staff, Brigadier General Eberhard von Mackensen, was also infuriated by the turmoil, and he issued orders on 19 September to bring the situation under control. Asserting that SS and police personnel were acting in violation of previous instructions from the Fourteenth Army to maintain order, Mackensen declared that all SS and army security forces in and around Przemyśl were to be placed under the direct authority of the city commander. These units, including the Security Police, could only carry out executions according to orders from the local military authority.[65] One day later Colonel Wagner requested that the Special Purpose *Einsatzgruppe* be withdrawn because of the "havoc" it had wreaked in the area.[66] Gestapo headquarters quickly acknowledged Wagner's demand and pulled von Woyrsch's unit back to Katowice on 22 September.

Unlike the relatively mild disagreements in Chełm and Sądowa Wisniza, the conflict between the army and the SS over the activities of the Special Purpose *Einsatzgruppe* (EG z.b.V.) was serious. Officers like General Mackensen and Major Schmidt-Richberg were infuriated by the seemingly pointless destruction and disorder that von Woyrsch's men caused in the region, and they moved rapidly to stop it. The fact that German troops and SS personnel had come to blows was also unacceptable in the eyes of German commanders, as were reports of widespread looting. Such acts suggested a breakdown of discipline in the ranks of locally stationed army units, and German officers moved swiftly to nip the problem in the bud. At the same time, certain commanders recognized that while the deeds of von Woyrsch's men were reprehensible, SS and police units also performed an important security function. For example, on the same day that Gestapo headquarters promised to withdraw von Woyrsch's force, Army High Command informed General Brandt in East Upper Silesia that command of the EG z.b.V. had been reassigned to Rasch and the unit was on its way to Katowice.[67] A short time later, General List petitioned to have the unit brought back to Przemyśl.[68] In an announcement to the enlisted personnel and officers under his command, List explained his reasons for attempting to recall the EG z.b.V.:

On the basis of repeated requests from the fighting troops, a special police unit was detailed for the clearing of bands, guerrillas, and plunderers from occupied areas. These police forces under the command of SS-*Obergruppenführer* von Woyrsch, which in the meantime have been pulled out [of the area], took ruthless action and essentially completed their tasks. Where abuses were alleged to have been committed (illegal shootings), investigations are underway.

The severe way in which these actions were carried out has also become known to the frontline troops, although frequently in exaggerated form. Because of this the result has been obvious discontent on many levels, which has come out in comments made by officers, noncommissioned officers, and the rank and file against all persons who wear the field uniform of the SS.

Intelligence officers were informed of the extraordinarily successful activity of this *Einsatzkommando* in the interest of the troops, as well as about its organization and tasks at a conference, which took place on 30 September. It was requested that this be explained to subordinate units in exactly the same way. The extensive support of the *Einsatzkommandos* [provided to the army] in fulfilling their frontier and state police tasks *is in the interest of the troops.*[69]

Therefore, at the same time that friction developed between the military authorities and the Operational Groups in southern Poland, certain other officers were facilitating SS efforts to make the southern section of the demarcation line *Judenfrei*. In some locations directly on the San River, such as Jarosław, for example, the expulsions were coordinated with local military commanders, while in others, like Tarnobrzeg, located on the Vistula River to the west of the San, the army expelled 4,000 Jews on its own initiative.[70] Discerning the total number of Jews forced over the San River by the SS and Wehrmacht is difficult, but according to the estimate of one former member of *Einsatzgruppe* I, it was no fewer than 18,000 people. Add to these the Jews who the German army pushed out of Tarnobrzeg and the total number expelled rises to at least 22,000.[71] Ironically, these people forced from their homes and communities were fortunate, as life for Jews under Soviet rule, while difficult, was undoubtedly preferable to living under the heel of the brutal SS.

In many ways, SS-army operations against Jews in northern Poland followed a similar pattern of cooperation and conflict. On or about 18 September, Lothar Beutel's *Einsatzgruppe* IV appeared in northeastern Poland and began its efforts against the Jews in communities along the demarcation line. Five days earlier, Beutel's men had departed from Bydgoszcz with General Braemer's forces and moved through East Prussia in the direction of Białystok as part of the Fourth Army's transfer to the northeastern section of the front. Traveling behind German lines via Graudenz (Grudziądz), Deutsch-Eylau (Iława), Osterode (Ostróda), Allenstein (Olsztyn), and Arys (Orzysz), Beutel's men moved into Poland on the extreme left flank of German forces and arrived in Łomza on 17 September. That day, Beutel received orders from the Fourth Army to proceed to Białystok, through which Army High Command assumed the German-Soviet demarcation line would run.[72] Once in Białystok, *Einsatzgruppe* IV again joined General Braemer's 580th Rear Army Area (*Korück 580*) and began policing the new eastern border.[73] Above all, Beutel's responsibilities included expelling Jews, orders that *Einsatzgruppe* IV received from Gestapo headquarters while en route to the city.[74]

Białystok was quiet when the Security Police arrived. The populace huddled behind closed doors because German troops passing through the city earlier had killed a number of people by firing randomly into homes.[75] Beutel quartered his men in a school, established an 8:00 P.M. to 5:00 A.M. curfew for the town's inhabitants, and initiated measures against the Jews. Squads of Security Police swept the city arresting Jewish men between the ages of fifteen and sixty. Homes and shops were also searched for weapons and valuables, and "a number of Jewish women were shot for refusing to part with their rings."[76] The action quickly grew from an "official" effort to confiscate Jewish wealth for the Reich into plundering for personal profit, which forced Beutel's deputy, Josef Meisinger, to search the cars of several *Einsatzgruppe* men for furs that a Jewish woman reported stolen. In what must have been a remarkable scene, Meisinger found the stolen furs and had the woman brought forward to pick the thieves out of a lineup. After identifying the perpetrators, Meisinger immediately placed the eleven policemen under arrest and sent them back to Germany under armed guard.[77]

Over the course of the next two days, Beutel's men collected several hundred Jews, marched them out of the city, and forced them at gunpoint to continue in an easterly direction. But before a large number of these Jews could be expelled, negotiations between newly arrived Russian officers, the local German commander, and Lothar Beutel made it clear that Białystok was in the Soviet zone of occupied Poland.[78] As a result, Beutel's men pulled out of the city on 21 September and arrived in Lyck (Ełk), East Prussia, shortly thereafter. For the next week, *Einsatzgruppe* IV traveled down the Narew River in the direction of Warsaw, stopping in Pułtusk and

Maków to confiscate valuables and push Jews over the river to the east. In Pułtusk, according to a former member of *Einsatzkommando* 1/IV, the Jews were told they could go to the Russian zone and bring with them what they could carry. After assembling on the market square, Security Police searched the bundles, confiscated anything of value, and sent the Jews east.[79] *Einsatzgruppe* IV reached the outskirts of Warsaw on 27 September and halted there briefly before reporting to the Eighth Army "for security police tasks after the occupation."[80] Overall, during this period of its operations in northeastern Poland, Lothar Beutel's *Einsatzgruppe* had no difficulties working with the military authorities.

The same cannot be said of the assignment of Ernst Damzog's *Einsatzgruppe* V to the Third Army in East Prussia. The Third Army's commander, General Georg von Küchler, was a career military officer, and he expected the men under his command to conduct themselves according to professional and ethical standards that sometimes ran counter to the SS's image of the ideologically motivated National Socialist fighter. It was almost certain, therefore, that General Küchler would not tolerate SS units terrorizing the Jewish population. After establishing his headquarters in Allenstein, Damzog's two *Einsatzkommandos* launched into Poland at different points. EK 1/V began the advance from Marienwerder (Kwidzyń) behind the assault of the 21st and 228th Infantry Divisions toward Grudziądz. Further to the east, EK 2/V started the campaign from Neidenburg (Nidzica) with orders to move directly south toward Mława behind the 61st and 11th Infantry Divisions and the SS Panzer Division Kempf. By 6 September, two subunits of EK 1/V had reached Grudziądz and a third was in Lubawa, while at the same time two *Teilkommandos* of EK 2/V were in Mława and another was in Działdowo with Damzog's group staff. Altogether, *Einsatzgruppe* V reported arresting only eight people, including three women, two priests, one teacher, and one postal agent.[81]

At this point, the local army commander in Grudziądz instructed Damzog's men to take twenty-five Poles hostage as protection against civilian attack.[82] Searches of government and religious buildings continued in the city as well, leading to the confiscation of documents, files, and other important official Polish records. In addition, the men of *Einsatzkommando* 1/V searched the synagogue and the offices of the Jewish community in Grudziądz, seizing records and lists of local members' names. The SD then selected two representatives for the Jewish community and gave them just fourteen hours to produce lists of families' names and Jewish-owned property in the city. This action was part of the overall "preparations for the deportation [*Abwanderung*] of the Jews" that were being carried out in the city by Heinz Graefe's subordinates.[83] By 9 September, Robert Schefe's *Einsatzkommando* 2/V had moved on to other locations, while *Einsatzkommando* 1/V remained in Grudziądz to implement further measures against the Jews. Ordering the Jewish community to prepare for deportation within three days, Graefe's men collected a communal fund of 20,000 Złoty under the pretext of facilitating the move.[84]

Reports from Damzog's *Gruppenstab* noted on 10 September that anti-Jewish measures were being instituted in the city of Mława as well. Of the 350 Jews still in Mława, "sixty-six men from the ages of fifteen to sixty-years-old and three women were taken into custody, and with the agreement of the local [Wehrmacht] commander *[Truppenführer]* were pushed *[abgeschoben]* southeast of Chorzele into unoccupied Polish territory."[85] Furthermore, "seventy Jews from Przasnysz were forced into Poland from the vicinity of Friedrichshof [in East Prussia some thirty-five miles to the northeast of Chorzele]. The remaining Jews in the district were then informed, with the agreement of local [military] commanders, of strict regulations the violation of which will be severely punished."[86]

Despite efforts by the Security Police to coordinate anti-Jewish measures with the proper local military authorities, these actions soon ran afoul of General Küchler. At the 1948 Nuremberg war crimes trial of Küchler and other ranking German commanders, Colonel Martin Grase testified that after the occupation of Mława, Küchler received news from his quartermaster, Lieutenant Colonel Friedrich Prüter, about the arrest and mistreatment of Jews by a police unit in the city. During the incident, several Jews had been gunned down in the street and buildings were burned to the ground. As Küchler himself described the anti-Jewish action in Mława during his testimony before the Allied military tribunal in Nuremberg:

> The Jews were herded together . . . [and told] that within two hours they were to report to the marketplace with only what they could carry. All other possessions were to be left behind and then removed. As my quartermaster [Prüter] reported to me, the scene soon became extraordinarily agitated. He told me on the telephone: "The people are standing here on the marketplace screaming and shouting, and the police—a number of shots have already been heard and a couple of houses are burning."[87]

Küchler then "authorized [Prüter] to bring up the nearest troops and disarm the police detachment. I gave the order that the next day the police detachment was to be sent back over the border—I believe they came from somewhere in East Prussia." In addition, he ordered that the Jews were to be set free and soon thereafter initiated court-martial proceedings against the commander of the police unit.[88]

At roughly the same time, another serious problem arose concerning actions against Jews by *Waffen*-SS troops with the SS Panzer Division Kempf, which was subordinated to the Third Army and part of the XXVI Corps, under the command of Major General Albert Wodrig. According to the Nuremberg testimony of Dr. Franz Hinz, a former member of the 12th Infantry Division's quartermaster staff, a man with the Reich Labor Service was "shot from a house . . . inhabited almost entirely by Jews" in the small town of Goworowo, which lay only a short distance east of Rózan.[89] The shooting took place in the immediate vicinity of personnel from SS Panzer Division Kempf, who spontaneously "retaliated" against the local Jews. Described by one officer as "running wild," the members of an SS artillery regiment in the vicinity, including one man with the army's Secret Field Police, killed nearly fifty Jews while brutally herding them into the town synagogue.[90] The portrayal of the scene offered in German sources falls short of adequately describing the actual horror of the events. Several Jewish survivors recalled the terror of that day in the memorial book dedicated to the memory of the Jews of nearby Rózan. As rendered by one of these witnesses, Rachel Weiser-Nagel, a refugee from Rózan,

> [In] Govorovo we were at once directed to the market square where the inhabitants had been assembled. After a long while people were ordered to gather at their places of worship: the Jews in the synagogue and the Christians in their church. As we entered the building I could see many Jews lying on the ground in the courtyard bleeding from severe wounds. . . . some had been shot in their faces, blinded and gored with broken skulls, past recognition. . . . When all the Jews were inside, the Germans sprayed the synagogue with kerosene and set it on fire. That very moment a car drew up and stopped. A shortish, rather fat officer stepped out and asked: "What's the matter here?" Lower ranked soldiers—his subordinates—explained: "Here we can destroy all the Jews at one stroke." He interrupted them and in a quiet, determined way told them: "This is too much." He gave the order to open the doors and shouted "out!"[91]

Minna Mlinek-Magnushever, a resident of Goworowo, recounted the incident similarly but added that she heard the German officer who set them free say, "'Throw them [the Jews] out. It's too soon yet!' And with a significant gesture towards the throat he added: 'They'll be slaughtered anyway. But not now—not yet!' Immediately his subordinates opened the doors."[92]

General Küchler reacted swiftly by contacting the SS division and ordering the immediate arrest and court-martial of the perpetrators. Other military commanders stationed in the area responded with similar indignation. As one of these officers later recalled, "Great agitation and outrage were expressed in the command staff, all the way up to the commanding general, Albert Wodrig. The disgust of our commanding general was so great that he, for example, refused to have the SS division serve under his command in the western offensive."[93] Werner Kempf, the commander of the SS panzer division, recounted his reaction to the events as follows:

> I remember the incident very well, during the occupation of a village near Rózan supply troops in the rear area of my division had murdered Jews. The incorrect viewpoint was prevalent in SS formations at the time that Polish Jews were participating in the fight against us and presented a danger to the troops. I fought against this viewpoint from the very first days and later forbade the arrest and herding together of Jews. In my opinion, it was never fully established how the horrible massacre came about. Members of the SS artillery regiment of my division began it, however, members of the army also participated. If I remember correctly, the intervening officers arrested five participants (four SS and one army soldier). The highest-ranking man arrested was a sergeant from the SS artillery regiment.
>
> I only learned of the event early the next morning. I reported it immediately to my superior officer [General Wodrig] and requested that the matter be investigated without delay. At midday on this day, the overall commander of the army, General von Küchler, arrived at divisional headquarters to speak with all of the SS commanders of units under my command. General von Küchler denounced the terrible deeds in the harshest terms. He impressed upon the commanders the wickedness, the barbarity, dishonorable, and beastly conduct of the culprits, making it clear that the crime of murder had been committed and that the honor of the troops had been most disgracefully sullied.
>
> Finally, he informed those present that these disgraceful fellows must be severely punished and that no sentence was too serious for them. He made it clear that the chief offenders must be punished with death for their barbaric crime. I must add that no one could have condemned and denounced this act more severely than General von Küchler did at this conference with the commanders of the SS formations.[94]

Predictably, the SS war court returned mild sentences against the offenders: it convicted the Secret Field Police officer of manslaughter and sentenced him to nine years' imprisonment. In addition, one *Waffen*-SS private
received a guilty verdict, with the court sentencing him to three years in
jail.[95] As its rationale for the especially light sentence of the SS private, the
court proffered the excuse that witnessing the cruelty of the Poles toward
ethnic Germans had agitated him. "As an SS man," the justification stated,
"he particularly felt that the Jews were hostile to Germans, which in his
youthful impetuousness he handled poorly."[96] General Küchler was appalled at the mild sentences, and as the senior commander in the area he
refused to confirm them, demanding instead that the offenders stand trial
before an army court-martial. Even the SS commander Werner Kempf declared the sentence "laughingly mild" and later stated that the entire
process was a sham.[97] For the second court-martial Küchler personally appointed the court's presiding officer to ensure a sentence more befitting the
crime. At this point, Himmler and the *Gauleiter* of East Prussia, Erich
Koch, intervened by paying Küchler a visit on 23 September to request that
he stop the court-martial.[98] General Küchler refused the request. However,
"before the court martial was able to take up its sessions, or before it was
able to pass sentence, Himmler took steps with Hitler for the SS to have
court martial jurisdiction of its own."[99] Eventually, the perpetrators were
completely pardoned as part of a general amnesty issued by Hitler on 4 October 1939.[100]

For its part, *Einsatzgruppe* V continued its security duties unhindered despite the conflicts in Mława and Goworowo. According to orders issued by
the Third Army on 14 September, "police forces in the rear" interrogated
"suspicious persons" and interned Polish and Jewish men.[101] The Security
Police continued to search for Jewish "opponents" as well, such as occurred
in Łomza on 19 September, when Damzog's men attempted to locate members of the Jewish intelligentsia by forcing representatives of the community
to draw up a list of Jews still in the city.[102] After the entry of the Soviets into
Poland on 18 September, the Third Army then utilized Damzog's men to control the growing flood of refugees and to question prisoners arrested by the
Military Police.[103] On 24 September, squads from *Einsatzgruppe* V began enforcing security along the Narew River in accordance with Wehrmacht orders that refugees of Jewish and Polish descent were to be prevented from
returning to German-occupied territory.[104] Security Police stationed in the
riverside town of Ostrołęka, for example, turned back Jews attempting to
cross over to the west.[105] These actions expanded five days later into full-
scale expulsions similar to those being carried out along the San River in the

south. As a report from *Einsatzgruppe* V noted on 29 September, "large columns of Jews are being pushed over the demarcation line."[106]

As this last series of orders illustrates, cooperation between *Einsatzgruppe* V and the Third Army remained generally uneventful concerning rear area security operations and the expulsion of Jews over the demarcation line. How can this be explained given Küchler's apoplectic reaction to SS atrocities against Jews in Mława and Goworowo? To begin with, there are indications that General Küchler did not disagree in principle with the overall policy of pushing Polish Jews over the demarcation line as long as these actions were carried out in an orderly fashion. Indeed, evidence of his anti-Jewish animus may be found in an announcement he issued on 22 July 1940 after learning that his troops were being transferred to Poland for occupation duty. Noting that "every soldier of the army, particularly every officer, [was to] refrain from criticizing the ethnic struggle being carried out in the Government General," Küchler argued that "[in] the treatment of the Polish minorities, and of the Jews, and the handling of church matters . . . the final ethnic solution of the ethnic struggle which has been raging on the eastern border for centuries calls for measures of such harshness and directness that one application of them will suffice."[107] Had the general changed his mind about the SS and thrown his full support behind the ethnic cleansing effort then under way in Poland? The assistance that his forces rendered to *Einsatzgruppe* V in expelling Polish Jews at the end of September 1939 certainly seems to have been the first step in such a direction.

On the other hand, General Küchler and other officers in the Third Army were clearly offended by the brutality that attended the actions of the Security Police against Jews in Mława and those of *Waffen*-SS personnel against the Jews of Goworowo. This disgust at the commission of unauthorized shootings and wanton barbarity by SS personnel reflected the fact that senior members of the officer corps took a very dim view of spontaneous violence against civilians. Brutality behind the lines suggested to men like Küchler that military discipline had broken down, and from there it was only a matter of time before atrocities such as those perpetrated in Mława and Goworowo caused general unrest, a potential state of affairs that many military commanders found intolerable. In this sense, Field Marshal Wilhelm Keitel offered an honest appraisal of the situation when in prison while on trial at Nuremberg he wrote, "Already while operations in Poland were in full swing, complaints were raised against the excesses of Himmler's police units *[Polizeiorgane]*, which took it upon themselves— without the agreement of Army High Command—to enforce 'calm and order' . . . behind the lines."[108] The SS's notion of calm and order clearly conflicted with that held by Wehrmacht commanders at the time, and it was on this point that conflicts like those between the SS and the Third Army erupted.

A heightened sense of institutional rivalry between the army and the SS probably also played a part in the case of General Küchler's energetic response to SS crimes. According to the postwar testimony of witnesses at Nuremberg, Küchler often went out of his way to antagonize the SS, such as during an inflammatory eulogy he delivered in September 1939 for General Werner von Fritsch, who was killed while leading troops on the siege lines outside of Warsaw.[109] As Karl Wilhelm Melior recalled, Küchler had at the time railed against those (i.e., Himmler and the SS) who "so maliciously and treacherously attacked and slandered" the honor of General Werner von Fritsch.[110] Küchler later claimed at Nuremberg that as a result of his actions against the SS and his statements at Fritsch's funeral he was punished by being the sole army commander not to receive a promotion after the campaign.[111] This argument was rather self-serving, however, as one year later Küchler played an important role in the conquest of Holland and the capture of Paris, achievements for which he was promoted to colonel general.[112] At this early stage of the war, it is thus likely that the ingrained disdain many German officers held for the rival *Waffen*-SS (including the SS Death's Head units) informed their attempts to punish SS personnel for their crimes. As General Küchler's response to the killings in Goworowo demonstrates, this tension between the army and the *Waffen*-SS and SS Death's Head units was so intense that conflicts between army rear area commanders and *Waffen*-SS formations often proved more severe than those between the army and the Security Police.

A serious clash that developed between Tenth Army headquarters and the SS *Leibstandarte* "Adolf Hitler" during the third week of the invasion is a case in point. Originally detailed to the Eighth Army's XIII Corps, the *Leibstandarte* was transferred to the Tenth Army after the end of the campaign's first week. Roughly ten days later, according to a report sent by Lieutenant General Joachim Lemelsen, the commander of the 29th Motorized Infantry Division, "*Obermusikmeister* Müller-John of the *Leibstandarte,* on the night of 18–19 September, in [the town of] Blonie, had fifty Jewish civilian prisoners shot. Müller-John claims to have acted according to orders from his superiors."[113] Lemelsen then noted that he had ordered Müller-John's arrest. Upon receiving Lemelsen's report, the commander of the Tenth Army, General Reichenau, informed Army Group South that "until this matter can be cleared up, I have ordered [Müller-John's] incarceration to remain in effect. The army has no knowledge of an order from above for Jewish prisoners to be shot. In a similar case, I let an officer be sentenced by a war court. I request instructions from the army group if the proceedings should be carried out."[114] The reply Reichenau received the next day confirmed that no one at Army Group South headquarters knew of an order to shoot Jewish prisoners; Müller-John was therefore to be court-martialed.[115] The trial never took place, however, due to Hitler's direct intervention. As Smilo Freiherr von Lüttwitz testified after the war, General Hermann Hoth, the commanding officer of the XV Corps, sent him to see Reichenau in order to stress the importance of having justice served in this "extraordinary case."[116] Colonel Lüttwitz found Reichenau "highly indignant" about the issue and awaiting further instructions from Berlin. Reichenau spoke with Armed Forces High Command several hours later and "shared with me [Lüttwitz] that on Hitler's order, the court martial was to be called off."[117]

Without doubt this incident was particularly galling to the officers who were prevented from exercising the army's executive authority. In taking it upon himself to have fifty Jewish prisoners killed without a prior court-martial, Müller-John had clearly flaunted the authority of Wehrmacht officers. However, it is impossible to know if General Reichenau was indignant about Müller-John's murderous behavior or simply about his blatant disregard for the army's authority. One suspects the latter, because neither Reichenau nor any other German officer ever voiced regret over the execution of Jewish civilians. Müller-John's defiance of authority was indiscipline so heinous that the punishment in this case would have undoubtedly been death by firing squad if his court-martial had been allowed to proceed.

Yet another episode of friction between the army and the SS is provided by problems that arose in the city of Włocławek (Leslau) one day after the 2d SS Death's Head Regiment "Brandenburg" carried out a large anti-Jewish action. Commanded by SS-*Standartenführer* Paul Nostitz, the 2d SS Regiment received instructions on 12 September directly from Himmler, via Theodor Eicke, to carry out "clearing and security measures" behind the Eighth Army.[118] Nostitz maintained after the campaign that the Eighth Army reiterated these instructions, which authorized his unit to "carry out house searches and arrests in order to free the area from insurgents, suspicious elements, and plunderers."[119] In an effort to coordinate security, the Eighth Army also informed units in the area on 15 September that these tasks were to be conducted in "close contact" with the commander of the 581st Rear Army Area (*Korück* 581), Lieutenant General Alfred Böhm-Tettelbach.[120] As an added measure, Himmler also dispatched SS-*Gruppenführer* Günther Pancke to Eighth Army headquarters in Łódź to act as a special commander of police *(Sonderbefehlshaber der Polizei)* and liaison officer between the army and the SS police forces operating behind German lines.[121]

Crossing into Poland on 14 September, Nostitz's men arrived in Ostrów the following day and from there carried out their duties in a number of locations, including Kalisz, Kolo, and Krosniewice, before arriving in Włocławek on 22 September. According to Böhm-Tettelbach, he had no prior warning that Nostitz's unit would be in Włocławek.[122] Orders issued the day before (21 September) made clear, however, that the Eighth Army had indeed instructed the 2d SS Regiment to "immediately transfer the necessary number of sections *[Hundertschaften]* to the area between Kutno-Lowicz-Sochaczew," just to the north of Włocławek, in an effort to "uncover bandit camps."[123] Upon reaching Włocławek, Nostitz reported to Böhm-Tettelbach that he intended to "comb the region, above all the forests around Włocławek."[124] On the following day (23 September), Pancke also arrived in Włocławek and confirmed the nature of Nostitz's orders to Böhm-Tettelbach. In an attempt to coordinate their activity, Böhm-Tettelbach and Nostitz then met on the morning of 24 September. As a result of this meeting, both men agreed that "searches should be carried out in Włocławek and in the surrounding area, especially in the forest south of the Vistula River along the stretch from Włocławek to Płock."[125] Böhm-Tettelbach later pointed out, though, that the 2d SS Regiment never carried out its assigned duties in the area, limiting itself instead to "actions against the local Jews."[126]

These actions began in the afternoon on 24 September after Nostitz received two orders via Pancke. The first was from Eicke at the Führer's headquarters to immediately detach two battalions of SS troops from his unit and send them to Bydgoszcz where a concerted action against the city's intelligentsia was under way. The second directive instructed Nostitz to "arrest all of the male Jews in the city in their homes and lead them to prison."[127] At 6:00 P.M., Nostitz deployed his three companies for the action. Two were used to encircle the city center, while the third was charged with "searching houses and apprehending Jews."[128] Jewish men were then driven from their homes toward the prison, and two were reported shot for allegedly attempting to escape. The city's two synagogues were also razed, as were two houses, and numerous buildings were plundered. With the approach of twilight at 8:30 P.M., Nostitz ordered an end to the action "because the prison was brimming" with Jews.[129] Altogether, between 800 and 1,000 Jewish men had been arrested.

Meanwhile, just after the operation began, Nostitz dispatched his adjutant, SS-*Obersturmführer* Reum, to Böhm-Tettelbach to ask what should be done with the prisoners. As Böhm-Tettelbach reported to the Eighth Army the next day, Nostitz

> sent his adjutant to my office to explain to my quartermaster, Colonel Wilck, his intention to have all of the city's male Jews arrested. Upon being told that this could mean perhaps ten thousand or more people had to be arrested, the incarceration of who was impossible, the adjutant answered that as many should be arrested as could be held in the prison, the rest could be shot. The quartermaster said he would not prevent the action, because canceling a raid that had already begun would embarrass the Wehrmacht in the eyes of the SS. He attempted, however, to limit the extent of the action, and expressing his regret that he had not received notification of the action before its initiation, offered the opinion that shooting all of the Jews was surely not the sense of the Führer's instructions.[130]

Apparently undecided about what to do with his prisoners, Nostitz transferred the Jews to Brigadier General Müller, who then ordered them released.[131] After the 2d SS Regiment "Brandenburg" departed Włocławek the next day, General Böhm-Tettelbach expressed to the Eighth Army his impression that "the unit had come here with the intention to undertake something against the Jews as a whole [*etwas gegen die Judenschaft als Ganzes zu unternehmen*]."[132] He then complained that the orders the SS regiment had received from a nonmilitary source led to misunderstandings between the Wehrmacht and the SS. These could have been clarified if only the army was informed beforehand about the tasks that Nostitz's unit was ordered to undertake. Nostitz had confirmed to Böhm-Tettelbach before departing that his unit was indeed subordinated to the Eighth Army, but then, Böhm-Tettelbach reported, "contrary to orders, he [Nostitz] had not busied himself with tasks that were in the interest of the army, but with special tasks that were outside of the army's jurisdiction."[133]

For their part, German troops also seem to have taken it upon themselves to harass Włocławek's Jews. Upon his unit's arrival in the city on 22 September, Nostitz informed Böhm-Tettelbach that while on his way to his quarters, he met "three or four soldiers with a group of [Jewish] civilians they had arrested." When he inquired what they were doing, Nostitz claimed,

> Sergeant Walter from an ambulance crew stationed in Włocławek explained to me that they had surprised the Jews at a meeting of some

kind and now thought that they should be brought to the SS. When they saw that they were dealing with a member of the SS, they asked me to take the Jews [off of their hands]. I took the Jews and led them to a yard. One of the Jews attempted to run at this point and he was shot. Meanwhile, I sent for a wagon from the 3d Company of the 2d SS Regiment in order to transport the imprisoned Jews and in addition ordered the block surrounded and searched because of Sergeant Walter's report that on this street there were mobs of Jews gathered in certain houses. With this, more Jews were taken into custody, of which a few again tried to flee. These few were shot during the attempt and one was wounded. The total number of those arrested was twenty-three.[134]

Further information about the involvement of regular German soldiers in events in Włocławek came to light in October 1939 during an SS investigation into allegations that Nostitz's men had plundered homes and shops in the city. In line with the twisted definitions of proper and improper behavior in the SS, authorities from Himmler down condoned the murder of Jews but abhorred crimes committed by SS men against Jewish property. In a letter dated 10 October, Heinrich Müller at Gestapo headquarters in Berlin warned Theodor Eicke that Heydrich was investigating rumors about the behavior of Nostitz's men in Włocławek. Recounting the events, Müller erroneously noted that out of revenge for the razing of the synagogue by unidentified perpetrators, the Jews had set fire to the houses that Nostitz reported burned. In response, the 2d SS Regiment had initiated an action against the city's male Jews leading to the arrest of nearly 1,000. During this action, Müller continued, "Jewish stores were plundered, including a jewelry shop."[135] Moreover,

in certain parts of the city, members of the armed forces distributed goods plundered from the shops to the Poles who ran away howling with them [*johlend abzog*]. According to the later report of a unit in Włocławek, the [2d SS] Death's Head Regiment left a building it had seized in indescribable condition. A wine locker had been found in the cellar of the house that was completely empty after the unit withdrew. Also, valuable paintings were found destroyed and worthless in rooms where SS men had been quartered.[136]

Müller concluded the letter by stating that he was informing Eicke so that he could be prepared in case third parties (probably the army) inquired about the incident.

Eight days later, on 18 October, Eicke sent a letter to Nostitz, who was stationed at the SS facility at Dachau, requesting that he take some action to deny that scandalous acts *(Schweinereien)* were perpetrated by the 2d SS Regiment in Włocławek. Important officials at the RSHA, Eicke stated, were inclined to believe that Nostitz's men were guilty of the offenses, necessitating that Nostitz report directly to Himmler to make his case.[137] Eyewitness statements, however, laid the blame for plundering squarely on the shoulders of Polish civilians and regular German soldiers stationed in Włocławek. In the words of one SS captain from the 2d SS Regiment,

> with the beginning of the action, I saw Poles and members of the Wehrmacht gathered on the Old Market Square. I approached them and asked the German troops to tell me where they bought the boots and shoes that they were carrying. A sergeant led me to a house where we met other German soldiers who were plundering. The sergeant told me there were also officers there who he had seen carrying shoes. They had emptied out the shop. I went from here back to the Old Market. There stood a First Lieutenant who saw the whole thing. I mentioned the acts of the soldiers to him and he said to me: "Unfortunately I can do nothing, for I have no men at my disposal."[138]

The participation of German soldiers and officers in the arrest of Jews and the plundering of Jewish businesses indicates there was some measure of agreement between SS and Wehrmacht troops on the status of Jews as targets for German harassment. As General Böhm-Tettelbach even noted in his report to the Eighth Army, "The Jews here and everywhere in Poland undoubtedly deserve harsh treatment."[139] But what bothered him was the violent and seemingly uncoordinated nature of the 2d SS Regiment's actions. Any measure against the Jewish population that had terror as its sole aim, he reasoned, "leads to unrest and the agitation of people who had been completely quiet" up to that point. Of course, Böhm-Tettelbach was unaware that terror was central to SS efforts to drive Jews out of German-occupied Poland. The general only saw the danger that uncoordinated actions presented to Germans given the "extraordinary weakness" of the military and police forces occupying the area.[140] To Böhm-Tettelbach, it would have been far more useful if "the proper professional organs, the SS Security Service and other police forces, sought out anti-German elements among the Polish and Jewish population."[141]

Upon reflection, it is evident that the incidents in Mława, Goworowo, Blonie, and Włocławek illustrate certain aspects of anti-Jewish actions that led to conflicts between the army and the SS during the German invasion. To begin with, although men like General Küchler were obviously disgusted by the murder of civilians, very few officers actually expressed outright disdain for SS atrocities based on ethical concerns. Wehrmacht commanders were instead far more worried about the potentially adverse effect that SS killings could have on military discipline. The focal point of this anxiety was a fundamental clash between the army and the SS over the definition of proper soldierly conduct. According to the SS, the soldier was first and foremost a National Socialist *Kämpfer* (fighter) who saw enemies in practical as well as in racial terms.[142] SS personnel thus defined Polish soldiers and the civilian population (Jewish and non-Jewish) alike as legitimate targets of aggression. This notion ran counter to the traditional ideal held by German army commanders of the ordinary soldier as a disciplined, professional warrior who did not kill civilians without just cause. Randomly perpetrated murders by Wehrmacht personnel, which occurred in large numbers, incidentally, implied a collapse of military discipline in the ranks. This prospect troubled many in the officer corps a great deal. It is no coincidence in this sense that German officers demanded orderly and disciplined behavior from German soldiers and SS personnel alike, and they frequently punished subordinates who transgressed against this code of conduct. Like the court-martial process and other formal procedures, regular army officers saw military discipline as the bedrock upon which the Wehrmacht was built, and SS actions represented an intolerable challenge to this principle.

Conflicts at the Top: SS Crimes, Army High Command, and the Reaction to Operation TANNENBERG

Equally important was the challenge that SS actions against Jews posed to the army's executive authority. Regardless of whether SS violence against Jews was part of the systematic terror ordered by Himmler or a spontaneous manifestation of SS anti-Semitism, these often chaotic operations offended officers who demanded calm and order in rear army areas. Unauthorized shootings, the looting of Jewish shops, and the destruction of homes and synagogues in explicit contradiction of orders represented insubordination of the highest degree, and Wehrmacht commanders simply could not tolerate it. Disagreements on precisely this score were particularly strident in Berlin, where concern about the numerous affronts to the army's institutional authority combined with the apprehension of some officers that the SS was embarking on an extensive killing program under the very noses of Wehrmacht commanders.

The rumbling began after Wilhelm Canaris provided Army High Command with information about Operation TANNENBERG that he received during a meeting with Reinhard Heydrich on 8 September. Heydrich informed Canaris at the time that the basic task of the *Einsatzgruppen* was "to render the leading class *[die führende Bevölkerungsschicht]* in Poland as harmless as possible."[143] Heydrich hinted that he wanted to directly involve the army in the killings by complaining bitterly that the army's court-martial process was too sluggish, even though military judges were sentencing to death an average of 200 Poles every day. The military justice system should be set aside, Heydrich argued, and "these people [i.e., insurgents . . . must be immediately shot or hanged without trial. We can show mercy to the common people, but the nobility, the Catholic clergy, and the Jews should be killed. After we enter Warsaw, I will reach an agreement with the army on how we should squeeze out all of these elements."[144] The next day (9 September), Canaris reported Heydrich's comments to Lieutenant General Karl-Heinrich von Stülpnagel, who in turn forwarded the information to General Halder. Yet it appeared that Halder already knew of these plans, telling Lieutenant Colonel Groscurth on 9 September that "the butchery of Poles behind the front was intensifying at such a rapid pace that the army would probably have to take steps against these acts soon."[145] Halder continued by stating, "It was Hitler's and [Hermann] Göring's intention to destroy and exterminate the Polish people." The rest of what Halder told him, Groscurth wrote in his diary, was so horrible it "could not be committed to paper."[146]

Canaris made a second attempt to raise the subject on 12 September. According to the *Abwehr* officer Lieutenant Colonel Erwin Lahousen, Canaris approached General Wilhelm Keitel, the head of Armed Forces High Command, while Hitler's headquarters train was stopped in the Silesian town of Ilnau. As Lahousen recalled, Canaris "warned Keitel very insistently that he was aware of steps, namely shootings and extermination measures, which were to be directed against the Polish intelligentsia, the nobility, and the clergy, as well as against all elements [of Polish society] that could be potential opponents."[147] Canaris further stated his firm belief that the "world would hold the Wehrmacht responsible for allowing these things to take place as it looked on." Keitel answered that General Brauchitsch had already made it clear to Hitler that the army wanted nothing to do with the killings. This policy had been decided by Hitler himself, however, and it was the Führer's opinion that if the army did not want to take part, it would have to allow the SS and Gestapo to carry out the liquidations independently. Hitler had ordered the shootings, Keitel elaborated, as part of the "political cleansing" of newly conquered Polish territory.[148] The Führer had decided that the responsibility for the "cleansing" actions would be transferred eventually to a civilian administrator assigned to each military district.

The military authorities attempted to get a handle on the situation one week later by arranging meetings with Heydrich and Hitler. Colonel Wagner spoke with Heydrich first on 19 September. Heydrich confirmed to Wagner that the "cleansing" of Jews, intelligentsia, clergy, and nobility from Poland was indeed planned. Wagner requested in response that Heydrich put off these measures until after a civilian government replaced the military administration in Poland.[149] Colonel Wagner's suggestion clearly echoed the intentions voiced by Hitler, which Keitel had revealed to Canaris one week earlier. In essence, Wagner was not attempting to prevent the intended liquidations, but he was taking steps to keep the army from being directly associated with them. The next day (20 September), General Brauchitsch went directly to Hitler to discuss the situation in Poland. During this meeting, Hitler confirmed to the general that Heydrich's *Einsatzgruppen* were implementing certain radical measures. Brauchitsch attempted to extract a promise from Hitler that any future instructions given to Himmler pertaining to the occupied territories would be shared with Army High Command. Brauchitsch then requested that Hitler order Heydrich to contact the army whenever radical policy initiatives were going to be undertaken.[150] The result would be closer consultation between the army and the SS on matters of executions and other police measures to be instituted for the "political cleansing" of Poland, consultation that would allow the military to steer clear of SS operations.

Brauchitsch distributed orders the following day to all senior level commanders in Poland informing them that "the *Einsatzgruppen* have been directed to carry out certain ethnic-political tasks [*volkspolitische Aufgaben*] in the occupied areas, according to instructions from the Führer." Because the tasks to which he was referring were "measures of an ethnic-political type," Brauchitsch noted that they remained "outside of the responsibilities of the local commanding officer" and were to be considered the exclusive domain of the *Einsatzgruppen*. Close consultation with the Security Police was to continue nevertheless so that police activities would not conflict with the needs of the army. In addition, Brauchitsch ordered that GFP and Military Police units were not to be made available for the special tasks being undertaken by the Security Police.[151] Also on 21 September, Himmler sent

Reinhard Heydrich to meet with Brauchitsch in order to calm the situation. During their meeting Brauchitsch made it clear to Heydrich that he wanted Himmler's 3 September "shoot-to-kill" order rescinded.[152] Heydrich replied that the order would be withdrawn but took the opportunity to complain about the deliberate pace of the court-martial process.[153] General Brauchitsch refused to concede the point, but stated that in order to expedite the trials he had authorized the formation of courts-martial as far down as the battalion level.[154]

The meeting ended with Brauchitsch having wrung concessions from Heydrich, although henceforth Heydrich was not going to allow the military justice system to operate smoothly. Several days later, he instructed *Einsatzgruppen* commanders to be sure that "the shooting [of insurgents] is only carried out in cases of emergency [e.g., escape attempts]. All other cases are to be given over to the courts martial. The courts martial must be so burdened with responsibilities that they can no longer function properly." Heydrich also demanded that a record was to be kept of verdicts issued by the army's courts so that he would be aware of judgments that did not call for the death penalty. In the end, however, his attempt to overwhelm the military justice system proved unnecessary owing to the general amnesty declared by Hitler on 4 October 1939, which pardoned all German military and SS personnel who had been found guilty of or punished for crimes against Poland's civilian population.

Although the clash in Berlin may have revealed General Brauchitsch's reluctance to consciously involve the army in SS killing operations, it does nothing to alter the conclusion that the German army cooperated extensively with the SS against Polish Jews. However, the basis for this collaboration differed from that which informed combined SS-army operations against Polish insurgents. In contrast to the draconian violence employed by the army against Polish guerrillas and the communities suspected of harboring them, several German commanders balked at the brutality of SS personnel against Polish Jews. The reason for this refusal lay in the fact that SS actions were typically not carried out in response to Jewish attacks on Germans. The chaos and destruction that characterized SS anti-Jewish operations meant instead that army field officers viewed these actions as a threat rather than as measures that were called for in order to provide security. Many Wehrmacht commanders were convinced that violence against the otherwise docile Jewish population provoked resistance against occupation troops and ethnic Germans. This viewpoint differed considerably from the opinions that would later become prevalent in the Wehrmacht in 1941, when German commanders agreed that Jews in the occupied Soviet Union and in Serbia presented the principal threat to German personnel. The widespread and deadly anti-Jewish animus that informed the Nazi crusade against Bolshevism simply was not as intense during the war in Poland. In 1939, German army commanders did not yet deem it necessary to physically liquidate Jewish communities as a preemptive defensive measure.

On the other hand, the cooperation of the two institutions on the demarcation line suggests that there was no fundamental disagreement on the need to reduce the number of Jews in German-occupied Poland. If anything, officers like General List and General Brandt, who had requested the court-martial of Udo von Woyrsch, agreed with the SS on the need to remove Jews and Poles from territory that was annexed to the Reich. At the end of September, for example, Brandt authored a curious document entitled "A Proposal for the Creation of a Buffer Zone," which foresaw the massive ethnic relocation program that Hitler would formally authorize Himmler to undertake in October 1939.[155] Claiming that "ethnic-political considerations *[bevölkerungspolitische Gesichtspunkte]* were the decisive factor" in solidifying Germany's hold on the area, he argued:

> The masses of Jews residing in the region between Chrzanów, Trzebinia, Sławków, Bedzin, and Myslowice . . . must be evacuated. In this regard, it is necessary to agree soon on a zone of evacuation for the population that is forced out. To avoid a later undesirable mixing of people it is necessary that the evacuation of ethnically foreign elements *[volksfremder Elemente]* and the return of German blood be carried out during wartime.[156]

For the moment, however, Brandt simply took steps to seal off Upper Silesia from so-called "undesirable elements" by ordering that "the flow of all Jewish refugees to eastern Upper Silesia is to be prevented by every means necessary."[157]

The complicated relationship between the army and the SS during the German-Polish conflict was thus filled with contradictions, particularly concerning actions against Jews. Clashes between ranking German officers and the SS over anti-Jewish violence demonstrate that some commanders were not prepared to support SS policies. In contrast, the expulsion of Jews over the demarcation line by the army, as well as its efforts to prevent the return of Jewish refugees, and the expression of opinions like Brandt's on how to deal with the Jews of East Upper Silesia suggest a measure of agreement on the need for a "territorial solution" to the Jewish question in Poland. The variety of reactions by Wehrmacht commanders to SS anti-Jewish policies makes it imperative that we resist the temptation to characterize opinion within the army officer corps as wholly and uniformly opposed to the SS.

Indeed, the cooperation of officers like Colonel Wagner, General Brandt, General List, and General Braemer in taking steps against Polish Jews indicates that there were officers in the army with whom the SS could work. Even commanders like General Küchler, who court-martialed SS men for their transgressions, saw fit to help the SS expel Jews over the demarcation line. Reinhard Heydrich understood the complications of the situation quite clearly. Writing to Order Police chief Kurt Daluege in July 1940 that "upper level commanders of the army held a fundamentally different concept" of the way enemies of the state should be fought, Heydrich pointed out nevertheless that Security Police "cooperation with troops below the staff level, and in many cases with the different staffs of the army themselves, was generally good."[158] The Security Police chief then added for good measure that "if one compares [the number of] physical assaults, incidents of looting, and atrocities committed by the army and the SS, the SS and police do not come away looking so badly." Heydrich's assessment of both the working relationship between the Security Police and German officers and the conduct of German troops during the war in Poland was accurate. The conflicts with military authorities notwithstanding, the seeds of successful collaboration between the army and the SS later in the war were sown in Poland in September 1939.

FIVE

INSTITUTIONAL BRUTALITY AND GERMAN ARMY REPRISAL POLICY

In recent years, scholars of the Holocaust have come to recognize that the retaliatory punitive measures *(Vergeltungsmassnahmen)* employed by the German army against civilians were a critical component of the racial-ideological warfare waged by the Third Reich in Eastern Europe between 1941 and 1945. During and after the military campaigns in the Balkans and the Soviet Union, German troops slaughtered civilians en masse as part of so-called reprisal actions. But while Slavs and others in occupied Southern and Eastern Europe suffered tremendous losses in the escalating spiral of German violence, it was above all the Jews whom German troops targeted during reprisals.[1] Underlying the elimination of the Jews was the belief held by Wehrmacht and SS commanders alike that all Jews were communists and partisans. German officers therefore justified the liquidation of entire Jewish communities as a measure necessary to defend Wehrmacht personnel.

In contrast to the clearly ideological nature of the German army's later campaigns in the east, however, German brutality in Poland in 1939 is typically characterized by western scholars as "naïve" and demonstrating "an unreflective trust in the methods of force" simply for "the maintenance of calm and order" rather than as a chronologically earlier manifestation of the criminal policies that were implemented elsewhere in Eastern Europe.[2] The importance of Wehrmacht reprisal policy as it was employed in Poland does not necessarily lie in the extent to which it revealed what Omer Bartov has called "the potential of ideologically determined brutality."[3] Its significance rests in recognizing that already in September 1939 the German army functioned according to a destructive modus operandi that was largely compatible with the violent methods and ideological goals of National Socialism.

Regulations developed by Army High Command (OKH) in the summer of 1939 were intended to help German troops deal with the challenge of fighting civilians. As one report produced by OKH in July 1939 stated, "The Polish population is fanatically incited and capable of sabotage as well as other types of attacks. The extensive evacuation of western sections of Poland and the demolition of all valuable industry and transportation centers is to be expected. The destruction and poisoning of food supplies is also to be considered [a possibility]."[4] In response to these expectations, army planners devised pacification measures for the invasion according to the guidelines for land warfare that had been promulgated at The Hague in October 1907.[5] The German interpretation of these guidelines allowed for the taking of hostages when security concerns made it necessary, but the execution of hostages was only permitted after authorization was received from Army High Command.[6]

On the battlefield, officers at the regimental command level and above could issue orders for the taking of hostages and have executions carried out after permission from above had been secured. German troops were expected to capture insurgents not killed in combat and bring them in for trial before a court-martial. Further rules required that lower ranking officers involve military and SS police forces against insurgents when they were available in an effort to "restore calm and order and ensure the security of the men."[7] Therefore, on the eve of the invasion, military personnel were clearly expected to act with restraint when faced with civilian resistance and to obey all regulations set out by OKH. Experience would demonstrate, though, that following these rules on the battlefield was impossible for German troops, in part because the chaotic reality of combat did not conform to the ideal scenarios envisioned by German commanders during the invasion's planning stages.[8] More important still was the inconsistency with which German officers implemented the regulations. Determined to put down civilian resistance as decisively as possible and completely indifferent to the suffering of noncombatants, commanding officers demanded ever-harsher reprisals and directed these at entire communities. Consequently, the intended capacity of regulations to control the troops was replaced by the calculated, even criminal logic of mass reprisals, which legitimized brutality on a broad scale and opened the door to mass murder.[9]

Wehrmacht formations advancing into Poland on 1 September took fire from armed civilians the moment they crossed the German-Polish border. As Lieutenant Colonel Alexander von Pfuhlstein, the chief of staff (Ia) of the 19th Infantry Division, noted in his unit's war diary, "civilians, including women . . . shot at troops from houses and hedges" when his men passed through the small towns in the area.[10] Pushing northeast toward Bełchatów the following day, the 19th Infantry continued to report attacks by civilians, claiming that "further defensive measures were necessary [because] terrorists *[Franktireure]* were shooting at units behind the lines."[11] Similarly, the 10th Infantry Division, operating to the north of the 19th Infantry, reported late on 1 September that "already for the entire day we took fire from farm houses. At night this guerrilla warfare intensified considerably."[12] These encounters preceded an incident the same night in Torzeniec, when the village's inhabitants greeted troops with the 41st Infantry Regiment (10th Infantry Division) and gave them shelter for the night. Just before midnight, villagers set upon some of the sleeping troops and shot them in their beds. One battalion alone lost three men killed and four men severely wounded in this encounter.[13] The 41st Infantry Regiment continued to meet significant opposition from irregulars the next day while it was occupied fighting regular Polish troops with the 4th Ulan Regiment. According to an official history authored by the commander of the 10th Infantry Division, General von Cochenhausen,

> on 2 September we fought against the *Narodna Obrana* [*sic*], a type of Territorial Army *[Landwehr],* and against insurgents. This demonstrated that the enemy had systematically organized a "People's War" *[Volkskrieg]* between the Prosna and Warta Rivers. One repeatedly found weapons, ammunition, and explosives stored in houses for arming the populace. The Poles would first let the infantry pass quietly through the villages and then when the artillery or other vehicles came up, they would suddenly be fired upon from all of the houses. A particularly heavy battle with guerrillas developed at night in Ostrowek. The 3d Company of the 10th Pioneer Regiment under Captain Bloch was working on rebuilding a bridge when they suddenly came under heavy fire from houses and bushes. Firing was constant throughout the night, pinning the company on the bridge. The next morning the bodies of three dead Poles who had tied themselves to trees were found. Along with that of a seventy-year-old man armed with a machine pistol, [were] those of two Polish women [found beside] a machine-gun.[14]

In addition to showing that they could be extremely clever in their methods of defense, Polish civilians also proved they could be tenacious opponents. For example, upon reaching the town of Tylice in the Polish Corridor on 7 September, the 3d Infantry Division encountered well-established and carefully laid out defenses manned by the town's inhabitants. The 3d Infantry's initial contact with these defenses came as a surprise: "With the entry of advance elements into Tylice, [we] were suddenly fired upon from all sides. Clearing this locale presented considerable difficulties, for the inhabitants had barricaded themselves into the houses, and without combat engineers [and their explosives] at hand, we did not have the means to open them up."[15] Taking such defensive positions necessitated difficult and dangerous house-to-house fighting, which resulted more often than not in the reduction of the given village to smoking rubble.

The official records of German field commands noted civilian resistance by using a variety of descriptive terms. The adjectives most often employed when referring to armed civilians were *Freischärler* (insurgents) and *Heckenschützen* (snipers). These relatively value-neutral terms were used throughout the war by both German military and civilian authorities. In addition, however, insurgents were alternately described as *bewaffnete Banden*, or "armed gangs," or *Soldaten in Zivilkleidung*, or "soldiers in civilian dress," terms that expressed the suspicion with which German officers viewed the civilian population and Polish methods of fighting the war.[16] Reports from many German units also referred to civilian assailants as "terrorists," such as an entry in the war diary of the 19th Infantry Division penned by Lieutenant Colonel Pfuhlstein, on 4 September. "The population east of the Warta River is much more peaceful than that on the western side," Pfuhlstein reported. "We only seldom meet terrorists *[Franktireurs]*. All of the local [ethnic German] inhabitants have fled into the forests because of numerous atrocities *[Gruelerzählungen]* committed [against them] by the Poles."[17]

Other reports commonly described potential enemies as *verdächtigen Personen*, or "suspicious persons," who were to be apprehended immediately. Those defined as "suspicious persons" included specific targets, such as the members of Polish political organizations like the nationalist Western Association *(Westmark Verband)*, or general categories of people, such as the entire male population of a locale. When German troops took large numbers of Polish men into custody, the military police and members of the *Einsatzgruppen* used ethnic German informants to question the prisoners in the search for *Hetzer*, or "agitators," and other *lichtscheues Gesindel*, or "light-shy riff-raff."[18]

The hunt for "terror groups" and "terrorists" during the campaign was an important area of cooperation between SS and Wehrmacht units, as was combating "established anti-German elements."[19] These tasks could often be carried out in a decidedly merciless manner. As one SD officer noted in a summary report on the activities of *Einsatzgruppe* II and the army in Częstochowa, "I am convinced that terrorist warfare *[Franktireurkrieg]* can be put to an end by the implementation of ruthless action *[rücksicht-*

lose Einschreiten]"—even after the army had already shot 100 civilians on 4 September.[20] These words echoed orders given by General Ernst Busch, the commander of the VIII Corps, who instructed his men that "every incident of terrorism *[Freischärlerunwesen]* is to be dealt with severely using the most drastic measures."[21] And as Lieutenant General Diether von Böhm-Bezing, the commander of the 252d Infantry Division, made unequivocally clear to his men, "Any Polish civilian who carries a weapon will use it against German soldiers. Therefore, no German soldier should hesitate to use his weapon, he should shoot first!"[22]

Typical military responses to civilian resistance were harsh and swift, entailing first the elimination of the immediate danger and then the permanent pacification of the area. The initial step in this process was to kill the assailant and destroy the individual house or farmstead from which the shots had been fired. German officers, though, soon moved beyond limited retaliation by ordering the summary destruction of entire villages in reprisal for civilian attacks. Like the execution of groups of people for the rebellious act of an individual, the razing of homes and even entire villages demonstrated the willingness of Wehrmacht officers to respond with collective punishment that far outweighed the crime in its severity. Field commanders never received specific instructions before the invasion regarding the summary destruction of homes and villages, indicating perhaps that the razing of villages was a spontaneous response to civilian resistance dictated by the cold logic of calculated brutality. As Lieutenant Colonel Pfuhlstein recorded in his unit's war diary on 2 September, "all of the villages [in the vicinity of Albertów] were razed so that there would be no danger of civilians shooting at advancing units."[23]

German officers usually placed the blame for having to implement extreme measures on the Poles themselves, particularly after the Polish government called for armed resistance by the populace on 9 September. The very same day, the commander of Army Group North, Field Marshal Fedor von Bock, issued instructions that stated in consideration of the Polish government's action any armed resistance by civilians was to be met with the severest measures.[24] On the following day, the 3d Infantry Division received orders from von Bock defining exactly what those measures were to be. Complaining that "the cowardly Poles have murdered a number of defenseless ethnic German civilians," he argued that "these acts compel me to order the following for the protection of the troops: 1) all those Poles capable of carrying arms should be arrested and sent to the rear, 2) if shots come from a house behind the Front, it is to be burned down. . . . if [the troops] are fired on from a house in a village behind the front, and it is impossible to determine from which house the fire came, the entire village should be razed to the ground."[25]

Von Bock's orders echo throughout the records of units that were part of Army Group North. For example, on 18 September, Captain Danke of the 208th Infantry Division forwarded an order to his men that "all civilians found carrying a weapon of any kind are to be shot on the spot. [Furthermore], any houses out of which shots are fired are to be burned to the ground."[26] A combat report of the 206th Infantry Division noted similarly on 16 September that "while the fight for some sections of the town [of Hajnówka] was still in progress, Sergeant Korty, on orders from Major [Walter] Nagel, arrested the mayor and four magistrates. He had them announce [to the inhabitants] that the entire city would be razed and the four hostages executed if another shot was taken at German troops in the already occupied parts of the city."[27]

No records remain documenting the dissemination of comparable orders to the troops of Army Group South for the burning of houses and villages. It is possible that a formal order never existed. Despite its absence, there is evidence that the personnel of Army Group South practiced the razing of houses just the same. On 4 September, Colonel Erwin Jaenecke, the Eighth Army quartermaster, asked the men to refrain from burning houses because in several cases Poles appeared to be shooting from the homes of ethnic Germans who had fled. Instead of razing houses, Jaenecke recommended that hostages be shot.[28] Later in the month, however, the chief of civil administration (CdZ) in Kraków received a report from the local administrator in Nowy Sącz indicating that two small villages had been burned, "one of which was destroyed as a reprisal measure *[Vergeltungsmassnahme]* for shots fired at German troops by terrorists."[29]

Wehrmacht commanders did not limit their methods for punishing defiant civilians to destroying property. It was, in fact, far more common for German officers to order the seizure of hostages. This policy seems to have served the dual purpose of providing security and suppressing civilian resistance. Take for example the occupation of the Poznań region, an area of Polish territory with the former German city of Posen at its center. The task of capturing and securing the region fell to three Frontier Guard units *(Grenzschutz-Abschnittskommandos)* that were attached to Army Groups North and South. These units were Lieutenant General Max von Schenckendorff's 13th Frontier Guards, Major General Hermann Metz's 12th Frontier Guards, and General Curt Ludwig Freiherr von Gienanth's 14th Frontier Guards.[30] The large amount of documentation for the 13th Frontier Guards that survived the war allows an examination of the experiences

A Wehrmacht firing squad executes two hostages (one Polish Christian and one Polish Jew) on Wolnosc Square in the town of Konin, September 1939. (Institute of National Remembrance, Commission for the Prosecution of Crimes against the Polish Nation; courtesy of the U.S. Holocaust Memorial Museum, Photo Reference Collection: WS 50294)

of Schenckendorff's group in particular. These experiences illustrate the typical German military reaction to civilian resistance.

A soldier since 1894, Max von Schenckendorff served in the kaiser's army and fought in the First World War as a battalion commander. By the end of the war he had attained the rank of major and continued to serve in the new *Reichswehr* under the Weimar Republic. Cashiered from the military in 1930, Schenckendorff reentered active service on the eve of the war with Poland and was promoted to lieutenant general in command of the 13th Frontier Guards. After the Polish campaign he went on to be named the commanding general of security troops in the rear area of Army Group Center, and while in the USSR, he initially demonstrated the same faith in collective reprisal measures that he had shown in Poland. Faced with the rapidly growing, powerful Soviet partisan movement, however, Schenckendorff became increasingly convinced before his death in 1943 that the Wehrmacht's policy of collective punishment was counterproductive.[31]

Like other Wehrmacht units, the *Gruppe Schenckendorff* received orders in the days before the campaign that all Polish and Jewish men between the ages of seventeen and forty-five who were capable of bearing arms were to be interned as prisoners of war. Schenckendorff was also informed that an *Einsatzgruppe* would be active behind the 13th Frontier Guards "fighting all enemies of the German people and state." Yet, in view of the potential threat from insurgents and the weakness of German security forces, he and his men were again warned to take appropriate defensive measures against the "cruel and cunning" Poles.[32] In addition, the Secret Field Police units assigned to Schenckendorff were charged with protecting the local *Volksdeutsche* "who were active in the fight for Germandom" *(Deutschtumskampf)*."[33]

While advancing toward Poznań, Schenckendorff recorded in his war diary that in the town of Wojnowice he and his men "learned for the first time how bestially *[viehisch]* the Poles had treated the ethnic German inhabitants."[34] During their retreat from the area, Polish troops had destroyed farms and killed the livestock of local *Volksdeutsche*. The following day (8 September), Schenckendorff's command entered Legnica and established a local headquarters there. Meanwhile, the 13th Frontier Guards had taken small-arms fire from civilians, and as a security measure Schenckendorff's men arrested all "suspicious persons" *(verdächtigen Personen)* in the immediate area, including those of military service age. Totaling 427 men, the *Gruppe Schenckendorff* "welcomed [the arrival of] an SS unit, which volunteered to transport the prisoners to the rear and search the area for more suspects."[35] General Schenckendorff's troops moved into Poznań on 11 September, and after organizing his headquarters in the Hotel Basar, Schenckendorff instituted several security measures. The city's Polish inhabitants were warned that searches of every home and building would take place and anyone found with a weapon in his possession or residence would be shot immediately. In addition, all street-side windows in homes and buildings were to remain closed. If German troops spotted any open windows, all the inhabitants of the house would be arrested and some or all of them would be shot. A curfew was also established, and all residents of the city were to be off the streets between the hours of 6:00 P.M. and 6:00 A.M. Last, hostages were taken, and any attack on German troops would lead to the immediate execution of ten of them in reprisal.[36]

The promised execution of hostages for attacks on German soldiers was a practice implemented throughout the Wehrmacht during the first days of the war in Poland. Regulations promulgated prior to the invasion made provision for the execution of hostages, but no specific mention was made regarding exactly how many should be shot in reprisal for the killing or wounding of either German troops or ethnic German civilians. General Walter von Reichenau, the commander of the Tenth Army and an officer who would go on to prove himself a zealous proponent of the War of Annihilation in the USSR until his death in January 1942, established as early as 4 September 1939 that for every German soldier killed or wounded by insurgents, three hostages taken from the local population were to be executed. In addition to promising reprisals for attacks on his men, Reichenau pledged to execute three hostages as well for every act of sabotage.[37]

General Schenckendorff, on the other hand, ordered the execution of ten hostages for every German soldier shot, thereby escalating the killing ratio. This development was consistent with others taking place elsewhere in occupied Poland. Facing resistance from the civilian population, Eighth Army command issued orders on 4 September stating that the process of arresting individuals guilty of attacking German troops had proved ineffective. Noting that the *Sicherheitspolizei* (Security Police) had already handled several cases of suspected insurgents turned over to them by German troops, the Eighth Army claimed that it was impossible to court-martial the alleged perpetrators because "only in the rarest of cases could proof of guilt be brought forward."[38] In view of the reality that "these kind of proceedings are impractical," the formal military judicial process was to be thrown out. The Eighth Army instead ordered its personnel to immediately shoot "assassins, insurgents, and civilians who are found possessing ammunition or weapons. Similar action is to be taken against Polish civilians who are found in houses or farms from which shots at our troops were fired. In every occupied area it is to be publicly announced that the populace will be held responsible for assassins in their ranks and will have to face the execution of hostages."[39]

Commanding officers in the Eighth Army thus not only showed themselves willing to jettison standing regulations; they also demonstrated a capacity for legitimizing what could be considered criminal behavior on the part of their men. Orders authorizing the summary execution of civilians who happened to be in a home from which shots had supposedly come paved the way for reprisals against all segments of the population, including women and children. In effect, Wehrmacht officers and enlisted men had been given permission to shoot noncombatants without having to prove their guilt. The intelligence officer (Ic) of the Eighth Army, Lieutenant Colonel Rudolf Schniewind, recognized the impact that these orders could have on the conduct of the troops, noting in a memorandum that "doubts" remained about the proper procedure for fighting insurgents.[40]

Schniewind attempted to clarify matters by reiterating earlier orders that insurgents could only be shot in combat. Army personnel were required to immediately bring captured insurgents before a court-martial. Should one not be convened in the area, Schniewind outlined an impromptu court-martial procedure. According to his suggestion, a regimental officer holding at least the rank of captain could call a field court-martial and, along with two men selected from the ranks, sit in judgment of the captured suspect. The defendant was to be represented by an officer and would be allowed a brief statement as well as the final word. As for a verdict, Schniewind's proposal continued, "the judgment, which can only be the death penalty, must be reached by majority vote," meaning that two of the three "judges" would have to vote for execution. This verdict would be recorded, along with a short explanation, and the prisoner would be kept in custody until the sentence could be confirmed by the commander of the army, in this case General Blaskowitz.

Although this procedure was clearly intended to prevent German troops from carrying out spontaneous shootings, its application effectively placed responsibility for authorizing executions on lower ranking combat officers. Moreover, the process was cumbersome and time-consuming for men on the move, as the German army in Poland constantly was. Other problems included the fact that Schniewind's proposal made no allowance for translators. If the accused perpetrator did not speak German, it was unlikely that he or she would get a fair hearing. It was also doubtful if soldiers on the spot would waste their time looking for someone to make an accurate translation when the only possible sentence could be death. Given the choice between immediately shooting the suspect and letting him go free, it seems highly unlikely that soldiers in the field would have opted against simply executing the individual. These informal courts-martial would also have faced the same burden-of-proof difficulties challenging standard courts-martial. Field courts-martial as formulated by Schniewind thus remained problematic to use, a reality confirmed by the fact that years of research by this author never turned up a single documented case of a field court-martial convened in Poland along Schniewind's guidelines.[41]

Rather than deal with cumbersome judicial proceedings, it was easier for field commanders to solve the problem of unapprehended perpetrators by ordering that a higher number of hostages be taken and a higher ratio of these be executed in reprisal. Lieutenant General Walter Petzel, the commander of the I Corps, chose just this course of action on 16 September after learning that Polish civilians shot and killed two sergeants in the town of Otwock. Petzel immediately ordered that 100 Polish men of all occupa-

A German soldier stands guard over Jewish men arrested in Aleksandrów Kujawski, September 1939. (Harry Lore; courtesy of the U.S. Holocaust Memorial Museum, Photo Reference Collection: ws 08767)

tional backgrounds *(nationalpolnische Männer aller Berufe)* who lived within 400 yards of the scene of the shooting were to be taken hostage. If the proper number could not be found within this area, men from the surrounding area were to be arrested and held. Once assembled, the names, birth dates, occupations, and religious affiliations of the captives were to be listed and the following message delivered to the mayor of Otwock. The mayor was then to inform the town's inhabitants that

> international law forbids the participation of the populace in hostilities. Whoever violates this will be punished according to the laws of war. On the 15th of September, German soldiers were shot from houses in Otwock. Because the guilty parties have not been arrested, the following measures have been ordered: (a) those guilty of the crime are to be turned in to the nearest German military authorities, (b) until the perpetrators are found, all of the hostages will remain in custody, (c) for every incident in the future when German troops are fired upon

from behind, ten hostages will be shot; for every German soldier wounded by being shot from behind, five hostages will be shot.[42]

Petzel's specification in this case that the men taken hostage come from all occupational backgrounds further illustrates the lack of formal guidelines designating the segments of Polish society from which hostages were to be seized. Typically, however, German officers sought out members of the intelligentsia and civil administration as hostages. For example, following his announcement of the initial security measures to be implemented in Poznań, General Schenckendorff collected from local ethnic Germans the names of prominent Polish citizens who could be used as hostages. Given that most prominent Poles had already fled the city, Schenckendorff complained about the difficulty he faced in finding the individuals named on his list. It was only after applying "extreme pressure" on the city's Polish mayor that he was able to secure twenty-five hostages. These men were then held in Poznań's city hall.[43] The records do not reveal if Schenckendorff ever had to order the execution of his twenty-five hostages, but several days later he made clear in his daily orders that the arrest of hostages still had not succeeded in securing the city. New attacks on his men by civilians caused him to believe that the "troops must devote even greater attention to fighting insurgents, criminals, and suspicious persons." A further radicalization of measures was necessary if the *Gruppe Schenckendorff* was to ensure "the protection and pacification of the city of Posen and its environs to the east."[44]

The selection of prominent local civilians as hostages occurred early in the campaign. On 4 September, the commander of the 21st Infantry Division, Lieutenant General Kuno-Hans von Both, called for the arrest of ten "respected" citizens in the city of Grudziądz. He announced publicly that these hostages would be shot if his men were fired upon or if his troops found weapons that were not turned in at a time designated by the divisional command. As soon as police forces entered the city, General Both instructed that they were to be entrusted with all further security measures.[45] Similarly, upon entering the town of Hajnówka on the morning of 16 September, advance elements of the 206th Infantry Division took four magistrates and the mayor hostage, promising to execute them if civilians resisted the occupation.[46] And on 11 September, the 59th Infantry Regiment (19th Infantry Division) reported the following incident in Mszczonów: "On the streets there were several armored cars that had entered the town the day before and then during the night were fired on or set on fire by Polish civilians. The panzer troops shot the priest, the mayor, and several other inhabitants of the place who had instigated the attack."[47]

Preinvasion guidelines concerning the arrest of hostages for reprisals said nothing specific about targeting prominent civilians, members of the clergy, the nobility, or the intelligentsia. Without doubt it was the visibility and reputation of local notables that determined the selection of these individuals by German officers. On the other hand, however, there is evidence to suggest that the German army did not target Poland's leading and educated classes for execution simply because it was convenient. The selection of local notables was instead an integral part of a larger program of pacification and repression. Take, for example, a document issued by the Fourteenth Army outlining the "re-establishment of security" in East Upper Silesia and Western Galicia:

> Those elements hostile to Germans *[Deutschfeindlich eingestellt]* in the countryside are teachers and the clergy, while it is largely the intellectual class in the cities. They are all the carriers of Polish chauvinism, the central focus of which is the city of Krakau. Passive resistance should therefore be expected from these circles as soon as the opportunity presents itself. Support for these activist elements, which would like to resurrect resistance based on Polish traditions, is possible and is to be expected. The *Abwehr* officers of the corps and divisions are [therefore] responsible for initiating defensive measures in connection with the GFP and the *Sicherheitspolizei*.[48]

In instructions he issued to the men of the 252d Infantry Division, Lieutenant General Böhm-Bezing demanded that "anyone found without proper identification should be arrested. It is eventually intended that all undesirables *[Missliebigen]*, Congress-Poles, and all those Jews who emigrated into the Posen province after 1918, will be deported to the Protectorate of Lodz."[49] Böhm-Bezing's orders continued as follows: "The clergy is frequently the source of anti-German propaganda. Polish-speaking German soldiers should therefore place them under surveillance. In the event that anti-German propaganda is mentioned, including the singing of anti-German songs, the priest is to be immediately arrested." And finally, regarding hostages, "with any sign of rebellion, or particularly strong resistance, the number of hostages is to be doubled. Whenever possible young intellectuals, Congress-Poles, students, and other anti-German elements are to be taken into custody."[50]

Officers like Böhm-Bezing clearly believed that priests and other segments of the intelligentsia were the focal points of Polish civilian resistance. As early as July 1939, instructions from Army High Command noted that

Wehrmacht guards look on as two ethnic German civilians question and search Poles arrested for the alleged murder of a fellow ethnic German in the town of Cyców, September 1939. The caption on the reverse of the original print reads: "Polish bandits that murdered a Volksdeutsche. Behind the headquarters building in Cyców." (Institute of National Remembrance, Commission for the Prosecution of Crimes against the Polish Nation; courtesy of the U.S. Holocaust Memorial Museum, Photo Reference Collection: ws 51291)

"the Catholic clergy is primarily responsible for nationalistic rabble-rousing *[nationalen Hetze]*."[51] Furthermore, officers were to remain on guard against expected attacks by secret Polish conspiratorial groups.[52] These terror groups had been organized on a national scale, and members of the local intelligentsia could be considered among the leaders. The impulse to make prominent local civilians and clergy pay with their lives for the defiance of the local populace appears to have arisen from cues given by Army High Command, knowledge of the Polish insurgent tradition, ingrained suspicion of the Poles, and a fundamental desire to destroy Polish political opponents. The tendency of German commanders to select the educated and leading classes of Polish society as hostages was thus an integral aspect of its overall policy of pacifying conquered territory, although ordinary Poles and Jews surely suffered as well.

It is impossible to accurately determine the frequency with which hostages were executed during the Polish campaign. However, the eminent Polish historian Czesław Madajczyk concludes that the German army and other units, including the police, SS, and *Selbstschutz* (ethnic German civilian militia) under its jurisdiction, carried out 764 shootings of varying scale between 1 September and 26 October 1939.[53] Of these, the Wehrmacht carried out 311 on its own, with the number of persons shot ranging from as few as 2, executed in Nierada/Zrebice, to as many as 900 executed in Przekopana.[54] Because of the principle of collective punishment, therefore, it is obvious that some communities paid dearly for the acts of impetuous individuals.

The Wehrmacht's use of collective punishment during the war in Poland was not without precedent. Prussian armies had executed civilians for the activity of irregulars during the war with France in 1870–1871. Similarly, the Imperial German Army used reprisals extensively during its advance through Belgium in August 1914, as well as in the violent suppression of Polish insurgents immediately after the First World War.[55] Upon its retreat from the Western Front in 1918, the kaiser's army again laid waste to the Belgian countryside and perpetrated atrocities against the civilian population. And in Lithuania, marauding *Freikorps* formations summarily executed thousands of civilians in Riga in 1919.[56] These incidents demonstrate that beginning in the late nineteenth century, the use of armed force against civilians by the German military became increasingly common. The behavior of German troops and officers in Belgium and Alsace-Lorraine in August 1914 is particularly worthy of further examination. During the period of mobile warfare on the Western Front at the outset of World War I, German officers ordered the summary destruction of villages and the shooting of hostages in response to civilian attacks, both suspected and real. These were not limited actions. For example, German troops slaughtered hundreds of Belgians during the sacking of Louvain and executed over 600 noncombatants in the town of Dinant.[57]

Scholars concerned with these events conclude that a wide variety of factors motivated the behavior of German soldiers and officers in August 1914, including drunkenness, nervousness, response to actual attacks, anti-Catholicism, and rumors circulated among German formations about civilians murdering and mutilating their comrades. Similar to the invasion of Poland, German military personnel in Belgium suspected that the Belgians had organized a "people's war" reminiscent of the Prussian Army's encounters with French guerrillas in 1870-1871.[58] The problem was that a "people's war" in Belgium did not really exist; it was a myth fabricated in the minds of German officers and enlisted men. However, because of the experience of the Franco-Prussian War, the memory of guerrilla warfare had become entrenched in the collective psyche of the German army officer corps and in the army's military culture. In turn, this tendency toward mythmaking had a tangible impact on the reaction of German officers to battlefield reports claiming that civilians had attacked German troops. As John Horne and Alan Kramer point out, in 1914 "reprisals of the kind ordered by Moltke the Elder in 1870—collective executions, arson, hostage-taking, and expulsions—remained the standard policy. . . . The German officer corps needed to do no more than consult its own past in response to its collective fantasy" and then lash out at civilians.[59]

The German experience of colonial warfare in Africa and Carl von Clausewitz's doctrine of total victory on German military thinking also influenced the Imperial Army's behavior in 1914. When Lieutenant General Lothar von Trotha eradicated the Herero in Southwest Africa between 1904 and 1907, General Alfred von Schlieffen of the General Staff in Berlin cabled congratulations to Trotha for "exterminating almost the entire people."[60] Horne and Kramer caution against drawing too clear a line of continuity from the Herero war to the commission of atrocities in Europe. Nevertheless, as they see it, the experience in Africa "gave German politicians greater freedom for experimentation in political and military conduct, and lowered the threshold to violence against European civilians ten years later."[61] The lowering of this threshold fit well into the supposedly Clausewitzian notion of *Vernichtungskrieg,* or war of annihilation, in which the enemy would be eradicated in quick battles.

But as Horne and Kramer note, Clausewitz's doctrine of *Vernichtungskrieg* was misinterpreted and perverted into a dogmatic view of offensive operations as the "concentration of forces with maximum efficiency in order to achieve victory."[62] In reality, Clausewitz argued, "the political purpose of war, and the social conditions of the societies waging it, limited how it was fought."[63] It was therefore due to the misreading of Clausewitz that the German officer corps in 1914 sought ways to achieve victory as rapidly and decisively as possible. Such thinking in Germany had the effect of justifying the use of draconian measures against civilian insurrectionists, whose operations behind the lines hindered the speedy conclusion of the military campaign. Ironically, then, many German officers came to view the forceful stamping out of civilian resistance as "a form of restraint . . . a 'German way of war' . . . [that consisted of taking] ruthless measures against civilians with the aim of keeping warfare in what . . . were deemed to be acceptable bounds."[64]

Pan-German prejudice and racism also proved influential in radicalizing the violent conduct of German troops in the early days of World War I. The willingness of Germans to be brutal toward Belgians and Alsatians arose out of the predominantly negative views of these peoples that were widely held by the soldiers and officers of the kaiser's army. (Some of these views were strikingly similar to opinions of eastern populations expressed by German military personnel in World War II.) For example, General Hans von Beseler wrote in August 1914 that the Belgians "made the impression they were of a lower race *[einer niedrig gehaltenen Rasse]*, and are physically of less value than Germans."[65] Moreover, given their mixed German-French origin, Alsatians were automatically considered suspect.[66] These prejudicial views were fostered by a "glorification of Germanism," which characterized German society prior to 1914. The exaltation of all things German, Roger Chickering concludes, led to the development of an "us and them" mentality and consequently a picture of the enemy as different and inferior. Fear of non-Germans also informed the behavior of German military personnel who habitually viewed Belgians, French, and Alsatians with suspicion.[67] In short, racial and ethnic prejudice went hand in hand with the increasing resort to violence already demonstrated by German officers in World War I.

Clearly, the tendency of Wehrmacht officers to use violence for suppressing civilian resistance in Poland proved to be part of the evolution of German military thinking before and during the First World War. It is important to recognize, though, that after 1933 dramatic changes had occurred in the political, cultural, and social context within which brutal reprisal policies were employed. Violence was venerated in the Third Reich. Nazi formations and the military establishment utilized force in German domestic life to persecute communists, socialists, Jews, and even members of the Nazi Party. This reliance on violence to destroy opposition also informed Hitler's plans for the ethnic reshaping of Poland following the German victory. As Hitler demanded of his officers on 22 August at the Berghof, the destruction of Poland was to be carried out with the "greatest brutality and without mercy."[68] Likewise, "pacifying" Poland's civilian population relied on the use of ruthless action against noncombatants by paramilitary formations like the *Einsatzgruppen* and SS Death's Head units.

Added to the veneration of ruthlessness and exaltation of violence was a heightening of the tendency to view the world beyond Germany's frontiers as filled with enemies. This outlook in 1939 was heavily informed by Nazi racial-biological principles. Evidence that National Socialism had already influenced many German officers along these lines can be found in the variety of orders given to rank-and-file troops regarding the treatment of non-German civilians in Poland. Preparations for the invasion included orientation sessions on the treacherous nature of the Polish and Jewish enemy. During the campaign, standing orders were followed for the summary imprisonment of all Polish and Jewish males between the ages of seventeen and forty-five.

These security precautions were based on a concept of Poles and Jews that incorporated ethnic stereotypes. Many Germans considered Poles aggressive and brutish, while Jews were thought to be underhanded and dangerous. These notions of the enemy based on stereotypes informed the deeply held insecurity of many German officers, automatically rendering suspect large parts of Poland's civilian population. Commanders in the Wehrmacht euphemistically described civilian resisters as "terrorists," "bandits," "agitators," and "riff-raff," terms that did not define them as people defending their homes and country, but as reprehensible criminals capable of any despicable act. Influenced by such negative attitudes, it was simple for hardened German field officers to authorize arrests and large-scale reprisal shootings in the name of restoring calm and order.[69]

In themselves, reprisal shootings and the retaliatory razing of homes and villages brutalized the soldiers instructed to carry them out. The use of these measures demonstrated to rank-and-file troops their officers' willingness to kill civilians and destroy property. Furthermore, the lack of respect for the lives and possessions of non-Germans demonstrated by German officers not only legitimized violent behavior but also gave soldiers the opportunity to perpetrate crimes against noncombatants under the pretext of retaliation. German documents, including the letters and diaries of German troops, do not typically describe reprisal shootings in detail, thus making it difficult to develop a mental image of the cruelty with which these actions were carried out. Fortunately, postwar investigations conducted by Polish authorities provide valuable insight into the details of reprisal actions, insight that comes from the testimony of witnesses themselves.

Władysława Bera was one such spectator. An inhabitant of the village of Widzów, located several kilometers south of Radomsko in western Poland, Bera looked on as German tanks and armored cars, elements of the 1st Panzer Division, passed through her village on 4 September 1939. According to Bera, an armored car stopped in front of her house, and a German tanker wearing a black uniform and black beret jumped out. The tanker shouted something in German to a man named Piotr Olczyk on the street. Simultaneously, other German soldiers from the column began shouting, and Bera saw several of her male neighbors coming out of their houses. Understanding that the Germans were calling men out into the street, Bera's husband Walenty and her stepson also answered the calls. Within minutes, Bera recounted to the investigator, the men were surrounded and ordered to raise their hands. They were driven to a site near the fire station and stood up against a fence. I ran to them to save my husband, threw my arms around him and begged for his life. I was eight months pregnant at the time, but [in spite of this condition] a German kicked me, I fell and lost consciousness. When I awoke the execution was over. I saw the bodies of the thirteen dead men. The Germans were no longer there. . . . my stepson was only fifteen-years-old.[70]

Incredibly, Władysław Wolda survived the execution in Widzów and later recalled what had happened. Upon hearing that the Germans were arriving, Wolda stated that people fled past him to hide in the surrounding meadows. He heard German soldiers shouting and saw men, women, and children coming out of their houses. Ignoring the women, the Germans kept calling for men to assemble, so Wolda left his horse to graze and answered the summons. German troops led him and the other men of Widzów to the village fire station and told them that they would all be shot. According to Wolda, "They then turned machine-guns on us and began firing. I fell heavily wounded in the head and side, but by some miracle survived."[71] Wolda went on to testify, as did Bera, that he could not understand why the Germans had done this to them because no one in the village had opposed them. Following the execution, Sofia Barska testified, German soldiers stopped to photograph the bodies, adding insult to the injury that had been inflicted on the small community.[72]

Reprisals by German troops against civilians were not always based on specific incidents, such as a shot from a house. Consider several incidents that took place in the village of Milejowiec, which the 1st Panzer Division completely destroyed in response to a Polish counterattack. Situated just to the south of Piotrków Trybunalski, units of the 1st Panzer occupied Milejowiec on 4–5 September. According to Regina Jakubiak, German tanks initially entered on 4 September and passed through the village without incident. That night, Polish forces attacked in the area, fought the Germans for two hours, and then retreated. The next morning, German troops arrived once again and began searching all of the houses, immediately killing by rifle shot or bayonet any man they found. The bodies were left in houses or out on the road that ran through the village. Finally, Jakubiak remembered German soldiers moving through the village in small patrols and systematically tossing hand grenades into the houses and farmsteads. This resulted in the razing of what Jakubiak estimated to be seventy-five to eighty farms altogether.[73]

Branisław Ganek also witnessed the destruction of Milejowiec and was fortunate to survive. A refugee from Krzyzanów, a village located several kilometers to the west of Milejowiec, Ganek and his family stopped for the night at the farm of a family friend named Koltunik. The Ganek family then tried to continue east through Milejowiec the following day but were stopped by a passing column of German armor. Fighting soon broke out and they took shelter. Polish soldiers who entered Milejowiec during the attack advised all the civilians to leave. Because of the fighting, however, neither Ganek nor any members of his family fled the village. The next morning after the gunfire stopped, German units once again entered Milejowiec and immediately began burning farms.

German troops seized Ganek and his family and ordered them to line up along the side of the road with the other townspeople. The soldiers separated the women and children from their men. Ganek and several other men were led away to the nearby village of Milejów, about one mile west of Milejowiec, where they were told to stand in a ditch by the side of the road. Shortly thereafter, a small group of Germans approached, told the men to raise their hands, and opened fire on them. Ganek received a hit in the arm and went down. Feigning death despite the pain, he recalled seeing a German soldier kicking the bodies and then delivering final shots to those still showing signs of life.[74] He remained there until nightfall and moved off toward the smoldering ruins of Milejów to find help. In Milejów, Ganek was fortunately captured by kinder German soldiers and led to a field hospital where he received medical attention. Upon returning to his home three months later, he learned that the Germans had killed his mother in Milejowiec on the day he was injured. According to witnesses, German troops told her to run once the men had been led away and they then used her for target practice, shooting her in the back as she fled.[75]

Arriving German panzers similarly caught Josef Bałata and his family in Milejowiec. Like Ganek, the Bałatas were also refugees from Krzyzanów. According to Josef Bałata, German soldiers began arresting males between the ages of ten and sixty upon entering the village. These prisoners, including Bałata himself, were held under guard in the garden of a local farmer. As night fell, Bałata estimated that the total number of civilian prisoners was around 100 people, including ten women and children.[76] Sometime late that night, as Bałata and the others waited, Polish units attacked the 1st Panzer Division and threw the Germans back. The prisoners escaped during the chaos that attended the Polish assault, but when dawn arrived, victorious German units returned to Milejowiec. Bałata recounted how the soldiers began burning the village and shooting all of the men they could find.[77] His own brush with death came while he and several other men were hiding in a barn. Seeing the buildings around them going up in flames, the men began to flee from their hiding places. Among them was Bałata's brother Marian, whom German troops caught and shot at close range after beating him severely. Bałata then noticed that the barn he was hiding in was on fire. He and two other men who had remained hidden decided to run, but as they fled, German soldiers spotted them and opened fire. Both of the men with Bałata died in the gunfire and he was wounded in the hand. Like Ganek, he only survived by feigning death.

Scenes like these occurred repeatedly in villages near Milejowiec as the 1st Panzer Division took vengeance on the civilian population for being attacked and momentarily thrown back by the Poles. On 5 September in the communities of Krzyzanów, Siomki, and Cekanów, marauding German troops murdered entire families, including women, children, and the elderly, on the streets and in the yards of their homes.[78] In Cekanów, an elderly father carrying home the body of his son was shot down on the street. Similarly, in Rozprza, German soldiers killed women in the street, and the body of Berek Rozenzweig, the Jewish owner of a local grocery store, was found in his shop with a gunshot wound to the head.[79]

The most atrocious crime in the area was perpetrated in Longinówka, when German troops locked forty people, among them nearly twenty Polish prisoners of war, inside the business of Wincenty Kałuznego and then set the building on fire. Panic quickly erupted as the captives struggled to escape the inferno. The Germans, who had formed a cordon around the building, including a tank posted outside the front door, opened fire on the escapees, killing them as they jumped through the windows.[80] South of Piotrków Trybunalski, the men of the 1st Panzer Division devastated a total of twelve villages altogether, including Longinówka, in the first days of September. Polish investigative authorities concluded that in Milejowiec alone, seventy-five people had been killed and 95 percent of the farms were razed because of German suspicions that the inhabitants had somehow aided Polish units in the area.[81] In the nearby village of Krezna, the Germans razed to the ground 82 of 100 farms.[82] Last, and most tragic of all, casualties among civilians were greatest among the elderly, women, and children.[83]

The merciless behavior of soldiers with the 1st Panzer Division during the Polish campaign foreshadowed activities that would become commonplace elsewhere in occupied Eastern Europe during the war. This reaction is not surprising given the hateful sentiments expressed by officers like General Schenckendorff, who publicly expressed the opinion on 24 September that "Germans are the masters and Poles are slaves."[84] In September 1939, the orders given by German officers clearly demonstrated an understanding that the pacification of the non-German population within the new German "living space" was the responsibility of the army and the paramilitary forces subordinated to it. Wehrmacht officers spared no effort to achieve this aim. Civilian resistance, or even the suspicion that civilians had participated in hostilities, was punished with force, a coldly logical conclusion that set the Wehrmacht on a slippery slope from punishing an individual perpetrator to exacting revenge on entire communities. This leaves the question of legality still to be answered. Given the frequently intense resistance of Polish civilians, can the German army's use of *Vergeltungsmassnahmen,* or punitive measures, against Poles and Polish Jews be considered criminal?

In his study of the history of German reprisal policy, Richard Fattig points out that the Hague Convention of 1907 said nothing about taking and shooting hostages because of the inability of the participating nations to agree on a fundamental policy.[85] Subsequently, in both World War I and in September 1939, German officers were convinced that taking and executing hostages was legal if these actions conformed to established procedures. The problem is that during the invasion of Poland, Wehrmacht commanders did not follow procedure. As has been discussed, Army High Command and ranking field officers relinquished their control over junior officers as well as their dependence on courts-martial to punish civilians. Instead German officers permitted their men to take matters into their own hands by allowing them to shoot insurgents and destroy farms and villages. Herein lay the beginning of the process by which German military personnel were released from their disciplinary obligation to respect the lives and property of noncombatants. This process would eventually be institutionalized by the promulgation of the so-called Barbarossa Decree in 1941, which legally sanctioned the concept that German soldiers would not be punished for crimes they committed against civilians during the war in the Soviet Union.

The nascent criminality of German reprisal policy in Poland is made even clearer concerning the treatment of Polish militia and the use of reprisals as set out in the Hague Convention. Article 1 of the code stipulated that militia members and volunteers were to be considered combatants if they wore a uniform, belonged to an organized force, and carried their weapons openly.[86] The members of Polish insurgent groups were indeed uniformed, wore armbands, and bore arms openly, yet they were not treated as prisoners of war. Rather, orders issued by German officers defined Polish militia as terrorists and criminals who were to be summarily executed.[87]

Regarding reprisals against the civilian population in general, article 46 of the Hague Convention was intended to limit the application of violence to individual perpetrators, while article 50 stated that communities could not be punished collectively for the act of an individual.[88] Germany had agreed to abide by these rules, and they were part of the Wehrmacht's legal code at the outset of the invasion. Within days of the invasion's opening, however, German officers consciously chose to ignore these rules and rely instead on collective measures to punish the civilian population. In this sense, the *Vergeltungsmassnahmen* implemented by the German army against Poles and Jews in September 1939 were fundamentally criminal in nature and amounted to nothing short of institutionally sanctioned mass murder.

Although the German army's policy of employing retaliatory violence to suppress civilian opposition antedated the advent of the Third Reich, it is clear from the opinions expressed by several Wehrmacht officers that National Socialism colored the notion of collective punishment by the time war with Poland broke out in 1939.[89] This result is to be expected given that the regime actively promoted a derogatory view of Poles and Polish Jews based on racial-biological principles. These views easily coincided with and intensified the bitterness that many Germans felt toward Poland's inhabitants after 1919. Generally speaking, such sentiments enabled the seamless confluence of pragmatically applied retaliatory violence and the racial prejudice promoted by National Socialism. To many German officers in 1939, therefore, Poland's inhabitants were not ordinary adversaries; they were also racial and ethnic enemies, and it was in part because of this ideologically oriented concept of the enemy *[Feindbild]* that German commanders repeatedly ordered their troops to act brutally in response to civilian attacks. The widespread hate for Poles and Jews based upon the prejudiced stereotypes common in nazified German society simply made it easier for Wehrmacht officers to order the destruction of villages and the slaughter of civilians whose lives were of questionable value. Of equal significance was the dramatic and negative effect that the use of *Vergeltungsmassnahmen* had on the behavior of German troops, as officers authorizing reprisals initiated a cycle of violence that quickly brutalized their men. The proliferation of officially sanctioned violence and the simultaneous relaxation of legal constraints presented the opportunity for German troops to act summarily against Poland's civilian population and as a result reprisals soon gave way to atrocities.

A REPRISAL IN CZĘSTOCHOWA,
4 SEPTEMBER 1939

On 3 September 1939, the 42d Infantry Regiment of the 46th Infantry Division entered the city of Częstochowa, Poland. The following day, members of the 42d took fire from an unidentified assailant. The gunshots came from the third floor of an apartment building on Strazacka Street. What happened next was captured by the camera of a German soldier from the 4th Machine Gun Company of the 42d Infantry Regiment. Following standard army policy, the men of the 42d emptied the building of its inhabitants, including Jewish and Polish men. The captives were divided into small groups, beaten, threatened, and herded at gunpoint to an open marketplace nearby. Eventually, German troops selected a large group of the prisoners (the exact number is unknown), led them into a nearby park, and executed them as punishment for the attack. Members of the 42d then razed the apartment building and the adjacent structures to the ground. This collection of photographs, donated by B. Ashley Grimes II and held in the Photo Reference Collection of the U.S. Holocaust Memorial Museum, is the only available visual evidence of the brutal reprisal action carried out by the men of the 42d Infantry Regiment on that day in Częstochowa.

German troops occupy defensive positions in a park across Strazacka Street, opposite the building from which they took sniper fire. The caption on the reverse of the original photograph reads: "Shot were fired at us from this house." (WS 26865)

German troops guard men pulled from the apartment building on Strazacka Street. The prisoners are facing the fence that enclosed the park across the street from the apartment building. At this point, the prisoners were searched for weapons and identification papers. (WS 26823)

The terrified captives await German orders. (ws 26822)

Two groups of prisoners wait to be "processed." The men in the group lying in the street have not been shot. They are waiting to be questioned and searched. Forcing captives to lay face down was a way of controlling their movement. (WS 26825)

Set aflame by German soldiers, smoke rises from the apartment building
out of which the gunshots were allegedly fired. (WS 26827)

A view down Strazacka Street toward the marketplace where German troops led the captives. Note the corpses of the prisoners lining the street. The caption on the reverse of the original photograph reads: "The dead on the street." (WS 26828)

German soldiers guard the prisoners on the marketplace. Note the man in the foreground photographing the scene. (WS 26829)

The execution of prisoners in the park adjacent to Strazacka Street. (ws 26830)

SIX

FROM RETALIATION TO ATROCITY: WEHRMACHT SOLDIERS AND IRREGULAR WARFARE

The policy of collective punishment demonstrated the German army's institutional dependency on violence to pacify Poland's civilian population. On an individual level, however, the implementation of retaliatory measures also reduced the power that German officers had over their men. As a result, the behavior of German troops in the field in Poland quickly grew out of control. When searching for the causes of German brutality toward civilians during the war in Poland, several factors must be taken into account. In the first place, the radicalization of German behavior toward noncombatants can be blamed in part on civilians who chose to involve themselves in the fighting. Such attacks heightened the nervousness of inexperienced German troops who were under the terrifying stress of combat for the first time. In response, these green soldiers lashed out indiscriminately at the civilian population. The impact of formally authorized punitive actions was also important, as these actions hardened German military personnel against the people they were ordered to kill. In addition, however, certain elements of German conduct toward Polish and Jewish civilians suggest the harmful influence of National Socialism, which denigrated Poles and Jews for their allegedly inferior racial-biological value while simultaneously glorifying German brutality against such people. Taken together, this combination of combat conditions and ideological influence proved decisive in sharpening the behavior of German military personnel against Poland's civilian populace. This phenomenon was particularly evident during the middle and latter phases of the campaign, when civilian involvement in combat decreased without bringing about an equivalent reduction in German violence. Put another way, atrocities became increasingly common throughout the invasion as German troops willfully destroyed communities and murdered Poles and Jews without any provocation whatsoever.

The Murderous March of the XIII Corps

A detailed example of the vicious cycle of German brutality can be found in the eastward advance of the XIII Corps into Poland during the first two weeks of the invasion. Commanded by General Maximilian Freiherr von Weichs, the XIII Corps counted among its units the 10th and 17th Infantry Divisions as well as the SS *Leibstandarte* "Adolf Hitler," a motorized *Waffen*-SS regiment assigned to it at the end of August 1939.[1] The XIII Corps was part of General Johannes Blaskowitz's Eighth Army and formed its primary striking force. As such, the XIII Corps had been instructed to direct its attack in a northeasterly direction, advancing first on Sieradz and from there on to Łódź and Warsaw. Commanded by Major General Conrad von Cochenhausen, the 10th Infantry Division began the invasion of Poland from a location several miles northwest of Gross Wartenburg (Syców). Stationed on its right flank was the 17th Infantry Division of Brigadier General Herbert Loch. The regiments of Loch's division straddled the road that ran east from Gross Wartenburg to the town of Kepno. Both the 10th and 17th Infantry Divisions pushed forward on the morning of 1 September. By midafternoon, the 41st Infantry Regiment of the 10th Infantry Division had reached the village of Torzeniec, which was located on the Kepno-Sieradz road, roughly eight miles north of Wieruszów. Passing to the east through Torzeniec, the 41st became heavily engaged fighting the 4th Polish Ulan Regiment, which had established a defensive position along the Prosna River.[2] Meanwhile, other elements of the 10th and 17th Infantry Divisions advanced slowly eastward from Kepno toward Wieruszów.

The 10th Infantry Division's three regiments took fire from houses and villages the entire day, and combat with insurgents escalated during the night of 2 September.[3] That evening in Torzeniec, Polish civilians fiercely attacked the 41st Infantry Regiment, prompting the troops to retaliate after three of their comrades were killed and four others were seriously wounded. In all, the 41st shot fifteen men, including three seventy-three-year-olds.[4] Pushing eight miles farther to the east, elements of the 10th Infantry Division entered the village of Ostrówek at around midday on 2 September. According to Aniela Hes, the first German soldiers to enter the village passed through without incident. That night, however, other troops began burning homes and randomly machine-gunning the inhabitants.[5] Realizing they should flee, Aniela and her seventy-seven-year-old father, Wojciech Góralski, tried to escape, but the Germans shot and killed Wojciech as he ran past the burning house of Walenty Juszczak. Another of Goralski's neighbors, her brother-in-law Michal Dulski, was also shot dead while

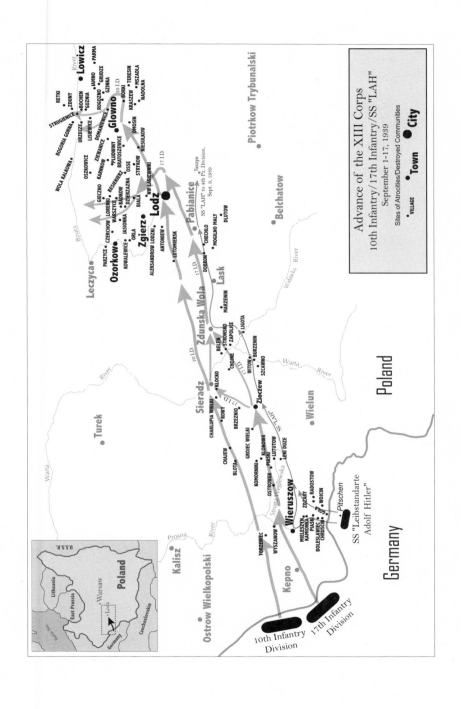

Advance of the XIII Corps
10th Infantry/17th Infantry/SS "LAH"
September 1-17, 1939

Sites of Atrocities/Destroyed Communities

• VILLAGE   • Town   ● City

looking out his window, and Aniela's married sister Józefa Binkowska was immediately killed by gunfire when she opened the door of her home to see what was happening.

In his official portrayal of the incident, General von Cochenhausen claimed that Polish civilians had fired on the 3d Company of the 10th Combat Engineer Battalion as it was rebuilding a bridge near Ostrówek, which lay on the west side of a small river called the Struga Węglewska.[6] Throughout the night the German engineers exchanged fire with armed civilians while at the same time working on the demolished bridge. The next morning, according to von Cochenhausen, his men discovered the bodies of three civilians who they had killed in the battle.[7] Janina Różanska, a member of the Tomała family, which owned a mill on the Struga Węglewska, later testified to Polish investigators that the bridge over the river was indeed destroyed when the Germans arrived. She also remembered German soldiers rebuilding the bridge after they arrived, but she then stated that the Germans suddenly opened fire on her family's home and business for no apparent reason. It was at this point that Różanska's sister and father were shot. As she recalled, "The buildings next to ours were burning and fearing that ours would soon catch fire, my father told us to run. He took our little sister in his arms and ran behind the stable. We ran after him, [and] when he got out into the open field he was shot in the left side, in the ribs. A bullet that hit her in the head killed my sister immediately."[8] Neither Hes nor Różanska remembered German soldiers being fired upon from Ostrówek, but the fact that inexperienced German troops were subjected to sniper fire earlier in the day makes it possible that they were nervous and killed the fleeing civilians entirely by mistake.

Elsewhere in the area, men with the 17th Infantry Division were involved in several incidents in the town of Podzamcze on 2 September. Residents later reported to Polish authorities that when the 17th Infantry moved into Podzamcze, a town located just on the western edge of Wieruszów, German troops killed several people in the street and set fire to a number of buildings. One of the victims was sixteen-year-old Agnieszka Wolna, who was at home looking out a window at the passing column of German soldiers when one of them shot her through the throat, killing her instantly.[9] German troops then broke into the house and took the whole family to the Protestant church in town where a large number of civilians were already gathered.[10] During her internment in the church, Zofia Monka saw German guards beating many of the local men they were guarding.[11]

In addition to these events, witnesses reported the murder of several other residents of Podzamcze. Among these unfortunates was practically the entire family of Kazimierz Hoffman. A wheelwright by trade, Hoffman and his family, including six children, were forced from their home by German troops and gunned down in their yard along with another woman named Maria Domgała.[12] The Germans also killed four other men at this time, including Franciszek Zawadzki, who was beaten and bayoneted to death.[13] Last, on the night of 2 September, German personnel dragged Tomasz Monka, the mayor of Podzamcze, and two other older men from their houses and took them to the brickyard of Stanisław Długoszewski. Once at the brickyard, German army interrogators beat the three men for twelve hours. It is probably not coincidental that all three of the men had participated in the Great Polish Insurrection of 1918–1919 in Poznań. Monka died from his injuries three days afterward, but there was no report on the fate of the other two individuals.[14]

Other incidents of civilians being murdered and villages destroyed in the first days of September were also reported in several locations south of Podzamcze and Wieruszów. This was the area in which the SS *Leibstandarte* "Adolf Hitler," under the command of SS-*Obergruppenführer* Josef "Sepp" Dietrich, was protecting the right flank of the 17th Infantry Division. Beginning the invasion from a point to the southwest of Bolesławiec, the *Leibstandarte* pushed into the area early on 2 September. According to Karol Musialek, "the first German patrol [arrived in Bolesławiec] at 5:00 A.M. [when] ten to fifteen motorcyclists came into the marketplace from the direction of Gola [a village to the south]. They drove around the marketplace three or four times and went back the same way."[15] The full complement of SS personnel arrived forty minutes later, and it was then that they perpetrated the first killings.

SS troops began to pull Jews and Poles out of their homes and assemble them on the marketplace. The SS men killed several individuals during this operation, including the father of Franciszek Lizon, who was shot while at his workbench, and Antoni Czubowicz, who an SS trooper shot in the back at point-blank range.[16] Tadeusz Kik, Czubowicz's grandson, could not explain why the SS killed his grandfather because he had not put up any resistance.[17] Once collected in the marketplace of Bolesławiec, the SS separated the civilians into two groups, one consisting solely of Jews and another of Poles. The prisoners were placed under guard and marched south toward the German-Polish border. As Franciszek Lizon recalled of this march, "We Poles were moving along in loose order and the Germans were not guarding us very closely. The Jews, however, were driven in front of us in a tight column while armed Germans and their dogs guarded them."[18] SS troops eventually drove the column of prisoners to the village of Gołkowice, on the German-Polish border, and held them there for two to three days. According to Lizon, mothers with children were given shelter in stables that he suspected the Germans had previously cleared of dung for the purpose of holding people.[19] The Jews, on the other hand, were forced to sleep in the open air. Karol Musialek was also on the march and remembered that shortly after arriving they were fed steamed potatoes. As for the Jews, Musialek recalled, "some 400 of them were assembled about forty yards away from us. They did not receive anything to eat and the Germans robbed them by searching their pockets and taking everything they found."[20] The Poles were released after two days, with the Jews following them one day later. Upon returning to Bolesławiec, many families found that in their absence the SS had burned their homes and farms.[21]

As the *Leibstandarte* moved to the north and east toward Wieruszów where it was to link up with the 17th Infantry Division, it razed a number of villages, including Żdżary, Piaski, and Mieleszyn. In the latter location, Henryk Okon and his family were preparing to leave when they and others with them were stopped by a patrol of soldiers wearing caps bearing Death's Head symbols. One of the SS men was questioning Okon's father Andrzej when another suddenly hit Andrzej in the back of the head with the butt of his rifle, knocking him to the ground.[22] The patrol then moved on, and the family started down the street toward the nearby shop of Jan Maczka. Outside the shop was another group of three SS troopers. These men seized Andrzej Okon and ordered him to tell Maczka to unlock the door and come outside. At the same time, one of the soldiers took aim and fired at sixty-year-old Tomasz Pasek, who lived across the street and was looking out his window at the group. The shots missed, but the SS man quickly ran across the street, broke into the house, and dragged Pasek out into the street. Throwing Pasek to the ground, the SS man bayoneted him in the side, seriously wounding but not killing him. Maczka then opened the door of his shop, and the SS trooper standing outside turned and quickly killed him with a bayonet thrust.[23]

Elements of the *Leibstandarte* rejoined the 17th Infantry Division in Wieruszów for the march east late in the day on 2 September. Shortly after their arrival in Wieruszów, SS troops participated in the roundup of civilians in the Protestant church that was being carried out by the 17th Infantry. SS personnel also used this opportunity to perpetrate crimes against local Jews, beating and murdering three members of the Lewi family, two men and one woman, on the street.[24] As the action against the inhabitants of Wieruszów was taking place, the leading regiments of the 17th Infantry Division, now joined by part of the *Leibstandarte,* continued to push east on the heels of retreating Polish forces. Moving through the village of Łęki Duże on 3 September, SS soldiers executed several civilians, among them Anna Ostrycharz, her child, and her brother Stanisław Luczak, who were shot outside their home near the village.[25] Their house was also burned down. According to other witnesses, random firing by SS troops into homes they passed also led to the deaths of Józefa Wysota and Leon Kowalski. Kowalski was shot in the head, but witnesses could not offer any rationale for the killing given that no one in Łęki Duże had fired at the German column.[26] Several additional murders took place in the communities of Debina, Józefina, and Piaksi, through which the 17th Infantry Division passed.[27]

By far, regular army soldiers and SS men committed the most heinous series of atrocities in the town of Złoczew on 3–4 September. The 95th Infantry Regiment and *Leibstandarte* reached the town, situated roughly fifteen miles southwest of Sieradz, on 3 September. Shortly after arriving in Złoczew, German troops and SS personnel engaged in an orgy of murder and destruction that resulted in widespread damage to the town and the deaths of almost 200 people.[28] According to Jan Korzuszek, a German bicycle patrol reached Złoczew as early as 2 September. The Germans stopped Korzuszek on the street and asked him if Polish forces still occupied the town. In addition, they asked him if he had any weapons and if there were any Jews in town.[29] Zofia Zasina, another resident of Złoczew, recalled that the next day, on 3 September, German soldiers began razing buildings and shooting people on the streets. Random firing by the soldiers into nearby houses resulted in the death of Zasina's husband, Michal. Neither Zasina nor other witnesses could recall why German soldiers did these things given the absence of resistance in the city.[30]

Janina Modrzewska also remembered the entry of German motorized units in Złoczew. Following the arrival of motorcyclists and bicyclists, Wehrmacht personnel ran amok as night fell. German soldiers fired on refugees in town, and Modrzewska saw the disemboweled body of a ten-year-old girl lying in the street. She had been shot through the back. Even more horrific, Modrzewska witnessed the murder of what she estimated to be a one-and-a-half-year-old girl by a German soldier who crushed her skull with the butt of his rifle.[31] Then there was the murder of Józefa Błachowska. A German soldier shot Błachowska in the arm and then threw her into a burning house. Numerous other witnesses in addition to Janina Modrzewska similarly reported seeing German troops firing indiscriminately at groups of refugees in Złoczew. One witness, Stanisław Ratajski, saw German soldiers order a wagon carrying refugees off the road into

Złoczew so German units could pass. Other soldiers who later marched by then suddenly lowered their weapons at the group and machine-gunned them to death.[32]

In a postwar investigation of these events, West German authorities decided that they could not establish a motive for the remarkably violent behavior of German troops and SS men in Złoczew. According to orders disseminated by the 17th Infantry Division on 2 September, military intelligence reports determined that Polish regiments had withdrawn from the area, leaving behind only a weak rear guard.[33] The XIII Corps command anticipated that the Poles would offer only sporadic and uncoordinated defensive action. It was highly unlikely, therefore, that the acts of violence against the inhabitants of Złoczew were committed accidentally during the heat of battle. West German investigators noted nevertheless that civilians had resisted the German advance with arms in the days before the 17th Infantry Division reached the city. Some of these encounters led to the deaths of military personnel, which may have enraged German soldiers who then took revenge on the people of Złoczew. Holes in the evidence, however, including a lack of documentation from the 17th Infantry Division itself, could neither confirm nor refute this claim, although the West German investigation also eventually concluded that "excesses [committed by] individual soldiers could not be ruled out," and there were indeed some clear-cut cases of murder, including the killing of children and the burning to death of Józefa Błachowska.[34]

The evidence collected by Polish legal authorities leads to a conclusion altogether different from that arrived at by the West Germans. In the preceding three days, regular army and SS forces had murdered people, machine-gunned refugees, and destroyed property in incidents that could not be directly attributed to retaliation for civilian attacks. Furthermore, if civilians were indeed shot in Złoczew under the rubric of retaliation for insurgent activity, the process by which these reprisals were carried out was not consistent with formal military policy at the time. Standing orders called for the arrest, court-martial, and execution of civilian assailants by German military personnel. Civilians in Złoczew were shot countless times without the benefit of a formal court-martial. The summary execution of noncombatants was never legal unless the assailant was killed while fighting. Neither Polish witnesses nor the existing German documentation makes note of German troops utilizing courts-martial during the occupation of Złoczew. Fighting also never took place in Złoczew because Polish forces withdrew to the east before the Germans arrived. German personnel simply killed civilians wherever they found them. Cecilia Korpecka, for example, stated that her husband Piotr was shot on the street for no apparent reason, and as Józef Krzec testified, his mother witnessed the random execution of five people by machine gun at close range, four of whom were women.[35]

West German authorities also discovered in the records of the 17th Infantry Division that the divisional command staff set up its headquarters upon arriving in Złoczew on 3 September.[36] If there was combat in the city, it is highly unlikely that a divisional headquarters would have been established there before Polish opposition was wiped out. In all, the available evidence points to the conclusion that Wehrmacht and SS soldiers ran amok in Złoczew. The destructive behavior of German personnel may indeed have been motivated by a desire for vengeance in response to attacks by snipers days before, but this conclusion cannot be firmly established. Whatever their motivation, the level of death and destruction caused by Wehrmacht and SS personnel in Złoczew was tremendous. When considered alongside the lack of evidence that the killings and arson were perpetrated under the rubric of formally guided reprisal actions, the only reasonable conclusion to be reached is that Wehrmacht soldiers and SS personnel maliciously and callously destroyed the property and took the lives of people they considered not worth sparing.

Following the occupation of Złoczew, the 17th Infantry Division pushed north and east toward Sieradz with the 10th Infantry Division on its left flank. For its part, the *Leibstandarte* once again took position on the right flank of the 17th Infantry, driving due east toward Burzenin before attempting to cross the Warta River. As the *Leibstandarte* advanced on 4 September, Brigadier General Loch's 17th Infantry Division drove north and east from Złoczew toward the Warta River. En route, Loch's regiments passed through the communities of Grójec-Wielki, Stanisławów, and Brzeznio. In Stanisławów, on the left flank of the 17th Infantry Division, through which the 21st and 55th Infantry Regiments marched, soldiers randomly fired on the houses of the inhabitants, setting alight the home of an ill Polish woman who subsequently died in the blaze.[37]

Still farther to the north, elements of the 10th Infantry Division moved through Komorniki and Klonowa. Rumors had already circulated among civilians that the Germans were killing men and burning homes, therefore many had fled east. German soldiers entered Klonowa and razed twenty houses altogether.[38] Two days later, on the morning of 4 September, troops with the 20th Infantry Regiment entered the village of Charlupia Wielka, located six miles southwest of Sieradz. According to local witnesses, the first German soldiers arrived on horseback and in automobiles. The infantry soon followed, and German soldiers went from house to house forcing the residents outside and ordering them to congregate in the town church.[39] Witnesses later told Stanisław Jaworski that his father Józef was standing outside his house when a German patrol moved up the street toward him.[40] Seeing this, Jaworski's wife Rozalia called him into the house just as the soldiers shouted for him to halt. The Germans pursued Jaworski and broke into the house. Józef and Rozalia fled into the kitchen and locked the door, forcing the Germans to begin hammering at it with their weapons. Unable to fully break down the door, one of the soldiers fired his rifle through it, hitting Józef in the head and covering Rozalia with blood.[41] After they broke through the door, the Germans saw Rozalia hiding under a table. One of the soldiers raised his rifle to shoot her as well when his comrade prevented it.[42] The men opted instead to take Rozalia from the house and put her with the other townspeople who the unit had collected in the local church.

With the occupation of Sieradz, the XIII Corps was poised to strike across the Warta River and drive toward Łódź, one of Poland's largest cities. German forces crossed the Warta at several points on 4–5 September, forcing the Poles to continue their retreat east. Less than ten kilometers to the south of Sieradz, the 21st and 95th Infantry Regiments made a difficult crossing of the river on the night of 4 September. Troops with the 95th crossed first and advanced to the village of Stronsko, while the 21st Infantry Regiment took the heights to the north, near the village of Belen.[43] The farming colony of Zagórzyce was also located near Belen, and when soldiers with the 21st captured the area, they razed all the farmsteads. Most of the inhabitants of Zagórzyce fled before the advancing Germans. However, seventy-year-old Józef Paszkowski did not, deciding instead to remain behind and help his neighbor whose wife was pregnant. After German troops set his neighbor's home ablaze, Paszkowski attempted to save the house and some possessions. Four Polish soldiers who had been detached from their unit and were hiding nearby saw German soldiers stop Paszkowski and run him through several times with their bayonets. They then shot and killed him.[44] The entire community of Zagórzyce was burned to the ground. Less than one mile to the south of Belen and Zagórzyce the 95th Infantry Regiment pushed Polish forces out of Stronsko, and German troops searched the area. One resident of Stronsko, sixty-four-year-old Marianna Krol, who had complained that she was too old to flee the Germans, instead decided to take cover in her potato cellar until the fighting passed the area. A German soldier discovered the cellar and ordered any occupants to come out. Krol responded that she was alone and too scared to move. Despite hearing the voice of a woman, the man threw in a grenade, killing her instantly.[45]

To the south, the *Leibstandarte* crossed the Warta River near Burzenin on 4–5 September. It then became detached from the 17th Infantry Division by straying too far south. As a motorized unit, the *Leibstandarte* was expected to advance faster than the infantry; yet it continued to lag behind the right flank of the 17th. Part of Sepp Dietrich's SS troops advanced toward the town of Widawa, while others turned toward the northeast to cross the Widawka River and reestablish contact with the 17th Infantry Division. As they moved to rejoin the XIII Corps, SS personnel found time to kill several more civilians, generally elderly individuals, in the villages of Witoldów and Wola Kleszczowa.[46] Parts of the *Leibstandarte* then crossed the Widawka and moved north toward Zdunska Wola and northeast toward Lask, which the 10th and 17th Infantry Divisions had occupied on 5 September.

On the road to Zdunska Wola, SS detachments arrived in Zapolice on 6 September, well behind the leading elements of the XIII Corps. Just outside the village, a German motorcyclist shot Józef Urbaniak off his bicycle as he pedaled toward his farm.[47] Near Zapolice, Józef Kuławiak and others witnessed the murder of Kuławiak 's brother Jan and father Stanisław by the village cemetery on 6 September. The Kuławiak family, accompanied by a man named Rojek, was returning to their home in Chojne, west of Stronsko, after having been overtaken by German troops. Rojek's daughter Józefa had already been killed in Zapolice, and the Kuławiaks were taking the body home when a detachment of mounted SS men stopped them.[48] The SS troops had been standing there looking at the bodies of Wehrmacht soldiers killed when the 95th Infantry Regiment fought its way through the area two days earlier. The SS riders halted the family as they approached, ordering them at gunpoint to get off the wagon. They then unharnessed the horses and led them away. Kuławiak recalled at this point that an SS man

> led us away from the wagon, ordering my brother Jan Kuławiak to keep his arms over his head, while kicking him at the same time. He then shot him with his rifle, killing him instantly. I was scared and hid under the wagon. The German pulled me out and told me to stand in the middle of the road. He then shot me in the left leg and I fell down crying. The officer sitting on his horse told him I was still alive and the soldier then kicked me in the head and abdomen, poked me in the ribs with his rifle, and then shot me twice more, once in the hand and once in the chest. I began to lose consciousness, but saw the same soldier go up to my father and hit him in the chest with his rifle. My father fell. The man ordered my father to get up and keep his arms above his head. He then shot him and my father fell dead on the spot.[49]

Kuławiak survived his wounds owing to treatment he received from a passing German army medic. He learned later, however, that Rojek had been shot in the face and died after suffering terribly.

Following the murder of civilians in Zapolice and other locations south of Zdunska Wola, the bulk of Sepp Dietrich's SS troops finally caught up with the 17th Infantry Division in time to participate in the assault on Pabianice, a large town located just beyond the southwestern outskirts of Łódź. The *Leibstandarte*'s days as part of the XIII Corps were numbered, however, due to complaints General Blaskowitz received about the combat performance of Sepp Dietrich's men. Strung out on secondary roads far from the right flank of the 17th Infantry Division, reports indicated that the *Leibstandarte* was advancing sluggishly and had failed to properly coordinate its movements. The *Waffen*-SS unit simply had not acquitted itself well to this point in supporting regular army units.[50] Sepp Dietrich was nevertheless ordered to bring up his battalions to participate in the attack on Pabianice. The Poles initially repulsed the assault on 7 September, but they were eventually overcome after difficult fighting and withdrew northeast through Łódź early the following day. Once again, regular army officers were critical of the *Leibstandarte*'s performance. These complaints led General Weichs to give the SS unit a secondary assignment for the attack on Łódź. Instead of participating in the primary assault, the *Leibstandarte* was detailed to clear the area south of the city, between Pabianice and Rzgów. In addition, the *Leibstandarte*'s artillery battalion was transferred to the 10th Infantry Division. Shortly thereafter, the entire unit was reassigned to the 4th Panzer Division where it would become General Reichenau's problem.

The participation of the *Leibstandarte* "Adolf Hitler" in the XIII Corps's advance through western Poland thus came to an ignominious end. Although SS troops demonstrated courage against Polish forces in several engagements, their willingness to perpetrate crimes against Polish and Jewish civilians was even more striking. The trail of destruction and death left by SS troops from the German-Polish border to the outskirts of Łódź did not escape the attention of Brigadier General Loch, who "complained about the *Leibstandarte*'s wild firing and tendency to reflexively set villages alight as they passed through them."[51] However, despite Loch's complaints, SS troops continued to shoot noncombatants in several villages east of Lask, including a number of Polish boy scouts from Pabianice who they murdered in a brickyard in Chechło.[52] The men of the *Leibstandarte* clearly fit the SS's definition of National Socialist fighters in this sense by proving their capacity to be hard and merciless toward their enemies, even if these were only women and children.

The *Leibstandarte*'s removal from the XIII Corps left the task of taking Łódź to the 10th and 17th Infantry Divisions. Faced with the prospect of difficult house-to-house fighting in the streets, German commanders employed a bold scheme to take the city with a minimum number of casualties. On 8 September, the 10th Infantry Division moved north around Łódź in order to outflank the Polish forces defending it. At the same time, Loch's 17th Infantry Division launched its assault, pinning down the city's defenders. The plan worked well, and by 8:00 P.M. on 8 September, the 10th Infantry was well behind Łódź, about seven miles south of Stryków.[53] Realizing their route of retreat was cut off, the Polish defenders collapsed, and the city was in German hands by early in the day on 9 September.

After bypassing Łódź, the 10th Infantry continued to pursue Polish forces to the northeast, reaching Skierniewice the following day (10 September). German troops en route to Skierniewice once again instituted measures against the civilian population by carrying out shootings and arrests and by destroying homes in several locations. Following a brief fight with retreating Polish units on 8 September, soldiers with the 10th Infantry Division arrived in the vicinity of Dmosin, a small town located several miles south of Głowno. Entering Dmosin late in the day, German troops fired incendiary shells into the cottage of Jan Nowicki and his neighbors. All of the homes burned to the ground.[54] Nowicki also witnessed the wounding of his neighbor, twelve-year-old Stefan Krakowiak, whom German soldiers shot while he was trying to save his family's cows from a burning barn. Last, Nowicki reported to Polish investigators the murder of Wiktor Cieslinski, the director of the local school. German military personnel took Cieslinski to the church in Dmosin as one of the many male hostages they arrested that day. Once there he was ordered to raise his hands, but because he had only one hand, Cieslinski did not raise both of his arms. The soldier giving the orders had Cieslinski killed on the spot for "disobedience."[55]

German soldiers arriving in Dmosin collected all of the inhabitants in the local church and systematically checked identification papers.[56] At one point during the German sweeps through the village, five teenage boys hiding in a stable attempted to flee.[57] They were seen by the soldiers and shot down. According to Marianna Dratek, who witnessed the shooting, the bullets only wounded two of the young men. German soldiers subsequently dispatched these individuals by striking each youth several times in the head with the butts of their rifles.[58]

While events in Dmosin were taking place, the 17th Infantry Division moved east from Łódź so that by 10 September it was in an area just to the northeast of Brzeziny. Any further movement toward Warsaw was made impossible at this point, however, owing to the beginning of a massive Polish offensive along the Bzura River. In a desperate attempt to break out of the ring into which the Wehrmacht was quickly enclosing them, several Polish divisions under the command of General Kutrzeba launched an assault over the Bzura River near Leczyca and slammed into the 30th Infantry Division. The attack quickly developed along a broad front from Leczyca to Łowicz, involving the 24th Infantry Division as well. With German forces reeling back on 10 September, the 17th Infantry Division was called upon to shore up the faltering 30th Infantry by moving west through Łódź and then north along the road from Łódź to Ozorków, which lay south of Leczyca. But before their departure from the area north of Brzeziny, troops with the 41st and 85th Infantry Regiments destroyed several villages, including Mszadła, Mikuly, and Teresin. The villages were razed in retaliation for two shots fired at German troops by unknown assailants. One of these shots was directed at German soldiers quartered in the orchard of a man named Wanios, located in Teresin.[59] The other was fired at German personnel in Mikuly, which lay just to the south of Teresin.[60]

In neither instance could the Poles who were present identify the assailants when the two incidents occurred. However, many witnesses steadfastly denied that any civilians had fired at German troops. The available evidence indicates that there were Polish troops in the area. Several witnesses actually recalled seeing German soldiers bringing in small groups of Polish prisoners of war. In one case, two Polish soldiers were captured soon after the shots had been fired; in retaliation, the Germans beat one of the men to death.[61] It seems probable, therefore, that the Polish soldiers in the area fired the shots, which did not matter to the Germans under attack. They immediately fanned out after the gunfire and began to collect men from the three villages. In the resulting bloodbath, rampaging German troops destroyed the three villages and killed forty-seven men. Squads of soldiers carried out much of the slaughter by summarily machine-gunning groups of local inhabitants. The youngest of the victims was a five-and-a-half-year-old girl killed on her family's farm along with her father and six-and-a-half-year-old brother.[62] Moreover, nearly twenty men were executed in the barn of Jan Kozlowski, after which the Germans who killed them were seen at a well washing blood from their hands.[63]

In the evening of 11 September, German forces south of the Bzura River launched a counteroffensive, and Polish forces spent from previous fighting began to collapse. On the right flank of this battle, troops with the 10th Infantry Division pushed through the village of Parma the next day (12 September). Henryk Pniewski recalled that as the German column moved through town, soldiers ordered several men to help them repair vehicles from a supply unit that had broken down.[64] A passing Polish patrol fired on the German column (Parma was very close to the front line), and the Germans' mood turned ugly.[65] They gathered several Polish men, including Pniewski's father, and lined them up against the wall of a house for execution. Pniewski and two other men were able to save themselves by pleading for their lives in German, but the firing squad shot the remaining men.[66] General Cochenhausen's men were still not finished punishing the inhabitants of Parma, though. They also seized Antoni Antosik and took seven other local men to the bank of the river that flowed through the village. At the riverside they threw Antosik and the others to the ground and opened fire on them. One of the soldiers then moved among the bodies kicking them to see if any remained alive. Somehow the hail of bullets did not hit Antosik, nor did the soldier checking the bodies kick him. He was nevertheless deeply shaken by the incident and remained prone among the cadavers until night fell.[67] Finally, the Germans razed Parma to the ground.

Polish defenses broke apart south of the Bzura on the afternoon of 14 September, and General Kutrzeba's forces began withdrawing north of the river. For their part, German units pursued the Poles to the southern bank of the Bzura and planned a coordinated attack across the river for the following day, 15 September. The initial attack failed because of desperate Polish resistance, and it was scheduled to resume once again on 16 September. Largely concentrated southwest of Sobota, the 10th Infantry Division was directed to make a difficult assault across the Bzura toward the northeast. In its path, on the far side of the river, lay the villages of Urzecze, Bogoria Górna, Strugiennice, and Zduny. On the morning of 16 September, Cochenhausen's men established a foothold on the north bank of the Bzura and then finally penetrated Polish defenses. This advance set the stage for a last series of shootings and razing of villages before the Polish surrender. Driving toward the northeast, the 10th Infantry Division first overran Urzecze, where Wehrmacht troops shot ten civilians, among them two women who attempted to flee after having been on a forced march from Bogoria Górna.[68] Bogoria Górna was located two miles to the north, and it too had fallen into German hands that day. Stanisław Jaros testified that when German soldiers arrived they immediately began burning all of the farms. He further recalled hearing from Józefa Slubski that

> at the Slubski's three men, two women, and a child were hiding in an underground shelter. German soldiers first put fire to the straw above the shelter and yelled "raus, raus" for the people to come out. [Walenty]

Bonczak, who had already been wounded by a grenade when he was
leading his horse from its stable, went out first and he was shot. Seventy-year-old [Piotr] Matych went out next and they shot him too.
[Piotr] Slubski then went third carrying his two-year-old son [Zdzisław
Slubski]. The Germans shot the child first and then the father. When
the father fell, the Germans saw that the child was still alive so they
shot him a second time.[69]

German soldiers also seized Wacław Walczak in Zduny, a village located
several kilometers to the east of Bogoria Górna. The Germans led him and
two other men to a nearby garden, gave Walczak a shovel, and ordered him
to dig a pit. After a while, one soldier noticed that Walczak was wearing
fine boots and told him to take them off. The soldier tried on the boots, but
they did not fit. After finishing the pit, Walczak and the other two men
were taken to a nearby stable and stood in a row in front of it. As Walczak
later testified:

> The three Germans who brought us there then lined up a few paces
> away and raised their rifles at us. I don't remember hearing any shots,
> but I felt heat and darkness enveloped me. After I regained conscious-
> ness, I realized that I was wounded. The bullet had entered my mouth
> and blood was streaming from my shattered palate and nose. I heard
> the voices of two Germans coming towards me. I heard one of them
> lean his rifle against the door of the stable; he then turned me over and
> searched through my pockets, pulled out my wallet, took my twenty
> Złotys, and threw my wallet away.[70]

While Walczak lay there in pain, he saw Wehrmacht personnel leading four
more men into the yard for execution. When the group approached the stable, the men saw the bodies and attempted to run. The soldiers guarding
them shot one in the head before he got even a few steps away and then
killed the other man. Seeing these two killed before his eyes, the third man
fell to his knees and begged for his life before being shot to death five times
at close range by the unsympathetic executioners.[71] All told, during the two
days (16–17 September) that the 10th Infantry Division was in the vicinity
of the Bzura River, German troops killed eighty-three civilians and destroyed six villages for reasons unrelated to combat. Many of the killings
appear to have occurred simply because of wanton German cruelty, as in
Baków Górny where two women and five children between the ages of four
and sixteen were shot dead.[72] And in the village of Retki, Józef Smiałek

witnessed three executions, during one of which he "saw four German soldiers shooting at six men in a neighbor's yard. The soldiers looked pleased with themselves and laughed when the bodies fell."[73]

Although Polish units within the Kutno-Bzura pocket formally surrendered on 19 September, the murder of civilians and Polish prisoners of war in the area occurred as late as 21 September in the towns of Sochaczew, Młodzieszyn, Jasieniec, and Rybno.[74] Polish authorities concluded in these cases that the perpetrators were not members of the 10th or 17th Infantry Divisions, but soldiers from the 4th Panzer Division, part of the XVI Corps, under the command of Major General Georg-Hans Reinhardt, which had closed on the Kutno-Bzura pocket from the east. Indeed, it is misleading to single out the divisions of the XIII Corps alone, for these were by no means the only German units guilty of deliberately murdering civilians and destroying property during the Polish campaign.

Different Units, Similar Behavior: German Army Crimes against Jews

German troops committed two particularly heinous killings on 9 September in the village of Swoboda during the Battle of the Bzura River. The area at the time was under the control of the 30th Infantry Division, which was commanded by General Kurt von Briesen, and part of General Wilhelm Ulex's X Corps. As the battle near the Bzura River ebbed and flowed, the Germans recaptured the villages of Biała, Dzierzazna, Badków, and Swoboda on 9 September and began to collect male civilians. They forced many of these detainees into a farmer's barn in Swoboda. Unaware that the owner was an ethnic German named Tischler, the soldiers formed a cordon around the barn and lobbed a hand grenade through the window. Those who were not immediately killed by the explosion died in the fire that erupted or were machine-gunned as they tried to escape the flames through the windows.[75] Jan Swiderski and several other witnesses reported that a similar crime was committed in Biała, when another group of Poles (between ten and fifteen), including a priest, were forced into the house of a man named Pabianczyk. The house was then razed, and several men were shot as they tried to escape.[76]

Like their fellow countrymen, Polish priests also suffered at the hands of German soldiers. Wehrmacht personnel executed five priests and one Polish prisoner of war on 12 September in the Puszcza Marianska, a forest near the village of Michalów. Jan Skrocki saw the priests being led to their deaths:

In the afternoon I saw four [*sic*] priests and a Polish soldier, I think he was an officer, walking along the road. Behind them walked two or three Wehrmacht soldiers with their rifles pointed down, and behind them drove a vehicle with German soldiers in it. I was then a little boy of nine-years-old and went out onto the road. One of the priests who passed me told me to pray for them because they were going to be shot. I watched the soldiers take the priests and the officer into the underbrush near the neighboring village of Michałów. After all of them had entered the bushes I heard shots. . . . three days later I went and saw a grave with a hand sticking out of it. Some weeks afterwards the Gestapo came to our house to ask my mother and me who shot the priests. We claimed not to know and one of the Gestapo men told me in Polish that I should grab a shovel and dig a pit for myself. While I was digging my mother spoke to one of the Gestapo men and told him that the grave was on land that we did not own. We could not know who was buried there. After the talk the Gestapo men spoke among themselves and told me to stop digging. They then left and went towards the Puszcza Marianska.[77]

In all probability, the perpetrators were soldiers with the 19th Infantry Division of Major General Günther Schwantes, which was part of the XI Corps of General Emil Leeb. Units from the 19th Infantry Division pushed through the area on 12 September while en route to battle near Sochaczew, where German forces were concentrating for a counteroffensive on the left flank of General Kutrzeba's Polish troops fighting along the Bzura River.[78]

Killings were also perpetrated in the city of Łowicz around this time. The 31st Infantry Regiment, which was part of the 24th Infantry Division, under the command of Major General Friedrich Olbricht, occupied Łowicz on 9 September.[79] Upon entering the city, German troops with the 31st Infantry began collecting civilians, both Poles and Jews, in the marketplace. The gathering of hostages did not go smoothly, however, and gunfire and explosions could be heard throughout the city, causing panic to sweep through the civilian population. Moving from street to street, German soldiers entered homes and forced the inhabitants out at gunpoint. In many cases, Wehrmacht personnel blindly threw grenades into homes without confirming that civilians were not present.[80] Several incidents of senseless violence attended the roundup as well. For example, an officer shot Stanisław Wolski at close range in front of his home at Łódźkiej Street 10. Other soldiers standing around had to hold back Wolski's wife, who screamed as she watched her husband die.[81] German troops also shot and killed sixteen-year-old Wacław Wolski (unrelated to Stanisław Wolski) on the same street.[82] And as Edward Wróbel recalled, he saw six Polish boy scouts under German guard being beaten and forced to march to the Neuman Brick Factory where they were eventually executed.[83] Polish investigators never confirmed the total number of noncombatants killed in Łowicz that day by the 31st Infantry Regiment.

The murders in Łowicz were not the first occasion when soldiers with the 24th Infantry Division had targeted Jews. Several Jewish men were also killed in the town of Lutomiersk (near Łódź) on 7 September when the 24th Infantry passed through. According to witnesses, Wehrmacht troops assembled the town's population in the marketplace and then divided them into groups of Jews and Poles.[84] Józef Wisnewski remembered that at that point a German officer with a pronounced Silesian accent addressed the groups in Polish, warning people to give up arms and ammunition under the threat of death if they failed to do so.[85] Some individuals did in fact hand over weapons, but none of these people were punished. Instead, the officer began selecting Jews from what looked like a prearranged list. Calling out names, the Germans chose eleven Jewish men altogether. Wisnewski described the scene to Polish investigators as follows:

> The soldiers passed by the Jewish group repeatedly and only after carefully considering each person, took the individual into the middle of the marketplace while kicking and shouting at them. In the Jewish group I also saw Jews from Zdunska Wola. I do not remember the number of Jews in the crowd because the Germans caused such fear in us that no one wanted to lift his eyes to look around. After the crowd was ordered to disassemble, only German soldiers and the group of Jews remained in the marketplace. The Jews were led to the synagogue and ritual bath (Mikvah) that stood nearby it and after a while shots were heard.[86]

Konrad Nowacka and Kasimierz Klimek actually saw the execution near the Mikvah take place. Nowacka recalled recognizing two of the Jews as Młody Toporek and his son. Both were pushed face first to the wall of the Mikvah when "little Toporek sensed what was about to happen and began crying and begging for his life. The Germans began hitting him and pulling at him so that the shirt he had on was ripped to shreds. Despite this he kept begging for his life and for that was shot no fewer than five times, after which his body slumped to the ground."[87] Klimek told Polish investigators it was his belief that an informant from the local ethnic German community was responsible for the deaths of the Jews, because "on various occasions the Jewish milk merchant Lepkowicz had showed him a postcard which when viewed straight on showed a pig's head, but if viewed from the side showed Hitler's face." Klimek stated as well that another of the local Jews shot that day was known as a vocal critic of Adolf Hitler.[88]

Other incidents suggest the viciousness with which German soldiers would at times treat Polish Jews, including events in Rawa Mazowiecka, which the 19th Infantry Division occupied on 9 September.[89] On 10 September a German army unit appeared in Rawa Mazowiecka leading a large column of Polish prisoners of war to a temporary internment camp that had been established there. As the column passed through, a German soldier ordered a Jewish boy who was standing beside the road to get him some water. The boy became frightened and turned to run away. When the boy fled, the man fired his rifle at the child. The shot missed the boy, but it hit and killed another soldier.[90] Chaos broke out next as other German soldiers who heard the shot and saw a comrade lying on the ground scattered and began to pull civilians from the houses flanking the road. Among these people were the Jewish boy and his entire family, all of whom the Germans shot on the spot. Civilians who the soldiers had collected and the POWs they brought with them were then forced to the marketplace and ordered to lay face down on the pavement.[91]

Ewa Sadzik recalled that as the large mixed group of Jews and Poles filled the marketplace, German soldiers fired randomly into the crowd, killing and wounding many.[92] A Jewish baker named Fluma, whom Sadzik knew, tried to run into his house, but a German who spotted him shot Fluma in the back. Wehrmacht personnel forced the remaining prisoners to lie down on the marketplace. The Germans screamed that whoever raised his head or tried to rise would be shot immediately. Troops then fanned out through the neighborhoods to chase people from their homes to the marketplace. As the group grew larger, women and children were separated from men, and Jews were separated from Poles. The situation rapidly deteriorated into an orgy of killing as German soldiers moved among the assembled Jews shooting at them. After a while, Sadzik lost count of those killed, but she estimated that the Germans shot to death at least 300 Jews.[93]

Other witnesses recalled shootings being simultaneously carried out elsewhere in the vicinity, including two groups of Poles, nine in the first and three in the second, whom German soldiers executed against a wall.[94] The Poles were constables from the local office of the forest service and were probably mistaken for militia because of their uniforms.[95] Jan Pawlewski also witnessed the murder of a mother and child whom German troops shot on the street.[96] Last, German soldiers took fifty Jews from the market square and locked them in a shack on the edge of Rawa Mazowiecka's Jewish cemetery. They set fire to the building and killed everyone inside.[97] Polish investigators never firmly established the number of people who lost their lives that day, either Polish or Jewish, opting instead to place the number at "scores of civilians."[98] Eyewitness statements indicate though that on this occasion German soldiers vented their anger about the murder of a comrade on the Jews of Rawa Mazowiecka to a far greater degree than on the non-Jewish population.

Jews were also specifically selected for execution in Kruszyna on 4 September. Located halfway between Częstochowa and Radomsko, German units passed through Kruszyna heading east toward Widzów when a soldier was shot and killed by an unidentified assailant.[99] In reprisal, the Germans took 300 people from their houses and assembled them in the town cemetery.[100] According to Józef Włodarek, "[Once we were] in the cemetery an officer announced we would all be put to death because one German soldier had been shot in the town of Kruszyna. . . . a Polish interpreter translated it to us. The Germans did not execute the sentence, however, because a car bearing three staff officers drove up and stopped it . . . but only for Poles. They shot all of the inhabitants of our village who were Jews."[101] German troops forced local Poles to dig the grave in the cemetery after which between twelve and fifteen Jews were executed.[102] The soldiers then moved on, razing the nearby village of Baby and killing twenty-five more Poles, including three children, before leaving the area altogether.[103]

The cases detailed here demonstrate that Wehrmacht personnel were at times willing to focus reprisals on Jews rather than Poles. Yet these incidents also seem to have been exceptions to the rule at this point in the war. When considered alongside the overall number of Wehrmacht actions against the civilian population in Poland, the shooting of Jews and the destruction of Jewish property during the Polish campaign does not seem to have occurred with any greater frequency than the killing of Poles and the devastation of their property. The example of Rawa Mazowiecka nevertheless illustrates that German military personnel were fully capable of vicious behavior when they found themselves among Polish Jews. In none of the other incidents described here thus far, not even in Złoczew, was such a large number of Poles systematically assembled, terrorized, and killed by German troops.

Eyewitness statements collected for *The Black Book of Polish Jewry* also tell of many incidents when Jews were tortured and mistreated by German troops during the Polish campaign. For example, on 2 September in the town of Wieruszów, soldiers with the 17th Infantry Division looted Jewish businesses and burned the beards off Jewish men.[104] Five days later, on 7 September, German soldiers burned the synagogue and tore down the prayer house of the Jewish community in Aleksandrów Łódźki.[105] And in Zgierź, just north of Łódź, the synagogue was razed and German soldiers tormented Jewish men in the streets by burning off their beards.[106] Similar acts of depravity and extreme cruelty toward Jews reportedly also took place in Piotrków Trybunalski, Częstochowa, Bielsko, Kalisz, Włocławek, Mielec, and Luków as well as in many other places, attesting to the widespread nature of such behavior.[107] In this sense, the conduct of German troops in Rawa Mazowiecka portended events to come elsewhere in occupied Eastern Europe, when it became standard practice for German police and military personnel to target Jews and their communities for collective annihilation.

Discipline and Brutality in the German Army during the War in Poland

The frequently barbaric conduct of German military personnel during the Polish campaign requires comment on the state of discipline in the Wehrmacht at that time. Scholars who have examined the enforcement of martial law in the German army and the relationship between the Wehrmacht's legal system and discipline in the ranks generally conclude that in 1939 German officers took a dim view of crimes committed by their men against the civilian population. Omer Bartov, for one, claims that "while [German] troops were not punished with inordinate cruelty [in Poland], the enemy's civilians and prisoners were also treated decently, and soldiers stepping out of line in their conduct toward the occupied were severely punished."[108] Similarly, Jürgen Förster argues that German officers absolutely forbid "unauthorized, spontaneous measures against Poles and Jews."[109] There are anecdotal examples that support these arguments. Toward the end of September, three soldiers were arrested and court-martialed for rape, robbery, and assaults against Jews, while two weeks earlier the Tenth Army court-martialed a reserve lieutenant for illegally using his weapon against Jews in the city of Konskie.[110] In addition, there are several well-known cases of SS personnel court-martialed by Wehrmacht commanders for crimes they perpetrated against civilians. Indeed, at least a portion of Brigadier General Loch's complaints about the SS *Leibstandarte* "Adolf

Hitler" concerned crimes that SS troops had perpetrated against civilians. These acts, and the *Leibstandarte*'s slipshod combat performance, provided more than enough reason for transferring the SS unit out of the XIII Corps.

An examination of German army records also yields multiple examples of officers attempting to limit the actions of their men, especially against the property of civilians. As early as 5 September, the Eighth Army's commander, General Johannes Blaskowitz, exhorted his field officers to keep their men from indiscriminately destroying houses and valuable food supplies.[111] Just over one week later, on 14 September, the intelligence officer of the 7th Infantry Division noted that looting, the needless slaughtering of livestock, and the unauthorized seizure of provisions from civilians were increasingly coming to his attention, and he demanded that they stop.[112] However, commanders did not limit their complaints about their men to property crimes. Many expressed dismay about summary killings as well. Lieutenant Colonel Hartwig Pohlmann, the chief of staff of the 31st Infantry Division, noted in his war diary on 3 September that

> the first days of the war have already shown that the troops and that part of the officers inexperienced in war were either not taught at all, or insufficiently trained in peacetime. The instinctive nervousness and insecurity and corresponding uninhibited shootings and incendiarism shames the discipline and reputation of the army, needlessly destroys quarters and provisions, and leads to hardships for the populace that doubtless could have been avoided.[113]

Brigadier General Otto von Knobelsdorff of the 3d Frontier Guards echoed Pohlmann's misgivings by ordering on 5 September that "the troops are to be told again that they may only fire when the identity of opponents is confirmed. It must be made clear to every soldier that shootings caused by nervousness offends the honor of his unit."[114] Finally, General Wilhelm List offered these comments to subordinate officers in the Fourteenth Army on 18 September: "There have been reports in the last few days about the lack of discipline, attacks, and summary measures instituted against the civilian population. . . . arbitrary shootings carried out without the judgment of a formal court-martial, the mistreatment of unarmed persons, rapes, [and] the razing of synagogues . . . demonstrate a recognizable slackening in the bearing and discipline of the troops."[115]

Clearly, Wehrmacht commanders were aware that military personnel were committing crimes against the civilian population. However, the evidence also suggests that the army's response to such behavior was not uniform. Statistics compiled by the Reich War Court *(Reichskriegsgericht)* show that between 26 August and 18 November 1939, courts-martial sentenced only thirteen men to the firing squad for looting.[116] This is a pitifully small number given the frequency with which German troops were warned about plundering and the fact that over 1.5 million men served in the Polish campaign.[117] On the other hand, the Reich War Court statistics suggest that military judges frequently imposed penalties less severe than death. For example, courts-martial sentenced a total of 27,212 German military personnel to prison terms between 24 August 1939 and 30 June 1940.[118] A breakdown of these statistics into specific categories of offenses does not exist, thus making it impossible to determine either the percentage of crimes that were committed against civilians or the average length of the prison sentence that was imposed. By and large, the reaction of many Wehrmacht officers in Poland to the atrocious conduct of German soldiers was similar to those later expressed by German commanders in the occupied USSR. Crimes were generally interpreted as resulting from failings in military discipline.[119] In response to this problem, General Brauchitsch demanded on 20 September that German troops maintain a "proper bearing" toward the civilian population in occupied territory.[120] General Halder offered further evidence of frustration at the top of the command structure, noting in his war diary on 5 October: "The murder of Jews—discipline!"[121]

The question remains whether Halder's appraisal of the situation in Poland was valid. Did the violent behavior of German personnel arise primarily from a lack of discipline or was their conduct the product of other influences, including the traumatizing effects of combat? German troops appear to have been deeply embittered toward the civilian population as a result of attacks by insurgents, but some commanders suspected that the nervousness of inexperienced combat troops and field officers might have also played a part in prompting shootings and incendiarism. Take for instance a complaint made on 6 September by Lieutenant Colonel Claus Kühl, the chief of staff of the 4th Infantry Division. Concerned that the escalating number of conflicts with Polish insurgents was leading to "shootings and the large-scale burning [of buildings]" motivated by fear and panic, Kühl concluded that there was a definite danger of so-called "guerrilla-psychosis *[Freischärler-Psychose]*" spreading throughout the ranks and officer corps.[122] Similarly, Major General Georg Brandt, the commander of the 3d Frontier Guards, noted on 4 September that the considerable fire German troops were taking from insurgents in Katowice was leading "nervous" German troops to respond with shootings.[123]

Despite their concerns about unauthorized killings and other random violence, German officers also repeatedly encouraged their men to be ruthless toward the civilian population. Brigadier General Knobelsdorff recommended on 4 September, for example, that Wehrmacht personnel "spare bloody losses" and immediately shoot civilians with weapons whenever they were encountered.[124] Likewise, General Brandt ordered a "merciless fight against insurgent activity."[125] These and similar exhortations undermined appeals for the troops to maintain discipline and contradicted instructions that German officers issued for military personnel to retain a "proper bearing" toward the civilian population. An excellent example of this contradiction can be found in orders handed down on 23 September by Major General Diether von Böhm-Bezing, the commander of the 252d Infantry Division. Noting first that the reputation and power of the Wehrmacht rested on the discipline of its soldiers, Böhm-Bezing ordered that incidents of plundering and the murder of civilians must cease or the perpetrators would be punished by court-martial. Nevertheless, his orders continued, "[German] soldiers should behave sharply and harshly towards the Polish population. Generosity and honorable treatment will be seen by the Poles as cowardice."[126]

The mixed message in Böhm-Bezing's instructions echoed similarly confusing instructions handed down by General Brauchitsch only three days earlier. Demanding that German personnel act with discipline, Brauchitsch added:

The German soldier is the representative of the German Reich and its power in occupied territory. He should therefore feel himself as such and act correspondingly. Any insult of or attack on the German armed forces and the German people is to be answered with the severest means. The German soldier should never forget that the civilian population . . . is inwardly hostile despite outward friendliness. [Furthermore,] the bearing of soldiers of the National Socialist Reich toward the Jews requires no special comment.[127]

Given these examples of contradictory orders and the evidence of German conduct offered earlier, it appears that military personnel often chose to selectively obey their commanders' orders. Instructions authorizing the use of collective punishment and exhorting German soldiers to be hostile toward Poles and Jews demonstrated the willingness of German officers to punish civilian resistance by devastating communities and ordering executions. The overall effect of such actions and orders was to reinforce the anti-Polish and anti-Semitic attitudes of German military personnel and undermine instructions that the men act in a disciplined manner.

Indiscipline, though, was certainly not the only factor that explains the frequently barbaric behavior of German military and SS personnel. The evidence suggests simply that many German troops and SS men killed Poles and Jews in cold blood and without provocation. Acts such as the murder of women and children, the machine-gunning of refugees, the beating and cruel treatment of civilians, the torture of Jews, and the random firing into homes and farm buildings without any reason often cannot be attributed to revenge for casualties inflicted by insurgents or to reprisals ordered by German officers. Even more telling in this regard is evidence of merciful behavior by some German personnel, behavior that demonstrates German troops could be considerate to civilians if they chose. In one instance, a German soldier warned Jan Szuminski of Nowe Grudze to find somewhere safe to hide because of combat in the area.[128] Also, Bronisław Panek of Krzyzanów was wounded in the arm during a reprisal shooting in his village and then left for dead by the German unit that carried out the killings.[129] After a few hours, another passing German soldier noticed that Panek was still alive and carried him to the nearest aid station.

Consider as well events during the initial occupation of Łowicz, when German personnel with the 24th Infantry Division moved through the city destroying houses and pulling Polish men into the street for internment in the city's synagogue. Several Poles were killed during these roundups, including the son of Marianna Wolski, whom German troops stood against the wall of his house and shot alongside several of his neighbors.[130] Appalled by the sight of her son's murder, Marianna attacked one of the Germans who did the shooting. As the man threw Marianna to the ground and lifted his rifle to kill her too, another soldier standing nearby intervened and saved her life. At this point, a staff car pulled up, and two officers ordered the soldiers not to kill the rest of the group but to take them to the synagogue with the rest of the prisoners.[131] The 24th Infantry released all of the hostages in Łowicz after several days.

The Wolskis' experience illustrates the positive impact that German officers could have on the behavior of their men if they chose to intervene. Władysław Pegiel of Dmenin claimed to owe his life to a German officer who released him after he and the other male inhabitants of the village were caught up in a German sweep. Pegiel, who understood German, witnessed the execution of ten of his countrymen and overheard the guards considering the execution of the rest of their prisoners before the officer appeared and ordered all of the prisoners let go.[132] Stanisława Mularczyk witnessed a similar incident on 6 September in the village of Grabek. After seeing German troops kill several children and throw a hand grenade down a shallow well, killing the family that was hiding there, she witnessed from her hiding place the preparation of a small group of men for execution against a fence. Just as the firing squad was forming up, a German officer drove up and questioned the soldiers. He disagreed with their reason for shooting the Poles, ordered the captives set free, and then detailed an army medic to treat the wounded civilians in the area.[133] Helena Stefanek of Wojcik similarly witnessed the shooting of several of her family members, including three children under the age of ten, by German panzer troops.[134] These shootings took place before a German officer arrived in a car bearing a Red Cross symbol on it. The officer angrily told the panzer troops to disperse and then tended to the wounds of an injured child. In contrast to those times when they encouraged barbaric behavior by their troops, these few incidents illustrate the key role that German officers could play in controlling their men. Discipline was easily imposed and lives could be saved when German personnel and especially lower ranking officers simply chose to do the right thing.

The treatment of Polish prisoners of war is also worth examining in this context for what it reveals about indiscipline and brutality during the German campaign in Poland. Scholars agree that unlike the war in the Soviet Union, when the deliberate maltreatment and execution of Red Army POWs caused millions of deaths, the German army in 1939 did not intend a similar fate for captured Polish soldiers.[135] The lack of an institutional impulse for mass murder notwithstanding, there were in fact hundreds of incidents during which Polish POWs were beaten, tortured, murdered, or otherwise mistreated by German troops. The Wehrmacht captured 694,000 Polish prisoners of war as a result of the invasion.[136] These POWs were supposed to have been guaranteed humane and decent treatment by the Geneva Convention of 1929, an international agreement signed by Germany stipulating that "prisoners should not be punished for the simple fact that they had borne arms and killed in the name of the state."[137] Moreover, the 1929 Convention also required that all captured soldiers were to receive adequate food and shelter as well as the right "to escape, to religious freedom, [and] rights under interrogation and access to external support," such as visits from the International Red Cross.[138] German troops were therefore expected at the outset of the invasion to show mercy to enemy soldiers who surrendered or were captured.

During the campaign, however, German troops frequently overlooked or disregarded these rules and regulations when Polish military personnel fell into their hands. Crimes against Polish prisoners were especially common in the wake of the Battle of the Bzura River, when large columns of

Thousands of Polish prisoners of war wait at an open-air holding center to be processed by German army authorities and sent to other POW camps, September 1939. The Germans will eventually release some of these men, but many others will be sent to Germany for forced labor. (Institute of National Remembrance, Commission for the Prosecution of Crimes against the Polish Nation; courtesy of the U.S. Holocaust Memorial Museum, Photo Reference Collection: WS 50191)

POWs were marched to internment camps behind German lines. One such camp was established in a park in Rawa Mazowiecka. A simple fenced-in area with no barracks or other shelter, this camp held nearly 4,000 Polish POWs for several weeks after the end of the war. The soldiers kept there were poorly fed once every two to three days, and medical attention was practically nonexistent. The German guards also enforced discipline very harshly. During his march to the camp at the end of September, Stanisław Smiałkowski witnessed how German guards immediately killed any prisoner who could not keep up with the column or who broke ranks to urinate or forage in cabbage fields for food.[139] Another POW, Franciszek Michalski, similarly witnessed German guards shooting POWs on the march. He even saw Poles who fell out of the ranks beaten to death by guards using the butts of their rifles. While in the Rawa Mazowiecka camp,

Michalski also saw German guards deliberately murder three Polish officers (a captain, a lieutenant, and a sergeant). The random shooting of small numbers of POWs occurred nearly every day, he reported, forcing the prisoners to live in daily fear for their lives.[140]

Conditions were no better for Polish prisoners held in the Sojki POW camp that was located outside of Kutno. At one point, Sojki contained as many as 10,000 captured Polish military personnel. Like the camp in Rawa Mazowiecka, the vast majority of these prisoners slept in the open air and received poor quality food, including moldy bread and soup made from rancid horsemeat.[141] Former Polish soldiers who had been held in Sojki also recalled the brutality of their guards. Already hungry after several weeks of fighting, Józef Maj remembered that food was distributed unevenly to the prisoners, and as a result many soon grew too weak to lift themselves off of the ground. Several times he saw German guards select weakened prisoners for forced labor and then kill these men when they could not respond to the summons.[142] Maj estimated that during his six weeks in Sojki he saw at least sixty prisoners killed for no reason by the German soldiers guarding the camp. Killings took place outside of the wire too, as happened on one occasion when guards gunned down sixteen POWs in the field next to the camp when one of the men refused to work.[143] Maj's fellow prisoner, Stanisława Kepinski, makes clear, however, that the German guards at Sojki did not necessarily need a specific reason to fire their weapons into the crowded compound and kill Polish POWs.[144] According to Kepinski, groups of prisoners were regularly executed as collective punishment for the escape of others. Standing up to walk also invited a German bullet, he recalled, forcing the prisoners to remain sitting or lying on the ground for days on end.

German troops commonly murdered Polish POWs on the battlefield as well. In the village of Radziwilka on 19 September, a group of twenty Polish soldiers abandoned their position in a farmhouse and came out into the front yard under a white flag. The German troops that the Poles had been fighting threw grenades into the group and killed most of them. Those Poles not killed in the explosions were finished off by machine-gun fire.[145] Even the symbol of the Red Cross was not enough in certain instances to keep German personnel from wantonly murdering injured Polish soldiers. Take, for example, events near Szwarocin on the morning of 16 September, when the wounded Tadeusz Starzynski noticed a dozen German tanks rolling toward the aid station where he was receiving medical attention.[146] Although the barn in which the aid station had been established was clearly marked by Red Cross signs on its sides and roof, the tanks turned off the

Colonel Wessel, commander of the 15th Motorized Infantry Regiment, gives the order for Polish prisoners of war to be executed near Ciepielów, 9 September 1939. Three hundred Polish POWs were shot during this action. (Institute of National Remembrance, Commission for the Prosecution of Crimes against the Polish Nation; courtesy of the U.S. Holocaust Memorial Museum, Photo Reference Collection: WS 50858)

road toward the barn and opened fire at a distance of about eighty yards. Starzynski watched in horror as Polish doctors and comrades were killed around him and the barn caught fire. Not severely wounded, Starzynski and another soldier took cover in a nearby ditch and observed how the tanks advanced toward the barn while firing at the wounded and screaming men crawling and hobbling out of the flaming structure. Several of these tanks rolled right up to the barn and crushed the life out of the handful of men

Troops with the 15th Motorized Infantry Regiment lead Polish POWs to their execution near Ciepielów, 9 September 1939. (Institute of National Remembrance, Commission for the Prosecution of Crimes against the Polish Nation; courtesy of the U.S. Holocaust Memorial Museum, Photo Reference Collection: WS 50852)

who had been able to escape. Between fifty and sixty men altogether died in Szwarocin on that day.

Perhaps the most infamous atrocity against Polish POWs was committed by the men of the 15th Motorized Infantry Regiment in the forest near Ciepielów on 9 September. The III Battalion of the 15th Infantry came under fire as it advanced and took fourteen casualties after an hour of fighting. The Polish defenders finally surrendered, and the furious regimental commander, Colonel Wessel, began to rage about his dead comrades and the fact that Polish troops had held up the regiment's advance. What happened next shocked an anonymous German eyewitness who took several photographs and recorded the following in his diary:

It did not matter to him [Wessel] that these were soldiers. He claimed he was dealing with partisans even though each of the 300 Polish prisoners was in uniform. They were forced to take off their tunics. Yes,

Soldiers with the 15th Motorized Infantry Regiment survey the bodies of Polish POWs they have just executed. The shooting of 300 Polish POWs at Ciepielów was one of the worst atrocities committed by German troops against prisoners of war during the war in Poland. (Institute of National Remembrance, Commission for the Prosecution of Crimes against the Polish Nation; courtesy of the U.S. Holocaust Memorial Museum, Photo Reference Collection: WS 81247)

now they looked more like partisans. Their suspenders were then cut, apparently to prevent them from running away. Next the prisoners were forced to march down the road single file. . . . Five minutes later, I heard the crash of a dozen German machine-guns. I ran towards them and a hundred yards back I saw the 300 Polish prisoners shot and lying in the ditch by the side of the road.[147]

The massacre of Polish prisoners of war at Ciepielów was not an isolated occurrence. In his work, Szymon Datner, the eminent historian of Wehrmacht war crimes in Poland, specifically identifies sixty-four separate incidents when German troops shot Polish prisoners of war either individually or en masse.[148] Another Polish scholar, Tadeusz Cyprian, notes that in the decades following World War II, Polish investigators uncovered substantial evidence that German troops had slaughtered Polish POWs in hundreds of locations during and after the campaign.[149] More than any other aspect of the Wehrmacht's campaign in Poland, the widespread nature of crimes against Polish prisoners of war demonstrates the already brutal conduct of the German army in 1939. Despite international legal constraints and the army's own regulations, of which every German soldier was aware, prisoners of war were mercilessly gunned down, starved, beaten, and abused on every day that the war in Poland was fought. From the handful of incidents described here, it is apparent that officers were sometimes complicit in these crimes; in cases when they were not, individual German soldiers took it upon themselves to willfully murder the prisoners to whom they were specifically ordered to show mercy.

In conclusion, it is obvious from the sheer weight of the available evidence that regardless of combat conditions or the extent to which German military personnel were infuriated by Polish attacks, they could choose how they acted toward the civilian population and prisoners of war. Some German soldiers took mercy on civilians caught in the fighting, and in certain cases Wehrmacht officers demonstrated the willingness to intervene when it appeared that their men were committing crimes against noncombatants. Unfortunately, it is just as clear that many German military and SS personnel were quite prepared to behave with incredible brutality toward Polish and Jewish civilians. The intensity of combat and the insecurity of German soldiers on foreign soil are likely reasons why such violence erupted, but another explanation can be found in the brutalizing influence of National Socialism, which valorized barbaric behavior against Germany's racial enemies as worthy and correct. In this sense, the conduct of many regular German troops was by comparison no different from that of the SS men in the *Leibstandarte* "Adolf Hitler," even though SS personnel were expected to treat Poles and Jews mercilessly. This reality did not bode well for future campaigns that the German army would fight in Eastern Europe when Slavs and particularly Jews would be subjected to violence that was terrific in scale and genocidal in intensity.

AN ATROCITY IN KONSKIE

Upon reaching the city of Konskie during the first weeks of the Polish campaign, German troops with the 8th Air Reconnaissance Unit took gunfire from snipers. Four men were killed, including one officer, and the bodies were mutilated before the arrival of German reinforcements. The soldiers entering Konskie on 12 September were incensed by the mutilations, and they gathered together a group of Jewish men (generally between thirty and fifty years of age) to dig a grave for the bodies of their comrades. The Jews were forced into a city park and beaten by German troops wielding rifles and slats ripped from a nearby fence. As the frightened Jews worked, a police major named Schulz approached the group and berated the men for their undisciplined behavior. The men agreed and begrudgingly stepped away from the grave to let the Jews go. However, when the Jews attempted to leave the scene, Reserve Lieutenant Bruno Kleinmischel took out his sidearm and fired two shots at the fleeing Jews. General firing then broke out, and in the chaos twenty-two Jews were killed. Kleinmischel was court-martialed by the Tenth Army for illegally using his weapon and for manslaughter. He was sentenced to a one-year imprisonment but likely was pardoned in the general amnesty issued by Adolf Hitler in early October 1939. The noted German filmmaker Leni Riefenstahl witnessed this murder of Jews in Konskie while she was in Poland with her crew to shoot scenes for a film about Germany's first military campaign of the war. Riefenstahl never completed the film.

German troops order Jewish men into a park in Konskie where they will be
forced to dig a grave for the bodies of German soldiers found in the area.
(Institute of National Remembrance, Commission for the Prosecution of Crimes
against the Polish Nation; courtesy of the U.S. Holocaust Memorial Museum,
Photo Reference Collection: WS 50414)

German military personnel look on as Jewish men dig a grave for the bodies of four German soldiers. (Institute of National Remembrance, Commission for the Prosecution of Crimes against the Polish Nation; courtesy of the U.S. Holocaust Memorial Museum, Photo Reference Collection: WS 50415)

Jewish men in Konskie wait their turn to dig a grave for the bodies of four German soldiers. (Institute of National Remembrance, Commission for the Prosecution of Crimes against the Polish Nation; courtesy of the U.S. Holocaust Memorial Museum, Photo Reference Collection: WS 50421)

Flanked by a member of her film crew, a distraught Leni Riefenstahl looks on during the murder of Jews in Konskie. Note the youth of the soldier in the foreground. (Bernhard Braun, Dresden, Stiftung Archiv der Parteien und Massenorganizationen der DDR im Bundesarchiv, Berlin; courtesy of the U.S. Holocaust Memorial Museum, Photo Reference Collection: WS 80965)

SEVEN

EXPLAINING GERMAN BRUTALITY

Wir Soldaten sind Dir Führer treu!
Wir schufen durch dich den Osten neu!
Ein Wort von Dir, wir sind bereit, zu
stürmen den Westen jederzeit.
Denn Du gabst uns die Glaubenskraft,
Du hast ein neues Deutschland geschafft,
Das stark genug zu jeder Zeit,
zu schlagen den, der an deine Ehre greift!
(A German soldiers' poem.[1])

In his important work on the German army's "war of annihilation" *(Vernichtungskrieg)* against the Soviet Union, Omer Bartov argues that the demodernization of combat conditions on the Eastern Front as well as the deepening nazification of German troops' attitudes combined to create a conflict of unprecedented barbarity and violence.[2] Yet the war in Poland exhibited many of the same characteristics as the later *Vernichtungskrieg*, despite the fact that it was fought nearly two years earlier. Episodes of spontaneous German brutality against civilians and prisoners of war were common during the brief conflict, while thousands of other innocent Poles and Jews fell victim to the draconian reprisal policy employed by the German army to suppress resistance. These killings also occurred within a context of heightened ideological, even quasi-genocidal, violence, as SS and police units, often assisted by the army, sought out and began to eliminate political opponents. Unlike the later campaign in the USSR, however, the war in Poland was a relatively quick and decisive triumph for the German army, and it was probably due to the rapidity of the Wehrmacht's victory that a "barbarization of warfare," as defined by Bartov, never took place there. Moreover, the war against Poland lacked the explicitly ideological dimension that was central to Nazi Germany's animus toward the Soviet Union.

The question then remains why the similarities in German behavior in Poland and elsewhere in occupied Eastern Europe were so striking if the conditions of warfare as well as the ideological nature of the adversary differed so significantly. A number of factors contributed to German brutality in 1939, including the fear and nervousness of troops experiencing combat for the first time, bitterness toward civilian assailants, a slackening of military discipline, and the institutional legitimization of violence against non-combatants. As important as these factors were, the merciless conduct of many soldiers toward Poles and Jews also suggests that there was an attitudinal basis for the atrocities that were committed, as German military personnel who had been exposed to virulent racism and anti-Semitism since 1933 expressed through physical violence the contempt they felt for the peoples who lived to Germany's east.

A measure of the extent to which at least some Wehrmacht personnel already by 1939 had internalized notions of militarism, hatred for Poles, anti-Semitism, and German cultural chauvinism can be gleaned from their writings. Three categories of documents are relevant in this regard, including *Feldpostbriefe* (letters), diaries, and experience reports called *Erlebnisberichte*, which were written shortly after the conclusion of the campaign. Previous scholarly analyses of German soldiers' letters and diaries from the Second World War have exposed several areas of agreement between the authors and the regime, among which were the perceived importance of Adolf Hitler to Germany, disdain for Jews, and a belief that the Third Reich was fighting a quasi-holy crusade against the Soviet Union.[3] It is therefore not surprising that many of the soldiers who chose to write about these subjects were likely to reflect positively on Nazi policies against Jews, Slavs, and others defined by National Socialism as "sub-human."[4] On the other hand, it is also important to keep in mind when reading the letters of German troops that these documents represent the opinions of only a segment of the military personnel who chose to commit their thoughts, impressions, and attitudes to paper. Indeed, most German soldiers limited their written remarks to descriptions of daily life at the front, the horrors of combat, and other banal subjects rather than ranting to loved ones at home about the decrepitude of East European villages or the discomforting physical appearance of orthodox Jews.

But what about the third category of relevant documents, the experience reports? Can these also provide a viable source for evaluating the opinions and mentality of at least some Wehrmacht personnel? German troops composed experience reports at the request of Army High Command, ostensibly for the purpose of providing the German people with descriptions of the war in Poland.[5] As raw material for their reports, military personnel often used their own diaries and letters. The experience of the Polish campaign also was not far removed for many of these authors because most of the *Erlebnisberichte* were written in October and November 1939. Like *Feldpostbriefe* and diaries, a number of these reports offer impressions of the people and communities that German soldiers encountered in Poland as well as reflections on the leadership of Adolf Hitler, the outbreak of war, and the righteousness of Nazi Germany's cause. The reports were intended for publication in newspapers (both military and civilian) and in special unit histories that commemorated the activities of German army units during the campaign.[6] Divisional commanders assigned regimental officers the task of collecting and censoring the reports written by their men, while instructions issued by army Chief of Staff Halder informed potential contributors of their "full responsibility for the accuracy of the portrayal."[7] General Halder further noted that the army especially desired portrayals of combat, as well as stories of individual heroism and tales of battle that stressed cooperation between infantry, armor, air power, and artillery.[8]

Completed experience reports were employed in the Wehrmacht's propaganda effort. According to Brigadier General Hasso von Wedel, the officer in command of the Wehrmacht Propaganda Office, a section of Armed Forces High Command, German troops' letters were used in a number of publications to raise public enthusiasm for the war effort. These reports were also important, so Wedel claimed, for maintaining the morale of combat troops by emphasizing the fighting prowess of German units and individual soldiers.[9] In spite of their later use as propaganda, however, there are several reasons why *Erlebnisberichte* written in October and November 1939 can be considered authentic expressions of the views held by many German troops. For one thing, contributors were not informed that their reports would be used in the Reich's propaganda efforts. The authors also never received more than the most general instructions on what information these reports should or should not contain. Then, too, multiple drafts of some *Erlebnisberichte* exist, and many of these contain editorial notations that can be analyzed. The mundane nature of these notes makes it quite clear that military editors were more concerned with the readability of the reports than with their content.[10]

In all, nearly 400 experience reports were examined for this book, with the majority of these written by men from the 1st, 2d, and 3d Mountain Divisions, also known as *Gebirgsjägerdivisionen*. Among the elite formations of the German army in 1939, these three divisions were composed of Austrians and ethnic Germans from the Sudetenland as well as Germans from Bavaria, Württemberg, and Baden, all areas known for their mountainous terrain. During the invasion of Poland, the mountain divisions fought as part of the XVIII Corps in the hills of southern Poland on the far right flank of General Wilhelm List's Fourteenth Army.[11] The content of these *Erlebnisberichte* will be examined alongside that of German soldiers' letters and diaries. These latter, contemporaneous documents provide a standard by which to compare the content of *Erlebnisberichte* that were written after the invasion. It should be stressed in this regard that unlike letters and diaries, many of which survived the war purely by chance, experience reports were written by a self-selected group of German military personnel. Because these men consciously chose to record their experiences, the resulting reports must be considered representative of the attitudes of only a segment of the German military personnel who participated in the Polish campaign.

By and large, the writings of many German troops reflect a tendency to view the conflict with Poland in terms similar to those expressed by Hitler and other Nazi leaders. According to Hitler, the Reich was forced into war by Poland's reluctance to negotiate on pressing territorial questions, such as the diplomatic status of Danzig and extraterritorial transportation routes through the Polish Corridor. Yet Hitler also rationalized the attack as a German response to atrocities that Poles were committing against Poland's sizable ethnic German minority. All that Hitler required once German military preparations were complete at the end of August was an incident to precipitate hostilities. This requirement was met on 31 August 1939 when reports arrived that Polish troops had allegedly attacked a German radio transmitter at Gleiwitz.[12] Several hours later, Hitler made the following radio address to German troops just prior to their advance over the border:

To the Armed Forces!
The Polish State has rebuffed my attempts to negotiate peaceful, neighborly relations; it has instead resorted to arms. Germans in Poland are being persecuted with bloody terror and driven from home and farmstead. A list of border violations unbearable for a great power proves that the Poles are not willing to observe the borders of the German Reich [and] I have been left with no other choice than to use force against force. The German armed forces will lead the fight for the honor and rights to live of Germans who reside outside of the Reich *[Lebensrechte des wiederauserstanden deutschen Volkes]*. I expect that in memory of the great, eternal military tradition of Germany, every soldier will perform his duty to the last. Always remain aware in every circumstance that you are representatives of Greater National Socialist Germany! Long live our people and our Reich![13]

Some of the troops could scarcely contain their joy upon hearing of the impending German assault. According to the diary entry of Lieutenant

Kleeberg, the communications officer for the 94th Infantry Regiment, as reprinted in his experience report hours before the "Polish" attack on Glei-witz, he received word that "tomorrow at 4:45 A.M. the attack on Poland begins. Finally, the long wait comes to an end. Tomorrow the theories of our soldierly trade will be put into practice, bloody practice. . . . tomorrow it at last goes off. Poland has not accepted the Führer's proposals for a peaceful settlement to the dispute."[14] Kleeberg's sentiments are echoed in the experience report of Sergeant Schade, an engineer with the 11th Engi-neer Battalion, who wrote: "It is a wonderfully sunny day dawning, the first of September 1939. The First Lieutenant read the Führer's proclama-tion to us. Now it is certain, with weapons in hand and by order of the Führer, we will protect our rights and the disgrace [*Schmach*] of Versailles will be atoned for in battle."[15]

Private First Class Mathias Strehn, an Austrian cavalryman with the 2d Mountain Division, agreed with Schade and Kleeberg that the time had fi-nally come to remove the stain of Versailles. Recalling that he and his com-rades received their mobilization orders with "joyful pride" *(freudigem Stolz)*, Strehn expressed satisfaction that he and others from the *Ostmark* (the Nazi term for post-*Anschluss* Austria) could finally serve their father-land. As he noted, "We wanted to prove that it was worthwhile for us to have been brought home into the Reich."[16] Strehn added his conviction that "the peace of Versailles forcefully ripped from us this land [in Poland] that had been ours for decades. Now we Germans stand at its doors with the firm will to take back what could not be peacefully secured."[17] Private Willi Romer of the 136th Mountain Rifle Regiment shared Strehn's pride in being called to armed service for the fatherland. Romer remembered the mood of his comrades when they received the order in Innsbruck to move out around midday on 29 August: "We were proud of that fact that we were the first company to hear the announcement. We were assembled on the city plaza and the commander led a triple cheer for Führer and father-land. We then marched to the train station."[18]

Many soldiers accepted Hitler's explanation that Poland had provoked Germany by violating its borders, necessitating that the Reich respond with force. Private Josef Heront, another member of the elite mountain infantry, declared: "It was clear to us from the beginning that the continued exis-tence of the Polish state would not be allowed if the Führer was forced to let German arms speak. The Poles should have learned from history that the German *Volk* is his sword to employ. Indeed, they [the Poles] are a de-luded people in decline, struck blind and deaf, and led by the British."[19] Contrary to the reality that it was Hitler who pushed Germany toward war,

Private W. B., serving with the 12th Company of the 98th Mountain Regiment, expressed his belief that "Poland is not ready to negotiate. . . . [it is] trying to make a greater nation of itself."[20] Incidentally, these sentiments expressed in postinvasion *Erlebnisberichte* were not too far removed from those also articulated in official Wehrmacht propaganda reports during the invasion itself. As Dr. Franz Pesendorfer concluded in one such report at the time, "Now every one of us knows that this struggle, which was forced on us, is a fight for the rights of Germans, rights that the German people would not have been given peacefully."[21]

An important part of the defensive struggle being waged on Germany's eastern frontier was the perceived need to protect ethnic Germans in Poland from the depredations of their Polish enemies. This perception was due in large part to the anti-Polish propaganda effort initiated by Reich Propaganda Minister Joseph Goebbels in the weeks before Germany's attack. Specifically, Goebbels issued a directive to German newspaper editors on 11 August 1939 ordering that "as of now, the first page should contain news and comments on Polish offenses against *Volksdeutsche* and all kinds of incidents showing the Poles' hatred of everything that is German."[22] German newspapers accordingly ran numerous stories on the murder of *Volksdeutsche* and the destruction of their farms and communities by the Poles. Hitler then reinforced this interpretation of events by mentioning during his radio address on 1 September the "bloody terror" being endured by ethnic Germans. There was some truth to the rumors that Polish police and soldiers were collecting and marching ethnic Germans to internment camps deep in the interior of Poland. In an environment of heightened tension and ethnic conflict, some of these actions were even attended by killings and the destruction of property.[23] Polish police were indeed forced in some cases to take measures against German communities after they received intelligence information on the activities of Nazi sympathizers in largely German-populated towns along the German-Polish border. In several locations, the Poles arrested members of secret German resistance groups and seized stores of weapons and ammunition.[24] The presence of an insurrectionist, ethnic German fifth column behind Polish lines was simply an intolerable danger given the possibility of war with Germany.[25]

Given the rhetorical ammunition supplied by the Poles in this case, the effect of Nazi propaganda on the opinions of Germans troops is clear. Many German soldiers remarked in their experience reports that their ethnic comrades in Poland were in great danger. Lieutenant Alexander Lernet-Holenia noted on 30 August that "the Poles have mobilized [and] one hears of murder and bloody atrocities [*Ausschreitungen*] against the Germans in Bromberg

[Bydgoszcz]."[26] Similarly, Lieutenant Schumann of the 99th Mountain Rifle Regiment wrote, "Every day the newspapers bring us new reports about the cruel treatment of Germans in Poland, about the threats against Danzig, and the insane, shameless comments made about the Reich by Polish warmongers. None of us was surprised therefore when on 25 August at 6:00 P.M. we received orders to prepare for departure [to the Polish border]."[27] Private Wilhelm Bechholds of the 3d Battalion, 179th Infantry Regiment, also recalled listening to Hitler's speech on 1 September and thinking that

> a decisive hour in the existence of our people stood before us. Spellbound, our eyes lifted towards the loudspeaker [as Hitler's] fateful words climbed to a decisive fanaticism: ethnic Germans persecuted and murdered throughout Poland, Polish soldiers across the border in six different places. As of 5:45 A.M. we are shooting back . . . bombs will be repaid with bombs. The sense of our power and strength coursed hot through us. We shuddered with pride before the godlike greatness of this man, who in this hour renewed his historic oath to his people. He is the first soldier of the Reich! We know that the hour has come for us to fight for Germany.[28]

Many German military personnel seem to have considered the Polish-German conflict a struggle between competing ethnic groups, an outlook reinforced by stories of the persecution of ethnic Germans. This inclination facilitated greater overall acceptance of the regime's definition of the war in racial-biological terms. Where members of the German "race" faced danger, all Germans were responsible for protecting them. Polish actions against ethnic Germans were thus affronts to the entire German people that demanded retaliation. As Private Erich Müller with the 309th Infantry Regiment recalled after crossing into Poland:

> The company commander greeted our now rescued *Volksdeutsche* brothers and sisters. . . . with a single enthusiastic voice, our company gave Adolf Hitler, the liberator of the German race [*Volksstum*], a triple "Sieg Heil"! A little further on we saw fruitful land dotted with small farms and bordered by small copses of trees. All of this is German again and will remain German for eternity. These are the things for which we, Adolf Hitler's soldiers, trouble ourselves.[29]

Another soldier put his feelings about the liberation of ethnic Germans in similar, if even more ideologically tinged, terms:

[Our] joy flowed over when a boy on the sidewalk raised up a portrait of Adolf Hitler [to the passing troops], next to which was the first German flag [we had seen]. The *Volk* returns home to the *Volk*. The voice of the community drowns out all else. Where are those people who at one time wanted to put boundaries around this land? Where are those who hated and scoffed at the voice of the people *[Volksstimme]* and who thought they could bind the displaced communities of a people in the chains of Versailles? The people rent its chains asunder, because the people is nature and nature never allows itself to be bound and chained.[30]

For his part, Corporal Kurt Schmoll of the 309th Infantry Regiment recalled of Poland's western frontier regions, "It was an odd feeling to be in so-called 'foreign territory.' The landscape is the same and the people are Germans like us. Satisfaction grew in us that now these people could be brought back home just as our brothers in Austria and the Sudetenland [had returned]. We did not receive any joyful cheers, but one could see in the eyes of the people what they really felt."[31]

The writings of many Wehrmacht troops portrayed Hitler as the liberator of Germans everywhere. Private Wallner claimed that "the Führer leaves no German in a bind. It is certain to us that we need only be called to protect German blood and German culture *[Kulturboden]* against untrammeled Polish despotism."[32] And Corporal Bürkhardt heartily greeted Hitler's call to arms: "At last the day arrived when we were to embark [to the front]. We had all feared that we wouldn't be needed. However, we were all proud and happy to follow the call of our Führer, who called on us to free our oppressed racial comrades *[Volksgenossen]* in enemy territory."[33] Finally, some of the writings of German troops showed a keen awareness of the long conflict that had been raging on Germany's eastern frontier since 1918. A soldier with the 151st Infantry Regiment concluded, "East Prussia was especially threatened. Since the re-creation of a Polish state, a tough, bitter border struggle has been waged against the Polish lust for conquest *[Eroberungslust],* which did not abate even during the period of German-Polish understanding *[Verständigungspolitik]*."[34] The officer responsible for the unit war diary of the 13th Infantry Regiment put it more succinctly, stating it was obvious to everyone that "the Polish question had to be clarified."[35]

But on 3 September, the stakes for Germany became much higher than simply settling the Polish question, as Great Britain and France declared war on Germany because of its invasion of Poland. Following his initial surprise at this turn of events, Hitler delivered a speech to his armed forces fighting in Poland that laid blame for the war entirely at Britain's feet and appealed to German suspicions that their nation was surrounded by enemies:

> Soldiers of the Eastern Army!
> For months now England has pursued a policy of isolating Germany, [a policy] for which it was well known before the World War. It attempted this with the aim of making every European state and people serve its needs. Poland was chosen to play an important role in this front encircling Germany *[Einkreisungsfront]* once the Soviet Union decided to subordinate English interests to its own. The continuing persecution of Germans in Poland, which tried by every means to attack the free city of Danzig, forced me to take measures on our eastern front to secure the Reich. As the most important element of British policies of isolation and destruction *[Vernichtungspolitik]*, Poland must be forced to sue for peace.[36]

Fed censored news and Nazi propaganda and therefore unaware of the truth, many German troops accepted Hitler's interpretation of events leading to war with the Western Powers. First Lieutenant Hans Eichhorn, an artillery officer with the 179th Infantry Regiment, believed that England's "imperialistic plans" included inciting the Poles to act against Germany. As for the Poles, Lieutenant Eichhorn argued that the "insane leaders of Poland threatened Germany's eastern frontier and endangered the security of Danzig" by initiating conflicts with German patrols and making incursions over the German border.[37] The perceived injustice of English plans to use Poland against Germany also influenced the opinion of an unidentified trooper with the 15th Motorized Infantry Regiment, who after fighting in Poland for more than a week railed against England. Suffering Polish refugees, the man wrote,

> accuse you [Great Britain]. See your work England, and the work of your creatures. Marshal Smigly-Rydz, what have you done to these people? Now England is far away and while its last—hopefully last—servant here on the Continent slowly bleeds to death, it looks on with indifference. What do the people in England know? What do the so-called upper classes, whose irresponsibility brought on insane chauvinism rather than understanding, know of the sorrow that has been brought to the mindless, stupid, miserable existence of these people. You have awakened feelings of hellish hate against us in the souls of

this people. You alone are guilty for the atrocities that the population perpetrated against us. Pilsudski's heirs have been betrayed by his incompetent successors. He himself considered it the tragedy of his people that they could only be the servants or slaves of others, never a nation in themselves.[38]

Such an outlook allowed German troops to legitimize the Reich's attack on Poland by explaining Polish belligerence as a result of English policies. Therefore, Polish civilians were sometimes to be pitied for the terrible end to which their leaders had brought them. As "England's vassal" the Poles had allowed their army to be destroyed and their country ruined, according to Otto Eder, a rifleman with the 137th Mountain Rifle Regiment.[39] The war was not Germany's fault, Eder concluded, but he was convinced that destroying Poland would have a positive result by creating "new living-space for the German people."[40]

In contrast to 1914, though, when widespread joy had been expressed in Germany over the prospect of war, the German populace in 1939 was far more subdued than the troops when sending its sons off to fight. As soldier H. H. wrote to his family on 12 September, "I want to briefly describe to you what we have experienced since our departure from Rostock on 9 August. From early in the morning until into the afternoon, the population waited to share the departure of its soldiers. Cigarettes, fruit, and chocolate were thrown into the ship in bunches . . . yet everyone knew, although no one spoke about it, that this time our war aims were serious and that many of us would not be making the trip home."[41] For another soldier with the 59th Infantry Regiment, the transport of his unit to the front was also a somber public occasion, but one that nevertheless aroused excitement in the men:

> On 26 August 1939 the decision came. The 9th Company was assembled in the school [and] it was here that we received our weapons and equipment. On 28 August, at 11:30 in the evening, the company marched to the freight-train station and there was arranged by battalion. Only a few passers-by escorted the marching troops. When we ascertained that the train was taking us to the east, we were filled with great joy. Through the villages and cities, in which the population happily greeted us, we rolled towards the border.[42]

The varying reactions of the German population to the beginning of the war reflected to a certain extent the mood of the men themselves. To some, the occasion elicited joy and excitement, while to others it brought grim apprehension of the fighting to come. In his diary, Rifleman Ludwig Plawitzki, another member of the 59th Infantry Regiment, thanked the men and women of Berlin for their ovation as his unit's train passed through the city.[43] On the other hand, First Lieutenant Edgar Alker of the 138th Mountain Rifle Regiment, recalled, "No festive parade like in the year 1914 eased our separation from our mountain home. The lack of inspirational inscriptions on the train cars showed that there was no romanticism. . . . it went all too matter of factly with many conscious of the seriousness of our difficult task—and it is better that this was so."[44] Last, a man named Kübler from the 98th Mountain Rifle Regiment noted that the departure of his regiment to the east presented a "disciplined and soldierly picture. In Mittenwald and in Garmisch members of the Party and state [administration] appeared at the train station, along with large sections of the population."[45] Tellingly perhaps, Kübler observed that these farewells were subdued affairs.

Lingering memories of the carnage of the First World War undoubtedly had an impact on the public mood as war approached as well as on the outlook of the soldiers moving toward the German frontier and an inevitable conflict with Polish forces. But instead of mourning family members lost in the last war, German troops took pride in the service their fathers had rendered to the Fatherland and hoped they could meet the high standards set for them by their predecessors. Ernst Bruzek recalled his battalion commander reminding the men of the last war:

He commented in his speech about the seriousness of the situation and admonished us to show the same bravery and determination to fulfill our duty that our fathers in the great World War had demonstrated. Afterwards, our regimental band played the *Deutschlandlied* and Horst Wessel song. We were all filled with enthusiasm . . . and waited only for the moment when for the first time we could prove to Führer and Fatherland that we were ready to show in deed as well as in word that we were prepared to fight for the Führer's ideas.[46]

Captain Heinz Winter of the 309th Infantry Regiment echoed these sentiments as he remembered his unit's departure for the border:

Old soldiers' songs from the [First] World War rang out, and along with those the songs of the [Nazi] movement. Everyone spoke in sequence about the Führer, *Volk,* and fatherland. The surge of enthusi-

asm was not so great as in 1914. This stood too clearly in the eyes of
those [comrades] who had participated in the World War. In its place
was a restrained passion, a decisive preparedness to settle accounts
with every loud-mouthed nation that had for months thwarted the
prospect for peace in Europe.[47]

After entering Poland, the names of rivers and towns further reminded
German troops of war stories they had heard as children. To a mountain
unit trooper named Stachelhaus, the soldiers of the kaiser's armies were
shining examples of German manhood.[48] And while marching over the San
River in southern Poland, Lieutenant Faber of the 136th Mountain Rifle
Regiment mentioned to his men that

> [our] fathers had already fought here in 1915/16. A reservist broke the
> silence with words that touched us all deeply. [He said] "My father fell
> here on the San, I don't know where, perhaps here." When on the next
> day another man in the company found a large, rusted, German steel
> helmet, every reservist held it long in his hands looking at it in silence.
> It became very clear to all of us that this was sacred ground, sacred be-
> cause it had already drank the blood of a generation before us. A lit-
> tle farther on it also became clear to us that we had to offer a blood
> sacrifice. This happened sooner than we thought it would.[49]

Private Peter Infeld and his comrades with the 137th Mountain Rifle Regiment were also aware that "on this historic ground [we fought] for a new,
Greater Germany. Galicia is saturated with blood. Our fathers fought well
here. . . . they stopped the Russian 'steamroller' . . . but could not bring
final victory home because they were forced by other insidious methods to
stack their weapons."[50] Here was a taste of bitterness over the "stab in the
back" legend, a bitterness that motivated Private Josef Heront to write:
"We German soldiers and with us the entire German people will stand before history and again make good what our people lost in 1918. The young
Greater German Reich . . . will prove to the world that it is capable of and
is resolved to . . . defend the rights of its people to exist and secure its living space [Lebensraum] for all time."[51]

In this case, the enemies against which German troops were defending
their people's interests were the Poles. With the commencement of the invasion, Polish authorities began implementing prearranged plans to neutralize the threat posed by Nazi sympathizers among the ethnic German
population. According to Christian Jansen and Arno Weckbecker, Polish

authorities arrested and force-marched to the east 10,000–15,000 ethnic Germans in the first days of September.[52] Poles in the city of Bydgoszcz also killed hundreds of ethnic Germans after fighting erupted between Polish troops and ethnic German insurgents. And thirty-four *Volksdeutsche* were executed in the town of Torun for allegedly having flashed light signals to German pilots circling overhead.[53] German troops advancing into Poland were soon confronted with evidence of atrocities committed by Polish soldiers and police against ethnic Germans, evidence many German soldiers thought demonstrated the barbaric racial character of Poles. Upon entering Drohobycz in eastern Galicia, Corporal Siebenpfund of the 199th Infantry Regiment wrote, "Charred corpses were the first witnesses of the animal subhumanity *[tierisch Untermenschentum]* of the Poles."[54] And Corporal Franz Ortner of the 137th Mountain Rifle Regiment declared, "These inhuman *[entmenschten]* Poles who fall into our hands, these Poles who bestially murder prisoners of war, who bayonet the wounded [to death] . . . should they be used for even the lowest work? No! It is ten times better to shoot them, shoot them to the last Pole, or to put it better, to the last bullet."[55]

In their experience reports and letters, German soldiers commonly described the actions of Poles against German civilians in terms reserved for animals. Lieutenant S. recorded in his diary on 7 September that upon entering Aleksandrów [Łódzki], his comrades realized the terror in which ethnic Germans had been living for several days. They soon discovered "victims of the inhuman cruelty" practiced by the Poles toward the *Volksdeutsche* as revealed by the bodies of "bestially murdered women and children" in the streets.[56] And Private W. K. of the 2d Motorized Infantry Division noted, "The devastation of German farms in the [Polish] Corridor caused by the Poles is animal *[viehisch]*."[57] To many soldiers, these encounters not only confirmed Polish inferiority but also made German troops want to lash out in retaliation. As Private Müller of the 179th Infantry Regiment wrote, "For us service in the POW camp was a touchstone of our dominance [over the Poles] as these depraved, brutal faces, some of them with hate-filled eyes and expressions distorted with rage, added to the knowledge that many of these soldiers had mistreated Germans in bestial ways. It would have been better if we could have beaten these cultureless beasts. We kept our cool, though, and these prisoners . . . were treated more than properly."[58]

The atrocities committed by Poles against ethnic Germans disgusted German troops, but their contempt paled in comparison to the disdain with which German military personnel viewed civilians who joined in the fighting. To men like Sergeant Wilhelm Hössmer of the 136th Mountain Rifle

Regiment, attacks on German columns by civilians were a characteristic "habit of the Polish mob *[ein Hauptgewohnheit des polnischen Gesindels]*," while to Corporal Herbert Franke, irregular warfare was a type of fighting specific to people like the Poles.[59] The involvement of civilians in combat confirmed to German troops the correctness of what their officers had told them at the start of the campaign. Poles were not to be trusted, the battalion commander of Lieutenant S. had warned on 30 August. Instead, the men should "see in every Polish citizen a fanatical enemy who will fight against you with every means possible!"[60]

The German suspicion of Polish civilians deepened as the fighting wore on, aided by rumors like that of a squad of SS men who were given shelter by sisters with the Red Cross and then fallen upon in the night by civilians who tore them to pieces.[61] Although outrageous, many rumors reflected the insecurity felt by Wehrmacht personnel who indeed came under attack by civilians. For example, on 29 September, two days after the surrender of Warsaw, the 41st Infantry Regiment, part of the 10th Infantry Division, reported that upon entering the Warsaw suburb of Mokotów, it became engaged in a fierce street battle "in which the entire population [including women] participated."[62] The 580th Field Police Section similarly reported to Army Group South on 16 September that several days before in an unidentified town a Jew had shot and wounded a sergeant in the foot. "The shot," the report continued, "was the signal for gunfire to start from different Jewish houses on the town market and also from the church. Seven people were shot during defensive action taken by the *Feldgendarmerie*."[63]

The rage of German soldiers subjected to such assaults is reflected in their experience reports. First Lieutenant Artmann railed at Polish prisoners about "your kind of warfare, you Polacks who first cower on rooftops and in hedges and then shoot us in the back. Then when we respond in earnest, you flee [and] set your houses on fire, leaving the people to their misery."[64] Similarly, Private Wilhelm Jahoda of the 82d Mountain Engineer Battalion wrote of the Polish "lust for murder," while Private Karl Patterer of the 111th Mountain Artillery Regiment noted, "Here and there we come upon fallen Poles [on whose] distorted faces one can still read the hate for Germans."[65] To some German troops it seemed that even in death the Poles were their mortal enemies. Civilian resistance to advancing German forces was particularly severe in the provinces of Poznań and East Upper Silesia and in the Polish Corridor. In addition to making Wehrmacht personnel nervous about being in the Polish countryside, resistance activity embittered German troops toward the majority of the population who did not participate in the fighting. Despite a frequent lack of direct evidence that

Polish civilians had fired on them, German soldiers assumed more often than not that all Poles were treacherous and underhanded. This tendency to presume that all Poles were cut from the same cloth pervades the language of German military personnel who committed their impressions to paper. To many soldiers, civilians were irrational fanatics who even razed their own homes with the approach of German units.[66]

Important in this context was the use of terms describing civilians that betrayed the ideological tint of German thinking. Much like the terminology used by SS and police personnel, German troops conducted sweeps of towns and forests in search of so-called "suspicious elements" *(verdächtigen Elemente)*, and as observers they noted how the police sorted "unpleasant elements" *(unliebsame Elemente)* from columns of Polish refugees.[67] According to Private Wilhelm Jahoda, one only seldom saw the inhabitants of villages, but those who did appear "made a frightening impression, with their unmistakably vengeful, brutal features."[68] These people, so different from Germans in the eyes of Wehrmacht personnel, were alternately described as "insidious" *(heimtückisch)*, "crafty" *(hinterlistig)*, and "despicable" *(niederträchtig)*.[69] German soldiers even declared friendly and nonthreatening Polish civilians to be "unbelievably decrepit and degenerate," their ranks filled with "many idiots, almost all of them hateful and strongly Catholic."[70] Some men, like Private Potesegger of the 137th Mountain Rifle Regiment, could not even bring themselves to recognize that Poles were human beings. Potesegger insisted instead that Poles were "a herd of living things [belonging to] the genus 'human.'"[71]

In the eyes of many German military personnel, behavior perceived as criminal was to be expected from a people whose homes, towns, and villages showed a striking level of decrepitude when compared to the standard of life in even the poorest sections of Germany. As Hans Oberheuer, an Austrian member of the 13th Company, 137th Mountain Rifle Regiment, noted regarding the involvement of civilians in fighting German soldiers: "I do not describe this type of fighting as cowardice, . . . [these] primitives prefer to die with the loss of their wretched hovels. In itself this behavior is not unique . . . but is rather characteristic of primitive peoples. We find it not only in the colonial wars [fought] in the so-called 'wild' but we also encountered it in the occupation of Bosnia [in the last war]. This is how it can be explained that the civilian population in the cities does not offer such resistance!"[72] The interpretation of Polish civilian behavior toward German troops as primitive was central to the overall German conception of the Poles as belonging to a lower cultural level. Captain Koerner of the 179th Infantry Regiment defined what he saw as "Polish non-culture" *(polnischer*

Unkultur), writing, "What we only fleetingly saw while on the march was neither civilization nor culture, but authentic Polish decay *(echt polnische Wirtschaft)*."[73] In a letter home on 8 September, Corporal K. A., a soldier with the Third Army fighting north of Warsaw, likewise associated the indescribably dilapidated condition of the roads and houses in Poland with the condition of the inhabitants. Describing the houses as "filthy, decrepit, and basically unreliable," K. A. concluded, "the population [is] exactly the same."[74]

Some German troops' comments on what they saw betrayed the close connection they had learned to make between the outward appearance of buildings and the racial character of the local population. Consider for instance a statement made by Corporal Franz Anderl, an Austrian and member of the Wehrmacht's elite mountain troops, who after searching a filthy hovel recalled the admonition of one of his former teachers that "people *[Personen]* and races *[Völker]* show their character in their living quarters."[75] Believing that his instructor had been proved correct, Anderl went on to claim that "the outer appearance of a people is the mirror of what lies on the inside. . . . one not only sees the difference between people in Polish and German houses, one also sees the difference between races" *(Unterschied zwischen den Völkern)*.[76] These contrasts between Poles and Germans were obvious to men like Corporal Hermann Ritter, who described Polish homes as "stinking dens" *(stinkigen Wohnlöcher)*.[77]

Such observations were generally similar in content to those made by German soldiers who fought in the east during the First World War, although there were differences in the type of expressions used. Klaus Latzel's detailed analysis of German soldiers' letters from the two world wars yields the conclusion that the terminology used by German soldiers in 1939 differed significantly from the language employed by their predecessors. The most striking dissimilarity in the writings was the incorporation of many of the stereotypes and the racism that became prevalent in Germany between the wars.[78] German soldiers' expressions of disdain for both Poles and their homes were indeed peppered with references to the biological racism common to discourse in Nazified German society. The writings of German military personnel who fought in Poland clearly conflated older notions about Polish culture and newer, racially oriented conceptions of Eastern Europe, thus demonstrating the fluid nature of the biological racism promoted by Nazism. As a central aspect of National Socialist ideology, the racist outlook fit well with other, earlier trends in German thought, and the two served as mutually reinforcing elements of a German conception of "the East" as a strange, alien place.

This notion of the east manifested itself in the writings of German troops primarily as a change in the way the men perceived their physical surroundings. Like their predecessors in World War I, many Wehrmacht soldiers argued that only German communities in Poland showed evidence of having culture.[79] As Sergeant Erich Hildebrand wrote, "After a round-trip march of some 500 kilometers [roughly 300 miles] through this Polish area, we can conclude with certainty that if there is culture here, it arises from Germans and [only] Germans are its representatives. Where the Polish element alone is present, everything is decrepit, dirty, and miserable."[80] Similarly, Lieutenant Kleeberg of the 94th Infantry Regiment confided to his diary on 8 September, "Early in the morning we marched from Ostrowite *[sic]* and reached Rypin, a place with a small German colony. Otherwise it was dirty *[dreckig]*, greasy *[speckig]*, and partially inhabited by Jews. When we crossed the former German-Russian frontier, the landscape—flat, monotonous, with poor soil—and the civilization—cottages with straw roofs, collapsing, and primitively constructed—changed. . . . the disgusting Polish decay *[die dreckige polnische Wirtschaft]* became even more Polish."[81] Similarly, to Lieutenant Alexander Lernet-Holenia of the 10th Mounted Rifle Regiment, writing on 12 September, "the endlessness of the eastern landscape impresses itself into our consciousness. This gigantic landscape stretches thousands of kilometers eastwards into the steppes of Asia."[82]

Corporal Kurt Schmoll of the 309th Infantry Regiment also considered the former German-Russian border of 1914 a reference point for the differences between the East and West. Following his unit's crossing of the frontier, Schmoll claimed, "The decades have not blurred [the differences]. What houses the people have here! The misery is inexpressible. German farmers live as always in between the Poles, their huts immediately recognizable by the autumn flower gardens in front. Once again the question comes to mind: 'what would the poorest farmer at home say about this Polish decay?' What does development *[Aufbau]* in the German sense mean here?"[83] A fellow soldier in the 309th Infantry, Sergeant Erich Hildebrand, shared Schmoll's observations: "The farther east we push, the weaker the German element we encounter becomes. Everyday after a daily march of some thirty kilometers the filth of the living conditions [increases] and the housing of the population becomes poorer. . . . the meanest [location] in this context was Grzybow, a small, Polish nest not far from the Vistula [River] that one can hardly describe as a village."[84] Given this outlook, *Volksdeutsche* villages that German troops encountered were understandably described as "oases" of culture in a desert of Polish filth and were indicative of the cultural struggle being waged in this territory between

Germans and Slavs.[85] Such was the conviction expressed by Corporal Siebenpfund of the 199th Infantry Regiment, who wrote that German operations in the East were a contemporary manifestation of "the eternal struggle of the German spirit and German culture in and around the areas east of the Reich."[86]

A defining element of the German concept of the east was the presence of Jews, whose total number of 3.35 million constituted over 10 percent of Poland's prewar population.[87] As might be expected, the reactions of German military personnel to the Polish Jews they encountered were uniformly negative, differing only in intensity from mild disgust to violent dislike. The expression of such sentiments was very common, revealing the detrimental impact that anti-Jewish propaganda had on many Germans in the years and decades before the war.[88] Without exception, Jews were described in the writings of German soldiers as a destructive influence in Poland, and their very presence was discomforting to troops who passed them on the street and saw them in the countryside. As Lieutenant H. A. of the 138th Mountain Rifle Regiment entrusted to his diary while waiting on the Slovak-Polish border for the invasion to begin, his commander "advised everyone to be careful and to keep their pistols close at hand because the place was full of Jews, Czechs, and Poles."[89] Moreover, to some soldiers it was the Jews and not the Poles or even the English and French who had actually precipitated the war. Private H. B. expressed to his relatives the hope that the French and English would see fit to avoid dying for the Jews of English high finance.[90] Corporal K. S. echoed this sentiment, arguing in a letter home that "Jews and war profiteers" financed efforts to incite a lust for war in the people of Europe.[91] And Private Potesegger believed the time had arrived for the "National Socialist people's army . . . to march against 'Juda' the world-enemy."[92]

Many German soldiers claimed that the corrupting influence of Jews caused Poland's disorderly economic state *(polnische Wirtschaft)*. Stationed in the city of Włocławek two weeks after the end of the campaign, Corporal A. K. wrote home on 12 October:

> We have become very familiar here with the meaning of "Polish decay." We are here in a city of some 70,000 inhabitants, 20,000 of which are Jews. The Jews here are all marked by a yellow triangle on their backs and they are forbidden to use the sidewalks. The city is beautiful, but somewhat seedy [and] . . . there are sections so filthy that one can almost not go there. It is never so dirty back at home, even if it had rained for four weeks. The population here is also en-

tirely different and all have treacherousness about them. It is high time
a change was made.[93]

Private Müller of the 179th Infantry Regiment agreed, describing the town
of Rudki in southern Poland as "a Jewish city . . . dirty and contaminated
[verpestet] with the well-known smell of Jews" that characterized "Polish,
or better put, Jewish decay."[94] Filth and decrepitude were to be expected,
of course, given that in the eyes of some German soldiers, Galicia and eastern Poland were at once the wellspring *(Urheimat)* of so-called world Jewry
and a "Jewish paradise."[95]

In his characterization of the town of Dukla, Captain Koerner similarly
expressed the conviction that the Jews were a destructive force. Located
near Krosno, in southeastern Poland, Dukla counted 1,800 Jews among its
2,000 residents. After speaking with a few of the Poles, using his limited
knowledge of the language, Koerner concluded that Jews there exercised an
"unhealthy influence" *(unheilvollen Einfluss des Judentums)* through their
economic exploitation of the non-Jewish population. This control explained
to Koerner the crushing poverty of Polish farmers, which kept them in a cultural position some 200 years behind the poorest farmer in Germany.[96] An
anonymous soldier fighting in southern Poland agreed with Koerner's assessment, writing that the foul air and taste left in one's mouth by the dust
in Galicia meant that "Jews ruled the land." Altogether, he continued,

> the villages through which we pass are filled with stained, black caf-
> tans. We see faces whose expressions are all the same and look into
> eyes one cannot describe. Cowardice *[die Feigheit]* is at home here.
> These people so slavishly follow to the commercial spirit *[Händ-
> lergeist]* that they will creep in the dust for the smallest profit. Pride is
> buried in this land; honor and beauty are strange notions. . . . is it any
> wonder that a yearning strengthens in and overpowers us? Yearning
> for German land, German cities, German villages, German people, and
> German orderliness. [One] must first travel through Galicia to under-
> stand the correctness of the proud words: "Germany, Germany above
> all." [One] must first see a Galician market or a ghetto to be thankful
> for Germany.[97]

Private First Class Hans Peinitisch also spoke for a good number of his
comrades when upon reaching the town of Nowy Sącz he wrote: "Here
was the same picture, the people depraved, the streets and houses filthy.
Should anyone wonder why when all one encounters on the corners and

alleys are Jews? Here is the clearest expression of the cultural gulf between East and West."[98]

German troops typically described Polish Jews in terms clearly drawn from Nazi propaganda rags like Julius Streicher's *Der Stürmer* and the official Nazi Party newspaper, the *Völkischer Beobachter,* that purveyed stereotyped images of *Ostjuden.* Hence, Grenadier Dreyer of the 48th Infantry Regiment wrote, "We met caftan-wearers [Jews] that we had only earlier seen pictured in *Der Stürmer.*"[99] And after relating how often the Jews allegedly cheated Poles, Private Potesegger declared, "Oh you poor Poles, how stupid you are, come and read *Der Stürmer* and see the proper remedy" for this problem.[100] Meanwhile, to Lieutenant Kleeberg, seeing Jews in Racięż step aside for a German patrol was like watching "apes make way," and to Private Mathias Strehn, the presence of Jews meant encountering "Jewish stench and beastliness."[101]

Wehrmacht troops taught to fear and hate Jews also instinctively assumed that all Jews were armed enemies, waiting only for the opportunity to murder Germans who let down their guard, as evidenced by the comment of Dr. Brachetka, a veterinarian with the 140th Mountain Rifle Regiment, who claimed that, upon entering Przemyśl, "the Jews shot treacherously [at us] from their houses."[102] Hans Geissler, a rifleman with the 99th Mountain Rifle Regiment, similarly stated that after he was captured by the Poles and led with other prisoners to the city of Lwów, "the civilian population, Jews and children, all armed, worked me over with the butts of weapons."[103] The widespread fear of Polish Jews caused some men, like Private First Class J. E., to immediately reach for their weapons upon seeing the "unkempt figures" in Polish towns.[104] To others, however, meeting Jews was an opportunity to humiliate them by cutting their beards and administering beatings. It was also common for soldiers to force Jews to do manual labor or to look on as the SS assembled Jews for work. This was a sight Private Müller savored, as "the Jews [of Rudki] received an actual tool for the first time and learned to use it."[105]

When faced with large numbers of *Ostjuden,* some of the men also expressed support for implementing a long-term policy against them. Private Herbert Nagl, stationed in Przemyśl on the San River, along the demarcation line between Soviet- and German-occupied Poland, energetically followed his orders not to allow Jews or Poles into German territory. After establishing that the ethnic identity of an individual was German, he or she was let across. Poles, however, were summarily turned away, and upon seeing Jews who were clearly identifiable, the only appropriate reply, Nagl wrote, was "Turn around—direction, Russia!"[106] And as Private Grömmer of the 111th Mountain Artillery Regiment put it,

German troops in Kielce amuse themselves by cutting the hair of a Jewish man, September 1939. The tremendous number of photographs showing the public humiliation of Jewish men suggests that the cutting of hair and beards, signifying emasculation and disdain for the "dirty Jew," was common practice among Germans who encountered Jews in Poland and elsewhere in "the East." The caption on the reverse of the original photograph reads: "The locks fall. Jewish rascals at the mobile barber shop." Note the gloves worn by the man cutting the hair, indicating his distaste for the Jew he had to touch. (Dr. Marvin Chadab; courtesy of the U.S. Holocaust Memorial Museum, Photo Reference Collection: ws 38097)

[In Poland] one can see these beasts [Jews] in human form. In their beards and caftans, with their devilish features, they make a dreadful impression on us. Anyone who was not a radical opponent of the Jews must become one here. In comparison to the Polish caftan-Jews, our own Jewish bloodsuckers [in Germany] are lambs. No wonder that after [only] twenty years the Polish State has become victim to these parasites. . . . we recognize here the need for a radical solution to the Jewish question.[107]

In general, the men who bothered to mention Poles and Jews in their letters, diaries, and experience reports considered themselves surrounded by nefarious enemies whose inherent racial character dictated that they fire at German columns and murder soldiers as they slept. The gunfire that Wehrmacht units sometimes took from houses and farms, as well as rumors about civilians mutilating wounded soldiers, only confirmed these suspicions. Other factors, like the physical appearance of Poles and Jews and the murder of ethnic German civilians in the first days of the war, further reinforced the impression among German troops that the conflict with Poland was indeed being fought against their bitter racial enemies. The only legitimate response to such enemies was violence. In the opinion of Private W. K., "We have become convinced that our kindness [towards the Poles] is too great," and as Corporal Richard Bremer put it regarding civilian resistance, "We are through with Polish nastiness [*Gemeinheit*]. The Poles will pay the bill, not us."[108]

A certain amount of German bitterness about the involvement of civilians in combat was to be expected and was perhaps even justifiable. The typical response to being fired on by snipers and guerrillas was to summarily destroy the building, or even the entire community, from which the shots had come. Yet as events during the Polish campaign demonstrated, the policy of reprisal could rapidly escalate out of control because it was often impossible to firmly establish if civilians had indeed fired on German troops. Most of the time, however, it did not matter if the assailant could be identified, because all civilians in the area were automatically considered guilty. Take, for example, an incident of revenge disguised as official reprisal policy that Lieutenant H. A. described in his diary. On 2 September, three of his men were murdered in their sleep, their throats cut during the night. In the eyes of the lieutenant, this experience revealed "the true face of the fleeing Polacks." Thus incensed by the attack, he and his men went to the nearest town on 3 September, gathered all of the men they could find, led them a short distance away, and executed them. The entire

German soldiers and civilians (likely ethnic Germans) look on as a Jewish man is forced to cut the beard of another Jewish man, September 1939. (Institute of National Remembrance, Commission for the Prosecution of Crimes against the Polish Nation; courtesy of the U.S. Holocaust Memorial Museum, Photo Reference Collection: WS 50978)

village was then razed to the ground, with Lieutenant H. A. adding afterward, "I had to remain very cautious that my people did not lynch on the spot every person they met who had a straight-razor [in his possession]."[109]

Without doubt, revenge played a part in some German reprisals against Polish and Jewish civilians. In this way, the ill-considered act of an individual civilian could bring down the wrath of an entire German unit on a community, inevitably leading to its devastation. Similarly, individual Polish soldiers or small squads of Polish troops detached from their units, who continued to fight behind German lines, could incite retaliatory acts against civilians. The fact that reprisals were fully sanctioned and in many cases were encouraged by commanding officers did nothing to help control the situation. As the orders of one regimental officer stated, "Be merciless against any irregular" *(Freischärler).*[110] Instructions like these allowed German troops the latitude to take matters into their own hands, which resulted in the razing of villages and shooting of civilians all over Poland.[111] The widespread occurrence of such behavior eventually led to complaints by some senior officers that their men were willfully destroying villages, even those inhabited by ethnic Germans.[112] As in the case described earlier by Lieutenant S., his comrades chose to be ruthless toward civilians and ignore their regimental commander's additional instructions to "be humane towards the non-combatant civilian population, above all women and children, and protect their possessions!"[113]

Anger over the loss of comrades and the involvement of civilians in combat clearly provoked much of the retaliatory action by German troops during the Polish campaign. However, many of the sentiments expressed in the correspondence, diaries, and experience reports examined above indicate that the brutal behavior of Wehrmacht personnel was also informed by images and stereotypes of Poles and Jews to which German soldiers were exposed before the war. A significant portion of the statements that German soldiers made about Poles and Jews in September 1939 closely resembles what Omer Bartov describes as the "striking inversion of reality" expressed by German troops fighting in the Soviet Union two years later.[114] Similar to that campaign in which the physical conditions were far more unforgiving, the stakes much higher, and the communist enemy more insidious, German soldiers in Poland attributed their own brutality to the inhuman nature of their enemy. In the minds of many German soldiers, Poles and Jews were not people, but beings whose behavior and appearance resembled that of beasts. The slaughter of ethnic Germans and the involvement of civilians in combat were clear evidence of the lower racial status of Poles and Jews. Of necessity, such an inhuman enemy had to be treated in an equally inhumane manner.

The diary entry of officer R. J. K., who served with the 101st Infantry Regiment as the regimental doctor, should be considered in this context. Upon reaching the town of Solec, the men of the 101st Infantry "arrested thirty Jews as hostages and placed them in a cellar near the church. One Jew was shot trying to flee, while a second escaped. Whenever one opened the cellar door, the Jews attempted to run. As a result they were driven back with hand grenades—a smoky knuckling down *[ein rauches Zupacken]*! However, there must be calm, in one way or another *[Aber es musste Ruhe werden, so oder so]*."[115] This man's callous disregard for the lives of the Jews of Solec mirrored many of the statements described in detail above. Because Germans considered the Jews' behavior and nature insidious, they were killed with hand grenades; in effect, the doctor claimed, his comrades had no choice.

To another soldier from the 15th Motorized Infantry Regiment, it was "the Polacks [with their] nasty, beastly gangs" *(ihren gemeinen viehischen Banden)* who did not know how to fight honorably.[116] They were the ones who treacherously attacked passing German columns, forcing soldiers to respond in kind. It was not the responsibility of German troops to exercise restraint when faced with enemies who were "fanatics" and "brutes."[117] The same could be said of Polish soldiers who fought "in violation of human rights," according to Lieutenant Alfred Detig, by shedding their uniforms and continuing to attack German units in civilian clothing. His comrades, Detig continued, thought it necessary to "act against this grave violation of human rights by [employing] the severest measures."[118] Hence, any Polish man found with a military pass, close-cropped hair, good quality boots, or even standard issue military-style underwear was immediately executed under suspicion of being an irregular.

These last examples and the numerous others described in the letters and experience reports above suggest that the behavior of many German troops in Poland was informed by a combination of influences that gave it a particularly destructive character. Young Wehrmacht personnel brought up in the 1920s and 1930s absorbed widely held sentiments that vilified and dehumanized Poles. Portrayed in schools, youth groups, popular politics, and by right-wing demagogues as culturally and racially inferior to Germans, Poles were seen by many Germans as barbaric enemies with aggressive and treacherous dispositions. By 1939, Germans had been told for twenty years that these were central elements of the Polish character. The impact of this indoctrination was also evident in the opinions of Germans who were not Wehrmacht soldiers. For example, in his diary of his days in Berlin during the Polish campaign, American foreign correspondent William L. Shirer recounted a discussion he had with his maid regarding the war. After she inquired why the French had declared war on Germany, Shirer asked the woman in return, "Why do you make war on the Poles?" A moment later she replied, "But the French, they're human beings." To which Shirer, now impatient with the woman, replied, "But the Poles, maybe they're human beings [too]."[119]

Although hate for Poles antedated the rise to power of National Socialism in Germany, after 1933 anti-Polish chauvinism was incorporated by the Nazis into overall instruction and propaganda about the supposed racial structure of reality. Ideologues from the NSDAP instructed teachers of all subjects to describe the world in terms of "ethnic types" and racial-biological classifications.[120] The introduction of "scientific" racism into all aspects of German life seems to have had an effect on the way in which a great many Germans conceived of their world. Persons defined by National Socialism as presenting a danger to the German *Volk*, either through their "asocial" behavior or hereditary deficiencies, were to be removed from society, while other people characterized as dire threats to Germany, in particular Jews and "racially inferior" Slavs, were to be isolated and eventually eradicated.

Without a competing message in German society powerful enough to contradict the institutionalized racism of the Nazi regime, ordinary Germans could not avoid being influenced to at least some extent by the propaganda. The way in which National Socialism focused anti-Polish sentiment and distorted reality is evident in samples from the writings of German soldiers that have been examined above. Wehrmacht troops marching into Poland came face to face with what they were told would be the reality of fighting against Poles and Jews. Since the end of the First World War, Poles had been characterized as ethnically inferior brutes engaged in a long-running conflict with Germans in the east. In like fashion, anti-Semites for decades had portrayed Jews as the mortal enemies of Germans, intent on Germany's ruin and willing to do harm to the German people in any way possible.

The stereotypes and images of reality in "the East" channeled and distorted the rage of German soldiers who were attacked by civilians and confronted with evidence of atrocities committed against their ethnic German comrades. German soldiers like the ones who submitted the experience reports above were thus prone to indiscriminately destroy entire Polish and Jewish communities and to slaughter civilians regardless of whether or not they were actually party to the attack. As these troops had learned before the war, the lives of Poles and Jews were of unequal value to the lives of Germans, so destroying them was of no consequence. Thinking in this fashion opened the doors to collective reprisals and the killing of several people for the wounding of even one German soldier. In short, Omer Bartov's conclusions about the ideologically influenced outlook of German troops fighting in the Soviet Union also apply to many of the German military personnel who fought in Poland.[121] Accordingly, it was not the Germans who were responsible for the brutality with which they conducted themselves; it was the fault of their "sub-human" enemies. In comparison, widespread destructive behavior and its attendant ideological outlook were absent during the German invasion of France and the Low Countries in the spring of 1940, when the Wehrmacht faced enemies of supposedly higher racial quality than Poles and *Ostjuden*.[122] Taken together, evidence of German troops' brutal behavior and the statements of a number of these men in their experience reports and letters indicate the detrimental impact that a combination of anti-Polish chauvinism, scientific racism, and anti-Semitism had on the conduct of at least some Wehrmacht personnel during the war in Poland.

To what extent was exposure to National Socialism responsible for the behavior and attitudes of German troops during the war? Omer Bartov suggests that Nazism was decisive in hardening Wehrmacht personnel against their enemies in the occupied Soviet Union. In particular, he points to the prewar membership and training of German troops in Nazi institutions like the *Hitlerjugend*.[123] Evidence concerning the age of German soldiers who fought in Poland indicates, however, that a considerable number of these men were old enough to have been partially socialized before the Nazis came to power in 1933. For example, a survey of the personnel complement of the 10th Infantry Division carried out at the end of January 1939 reveals that the largest percentage of its soldiers were probably too old to have ever been members of the Hitler Youth. The age limit for belonging was eighteen, but the highest percentage of men in the three combat regiments of the 10th Infantry Division were born in the years 1916 and 1915, making them seventeen and eighteen years old in 1933 and twenty-three and twenty-four years old on the eve of the war in 1939.[124] Leaving aside officers, there were 2,198 men in the 20th Infantry Regiment, of which 1,072 (48 percent) were born in 1916 and 1915. In the 85th Infantry Regiment, 1,029 of 2,284 men (45 percent) were born in 1916 and 1915. And in the 41st Infantry Regiment, the cohort of older men born in 1916 and 1915 was even larger, meaning 1,770 of 3,251 men (54 percent) were too old to have belonged to the *Hitlerjugend*.[125]

As might be expected, combat officers in the 10th Infantry Division were of even higher average age than rank-and-file troops. The available statistics unfortunately are incomplete, making it possible to examine only the ages of men who had attained at least the rank of corporal by 1936 in two companies of the 41st Infantry Regiment. Of twenty-four noncommissioned officers (corporals and sergeants) in the 13th Company, five were born in 1909, four in 1911, two in 1912, three in 1913, two in 1914, and one in 1915.[126] The ages of twenty-four corporals and sergeants in the 14th Company showed a similar, if not greater, discrepancy. One man was born in 1904, one in 1905, two in 1908, one in 1909, one in 1910, two in 1911, three in 1912, one in 1913, two in 1914, and one in 1915 (this man was listed as a private first class).[127] Therefore, by the outbreak of the war in 1939, these noncommissioned officers born between 1904 and 1915 would have been twenty-four to thirty-five years old.

On the other hand, millions of German youth did pass through Nazi institutions like the *Hitlerjugend* and especially the *Reichsarbeitsdienst,* or Reich Labor Service, before entering the Wehrmacht. Statistics adequately demonstrate the extent to which Nazi organizations spread throughout

German society in the years before the outbreak of war in 1939. At the end of 1933, there were roughly 7.5 million boys in Germany between the ages of ten and thirteen. Of these, 2.3 million, representing roughly 30 percent, were in the *Hitlerjugend*.[128] By 1939, this situation had changed dramatically as the Hitler Youth extended its influence throughout the country: at the beginning of that year, 8.7 million of Germany's 8.8 million boys between the ages of ten and thirteen were members.[129]

These youths were exposed to a world of paramilitary exercises, including shooting, map reading, hiking, camping, and group sports, that intended to instill in them a sense of camaraderie, physical well-being, and preparation for military service. As the "spiritual school of German youth," the *Hitlerjugend* was a training institution that aimed to create a "fighter's bearing" in its members.[130] It is understandable, therefore, that Wehrmacht commanders took a keen interest in directing the paramilitary training of *Hitlerjugend* and established a system of liaison officers in regions where both divisional commands and camps were located.[131] These divisional commands arranged for liaison officers *(Verbindungsoffiziere)*, typically lieutenants or captains, to act as sponsors for local *Hitlerjugend* groups, called *Banne*.[132] Altogether, the goal of training directed by Wehrmacht officers was to promote soldierly bearing, willingness to take up arms, and readiness to sacrifice for the *Volk* and the fatherland.[133] In time, the aim was to develop these qualities in each member by the moment of his release from the organization at age eighteen.[134]

Members received thorough ideological instruction in addition to physical and military training. For those younger German soldiers who spent several years in the organization, this indoctrination frequently translated into what has been described as "an exhilarating and fanatical devotion, [as well as a] commitment to destroying the present and building the future . . . accompanied by a fascination with death [that] was at the very heart of the Nazi takeover of Germany's youth and future soldiers."[135] The result was thus a potentially destructive combination of blind loyalty to Adolf Hitler, complete, unthinking obedience to orders, and eventually a willingness to annihilate racial enemies in defense of the *Volk*. Yet only a small percentage of the soldiers enlisted in the 10th Infantry Division at the beginning of 1939 seem to have been the proper age to belong to *Hitlerjugend* for at least some of their teenage years. According to the division's count, of the 2,198 men in the 20th Infantry Regiment, 274 were born between 1919 and 1921, making them eighteen to twenty years old in 1939.[136] This 13 percent of the regiment's manpower would have been between twelve and fourteen years old in 1933 or from fourteen to sixteen years old by 1936 when the state increased pressure on German youth to join. Still smaller percentages can be found in the other two regiments of the 10th Infantry Division. In the 41st Infantry Regiment, 307 out of 3,251 men were born between 1919 and 1921, meaning only 9 percent could have belonged to the organization. And in the 85th Infantry Regiment, only 187 of 2,284 men, or just 8 percent, could have legitimately spent any time in *Hitlerjugend* by the outbreak of the war.[137]

These statistics do not rule out the possibility that in their late teenage years many of these men could have belonged to other Nazi organizations, such as the SA (storm troopers) or Reich Labor Service, which were also organized in military fashion and oriented toward training their members for military service.[138] In addition to the older men totaled above, there were other Wehrmacht personnel who may have not been members of the Hitler Youth but were nevertheless of the appropriate age to have joined other Nazi Party formations. Recruits falling into this category were born in 1918 and 1917, making them twenty-one and twenty-two years old in 1939. In the 20th Infantry Regiment, 480 out of 2,198 men (22 percent) were of this age.[139] Percentages in both the 41st and 85th Infantry Regiments were comparable, with 630 of 3,251 men (19 percent) in the former regiment and 517 of 2,284 (23 percent) in the latter.[140]

The German army does not seem to have kept statistics on the number of recruits it conscripted directly from Nazi Party organizations. Conan Fischer suggests in his study of the SA, however, that the influx of Nazi storm troopers into the armed services was considerable.[141] For example, in the year following Hitler's purge of the SA in 1934, 60,000 former SA men entered the Wehrmacht. With the reintroduction of conscription in March 1935, 20,000 more were drafted into the German Air Force reserve. And in the following October and November, the army drafted another 26,000 men into its ranks.[142] Similar figures are not available for *Hitlerjugend*. We can only assume, therefore, that troops who were of the appropriate age to have been members of the organization did indeed join because of state and societal pressure. The youngest of this smaller percentage of men would then have received at most four years of instruction from Nazi Party youth leaders and Wehrmacht liaison officers by September 1939, while others would have had at best two years in the Hitler Youth. Documentation on the background and ages of military personnel in the 10th Infantry Division, or any other units for that matter, is also missing for later in 1939. It is thus impossible to determine the exact influx and ages of men into the German army in the final months before the war with Poland.[143]

Concerning noncommissioned officers in the German army, evidence presented by Bernhard Kroener and Omer Bartov points to the conclusion that men from the ages of twenty-one to twenty-five years old who became frontline officers in the late 1930s were more inclined than older, higher ranking officers to accept the National Socialist worldview. As statistics from the 10th Infantry Division show, these men would have been too old on average to have spent much time in the Hitler Youth, although membership in the Nazi Party and any of its other organizations was certainly possible. The number of officers in the German army rose tremendously in the 1930s, from 3,858 on 1 May 1933 to 89,075 by 1 September 1939.[144] As Bartov suggests, the typical lower ranking German officer of the late 1930s was relatively well educated and generally came from the ranks of army reservists. These men were more inclined to have been members of the Nazi Party before joining the army and thus responsive to its ideology.[145] Bernhard Kroener similarly argues that "the educational mechanisms of the prewar period had an especially intense effect" on men born between the years 1914 and 1918, leading to the conclusion that even indirect exposure to Nazism had a discernible impact on their outlook.[146]

In essence, if the 10th Infantry Division can be considered representative of other frontline infantry divisions in the German army, combat troops in September 1939 were generally older men whose socialization was partially complete by the time Hitler came to power in 1933.[147] For the smaller percentage of men who were adolescents introduced to the Hitler Youth in its first years of existence, the organization was exciting and opened new possibilities.[148] Some of the evidence presented above, including the influx of SA men into the army, suggests that exposure to National Socialism, especially in the early years of the Third Reich, probably had an impact on the outlook of many German military personnel. Nevertheless, because of sizable holes in the evidence, it is difficult to establish a direct, causal connection between the formal indoctrination of German troops by Nazi institutions and their later destructive behavior in Poland.

This deficit leaves open the likelihood that many German soldiers passively absorbed Nazified racist sentiments and prejudice through repeated and constant exposure to them. Klaus Latzel reaches a similar conclusion in his investigation of the attitudes expressed by German soldiers in their writings. Although the letters and diaries of many German military personnel convey at least a "partial identification" with Nazi ideological precepts, Latzel points out that these expressions do not in themselves form a coherent ideological worldview, but rather an "agreement with National Socialism in a set of attitudes."[149] Given the available evidence, therefore, it seems that although Nazism may have had an impact on some of the attitudes expressed by Wehrmacht soldiers, other tendencies in German society during the 1920s and 1930s also affected the outlook and behavior of German soldiers who fought in Poland.

Among these other influences was a culture of anti-Polish attitudes that antedated Hitler's rise to power. Germans coming to adulthood in the decades before 1939 were raised in an atmosphere of extreme disdain for the Poles that had its origins in the eighteenth and nineteenth centuries.[150] For nearly 200 years, Prussian and imperial German regimes actively strove to "germanize" eastern regions of the country that were heavily populated by Poles. But these efforts at "civilizing the East" were largely unproductive, succeeding only "in raising the nationality conflict to fever pitch" by the beginning of the First World War.[151] The outbreak of war in 1914 further heightened tensions in the eastern territories. Polish underground organizations resisted German forces and planned for a popular revolt. The army's reaction to this resistance was swift and brutal, as leading Polish insurgents were arrested and the city of Kalisz was razed in retaliation for shots that were fired at German soldiers.[152]

Germany's defeat in 1918 significantly worsened the situation in the east. Inspired by the Allied victory, Poles seized the chance to finally throw off German rule by staging revolts in the provinces of Poznań and Upper Silesia. Bitter fighting continued in and around Poznań throughout December 1918 and into early 1919, only to be ended by the Trier Armistice signed in February 1919 by the new Socialist German government.[153] To those on the political right and in the army, the Trier Armistice was unacceptable because it prevented Germany from using military force against the Poles. For all practical purposes, the Poznań province was left in Polish hands, and the Weimar regime was forever linked to the loss of German territory in the east. This stigma was subsequently reinforced by the conclusion of the Versailles Peace Treaty in 1919, according to which Germany formally relinquished control over Danzig, Poznań, and West Prussia.[154]

Despite the settlement at Versailles, bloodshed along the new German-Polish frontier did not end until the middle of June 1921. One month earlier, a Polish insurrection in Upper Silesia led to considerable fighting between Polish insurgents, ethnic German self-defense *(Selbstschutz)* units, and volunteers with various right-wing *Freikorps* formations.[155] Following a bitterly contested plebiscite in the region, Poland then formally annexed parts of East Upper Silesia, solidifying the shape of the German-Polish frontier until September 1939. These events at the end of the First World War had a decisive impact on anti-Polish sentiment in Germany, which rose dramatically after 1918.[156] Throughout the 1920s, Germany and Poland waged a war of words and the Weimar government pursued a policy of economic warfare against the Poles. This increase in anti-Polish sentiment also proliferated in German popular consciousness. For the entire interwar period, the German press referred pejoratively to the Polish uprisings as "bandit warfare" *(Banditenkrieg)* and as part of a "war of conquest" *(Raubkrieg),* indicating that they were criminal wars of aggression rather than legitimate revolts by an oppressed people. These allegedly criminal acts severed communal ties in the east, led to economic depression, and created a so-called "bleeding frontier" in eastern Germany.[157]

Poles were similarly said to be responsible for perpetrating numerous atrocities against Germans, both during the revolts and in the years afterwards. These claims were expressed in vicious and derogatory terms describing Poles as "Asiatic" and "semi-Asians" who inhabited dens and resembled animals.[158] In books and newspaper articles alike, German writers portrayed Polish homes and communities as filthy and decrepit, bereft of culture, and barren of prosperity. These were all characteristics of so-called "Polish decay" *(polnische Wirtschaft),* a tenuous state of existence that indicated the alleged backwardness and poor economic management skills of the Poles. According to scientists and scholars like Albrecht Penck, a Berlin geography professor, Germans had created the only culture that existed in Poland. As evidence Penck cited differences in the physical appearance of "tidy" German villages and the "frequently wretched Polish villages" in the Poznań province.[159]

Prejudice and hostility toward Poles and Poland were also common in German schoolbooks at the time. From 1933 to 1936, the Polish Subcommission for the Examination of Foreign Schoolbooks, working under the auspices of the League of Nations, examined the content of nearly 200 German schoolbooks. The subcommission found that well into the Nazi period, German schools continued to use old books from the Weimar era.[160] Therefore, the information regarding Poland in many of these books was indicative of aspects of German education before 1933, as well as the more explicitly racist instruction implemented during the Nazi period. The subcommission discovered numerous errors in these books, most of which concerned faulty historical information. Even more insidious were textbook authors' frequent proposals that teachers encourage hostility to Poles and Poland in their classes. Instructions in many books directed teachers to stress that Slavs (i.e., Poles) had "invaded" eastern territory that was historically and rightfully German.[161]

Many books depicted Slavs as lesser beings, claiming they were fundamentally inferior to Germans in every aspect of social and economic life. Being Slavs, Poles were thus said to be less educated, less cultured, slovenly, and utterly deficient in habits of personal hygiene. Furthermore, Poles were commonly portrayed as dangerous and aggressive, as beasts, thieves, and criminals, who stole territory from Germany at its moment of weakness despite all it had done to bring them civilization and culture.[162] Children's school atlases proved to be just as biased in proclaiming that lost eastern territory was still culturally German and had always belonged to Germany. Illustrations depicting Polish troop concentrations along the "bleeding frontier" purported that the brutal and aggressive Poles awaited only the opportunity to once again strike at Germany. German pupils were taught in this sense that the absence of hostilities between Germany and Poland was only a temporary cease-fire in the long ethnic conflict that raged along the broken eastern frontier.

Of course, German students who did not get enough of this propaganda in their studies received exposure to it in the various youth groups to which many of them belonged.[163] A great number of these organizations were *völkisch*, anti-Semitic, and nationalist in nature. Groups would organize excursions to the "bleeding frontier," and members would attend lectures where speakers would rail against Poland and the Versailles Treaty that had created it.[164] In their schooling and social lives, there was no lack of opportunity for Germans growing up in the 1920s and 1930s to absorb revanchist sentiments and develop a thorough hatred for Poland and its people. Indeed, these lessons were not lost on the young people of that time. Werner B., a *Gymnasium* student in March 1939 before being drafted into the Wehrmacht, recalled that "to me 'Versailles' was not some castle or French tradition. . . . it was the embodiment of German shame."[165] Disdain for the postwar settlement extended to a common conception of Poland as a monstrosity born out of Versailles and forced upon the proud German people. Gerhard S., a classmate of Werner B. and also a soldier who served in Poland, later remembered, "I found myself for a long time in [Polish] territory that my school atlas had marked as German territory." He then candidly remarked how well he had been taught to think of culture in Poland as stemming solely from German origins: "I saw large, artistic buildings there [in Poland], and said to myself, 'here we Germans also proved our architectural skill.'"[166]

Prejudicial instruction by German teachers seems to have fully achieved the aim of raising public agreement for a revision of Versailles, including demands for reclaiming territory lost on the eastern frontier. Rolf F. stated that geography instruction in his school was a type of optical illusion, which had a tremendous impression on him as a student: "With a look at the map [of Germany] I thought to myself, as any child would, 'that area actually belongs to us and must once again be returned to us.' I had always thought that."[167] To Otto M., a classmate of Rolf F., these lessons translated into support for the German cause and full belief in the righteousness of German claims. Upon the outbreak of war, Otto M. explained, "I was convinced, as were my parents, that Germany would have justice before the world. The Versailles Treaty must be revised and lost territory reconquered."[168] Part of reclaiming lost German territory entailed the return of ethnic Germans to their blood homeland, a lesson German teachers also imparted to their students. As Rolf F. recalled, one of his teachers, a professed German nationalist, placed lighted blue candles in the windows of the classroom in honor and memory of ethnic Germans living outside of the Reich's borders.[169]

Throughout the 1920s and into the 1930s, frequent calls in Germany for a renewed "Push to the East" against the Poles perpetuated the notion that ethnic conflict on Germany's eastern frontier was a constant fact of life. These calls could be heard on all levels of German society and in speeches made by public figures from every part of the political spectrum. Demands for a revision of the eastern frontier were of course most strident on the political right, where a large variety of social groups, from hunting clubs to singing groups, carried on the idea of an eventual reckoning with the Poles.[170] All over Germany, but especially in the eastern provinces, agitation for a revision of the frontier was also egged on by the large community of German refugees who had immigrated at the end of World War I. According to Richard Bessel, the roughly 750,000 refugees from former German provinces provided a sizable "reservoir of right-wing and anti-Polish sentiment" upon which radical parties like the NSDAP could draw.[171] Moreover, energetic agitation by refugee groups like the Eastern Association *(Ostbund)* and the German Home Association of Poznań Refugees *(Deutscher Heimatbund Posener Flüchtlinge),* to name only two, heightened public awareness of the supposed persecution to which the just over 1 million ethnic Germans still in Poland were being subjected.[172] According to nationalist refugee groups, ethnic Germans left behind in Poland were being systematically terrorized. In addition, Polish authorities were actively "Polonizing" *Volksdeutsche* by closing their schools and churches, murdering members of German political groups, and forcing Germans to only speak Polish.

Some radical right-wing groups went further than preaching hate for Poland by leading incursions against Polish border patrols. Members of the Steel Helmet *(Stahlhelm),* a nationalist veterans group, and detachments of the Nazi Party's SA, which provided manpower for the German border guard *(Grenzschutz)* units that patrolled the frontier, frequently attacked Polish border posts in the 1920s and early 1930s.[173] The anti-Polish activities of the SA were especially provocative. *Sturmabteilung* detachments often harassed Polish communities in eastern Germany by carrying out searches of homes and marching through towns while singing "if Polish blood spurts from the knife, then so much the better."[174] After Hitler came to power in January 1933, these incidents became so numerous and aggravated tensions along the eastern frontier to such an extent that the new Nazi government was forced to forbid SA members from wearing their uniforms or holding SA marches anywhere within six miles of the German-Polish border.[175]

A rise in anti-Polish sentiment also initially accompanied the rise of Adolf Hitler to power. However, because Hitler could not afford to jeopardize his political position while he was still consolidating power, he quickly moved to calm tensions between Poland and Germany by signing a nonaggression pact in January 1934.[176] Yet, while Hitler's attempt to normalize relations with Poland stifled violent actions against Poles by Nazi Party formations like the SA, it had no real impact on German popular opinion toward Poland and its people.[177] Propaganda on the supposed racial inferiority of Poles continued to intensify, and demands for a revision of Versailles and Germany's eastern frontier with Poland did not abate. Moreover, notes the Polish scholar Tomasz Szarota, "Nazi propaganda took over several myths spread during the period of the Weimar Republic" that perpetuated commonly held stereotypes about Poland and the Polish people.[178]

Poland was still portrayed as a state created through criminal means, a so-called *Raubstaat,* constructed at the whim of the Western Allies. Some of the central characteristics of Poland's illegitimacy, Nazi propagandists claimed, were the backwardness of its culture and economy and the fact that it persecuted its German citizens. Poles supposedly did not abide by ethical norms because of their barbaric ethnic character, which Nazi propagandists defined as criminal, treacherous, and aggressive. Positive human qualities were never attributed to Poles. Instead they were portrayed as base and animalistic, fully capable of murder, and undeserving of equal treatment or respect.[179] In short, Poles were depicted as mortal enemies of the Reich engaged in an ongoing ethnic struggle against the German race.

The specific vilification and dehumanization of Poles (not to mention Jews) paralleled general trends in Nazified German society toward applying scientific racism to categorize, ostracize, and eventually eliminate people defined as "others." Detlev Peukert notes that these efforts were part and parcel of the overall Nazi effort to reshape German society into a *Volksgemeinschaft,* or racially homogeneous ethnic community, by formally categorizing human beings according to their biological value.[180] Certain aspects of this trend antedated the Nazi assumption of power, particularly in the areas of health and education policy but also in the proposed "euthanizing" of persons whose lives were deemed "not worth living."[181] The Nazis kept public approval in mind, however, and the regime implemented policies in steps, always with an eye toward "what German citizens would support, or at least tolerate."[182]

The forced sterilization of nearly 400,000 German men and women, including the mentally ill, those with hereditary physical problems, alcoholics, and others, formed one such policy.[183] This program continued throughout the existence of the Third Reich, and, according to Robert Gellately, "it is very likely that the idea of a sterilization law was quite popular."[184] Indeed, popular protest never arose in response to the sterilization program, indicating that even if most Germans did not fully accept the violence of proposed Nazi "solutions" to certain problems, many seem to have thought in broad categories that accepted the racial-biological superiority of some people and the inferiority of others. In short, to quote Detlev Peukert, "When the Nazis came to power in 1933, the paradigm of selection and elimination, already dominant, [became] absolute."[185]

This, then, was the context within which young German men were raised between 1919 and 1939. Active indoctrination by the Nazi Party went hand in hand with the passive intake of popular sentiments that devalued human life and valorized racial hatred, militarism, and revanchism. After years of exposure to such derogatory sentiments, it should come as no surprise that with the outbreak of war, military discipline quickly broke down and German officers were generally unable to control the behavior of their men. The barbaric conduct of German soldiers during wartime was in many ways a consequence of the "cult of violence" that had developed in Germany since the rise of Hitler in 1933.[186] When war came in 1939, it indeed brutalized German military personnel. In the final analysis, however, the incredibly violent conduct of German soldiers so early in the conflict suggests that it was not simply combat itself that unleashed the beast in many German men. The war instead provided a fitting context for the explosion of attitudes that had been deeply poisoned by prejudice, racism, and the exaltation of violence toward "others." In many ways, therefore, the viciousness of many German soldiers in 1939 proved a foreshadowing of still greater violence to come, violence that provided a foundation for the "war of annihilation" and the genocide of the Jews.

CONCLUSION

For all of Poland's inhabitants, both Gentile and Jewish, the German invasion in September 1939 was a catastrophe of unparalleled proportions. During the five-year occupation, Nazi resettlement and pacification policies displaced and killed millions of Polish Christians. Germans hardened by anti-Polish prejudice demonstrated a nearly unlimited capacity for brutality, and accordingly they devastated Poland's cities and ruined innumerable villages in the countryside.[1] Still worse was the suffering of Polish Jewry, which the Germans effectively wiped out as part of their so-called "Final Solution to the Jewish problem" in Europe.[2] Of all the Jewish communities to fall under German control during the war, only those in the Baltic states suffered a higher proportion of losses than the Jews of Poland.[3]

Looking back at these events, it is difficult to characterize the 1939 war in Poland as normal. Indeed, when compared to the war in Western Europe one year later, the shocking level of barbarity with which the SS and German army conducted the invasion suggests that the Polish campaign was anything but typical. The measures implemented by the SS and Wehrmacht against Polish political figures, the collective punishment of civilians, and the violent expulsion of Jews from occupied Poland all clearly revealed the harsh character of the new conflict that Nazi Germany intended to fight in the east. Already in 1939, Hitler's forces waged war against enemies that National Socialism defined in racial-biological as well as military-political terms. The war against Poland was, therefore, a critical first step in the amalgamation of Nazi ideology and military practice that would be central to Germany's *Vernichtungskrieg* against the Soviet Union and brutal anti-partisan campaigns in Serbia.

Well before the first shot was fired, Adolf Hitler described Germany's objective for the invasion as the utter annihilation of Poland's "living forces." It was for this reason that in late August Hitler had exhorted his subordinates in the SS and Wehrmacht to view the impending attack as an exercise in killing the enemy and not as a traditional military-diplomatic campaign with larger geopolitical ramifications. Concerning the SS in particular, it is clear from Hitler's comments, as well as from the steps taken by Reinhard

Heydrich, that the police forces that constituted the *Einsatzgruppen* were intended to be the vanguard of Nazi executive authority in occupied Polish territory. As the first representatives of the Gestapo and Security Police apparatus in Poland, *Einsatzgruppen* personnel received instructions from Heydrich to implement what he himself described as the "extraordinarily radical" policy of eliminating those segments of Polish society that could challenge German rule.[4] In this sense, Operation TANNENBERG represented an entirely new phenomenon in the history of modern warfare. Although the Nazis regularly employed violence against their enemies, never before had Hitler charged his SS and security forces with so extensive and merciless a mission as the murder of Poland's leading and educated social-political classes.

The task was so radical, in fact, that Heydrich and Werner Best took pains to recruit personnel ruthless enough to carry it out. Of necessity, the men chosen from the SS and police leadership cadre to command the *Einsatzgruppen* and *Einsatzkommandos* had to have proven their dedication to the Nazi cause, either through direct experience in the *Freikorps* fighting the Poles or by years of service combating domestic political opponents. The practice of identifying and selecting the proper men for the job demonstrates beyond a doubt that the escalation of violence against Germany's "racial" enemies did not occur because the war brutalized SS and police personnel. Instead, leading figures in the SS and police apparatus intentionally took steps before the outbreak of hostilities with Poland to sharpen the regime's racial-political polices. Hitler, Heydrich, Best, and many others in the Nazi Party unequivocally viewed the war against Poland as a *Volkstumskampf*, or ethnic conflict. According to convinced National Socialists, the Poles were Germany's ethnic (i.e., racial) enemies as well as a military-political threat. It followed, then, that the slaughter of Poland's leading and educated social-political classes was a *volkspolitische Aufgabe*, or ethnic-political task, necessary to secure Germany's hegemony over the conquered territory.[5] In effect, already in 1939 the conflation of Nazi racial-biological maxims and power political concerns raised mass murder to the status of a military-security operation.

The fact that the SS leadership and officers in the Operational Groups considered Operation TANNENBERG a dimension of the war is illustrated by Heydrich's demand for the men chosen to command the *Einsatzgruppen* to have combat experience or formal military training. A former German naval officer himself, he undoubtedly understood the power of military discipline to shape men's behavior.[6] In addition to finding it easier to work with the Wehrmacht, Heydrich also probably suspected that those who possessed such a background were more likely to follow orders to liquidate civilians out of a sense of obedience similar to that found in the German armed forces. This tendency toward militarizing murder is evident in speeches delivered by Helmut Bischoff and Otto Hahn during the campaign. In Bischoff's case, he exhorted his men to obey their orders and to execute them mercilessly when clearing adult Polish males from the Schwedenhöhe district of Bydgoszcz. Similarly, Otto Hahn reminded his *Einsatzkommando* personnel of their obligation to follow orders and act ruthlessly against Polish insurgents, prisoners of war, and other civilian targets prior to entering Katowice. Both of these SS officers warned their subordinates that martial law was in force as of the war's outbreak on 1 September. Those who did not obey their orders could be punished for dereliction of duty even though they were engaged in what amounted to organized killing actions directed against civilians and not formal military operations.[7]

Legitimizing the murder of civilians as a military operation went hand in hand with the overall process of militarizing the police that began in the 1930s.[8] Once war broke out, the militarization of SS and police units had two benefits for the implementation of harsh racial-political policies by the Nazi regime. The first of these was organizational. By virtue of their organization, militarized SS and police units could operate more efficiently in the field, a benefit that facilitated cooperation with the German army. But as events during the Polish campaign also demonstrated, militarized SS and police units could be used effectively for killing operations because it was possible for SS commanders to couch orders for the murder of civilians, meaning ethnic and racial enemies, in terms of military necessity. Policemen organized in a unit along military lines, executing an "operation" like TANNENBERG, and killing "enemies" according to orders handed down through a formal military-style chain of command were not likely to question the legality of their tasks. The structure of the Operational Groups and wartime context within which Operation TANNENBERG was implemented thus reduced the likelihood that SS and police personnel would feel individually responsible for the criminal instructions they were ordered to carry out.[9] To a considerable extent, therefore, the militarization of the attitudes of SS and police personnel helped render the *Einsatzgruppen* flexible and deadly instruments in the prosecution of Nazi Germany's first racialized military campaign.

As for the Wehrmacht and its role in the *Volkstumskampf* against the Poles, in contrast to the later war against the USSR, the Army High Command did not prepare for the Polish campaign by promulgating criminal orders that sanctioned the murder of communist functionaries and permitted violence against civilians.[10] Events in September showed, though, that explicitly criminal orders were not necessary in order to motivate German troops and officers in the fight against Polish guerrillas. Nor were such instructions required to unleash a murderous wave of violence against Poland's civilian population. German officers, from Army High Command down through the ranks, were fully prepared to utilize SS units and work with Heydrich's Security Police in order to neutralize Polish opposition groups. This cooperation included providing the Gestapo with the names of known Polish enemies and saboteurs, as well as actively using the *Einsatzgruppen* during the fighting to eliminate insurgents. Some friction between the army and the SS did arise when SS and police personnel tried to carry out their orders to kill groups of Poles and Jews targeted as part of Operation TANNENBERG.

Offering generalized conclusions about the origin and nature of the conflicts between the Wehrmacht and the SS is problematic, however, largely because the circumstances surrounding these conflicts differed from situation to situation. Clearly, many German army officers were ready to use extremely violent measures to suppress Polish opposition groups, including retaliatory shootings and incarcerating Polish enemies in concentration camps. On the other hand, most army officers were not prepared to permit the wholesale slaughter of tens of thousands of innocent civilians.[11] This reluctance to participate in the most radical dimension of the *Volkstumskampf* in 1939 was a central difference between the Polish campaign and the later Russian campaign, during which all legal and psychological constraints against the murder of Soviet Jews and Red Army POWs were systematically ignored.

Army and SS collaboration in Poland proved most effective when German troops encountered armed resistance from the civilian population. This opposition typically prompted a vicious response from the representatives of both institutions, although German army officers frequently responded to Polish civilian attacks with a callousness that exceeded even the retaliatory measures employed by the Security Police. In cities like Częstochowa, Bydgoszcz, and Katowice, as well as in many other locations, the army immediately resorted to mass shootings and the summary destruction of property to quell resistance. And while this policy of *Schrecklichkeit,* or using terror against civilians, was generally directed at all levels of Polish society, more often than not, local notables and members of the Polish intelligentsia were the first people placed in front of German firing squads.

Polish civilian attacks on German personnel may have precipitated Wehrmacht reprisals, which gave the violence of retaliatory actions a pragmatic, defensive, and nonideologically influenced dimension. Nevertheless, the line between the pragmatic brutality of *Schrecklichkeit* and violence informed by National Socialism was frequently unclear. Many commissioned and noncommissioned officers voiced negative opinions about Poles and Polish Jews during the invasion, a reality that can only lead to the conclusion that deep-seated anti-Polish and anti-Semitic prejudices sharpened the response of these men to civilian aggression and informed their willingness to use extremely violent methods.

A similar combination of prejudiced attitudes and chaotic battlefield conditions also seems to have influenced the behavior of many ordinary German military personnel. The activity of civilian snipers and saboteurs validated to rank-and-file troops the often repeated warnings of their officers that Poles and Jews were treacherous and dangerous opponents. Moreover, to many Germans, the murder of *Volksdeutsche* confirmed the stereotyped image of Polish and Jewish barbarism that was purveyed on all levels of Nazified German society. When combined with the experience of "Polish brutality" in battle, these preconceived, negative opinions prompted many German military personnel to lash out at the civilian population. The use of massive retaliatory and punitive measures made it abundantly clear to the men that their commanding officers sanctioned summary executions and the destruction of property. From this point it was only a short step to the outright commission of atrocities against the civilian population. Consequently, although intense civilian resistance subsided after the first week of the war, many German military personnel continued to shoot, beat, and torture civilians indiscriminately throughout the month of September. This tendency to use violence summarily implies not only the profoundly debasing impact of combat and the breakdown of discipline in the Wehrmacht, but also the operation of anti-Polish and anti-Jewish attitudes for the duration of the campaign.

The opinions expressed in the writings of many German troops strongly imply that behaving violently toward Poles was acceptable to Wehrmacht personnel within the context of warfare in what they considered to be the unusual and backward social-cultural conditions of "the East."[12] As a cultural and psychological construct, the notion of "the East" as a strange land populated by hostile and inferior people and cultures enabled Germans (and Austrians) convinced of their own racial and cultural superiority to believe they were not constrained by the moral and ethical norms that guided behavior toward other Germans. Accordingly, to those who held this concept of the east, Poles and Jews were more closely related to animals than to human beings, meaning that these "quasi-people" did not deserve decent treatment. The only authority that could have countered the detrimental impact of this notion during the Polish campaign was the energetic enforcement of martial law by German officers. But even this deterrent proved largely ineffective due to the inconsistency of German officers responding to the actions of their men. As has been described, officers who chose to intervene for good were able to prevent atrocities from occurring and thereby save civilian lives. The same held true for individual German soldiers who were able to dissuade their comrades from killing civilians and prisoners of war. Unfortunately, the converse was also true. Far too few German officers and enlisted men took steps to prevent violent acts by their countrymen, and as a result German troops killed thousands, perhaps even tens of thousands, of civilians in incidents that were unrelated to combat.

Predominantly negative preconceptions of "Eastern Jews" *(Ostjuden)* deeply informed the violence of Wehrmacht and SS personnel against Jews during the invasion. Anti-Jewish attitudes based on the stereotypes purveyed in Nazi propaganda could on occasion inspire German brutality directly against Jews and not Poles, such as occurred when German troops in Rawa Mazowiecka and Częstochowa focused on killing Jews during reprisal actions. Without doubt a similar hate of Jews also underlay the SS terror operations that were calculated to spur the flight of Jews from German-occupied Poland, such as occurred in Przemyśl and Włocławek. Yet, to many commanders in the German army, it mattered little if anti-Jewish violence was either spontaneous or planned. Most officers tended to frown upon these incidents because they caused unrest behind the front line. Particularly at issue was the fact that Wehrmacht commanders considered violence against Jews to have a detrimental effect on the discipline of rank-and-file military personnel. Fearing a loss of control over their men and under the impression that SS violence against Jews was unauthorized, some German officers took energetic steps to restore order by commanding that SS and Wehrmacht personnel be court-martialed for their transgressions against Polish Jews. This situation, too, differed considerably from what occurred during the *Vernichtungskrieg,* when German military commanders, had they been so inclined, could not court-martial SS or even Wehrmacht personnel for their crimes against the civilian population, Jewish or otherwise.[13]

An ominous exception to the attempts by some German officers to limit anti-Jewish violence can be found in army-SS cooperation against Jewish communities along the German-Soviet demarcation line. Apart from the complaints of a few ranking commanders, a majority of German officers had no qualms about helping the SS expel Jews from the German sphere of interest in Poland. In itself, the policy of using terror to eject Jews en masse from German-occupied territory was a radicalized continuation of methods that had been utilized by the SS and police since autumn 1938 to drive Jews from the Reich and incorporated territories. It is important to recognize, though, that anti-Jewish policy during the Polish campaign differed considerably from what it later became during the war in the Soviet Union. In 1939, expulsion and resettlement were the order of the day, with physical violence, the destruction of property, and intimidation being instruments used by the SS and, to a lesser degree, the Wehrmacht, in order to meet the goal of making the German Reich *Judenfrei*. By contrast, the terrorization and murder of Jews became ends in themselves in late summer 1941. It is therefore imperative to retain the proper historical perspective by judging events in 1941 from an understanding of what took place in 1939 and not the other way around. Forcing the emigration of Jews and resettling them in the General Government remained the central components of anti-Jewish policy until the invasion of the Soviet Union ushered in the policy of genocide.[14] The eradication of European Jewry would not become an explicit goal of the regime for another two years, but the outbreak of war in 1939 was a watershed event nonetheless in that it signaled a decisive escalation of the "violent solution" to the "Jewish problem" as well as the German army's deepening involvement in the implementation of anti-Jewish policy.

A key reason for the differences in anti-Jewish policy between 1939 and 1941 was the nature of the ideological campaign that the SS was fighting when the war with Poland broke out. According to Heydrich and others in the SS and police hierarchy, Germany's primary enemies at the time were ethnic Poles and not Polish Jews. As Jakob Lölgen, the SD commander in the Bydgoszcz region, noted to his men following Poland's capitulation, "It is the Führer's wish that a Germanized West Prussia be created out of Polish Pomerania as soon as possible." In order to carry out this task, Lölgen continued, "the following measures are necessary: 1) the physical liquidation of all Polish elements that a) were formerly leaders in Polish society or b) which could lead Polish resistance in the future. These liquidations must be carried out in the shortest time possible."[15] Not surprisingly, the desired speed of the killing campaign mentioned in his orders echoed instructions that Heydrich issued on 16 October for "the liquidation of the Polish leadership to be completed by 1 November 1939."[16]

Given the ferocity of Polish civilian opposition during the invasion and the danger to the purity of German blood that Poles were perceived to pose, it made sense from a Nazi standpoint to subdue the Polish nation (ethnically defined) by selectively liquidating certain social-political classes of Polish society. However, fulfilling this goal required manpower that the SS lacked. In addition, although disdain for Poles was widespread throughout the army officer corps, many German officers remained unwilling to become involved in killing Polish leaders, educators, clergy, nobility, and intellectuals. The combination of the logistical difficulties, the ideological priorities, and the speed of the slaughter demanded by Heydrich necessitated that the SS focus its efforts on destroying the potential for Polish resistance in 1939. Consequently, the SS murder campaign escalated precipitously throughout the autumn and early winter of that year until by December 1939 the SS and their ethnic German auxiliaries had slaughtered as many as 50,000 people. At least 7,000 of these victims were Polish Jews.[17] The roughly 4 to 1 ratio of Polish Christian deaths to Polish Jewish deaths suggests the decidedly anti-Polish, and not anti-Jewish, animus of the killing program of the SS in those early months of the war.

To point out the butchering of Polish Christians by the SS does not minimize the suffering of Polish Jews, nor does it deny the ferocity of SS anti-Jewish policies early in the war and the later evolution of these policies into genocide. On the contrary, it provides a line of continuity between the initial slaughter of Polish Gentiles by the SS and the subsequent heightening of its killing campaign against the Jews. In targeting the leading classes of Polish society for elimination and in carrying out the task through mass shootings, SS killings in Poland bore a striking resemblance to later efforts by Heydrich's Security Police to decapitate Soviet society by eliminating Jewish men and communist leaders between 22 June and mid-August 1941.[18] It goes without saying that significant differences existed between Operation TANNENBERG and Operation BARBAROSSA. The latter was far larger in scale, and the targets in the killers' gun sights had by mid-1941 shifted decisively to Jews. Still, before the SS embarked on its program to completely eradicate Soviet Jewry by shooting all Jews regardless of age or sex, its policy of using mass murder to pacify conquered territory was applied in a relatively similar fashion in both Poland and the USSR, occasionally even including the transfer of hardened SS killers from Poland to the Eastern Front where they then murdered Jews.[19]

The similarities and connections between the two killing programs suggest that Operation TANNENBERG and the butchery of Poles in 1939 served as a kind of dress rehearsal for the initial wave of murder that later engulfed Soviet Jewry during the opening phase of Operation BARBAROSSA. Just as the killing of the mentally ill and infirm in the gas chambers of Grafeneck, Hartheim, Sonnenstein, and other institutions in Germany led eventually to industrialized killing in the death camps of the General Government, the methods of mass shooting utilized to such devastating effect in the USSR were first proved viable against non-Jewish Poles in the forests of occupied Poland.[20]

In the final analysis, the responsibility for unleashing this series of catastrophes can only be assigned to Adolf Hitler. Only Hitler's vision of Germany's new war in Eastern Europe was influential enough to incorporate and encourage resettlement and mass murder as its crucial components. Accordingly, Germany's military campaigns in Poland and elsewhere to the east were conducted as hard, merciless, ideological battles against perceived ethnic and racial enemies. The Polish campaign was thus pivotal in that it initiated Hitler's new war. The assistance given by the German army to the SS, the violence directed against civilians, and the xenophobic, anti-Semitic, and racist attitudes of many German military personnel, when taken to the extreme, would later become integral parts of the Wehrmacht's *Vernichtungskrieg* against the Soviet Union as well as of the antipartisan warfare that German troops and the SS would fight in the Balkans. In this sense, the brief war with Poland in September 1939 was the first step in the overall escalation of National Socialist racial and occupation policies during World War II that ultimately resulted in genocide.

NOTES

Abbreviations Used in Notes

Abt.	Abteilung (Administrative Section or Branch)
Abw.	Abwehr (Military Counterintelligence Office)
AK	Armeekorps (Army Corps)
AOK	Armeeoberkommando (Field Army Command)
BAK	Bundesarchiv Koblenz (German Federal Archives, Koblenz)
BA/MA	Bundesarchiv/Militärarchiv Freiburg (German Federal Archives/Military Archives, Freiburg)
BDC	Berlin Document Center
BfZ	Bibliothek für Zeitgeschichte, Stuttgart (Library for Contemporary History)
BPP	Bavarian Political Police
CdZ	Chef der Zivilverwaltung (Chief of Civil Administration)
EG	Einsatzgruppe (Operational Group)
EK	Einsatzkommando
GAK	Grenzschutz-Abschnittskommando (Frontier Guard Unit)
Gen.St.d.H.	Generalstab des Heeres (General Staff of the Army)
Gestapo	Geheime Staatspolizei (Secret State Police)
GFP	Geheime Feldpolizei (Secret Field Police)
GStA	Generalstaatsanwaltschaft (General State Attorney's Office)
HA-Sipo	Hauptamt-Sicherheitspolizei (Security Police Headquarters)
HGr.Kdo	Heeresgruppenkommando (Army Group Command)
Ia	Operations Officer
Ic/AO	Intelligence Officer
I.D.	Infantry Division
IMT	*Trial of the Major War Criminals before the International Military Tribunal*
I.R.	Infantry Regiment
Kdr.	Kommandeur (Commander)
Korück	Kommandant des rückwärtigen Armeegebietes (Rear Army Area Commander)
Kripo	Kriminalpolizei (Criminal Police)
KTB	Kriegstagebuch (War Diary)
MCC	Main Commission for the Investigation of Nazi Crimes in Poland
NARA	National Archives and Records Administration, College Park, MD
NSDAP	Nationalsozialistische Deutsche Arbeiterpartei (Nazi Party)
Ob.d.H.	Oberbefehlshaber des Heeres (Commander in Chief of the Army)
OKH	Oberkommando des Heeres (High Command of the Army)

OKW   Oberkommando der Wehrmacht (High Command of the Armed
          Forces)
Orpo   Ordnungspolizei (Order Police)
POW   Prisoner of War
PPS   Protokół Przesłuchania Świadka (Protocol of a Witness Statement)
Qu.   Quartermaster
RFSS   Reichsführer SS (Reich Leader SS Heinrich Himmler)
RG   Record Group
RH   Divisional Records held in the BA/MA Freiburg
RSHA   Reichssicherheitshauptamt (Reich Security Main Office)
SA   Sturmabteilung (Storm Troops)
SD   Sicherheitsdienst (Security Service of the SS)
Sipo   Sicherheitspolizei (Security Police of the SS)
SS   Schutzstaffeln (Protective Squads)
SSTV   SS-Totenkopfverbände (SS Death's Head Units)
StA   Staatsanwaltschaft (State Attorney's Office)
TWC   *Trials of War Criminals before the Nürnberg Military Tribunals*
USHMMA   U.S. Holocaust Memorial Museum Archive
WPr.   Wehrmachtpropagandaamt (Wehrmacht Propaganda Office)
z.b.V.   zur besonderen Verwendung (for special purpose)
ZStL   Zentrale Stelle der Landesjustizverwaltungen, Ludwigsburg (Cen-
          tral Office of Justice Administration for the German States)

Chapter 1. The Ideological Dimensions of War with Poland

1. Document R-100, "Führer to the Commander-in-Chief (Brauchitsch)," 23 March 1939, in *Trials of War Criminals before the Nürnberg Military Tribunals* (hereafter cited as *TWC*), vol. 10 "The High Command Case" (Washington, DC: Government Printing Office, 1951), p. 648.

2. Szymon Datner, *Crimes Committed by the Wehrmacht during the September Campaign and the Period of Military Government* (Poznań: Institute for Western Affairs, 1962).

3. Based upon their analysis of several sources, Christian Jansen and Arno Weckbecker, *Der "Volksdeutsche Selbstschutz" in Polen 1939/40* (Munich: Oldenbourg, 1992), p. 20, conclude that the number of ethnic Germans living in Poland at the outbreak of the war cannot be determined exactly, but they estimate that the number stood between 727,000 and 1.6 million.

4. Document L-79, "Minutes of Führer Conference," 23 May 1939, in *TWC*, vol. 10, p. 673.

5. Although oppressive and stridently anti-Catholic, traditional Prussian, and then German, policy toward the Poles and their lands between the late eighteenth and the early twentieth centuries was far less brutal than *Polenpolitik* as implemented by the Nazis. For more on Prussian and Imperial German Polish policy, see Martin Broszat, *Zweihundert Jahre deutsche Polenpolitik* (Frankfurt/Main: Suhrkamp, 1972), or William W. Hagen, *Germans, Poles, and Jews: The Nationality Conflict in the Prussian East, 1771–1914* (Chicago: University of Chicago Press, 1980).

6. Hans-Adolf Jacobsen, *Nationalsozialistische Aussenpolitik, 1933–1938* (Frankfurt/Main: A. Metzner, 1968), p. 404f.

7. See Manfred Messerschmidt, "Foreign Policy and Preparation for War," in *Germany and the Second World War,* vol. 1, *The Buildup of German Aggression,* ed. Wilhelm Deist et al., trans. P. S. Falla, D. S. McMurry, E. Osers, and L. Wilmot (New York: Oxford University Press, 1990), pp. 590ff, for the importance Hitler placed on concluding a nonaggression pact with Poland to buy time for German rearmament.

8. Ibid., p. 592.

9. Klaus Hildebrand, *The Foreign Policy of the Third Reich,* trans. A. Fothergill (Berkeley: University of California Press, 1973), p. 33.

10. Ibid. Comments that Hermann Rauschning, *Hitler Speaks: A Series of Political Conversations with Adolph Hitler on His Real Aims* (London: Thornton Butterworth, 1939), p. 123, attributes to Hitler in 1934 suggest that the Nazi leader indeed considered a rapprochement with the Poles a temporary convenience to be discarded when the opportunity presented itself to pursue a more radical policy. As Hitler allegedly assured Rauschning at the time, "All our agreements with Poland have a purely temporary significance. . . . I have no intention of maintaining a serious friendship with Poland." When Rauschning pressed him on the issue, Hitler responded by saying that he would maintain cordial relations with the Poles until Germany was militarily prepared to confront all of its enemies, including Poland, France, and Great Britain.

11. Hitler and Darré became close in 1930 as a result of the latter's influential writings on the alleged connections between race and agriculture. In fact, it was Hitler who brought Darré into the Nazi fold by assigning him the task of organizing rural policies for the NSDAP. See Donald E. Thomas Jr., "Richard Walther Darré and the Doctrine of Blood and Soil" (Master's thesis: University of Chicago, 1962), and Gustavo Corni and Horst Gies, *Blut und Boden: Rassenideologie und Agrarpolitik im Staat Hitlers* (Idstein: Schulz-Kirchner Verlag, 1994).

12. Karl Dietrich Bracher, *Die Deutsche Diktatur: Entstehung, Struktur, Folgen des Nationalsozialismus* (Cologne: Kiepenheuer and Witsch, 1969), p. 169.

13. Adolf Hitler, *Mein Kampf,* trans. R. Manheim (London: Pimlico Edition, 1992), pp. 123ff.

14. Jerzy Marczewski, "The Nazi Concept of *Drang nach Osten* and the Basic Premises of Occupation Policy in the 'Polish Question,'" *Polish Western Affairs,* 8, no. 2 (1967): 289–324, offers a detailed examination of the continuities and differences in German eastern policy from the German empire to the Third Reich.

15. Hitler, *Mein Kampf,* p. 354f.

16. Adolf Hitler, *Hitlers Zweites Buch: Ein Dokument aus dem Jahr 1928* (Stuttgart: Deutsche Verlags-Anstalt, 1961), p. 81.

17. Gerhard L. Weinberg, *The Foreign Policy of Hitler's Germany: Diplomatic Revolution in Europe, 1933–36* (Chicago: University of Chicago Press, 1970), p. 25f. See also Thilo Vogelsang, "Neue Dokumente zur Geschichte der Reichswehr 1930–1933," *Vierteljahrshefte für Zeitgeschichte* 2, no. 4 (October 1954): 435.

18. Joachim von Ribbentrop, *The Ribbentrop Memoirs,* trans. O. Watson (London: Weidenfeld and Nicolson, 1954), p. 45.

19. Document 386-PS, "Hossbach Memorandum," 10 November 1937, in *Trial*

of the Major War Criminals before the International Military Tribunal, Nuremberg, 14 November 1945–1 October 1946 (hereafter cited as IMT), vol. 25 (Nuremberg: International Military Tribunal, 1947), pp. 403, 408.

20. Gerhard L. Weinberg, *A World at Arms: A Global History of World War II* (New York: Cambridge University Press, 1994), p. 22, reaches a similar conclusion, stating that "[Hitler's] wars would start at the times of his choosing and accordingly with incidents of his creation."

21. Richard Breitman, *The Architect of Genocide: Himmler and the Final Solution* (New York: Alfred Knopf, 1991), p. 62.

22. Ibid., p. 63.

23. Weinberg, *World at Arms*, p. 29.

24. Ibid.

25. Gerhard L. Weinberg, "A Proposed Compromise over Danzig in 1939?" in *Germany, Hitler, and World War II: Essays in Modern German and World History* (New York: Cambridge University Press, 1995), p. 128. Also see Messerschmidt, "Foreign Policy and Preparation for War," p. 686f.

26. Hildebrand, *Foreign Policy*, p. 82.

27. Gerhard L. Weinberg, *The Foreign Policy of Hitler's Germany: Starting World War II, 1937–1939* (Chicago: University of Chicago Press, 1980), p. 557f. See also Messerschmidt, "Foreign Policy and Preparation for War," p. 705.

28. Robert G. L. Waite, *Vanguard of Nazism: The Free Corps Movement in Postwar Germany, 1918–1923* (New York: W. W. Norton, 1952), p. 96 n. Also see Martin Broszat, *Zweihundert Jahre deutsche Polenpolitik* (Frankfurt/Main: Suhrkamp Taschenbuch, 1972), p. 210f and T. Hunt Tooley, *National Identity and Weimar Germany: Upper Silesia and the Eastern Border, 1918–1922* (Lincoln: University of Nebraska Press, 1997).

29. Carl Dirks and Karl-Heinz Janssen, *Der Krieg der Generäle: Hitler als Werkzeug der Wehrmacht* (Berlin: Propyläen, 1999), p. 18.

30. Hans Mommsen, *The Rise and Fall of Weimar Democracy*, trans. E. Forster and L. E. Jones (Chapel Hill: University of North Carolina Press, 1996), pp. 104, 201.

31. Geoffrey P. Megargee, *Inside Hitler's High Command* (Lawrence: University Press of Kansas, 2000), p. 12.

32. Christian Hartmann and Sergei Slutsch, "Franz Halder und die Kriegsvorbereitungen im Frühjahr 1939. Eine Ansprache des Generalstabschefs des Heeres," *Vierteljahrshefte für Zeitgeschichte* 45, no. 3 (July 1997): 479.

33. Ibid., p. 482.

34. Ibid., p. 486.

35. Ibid., pp. 489, 495.

36. Quoted in Gerd R. Ueberschär, "Militäropposition gegen Hitlers Kriegspolitik 1939 bis 1941," in *Der Widerstand gegen den Nationalsozialismus*, ed. J. Schmädeke and P. Steinbach (Munich: Piper, 1986), p. 348.

37. Erich von Manstein, *Lost Victories*, ed. and trans. A. G. Powell (London: Arms and Armour Press, 1982), p. 27.

38. Document PS-3706, Affidavit of Blaskowitz, 10 November 1945, in IMT, vol. 32 (Nuremberg, 1948), p. 467f.

39. Document PS-3704, Affidavit of von Blomberg, 7 November 1945, in IMT, vol. 32 (Nuremberg, 1948), p. 464f.

40. Theodor S. Hamerow, *On the Road to the Wolf's Lair: German Resistance to Hitler* (Cambridge, MA: Belknap Press of Harvard University Press, 1997), p. 262.

41. Elisabeth Wagner, ed., *Der Generalquartiermeister: Briefe und Tagebuchaufzeichnungen des Generalquartiermeisters des Heeres General der Artillerie Eduard Wagner* (Munich/Vienna: Olzog Verlag, 1963), p. 109.

42. IMT, vol. 1, p. 199. See also Megargee, *Inside Hitler's High Command,* pp. 67ff, which details German military preparations for the attack.

43. Document L-079, "Little Schmundt Report," 23 May 1939, in IMT, vol. 37, p. 548, and Document L-79, "Minutes of Führer Conference," 23 May 1939, in *TWC,* vol. 10, p. 673.

44. Ibid.

45. *TWC,* vol. 10, p. 674.

46. Ibid., p. 673.

47. Document PS-798, "Führer's Speech to the Commanders-in-Chief," 22 August 1939, in *TWC,* vol. 10, pp. 698ff.

48. The Nazi-Soviet Pact was in fact signed the following day, on 23 August 1939. For more on the details of the agreement, see E. Oberländer, ed., *Hitler-Stalin Pakt 1939: Das Ende Ostmitteleuropas?* (Frankfurt/Main: Fischer, 1989).

49. Document PS-1014, "Führer's Speech (Second) to the Commanders-in-Chief," 22 August 1939, in *TWC,* vol. 10, p. 702. By "living forces," Hitler presumably meant Polish troops.

50. Notes from Admiral Wilhelm Canaris's diary quoted in Winfried Baumgart, "Zur Ansprache Hitlers vor den Führern der Wehrmacht am 22. August 1939," *Vierteljahrshefte für Zeitgeschichte* 19, no. 2 (July 1971): 303.

51. Document 193, "Zweite Ansprache des Führers am 22. August 1939," IMG Nürnberg 1014-PS, in *Akten zur deutschen Auswärtigen Politik 1918–1945,* Series D (1937–1945), vol. 7, "Die letzten Wochen vor Kriegsausbruch 9. August bis 3. September 1939" (Baden-Baden: Imprimerie Nationale, 1950), p. 171. In his detailed analysis of the documentation surrounding the 22 August conference, Winfried Baumgart was unable to confirm if Hitler actually referred to orders for the SS to kill Polish men, women, and children. The statement originates from a document given to the American journalist Louis Lochner by Hermann Maass in 1939. Maass himself had been asked to forward the document to Lochner by Colonel General Ludwig Beck, a known member of the military opposition, who claimed an "unnamed" officer as his source. The cloudy origin of the document, incidentally, is likely the reason why it was not entered as evidence at the Nuremberg War Crimes proceedings. See Baumgart, "Zur Ansprache Hitlers," p. 121.

52. Jansen and Weckbecker, *Der "Volksdeutsche Selbstschutz" in Polen,* p. 29, quote Franz Halder as having stated "Die Physische Vernichtung der Bevölkerung polnischer Abstammung."

53. Von Bock recounted Hitler's comments during the trial of Karl Wolff for participation in mass murder. See Public Prosecutor's Office, Provincial Court Munich II, Ref. 10a JS 39/60, p. 86. Also see Zentrale Stelle der Landesjustizverwaltungen, Ludwigsburg (hereafter cited as ZStL), "Einsatzgruppen in Polen: Einsatzgruppen der Sicherheitspolizei, Selbstschutz und andere Formationen in der

Zeit vom 1. September 1939 bis Frühjahr 1940," 10 June 1962, p. 122, and Heinz Höhne, *The Order of the Death's Head: The Story of Hitler's SS,* trans. R. Barry (New York: Ballantine, 1971), p. 336.

54. The "Führer's Speech to the Commanders-in-Chief," 22 August 1939, in *TWC,* vol. 10, p. 702.

55. By 1939 the command structure of Nazi Germany's armed forces was split between two different offices. The Oberkommando des Heeres, or OKH, also known as Army High Command, directed all of Germany's land forces, with the exception of the Waffen-SS. Beginning in February 1938, the Oberkommando der Wehrmacht (OKW), or Armed Forces High Command, coordinated the activities of Germany's air force, navy, and land forces and stood directly under the command of Adolf Hitler. See Megargee, *Inside Hitler's High Command,* pp. 1–61.

56. Hartmann and Slutsch, "Franz Halder und die Kriegsvorbereitungen," p. 493.

57. SS Aktenvermerk, Berlin, 4 July 1940, Berlin, in ZStL, 211 AR-Z 13/63 Strafverfahren gegen Lothar Beutel, Helmut Bischoff, Dr. Walter Hammer, Erich Preckel und andere Angehörige der Einsatzgruppe IV wegen Mordes (NS-Gewaltverbrechen in Polen 1939), p. 21.

58. Michael Wildt, "Radikalisierung und Selbstradikalisierung 1939: Die Geburt des Reichsicherheitsamtes aus dem Geist des völkischen Massenmords," in *Die Gestapo im Zweiten Weltkrieg: Heimatfront und besetztes Europa,* ed. Gerhard Paul and Klaus-Michael Mallman (Darmstadt: Wissenschaftliche Buchgesellschaft, 2000), p. 16. See also Lutz Hachmeister, *Der Gegnerforscher: Die Karriere des SS-Führers Franz Alfred Six* (Munich: C. H. Beck, 1998), p. 205. Also, according to the Vermerk, II 112 *Betr.* Verbindungen nach Polen, 9 May 1939, Berlin, in Bundesarchiv Koblenz (hereafter cited as BAK), R 58/954, frame (hereafter fr.) 179, the Zentralstelle II P was already in existence by 7 May 1939. I am grateful to Dan Michman of Bar-Ilan University for this citation.

59. Wildt, "Radikalisierung," p. 16.

60. "in Polen Personen zu kennen, die genaue Auskünfte zu einer vollständigen Erfassung des Judentums im Polen geben können." See Vermerk, II 112 *Betr.* Verbindungen nach Polen, 9 May 1939, Berlin, in BAK, R 58/954, fr. 179.

61. Wildt, "Radikalisierung," p. 16. See Vermerk, II 112 *Betr.* Verbindungen nach Polen, 9 May 1939, Berlin, in BAK, R 58/954, fr. 180.

62. Wildt, "Radikalisierung," p. 16.

63. SS Aktenvermerk, 8 July 1939, Berlin, in U.S. Holocaust Memorial Museum Archive (USHMMA), RG 15.007M (Records of the Reichssicherheitshauptamt—RSHA), reel 11, file 154. Werner Best, Heinz Jost, Heinrich Müller, Walter Schellenberg, and Heydrich's adjutant, Hans-Hendrik Neumann, were also in attendance at this meeting.

64. The departments for which Best was responsible were HA-Sipo Amt V: Verwaltung und Recht; Gestapo Abteilung I: Organisation, Personalien, Verwaltung und Recht; and Gestapo Abteilung III: Abwehrangelegenheiten. For more on the positions of responsibility occupied by Best, see ZStL, VI 415 AR 1310/65 E16 (GStA. beim Kammergericht Berlin—1 Js 12/65 [RSHA] Anklageschrift in der Strafsache gegen Dr. Werner Best wegen Mordes vom 10.2.1972), pp. 265ff, and Ulrich Herbert, *Best: Biographische Studien über Radikalismus, Weltanschauung und Vernunft, 1903–1989* (Bonn: J. H. W. Dietz Nachfolger, 1996), p. 580 n. 171.

65. Ibid. Tesmer's offices were HA-Sipo Referat V 3, Personal and Gestapo Referat I E, and Personalangelegenheiten der höheren Beamten des Gestapa, respectively. See also Geschäftsverteilungsplan des Geheimen Staatspolizeiamtes. Stand vom 1 July 1939, Gestapa, B.Nr 8/39 IAg in USHMMA, RG 11.001M.01 (Selected records from the "Osobyi" Archive in Moscow), reel 1, folder 38a, p. 4f.

66. ZStL, VI 415 AR 1310/65 E16 (GStA. beim Kammergericht Berlin—1 Js 12/65 [RSHA] Ermittlungsvermerk vom 1 December 1963, Verfahren gegen Dr. Werner Best, u.a.), p. 61.

67. Besprechung über Grosseinsatz, Kalendarnotiz of Dr. Best, 14 July 1939, cited in ZStL, VI 415 AR 1310/65 E16 (GStA, Kammergericht Berlin—1 Js 12/65 [RSHA] Anklageschrift in der Strafsache gegen Dr. Werner Best wegen Mordes, 10 February 1972), p. 392.

68. Aufstellung ständiger Einsatzkommandos für den SD-RFSS, 22 July 1939, Schellenberg to SS Brigadeführer Jost, Berlin, in USHMMA, RG 11.001M.01 (Selected records from the "Osobyi" Archive in Moscow), reel 1, folder 20.

69. Until recently, scholars thought that the commander of Einsatzgruppe III was Dr. Herbert Fischer. See Michael Wildt, "Radikalisierung und Selbstradikalisierung 1939: Die Geburt des Reichssicherheitsamtes aus dem Geist des völkischen Massenmords," in *Die Gestapo im Zweiten Weltkrieg,* Paul and Mallman, p. 19.

70. Due to a lack of documentation and the late formation of Einsatzgruppe VI, only six of the seven Einsatzgruppen deployed in Poland are examined here. Einsatzgruppe VI was commanded by SS-Oberführer Erich Naumann, formed on 12 September 1939 and deployed in the Poznań district during the second week of the campaign.

71. The approximately 200 police in Einsatzgruppe VI have been included in this numerical total. Several small Einsatzkommandos were also formed in the region of Western Pomerania during and after the campaign. The number of personnel in each has not been included here. Those interested in learning more about EG VI and the other EKs deployed in Poland should refer to ZStL, "Einsatzgruppen in Polen," Jansen and Weckbecker, *Der "Volksdeutsche Selbstschutz" in Polen,* or Dieter Schenck, *Hitler's Mann in Danzig: Albert Forster und die NS-Verbrechen in Danzig–Westpreussen* (Bonn: J. H. W. Dietz Nachfolger, 2000).

72. Fall Weiss—Sonderbestimmungen zu den Anordnungen für die Versorgung, OKH/6.Abt., Gen.St. d.H., 24 July 1939, in National Archives and Records Administration, College Park, MD (NARA), RG 242, T-78, reel (hereafter r.) 351, fr. 6310574–81.

73. Ibid., fr. 6310576–77.

74. "Die Polizeigewalt steht allein den Inhaber vollziehender Gewalt zu. Zu ihrer Ausübung verwenden sie im eigenen Lande im allgemeinen die zuständigen Behörden, in Feindesland die von ihnen betrauten Organe. Alle Polizeikräfte haben demnach nach den Weisungen und im Sinne der Inhaber der vollziehenden Gewalt und der ihnen verantwortlichen Persönlichkeiten zu arbeiten" (ibid., fr. 6310580–81).

75. Ibid.

76. Richtlinien für den auswärtigen Einsatz der Sicherheitspolizei und des SD, 31 July 1939, in ZStL, VI 415 AR 1310/65 E16, 10 February 1972, p. 393.

77. "Aufgabe der sicherheitspolizeilichen Einsatzkommandos ist die Bekämpfung aller reichs- und deutschfeindlichen Elemente in Feindesland rückwärts der fechtenden Truppe." These regulations were also formalized in Schreiben des OKH (6.Abt.-II-Gen.St.d.H., Nr. 1299/39 G.Kdo.), 31 July 1939. See ibid. as well as Helmut Krausnick and Hans-Heinrich Wilhelm, *Die Truppe des Weltanschauungskrieges: Die Einsatzgruppen der Sicherheitspolizei und des SD, 1938–1942* (Stuttgart: Deutsche Verlags-Anstalt, 1981), p. 36.

78. Richtlinien für den auswärtigen Einsatz der Sicherheitspolizei und des SD, 31 July 1939, in ZStL, VI 415 AR 1310/65 E16, p. 394.

79. Ibid., p. 395.

80. Ibid., p. 397.

81. Ibid., p. 397f.

82. Breitman, *Architect*, p. 68.

83. "Die Weisungen, nach denen der polizeiliche Einsatz handelte, ausserordentlich radikal waren (z.B. Liquidationsbefehl für zahlreiche polnische Führungskreise, der in die Tausende ging)." See Schreiben des Chefs der Sipo und des SD an SS-Obergruppenführer General Kurt Daluege, 2 July 1940, in ZStL, Der Generalstaatsanwalt bei dem Kammergericht—1 Js 12/65 (RSHA)—Ermittlungsvermerk, 1 December 1968, Verfahren gegen Dr. Werner Best u.a. ASA 179, p. 128.

84. Besprechung über Grosseinsatz, Kalendarnotiz of Dr. Best, 14 August 1939, in ZStL, VI 415 AR 1310/65 E16, p. 401. It is not clear if Heydrich was present at these meetings.

85. Testimony of Lothar Beutel, 20 July 1965, in ibid., p. 408.

86. Names compiled from the testimony of Lothar Beutel and Emanuel Schaefer in ibid., pp. 401ff.

87. Testimony of Lothar Beutel, 20 April 1971, in ibid., p. 411.

88. Another participant in the conference also recounted this list of enemies. See Testimony of Dr. Ernst Gerke, 2 November 1966, in ibid., p. 414.

89. Testimony of Lothar Beutel, 20 July 1965, in ibid., p. 408. Regarding the targeting of the Polish intelligentsia for elimination, Beutel reiterated in testimony he gave several years later: "Für die Teilnehmer an dieser Besprechung war danach klar, dass die Einsatzgruppen im besonderes Augenmerk auf diese Gruppen zu richten hatten" (20 April 1971, in ibid., p. 412).

90. Testimony of Dr. Ernst Gerke, 2 November 1966, in ibid., p. 414.

91. ZStL, Der Generalstaatsanwalt bei dem Kammergericht—1 Js 12/65 (RSHA)—Ermittlungsvermerk, 1 December 1968, Verfahren gegen Dr. Werner Best, u.a., ASA 179, pp. 60f. The estimate of 61,000 names comes from the research of Polish historian P. Dubiel and is cited in Sybille Steinbacher, *"Musterstadt" Auschwitz: Germanisierungspolitik und Judenmord in Ostoberschlesien* (Munich: K. G. Saur, 2000), p. 54.

92. Evidence is provided in Herbert, *Best*, p. 236, that the Security Police began collecting the names of Poles in 1936, and particularly "since June 1938 the names of the leading representatives of Polish clubs and associations in Upper Silesia were compiled." The creation of specific Sonderfahndungsbücher for Poland began in June 1939, according to Christoph Klessmann and Wacław Długoborski, "Nationalsozialistische Bildungspolitik und polnische Hochschulen 1939–1945," *Geschichte und Gesellschaft* 23, no. 4 (1997): 536.

93. Testimony of Werner Best, 10 June 1969, in ZStL, VI 415 AR 1310/65 E16, p. 380.

94. Ibid.

95. Ibid., p. 381.

96. Testimony of Walter Huppenkothen, 11 August 1960, in ZStL, 8 AR-Z 52/60 (StA. Würzburg—1 Js 2469/60—Verfahren gegen Dr. Alfred Hasselberg wegen Mordes), vol. 1, p. 175.

97. Vermerk OKW/Abwehr, 26 August 1939, in NARA, RG 242, T-312, r. 47, fr. 7559979.

98. Robert M. Citino, *The Path to Blitzkrieg: Doctrine and Training in the German Army, 1920–1939* (Boulder, CO: Lynne Rienner Publishers, 1999).

99. I am grateful to Dennis Showalter for this phrase.

100. Sonderbestimmungen zu den Anordnungen für die Versorgung, AOK 4, August 1939, in NARA, RG 242, T-314, r. 846, fr. 1123.

101. Besondere Anordnungen für die Heeresversorgung AOK 8, Beilage 1 zu Anlage 5 "Sonderbestimmungen," 16 August 1939, in NARA, RG 242, T-312, r. 39, fr. 7548618-20.

102. Sonderbestimmungen zu den Anordnungen für die Versorgung, 6.Abt., OKH, Gen.St.d.H., 21 August 1939, in NARA, RG 242, T-311, r. 236, fr. 1034.

103. Kriegstagebuch Ic/AO, AOK 14, 26 August 1939, in NARA, RG 242, T-312, r. 477, fr. 8068051.

104. Bekämpfung aller volks- und staatsgefährdenden Bestrebungen im Operationsgebiet des AOK 8, 28 August 1939, in NARA, RG 242, T-314, r. 870, fr. 64. Incidentally, these orders also required the men to report on any case of espionage or treason within their own ranks.

105. Klaus Gessner, *Geheime Feldpolizei. Zur Funktion und Organisation des Geheimpolizeilichen Exekutivorgans der Faschistischen Wehrmacht* (Berlin: Militärverlag der DDR, 1986), and Klaus Gessner, "Geheime Feldpolizei—die Gestapo der Wehrmacht," in *Vernichtungskrieg. Verbrechen der Wehrmacht 1941–1944,* ed. H. Heer and K. Naumann (Hamburg: HIS Verlagsges, 1995), pp. 343–357.

106. Gessner, *Geheime Feldpolizei,* p. 34.

107. Ibid., pp. 37, 42.

108. Gessner, "Geheime Feldpolizei—die Gestapo der Wehrmacht," p. 346.

109. Gessner, *Geheime Feldpolizei,* p. 38.

110. Paul Brown, "Forester to *Feldpolizeichef*: The Life and Counterintelligence Career of Wilhelm Krichbaum," (Master's thesis, Southern Illinois University, 1999), pp. 41ff.

111. Ibid., p. 44, suggests that Krichbaum's appointment as head of the GFP by Canaris may indeed have been motivated by the fact that he was close to Best and Heydrich, which allowed Canaris to coordinate counterintelligence efforts between the Security Police and GFP as well as keep tabs on the activities of the Einsatzgruppen.

112. Sonderbestimmungen zu den Anordnungen für die Versorgung, 6.Abt., OKH, Gen.St.d.H., 21 August 1939, in NARA, RG 242, T-311, r. 236, fr. 1034.

113. Bekämpfung aller Volks- und Staatsgefährdenden Bestrebungen im Operationsgebiet des AOK 8, 28 August 1939, in NARA, RG 242, T-314, r. 870, fr. 62.

114. Ibid., fr. 63–64.

115. My emphasis. Vortrag des Ministerialrats Dr. Danckwerts über "Die Stellung und die Aufgaben des Chefs der Zivilverwaltung," 26 February 1936, in NARA, RG 242, T-77, r. 1432, fr. 296. This report was produced in the Reich War Ministry, which was dissolved in 1938.

116. Generaloberst Franz Halder, *Kriegstagebuch*, vol. 1, *Vom Polenfeldzug bis zum Ende der Westoffensiv (14.8.1939–30.6.1940)* (Stuttgart: W. Kohlhammer Verlag, 1962), p. 32.

117. A detailed explanation of the authority held by the CdZ can be found in Hans Umbreit, *Deutsche Militärverwaltungen 1938/39: Die militärische Besetzung der Tschechoslowakei und Polens* (Stuttgart: Deutsche Verlags-Anstalt, 1977), pp. 13–24.

118. Klaus-Jürgen Müller, *Das Heer und Hitler: Armee und nationalsozialistisches Regime, 1933–1940* (Stuttgart: Deutsche Verlags-Anstalt, 1969), p. 426, notes that Hitler made clear the authority of the CdZ vis-à-vis the army on 8 September, thereby challenging the military's claim to be the sole holder of executive authority.

119. ZStL, "Einsatzgruppen in Polen," p. 96.

120. Müller, *Das Heer und Hitler*, p. 426. See also Umbreit, *Militärverwaltungen*, p. 86.

121. Schenk, *Hitler's Mann in Danzig*, p. 145.

122. Krausnick and Wilhelm, *Die Truppe*, pp. 87ff.

123. Halder, *Kriegstagebuch*, p. 30.

124. Charles W. Sydnor Jr., "Theodor Eicke: Organisator der Konzentrationslager," in *Die SS: Elite unter dem Totenkopf 30 Lebensläufe*, ed. R. Smelser and E. Syring (Paderborn: Schöningh, 2000), pp. 147–159.

125. Charles W. Sydnor Jr., *Soldiers of Destruction: The SS Death's Head Division, 1933–1945*, rev. ed. (Princeton, N.J.: Princeton University Press, 1990), p. 35. See also Bernd Wegner, *Hitlers Politische Soldaten: Die Waffen-SS, 1933–1945* (Paderborn: Schöningh, 1990).

126. According to Richard Breitman, *Official Secrets: What the Nazis Planned, What the British and Americans Knew* (New York: Hill and Wang, 1998), p. 32: "On August 25, 1939, Himmler's chief of staff, Karl Wolff, following Himmler's instructions, wrote to Daluege, Heydrich, and Eicke to have them pass sealed envelopes along to the commanders of various police and Waffen-SS units to be used in Poland; these envelopes contained what Wolff described only as an SS order. The commanders were to open the envelopes and alert their men to the contents just before operations began." Although copies of these documents no longer exist, it is plausible to suggest from the operations of the SSTVs and Einsatzgruppen in Poland that Himmler's instructions ordered SS commanders to terrorize Polish Jews in order to force their flight east from German-held Poland to Soviet occupied territory. See Chapter 4 of this book on anti-Jewish policy.

127. Rudolf Höss, *Kommandant in Auschwitz: Autobiographische Aufzeichnungen von Rudolf Höss*, ed. M. Broszat (Stuttgart: Deutsche Verlags-Anstalt, 1958), p. 72.

128. Ibid.

129. Field Marshal Wilhelm Keitel testified at Nuremberg that Brauchitsch pressed Hitler to grant the army executive authority in response to the complaints of many German officers about excesses committed by the SS during the occupa-

tion of Czechoslovakia in March 1939. Keitel claimed that SS activities had shocked many in the officer corps and that they did not want a repeat of these crimes in Poland. See Krausnick and Wilhelm, *Die Truppe,* p. 39. Keitel's claim is curious considering that the military had participated in helping the SS identify and arrest thousands of suspected Czech communists in 1938 and 1939. For more on this see Umbreit, *Militärverwaltungen,* p. 57.

130. The 26 August notation in Halder's war diary specifically mentions discussing the question of the army's executive authority with Wagner; see *Kriegstagebuch,* p. 32.

131. *Der Generalquartiermeister,* p. 103.

132. Wagner cited in Krausnick and Wilhelm, *Die Truppe,* p. 40.

133. The phrase Halder recorded in his diary was "Festnahmen nach A-1 Kartei" (*Kriegstagebuch,* p. 44).

134. Ibid.

135. Ibid.

136. ZStL, 211 AR-Z 13/63 Strafverfahren gegen Lothar Beutel et al., p. 15.

137. Helmut Krausnick, "Hitler und die Morde in Polen: Ein Beitrag zum Konflikt zwischen Heer und SS um die Verwaltung der besetzten Gebiete," *Vierteljahrshefte für Zeitgeschichte* 11, no. 2 (April 1963): 198.

138. Die polnische Armee, 8 August 1927, Reichswehrministerium (Heer), Heeres-Statistisches-Abteilung, Nr. 550.27.geh.T3. Berlin, in NARA, RG 242, T-79, r. 53, fr. 000237. Congress Poles were those who inhabited the regions of Poland that were formerly part of the Russian empire.

139. Ibid., fr. 000238. Units composed of troops from Congress Poland were said to have "often collapsed" during the Russo-Polish war.

140. Ibid., fr. 000238.

141. Taschenbuch: polnisches Heer, 10.Div., Ia, Nr. 947 G.Kdo., Regensburg, 24 July 1939, in NARA, RG 242, T-79, r. 131, fr. 000595.

142. Ibid.

143. Ibid., fr. 000596–97.

144. Ibid.

145. Ibid.

146. Polen, Staatsgebiet und Bevölkerung, Wehrmacht Propagandaamt, OKW, 25 August 1939, in NARA, RG 242, T-312, r. 45, fr. 7557429.

147. Ibid.

148. Ibid.

149. Those interested in a map of German settlements in Poland created by the Wehrmacht Propaganda Office for the campaign should refer to "Karte der Deutschen Siedlungen in Mittelpolen," Wehrmacht Propagandaamt, OKW, August 1939, in NARA, RG 242, T-79, r. 154, fr. 498.

150. For more information on the Wehrmacht's role in establishing an ethnic German militia in western Poland, see Jansen and Weckbecker, *Der "Volksdeutsche Selbstschutz" in Polen,* p. 46f.

151. Merkblatt zur Bekanntgabe an die gegen Polen eingesetzten Truppen, AK VI, 22 August 1939, in NARA, RG 242, T-314, r. 846, fr. 1042.

152. Deutsches Volkstum in Polen, AOK 8, 26 August 1939, in NARA, RG 242, T-314, r. 870, fr. 197–212.

153. Polen-Orientierungsmaterial für die Unterrichtung der Truppe, Wehrmacht Propagandaamt, OKW, 23 August 1939, in NARA, RG 242, T-312, r. 46, fr. 7558115.

154. Ibid.

155. Merkblatt über Eigenarten der polnischen Kriegsführung, 12.Abt.(III), OKH, Gen.St.d.H., Nr. 1343/39g, Berlin, 1 July 1939, in NARA, RG 242, T-79, r. 131, fr. 000525.

156. Ibid.

157. Besondere Anordnungen für die rückwärtigen Dienste Nr. 1, 24 August 1939, Anlage 1, Merkblatt zur Bekanntgabe an die gegen Polen eingesetzten Truppen, AOK 8, in NARA, RG 242, T-312, r. 39, fr. 7548860.

158. One particularly feared Polish group was the "Taschna Organizacja Konspiracyna," an organization formed primarily of Poles from Pomerania who were well trained in the use of explosives and guerrilla tactics. See Polnisches Sabotageorganisation, Ic/AO, AOK 10, Nr. 206/39, Abw. IIIg., Oppeln, 31 August 1939, in NARA, RG 242, T-79, r. 8, fr. 001223.

159. Anlage 6 zu Hgr.Kdo.3 Ia Nr.150/39. G.K.Chefs.v., 14 June 1939, in *TWC*, vol. 30, Document 2327-PS, p. 192.

160. Halder, *Kriegstagebuch,* p. 19.

161. Sonderbestimmungen zu den Anordnungen für die Versorgung, O.Qu., AOK 4, August 1939, in NARA, RG 242, T-314, r. 846, fr. 1121.

162. Besondere Anweisung zum Merkblatt Ziff.7a und b. für die Ic A/O der AOKs und Generalkommandos und die Ic der Divisionen, OKH, 22 August 1939, in NARA, RG 242, T-77, r. 1501, fr. 964.

163. Bekämpfung aller Volks- und Staatsgefährdenden Bestrebungen im Operationsgebiet des AOK 8, 28 August 1939, in NARA, RG 242, T-314, r. 870, fr. 61.

164. Propaganda Report from Propagandakompanie 689 entitled "Gewehr bei Fuss," 29 August 1939, in BA/MA, RW 4/v.261. "Wohin unser March geführt hatte überall waren wir die Zeugen des Aufmarsches gegen die polnische Frechheit."

165. Kriegstagebuch der 21 Infanterie Division vom Einsatz im Polenfeldzug, 25 August–30 September 1939, p. 6, in BA/MA, RH 26-19/2.

Chapter 2. Nazi Radicals and SS Killers

1. Christopher R. Browning, *Ordinary Men: Reserve Police Battalion 101 and the Final Solution in Poland* (New York: HarperCollins, 1992), and Daniel Jonah Goldhagen, *Hitler's Willing Executioners: Ordinary Germans and the Holocaust* (New York: Alfred Knopf, 1996).

2. SS Aktenvermerk, Berlin, 4 July 1940, Berlin, in ZStL, 211 AR-Z 13/63, Strafverfahren gegen Lothar Beutel, Helmut Bischoff, Walter Hammer, Erich Preckel und andere Angehörige der Einsatzgruppe IV wegen Mordes. (NS-Gewaltverbrechen in Polen 1939), p. 21.

3. Schellenberg an die Zentralabteilung III 2, SS-Brigadeführer Jost, Berlin, 22 July 1939, Stabskanzlei IL 1939/0 in USHMMA, RG 11.001M.01 (Selected records from the "Osobyi" Archive in Moscow), reel 1, folder 20.

4. Sonderreferat "Unternehmen Tannenberg" (SV1 Nr. 86/39-151-9), 25 Au-

gust 1939, in ZStL, VI 415 AR 1310/65 E, 16 Anklageschrift in der Strafsache gegen Dr. Werner Best wegen Mordes vom 10.2.1972, p. 291.

5. Ibid. The staff of the Sonderreferat "Unternehmen Tannenberg" included Dr. Heinrich Meyer, Dr. Rudolf Bilfinger, Kurt Hafke, Heinz Engelmann, Erwin Jarosch, Dr. Theodor Paeffgen, Walter Renken, Albert Reipert, Dr. Johannes Viegene, and Rudi Moser.

6. See Generaloberst Franz Halder, *Kriegstagebuch, Band. I: Vom Polenfeldzug bis zum Ende der Westoffensiv (14.8.1939–30.6.1940)* (Stuttgart: W. Kohlhammer Verlag, 1962), pp. 31–40, in which the army commander in chief, Field Marshal von Brauchitsch, confirmed 1 September as the new date for the attack.

7. Lebenslauf of Bruno Streckenbach, NARA, RG 242, Records of the Berlin Document Center (BDC) file of Bruno Streckenbach, A3343 SSO-165B, fr. 1152.

8. Ibid.

9. Ibid.

10. Led by Wolfgang Kapp and General Walther von Lüttwitz, the right-wing attempt to overthrow the Weimar Government on 13 March 1920 using Freikorps formations from all over Germany resulted in failure owing to internecine squabbling and a lack of clear goals. See Robert G. L. Waite, *Vanguard of Nazism: The Free Corps Movement in Postwar Germany, 1918–1923* (New York: W. W. Norton, 1952), pp. 140–182.

11. Ibid.

12. SS Stammrollenblatt of Bruno Streckenbach, 19 April 1934, in NARA, RG 242, BDC File of Bruno Streckenbach, A3343 SSO-165B, fr. 1403.

13. ZStL, VI 415 AR 1310/63 E 32 (StA. Hamburg—147 Js 31/67 Anklageschrift gegen Bruno Streckenbach vom 30.6.1973), p. 5f.

14. Ibid. See also NARA, RG 242, BDC File of Bruno Streckenbach, p. 1147.

15. SS Stammrollenblatt, 19 April 1934, fr. 1403, and Streckenbach an das SS-Hauptamt, 2 December 1936, in ibid., fr. 1186.

16. ZStL, "Einsatzgruppen in Polen: Einsatzgruppen der Sicherheitspolizei, Selbstschutz und andere Formationen in der Zeit vom 1. September bis Frühjahr 1940," 10 June 1962, pp. 32ff.

17. Lebenslauf, 20 April 1934, in NARA, RG 242, BDC File of Ludwig Hahn, A3343 SSO-053A, fr. 136. Hahn described his father as a farmer, whose land included 150 hectares.

18. Ibid., fr. 137, and Fragebogen, 10 August 1937, in ibid., fr. 133.

19. Ibid., fr. 139.

20. SS Stammrollenauszug, 15 February 1937, in ibid., fr. 147, 170.

21. Ibid., fr. 126.

22. Ibid., fr. 162, 170.

23. Personal-Bericht, 28 December 1937, in ibid., fr. 130, 139.

24. Personal-Bericht, 15 June 1936, in NARA, RG 242, BDC File of Bruno Müller, A3343 SSO-327A, fr. 864.

25. SS Stammrollenauszug, 29 October 1934, in ibid., fr. 912.

26. Ibid.

27. Beurteilung, 23 April 1936, in ibid., fr. 883.

28. Fragebogen, 22 October 1936, in ibid., fr. 854.

29. Ibid., fr. 852.

30. Personal-Bericht, 13 May 1938, in ibid., fr. 880.

31. Beurteilung, 23 April 1936, in ibid., fr. 883.

32. Lebenslauf in NARA, RG 242, BDC File of Alfred Hasselberg, A3343 SSO-068A, fr. 1189.

33. Ibid.

34. Ibid., fr. 1190.

35. Ibid.

36. Ibid.

37. Ibid., fr. 1188, 1190.

38. Ibid., fr. 1191.

39. Ibid.

40. Ibid., fr. 1178.

41. Ibid.

42. Personal-Bericht, in ibid., fr. 1185.

43. Lebenslauf, 17 April 1934, in NARA, RG 242, BDC File of Karl Brunner, A3343 SSO-112, fr. 113. Brunner's father's civil service position put his family solidly into the upper middle-class in imperial Germany. Also see Jens Banach, *Heydrichs Elite: Das Führerkorps der Sicherheitspolizei und des SD, 1936–1945* (Paderborn: Schöningh, 1998), p. 42.

44. Lebenslauf, 17 April 1934, in NARA, RG 242, BDC File of Karl Brunner, A3343 SSO-112, fr. 113.

45. Ibid.

46. Ibid.

47. Ibid.

48. Ibid.

49. SS Stammrollenauszug in ibid., fr. 160.

50. Ibid., fr. 103.

51. Dienstlaufbahn, in ibid., fr. 108.

52. Personal-Bericht, 1 March 1936, in ibid., fr. 114.

53. ZStL, 201 AR-Z 76/59 (StA. Hamburg—141 Js 31/67 Verfahren gegen Bruno Streckenbach), vol. 1, p. 126.

54. Testimony of Dr. Ludwig H., 20 July 1960, in ZStL, 8 AR-Z 52/60 (StA. Würzburg—1 Js 2469/60 Verfahren gegen Dr. Alfred Hasselberg wegen Mordes), vol. 1, p. 148f. See also ZStL, 211 AR-Z 13/63 (StA. Berlin—3P[k] Js 198/61—Schlussvermerk in dem Strafverfahren gegen Lothar Beutel und andere Angehörige EG IV wegen Mordes vom 29 January 1971), pp. 12ff.

55. Ibid.

56. ZStL, "Einsatzgruppen in Polen," p. 22.

57. Testimony of Heinrich Johann zum Broock, 6 November 1963, and testimony of Walter Huppenkothen, 28 October 1964, in ZStL, 201 AR-Z 76/59, vol. 2, pp. 219, 221, and 252.

58. Personalangaben, 19 November 1941, in NARA, RG 242, BDC File of Johann Schmer, A3343 SSO-083B, fr. 660.

59. Personal-Bericht, 4 December 1941, in ibid., fr. 674.

60. For more on the Nazi consolidation of police power and the BPP, see Shlomo Aronson, *Reinhard Heydrich und die Frühgeschichte von Gestapo und SD* (Stuttgart: Deutsche Verlags-Anstalt, 1971), pp. 98ff, and George C. Browder,

Hitler's Enforcers: The Gestapo and the SS Security Service in the Nazi Revolution (New York: Oxford University Press, 1996), pp. 40ff, 204f.

61. NARA, RG 242, BDC File of Johann Schmer, A3343 SSO-083B, fr. 659.

62. Testimony of Johann Schmer, 27 September 1960, in ZStL, 8 AR-Z 52/60, vol. 2, p. 302. Information on the deployment of SS Einsatzgruppen in Austria and Bohemia/Moravia can be found in Helmut Krausnick and Hans-Heinrich Wilhelm, *Die Truppe des Weltanschauungskrieges: Die Einsatzgruppen der Sicherheitspolizei und des SD 1938–1942* (Stuttgart: Deutsche Verlags-Anstalt, 1981), pp. 19–31, and Hans Umbreit, *Deutsche Militärverwaltungen 1938/39: Die militärische Besetzung der Tschechoslowakei und Polens* (Stuttgart: Deutsche Verlags-Anstalt, 1977), pp. 30–62.

63. Testimony of Johann Schmer, 27 September 1960, in ZStL, 8 AR-Z 52/60, vol. 2, p. 302f.

64. Testimony of Bruno Streckenbach, 1 November 1961, in ZStL, 201 AR-Z 76/59, vol. 1, p. 126.

65. Ibid., p. 128, and Abwehrbericht, AOK 14, Ic/AO an der Ic/AO der Heeresgruppe Süd, 2 September 1939, in NARA, RG 242, T-311, r. 265, fr. 143. See also ZStL, "Einsatzgruppen in Polen," pp. 33ff.

66. Testimony of Bruno Streckenbach, 1 November 1961, in ZStL, 201 AR-Z 76/59, vol. 1, p. 126.

67. Testimony of Emanuel Schaefer, 25 November 1960, in ZStL, 8 AR-Z 52/60, vol. 2, p. 347, during which he stated that EG II was "eine völlig zusammengewürfelter Haufen" ("a completely thrown together crowd").

68. Testimony of Richard Schulze, 29 July 1960, in ZStL, 201 AR-Z 76/59, vol. 1, p. 126. The HA-Sipo ordered Schulze to report to Oppeln on 22 August. "Kriminalrat" translates roughly as "criminal councillor" and is equivalent to the military rank of captain.

69. Testimony of Hellmut R., 24 August 1960, in ZStL, 8 AR-Z 52/60, vol. 2, p. 242f.

70. NARA, RG 242, BDC File of Emanuel Schaefer, A3343 SSO-066B, fr. 004.

71. Ibid., fr. 005.

72. Lebenslauf, 6 May 1937, in ibid., fr. 008.

73. Christopher R. Browning notes that Schaefer "left the *Stahlhelm* in 1928 because he had 'the impression that the *Stahlhelm* was atrophying'" (*Fateful Months: Essays on the Emergence of the Final Solution* [New York: Holmes and Meier, 1985], p. 73).

74. Eric A. Johnson, *Nazi Terror: The Gestapo, Jews, and Ordinary Germans* (New York: Basic Books, 1999), p. 54.

75. NARA, RG 242, BDC file of Emanuel Schaefer, A3343 SSO-066B, fr. 4, and Personal-Bericht, 12 July 1937, Breslau, in ibid., fr. 47. Schaefer actually adopted Lutheranism in 1926 but became an agnostic in May 1928.

76. Johnson, *Nazi Terror*, p. 55.

77. Ibid., p. 53.

78. NARA, RG 242, BDC File of Emanuel Schaefer, A3343 SSO-066B, fr. 004, lists Schaefer's promotions as SS-Untersturmführer (September 1936), Obersturmführer (April 1937), Hauptsturmführer (August 1938), and Obersturmbannführer (10 September 1939).

79. For the best short description of events surrounding the Gleiwitz "attack," see Jürgen Runzheimer, "Die Grenzzwischenfälle am Abend vor dem deutschen Angriff auf Polen," in *Sommer 1939: Die Grossmächte und der Europäische Krieg,* ed. W. Benz and H. Graml (Stuttgart: Deutsche Verlags-Anstalt, 1979).

80. Lebenslauf, 23 March 1937, in NARA, RG 242, BDC file of Otto Sens, A3343 SSO-133B, fr. 115.

81. Ibid.

82. Ibid., fr. 116. Sens never attended a university.

83. Dienstlaufbahn Otto Sens in ibid., fr. 102.

84. Ibid.

85. Personalangaben, 17 March 1939, in NARA, RG 242, BDC file of Karl-Heinz Rux, A3343 SSO-068A, fr. 679.

86. Ibid., fr. 680.

87. Ibid., fr. 666.

88. Ibid., fr. 680.

89. Dienstlaufbahn in ibid., fr. 669.

90. Unternehmen Tannenberg–Tagesbericht, HA-Sipo (s.V.1-S.Nr. 57/39), 6 September 1939, in USHMMA, RG 15.007M (Records of the Reich Security Main Office–RSHA), File 1, R. 2, p. 1, indicates that Sens's EK closely followed the IV Corps into Poland.

91. ZStL, "Einsatzgruppen in Polen," pp. 40ff.

92. Recent research carried out by Klaus-Michael Mallman and Michael Wildt has revealed that the commander of Einsatzgruppe III was indeed Hans Fischer and not Dr. Herbert Fischer, as was previously thought. See Michael Wildt, "Radikalisierung und Selbstradikalisierung 1939: Die Geburt des Reichsicherheitsamtes aus dem Geist des völkischen Massenmords," in *Die Gestapo im Zweiten Weltkrieg: Heimatfront und besetztes Europa,* ed. Gerhard Paul and Klaus-Michael Mallman (Darmstadt: Wissenschaftliche Buchgesellschaft, 2000), p. 19.

93. Lebenslauf in NARA, RG 242, BDC File of Hans Fischer, A3343 SSO-208, fr. 536.

94. Ibid., fr. 487. Fischer also joined the NSDAP three months later in May 1932.

95. See Stellenbesetzung, 8 March 1935, in ibid., fr. 487, 513.

96. Schreiben Personalkanzlei v.3.IX.1935, Tgb. Nr. 19658, 20 September 1935, in ibid., fr. 532.

97. Ibid., fr. 487.

98. Personal-Bericht in ibid., fr. 495.

99. Testimony of Leo Stanek, 24 March 1960, in ZStL, 8 AR-Z 52/60, vol. 1, p. 20.

100. Testimony of Alois Globisch, 28 September 1960, in ibid., p. 308.

101. Testimony of Josef Maurer, 20 September 1960, in ibid., p. 289.

102. Testimony of Georg Lothar Hoffmann in Vermerk, 19 July 1960, in ibid., p. 113. Alois Globisch similarly recalled that the majority of men in EG III were from Silesia; ibid., p. 308.

103. Lebenslauf, 6 October 1939, in NARA, RG 242, BDC File of Wilhelm Scharpwinkel, A3343 SSo-071B, fr. 291. See also Personalangaben, 3 April 1939, in ibid., fr. 295. Scharpwinkel's father was a sales employee.

104. Ibid., fr. 295.

105. Scharpwinkel worked for the Reichsanstalt für Arbeitsvermittlung und Arbeitslosenversicherung, in ibid., fr. 294, 306.

106. According to ibid., fr. 307, the transfer from Breslau to Liegnitz took place on 15 July 1939.

107. Ibid.

108. Lebenslauf, 16 August 1938, in NARA, RG 242, BDC File of Fritz Liphardt, A3343 SSO-268A, fr. 138.

109. Ibid., fr. 114.

110. Beforderungsvorschlag, 1 September 1938, in ibid., fr. 132.

111. Personalangaben, in ibid., fr. 143.

112. Personal-Bericht, in ibid., fr. 136.

113. ZStL, "Einsatzgruppen in Polen," pp. 46–54.

114. See Gail H. Nelson, "The Molding of Personality: SS Indoctrination and Training Techniques" (Master's thesis, University of Colorado at Boulder, 1966), pp. 64ff, for more on the Ordensburg at Krössinsee. The town of Dramburg (Drawsko) is commonly cited as the location where EG IV assembled. The testimony of Lothar Beutel and many other members of his Operational Group makes it clear, however, that the Ordensburg of Krössinsee was the assembly point for Einsatzgruppe IV.

115. NARA, RG 242, BDC file of Lothar Beutel, A3343 SSO-066, fr. 265. According to Waite, *Vanguard,* pp. 198ff, the Orgesch was a nationwide combination of groups called Civil Guards that, although filled with nationalistically inclined veteran volunteers, were not as radically violent as many of the Freikorps formations that fought in the east from 1919–1921.

116. NARA, RG 242, BDC file of Lothar Beutel, A3343 SSO-066, fr. 264f.

117. Testimony of Lothar Beutel, 27 January 1964, in ZStL, 211 AR-Z 13/63 (StA. Berlin—3P[k] Js 198/61—Schlussvermerk in dem Strafverfahren gegen Lothar Beutel und andere Angehörige EG IV wegen Mordes vom 29 January 1971), vol. 8, p. 1729. Beutel never specified the name of the university where he was trained.

118. Ibid.

119. Ibid., p. 1730.

120. NARA, RG 242, BDC file of Lothar Beutel, A3343 SSO-066, fr. 264.

121. ZStL, "Einsatzgruppen in Polen," p. 56, incorrectly lists Hammer as the commander of EK 1/IV and Bischoff as the head of EK 2/IV. Hammer confirmed his assignment as head of EK 2/IV in his interrogation on 13 January 1964, in ZStL, 211 AR-Z 13/63, vol. 1, p. 7.

122. Lebenslauf, 18 August 1937, in NARA, RG 242, BDC File of Helmut Bischoff, A3343 SSO-073, fr. 290.

123. Beförderung des SS-Sturmbannführers Helmut Bischoff, RSHA I5a, Az: 1702, 31 March 1943, in ibid., fr. 294.

124. Ibid.

125. Fragebogen, 15 August 1939, in ibid., fr. 284.

126. Lebenslauf, in NARA, RG 242, BDC File of Walter Hammer, A3343 SSO-058A, fr. 766.

127. Testimony of Walter Hammer, 13 January 1964, in ZStL, 211 AR-Z 13/53, vol. 1, p. 7. According to Hammer's Lebenslauf, in ibid., fr. 767, he also became a member of the SS in December 1936.

128. Testimony of Walter Hammer, 13 January 1964, in ibid., p. 7. Also see "Personalangaben, 30 September 1938," in NARA, RG 242, BDC File of Walter Hammer, A3343 SSO-058A, fr. 762, which notes that Hammer completed two months of training with the 1st Flak Regiment–Gotha in early 1938.

129. Testimony of Erich Müller, 30 November 1964, in ZStL, 211 AR-Z 13/53, vol. 1, p. 113.

130. West German investigators never determined accurate numbers of personnel from the offices in Köslin and Schneidemühl.

131. Testimony of Fritz Kruttke, 15 May 1967, in ZStL, 211 AR-Z 13/53, vol. 7, p. 1474.

132. Testimony of Erich Müller, 30 November 1964, in ZStL, 211 AR-Z 13/53, vol. 1, p. 113.

133. Testimony of Bischoff quoted in Schlussvermerk, 29 January 1971, in ZStL, 211 AR-Z 13/53, vol. 1, p. 103.

134. Testimony of Heinz Schmidt, 8 January 1963, in ZStL, 211 AR-Z 13/53, vol. 1, Anlage A, p. 26.

135. ZStL, "Einsatzgruppen in Polen," p. 56.

136. NARA, RG 242, BDC file of Ernst Damzog, A3343 SSO-135, fr. 323, notes that Damzog was promoted to Standartenführer on 10 September 1939, during the invasion of Poland.

137. Lebenslauf des Kriminal-Direktors Damzog, 20 June 1933, in ibid., fr. 332.

138. Ibid., fr. 316.

139. Aronson, *Heydrich und die Frühgeschichte von Gestapo und SD*, pp. 157f. See also Geschäftsverteilungsplan des Geheimen Staatspolizeiamtes, Stand vom 1 July 1939, Gestapa, B.Nr 8/39 IAg, in USHMMA, RG 11.001M.01 (Select records from the "Osobyi" Archive in Moscow), r. 1, folder 38a, p. 17.

140. Personal-Bericht, 19 June 1938, in NARA, RG 242, BDC File of Ernst Damzog, A3343 SSO-135, fr. 325. See also Banach, *Heydrichs Elite*, p. 298.

141. ZStL, "Einsatzgruppen in Polen," p. 67. Two other small units, Einsatzkommando 11 and Einsatzkommando 12, were likely assigned to Einsatzgruppe V as well.

142. NARA, RG 242, BDC File of Dr. Heinz Graefe, A3343, SSO-026A, fr. 841.

143. Lebenslauf, 29 August 1938, in ibid., fr. 853.

144. Ibid., fr. 854.

145. Beförderung des SS-Sturmbannführers Dr. Heinz Graefe, 15 March 1943, in ibid., p. 871.

146. Lebenslauf, 29 August 1938, in ibid., fr. 854.

147. Personalangaben, 30 August 1938, in ibid., fr. 856.

148. NARA, RG 242, BDC File of Dr. Heinz Graefe, A3343 SSO-026A, fr. 867.

149. Personal-Bericht, n.d., in ibid., fr. 850.

150. NARA, RG 242, BDC file of Dr. Robert Schefe, A3343 SSO-072B, fr. 1445.

151. Ibid., fr. 1440.

152. Ibid., fr. 1441.

153. ZStL, "Einsatzgruppen in Polen," p. 66f.

154. Ibid., p. 65.

155. ZStL, 205 AR-Z 302/67 (StA. Stuttgart—85 Js 49—53/74—Verfahren gegen Udo von Woyrsch), vol. 3, p. 80of.

156. Hellwig was the commanding officer of the Führerschule der Sipo in Berlin-Charlottenburg. See Testimony of Kurt J., 12 December 1961, in ZStL, 205 AR-Z 302/67, vol. 1, p. 79.

157. Testimony of Fritz S., 30 October 1963, in Aktenvermerk der ZStL, 205 AR-Z 302/67, vol. 1, p. 139, and Brief der Landeskriminalamt Baden-Württemberg an die Zentrale Stelle, 5 February 1964, in ZStL, 205 AR-Z 302/67, vol. 1, p. 157.

158. ZStL, "Einsatzgruppen in Polen," pp. 85, 200. Also worth noting are the central roles that Hellwig, Trummler, and Rasch played in contriving the Polish "attacks" on German border posts on 31 August. These attacks were used by the regime as a pretext for the German invasion, which the German press portrayed as retaliatory and defensive. The personnel used to stage the attacks came from the contingents of Sipo cadets commanded by Hellwig and Trummler. According to Runzheimer, "Die Grenzzwischenfälle," pp. 113ff, the number of cadets involved totaled 150.

159. Hans-Joachim Neufeldt, Jürgen Huck, and Georg Tessin, eds., *Zur Geschichte der Ordnungspolizei, 1936–1945* (Koblenz: Schriften des Bundesarchivs, 1957), p. 33.

160. These figures come from Winfried Nachtwei, "Ganz normale Männer: Die Verwicklung von Polizeibataillonen aus dem Rheinland und Westfalen in den nationalsozialistischen Vernichtungskrieg," in *Villa Ten Hompel: Sitz der Ordnungspolizei im Dritten Reich,* ed. Alfons Kenkmann (Münster: Agenda Verlag, 1996), pp. 54–77.

161. Some of the information presented in Neufeldt, Huck, and Tessin, *Zur Geschichte der Ordnungspolizei,* on the police battalions in the Einsatzgruppe z.b.V. does not agree with the original documentation. The authors note that the five police battalions under von Woyrsch were designated the First Police Group. However, documents from both the RSHA and the army's VIII Corps refer to the unit as the Third Police Regiment. See Meldung des Polizeiregiments 3, Kdo. Ia, 5 September 1939, quoted in Krausnick and Wilhelm, *Die Truppe,* p. 51.

162. NARA, RG 242, BDC file of Udo von Woyrsch, A3342 SSO-013C, fr. 970.

163. Holger H. Herwig, *The First World War: Germany and Austria-Hungary, 1914–1918* (New York: St. Martin's Press, 1997), p. 93.

164. NARA, RG 242, BDC file of Udo von Woyrsch, A3342 SSO-013C, fr. 956.

165. ZStL, 205 AR-Z 302/67, vol. 2, p. 233f.

166. Wittje an SS-Obergruppenführer von Woyrsch, 20 December 1934, in NARA, RG 242, BDC file of Udo von Woyrsch, A3342 SSO-013C, fr. 962.

167. Kelz an von Woyrsch, 1 April 1936, in ibid., fr. 963.

168. Himmler an Daluege, 20 October 1938, in ibid., fr. 965.

169. NARA, RG 242, BDC file of Emil Otto Rasch, A3343 SSO-007B, fr. 836; see also Lebenslauf, 28 August 1937, in ibid., fr. 846.

170. Fragebogen, 2 March 1937, in ibid., fr. 843.

171. Ibid, fr. 837. Rasch served alongside Otto Sens, the commander of Einsatzkommando 1/II, who was also a member of the Brigade von Loewenfeld Freikorps.

172. Lebenslauf, 28 August 1937, in ibid., fr. 848.

173. Heydrich an Rasch, 3 February 1939, in ibid., fr. 875, and Banach, *Heydrichs Elite,* p. 189.

174. NARA, RG 242, BDC file of Emil Otto Rasch, A3343 SSO-007B, fr. 850.

175. Lebenslauf des Regierungsrates Otto Hellwig, 1.7.35, in NARA, RG 242, BDC File of Otto Hellwig, A3343 SSO-083A, fr. 016.

176. Ibid.

177. The Rossbach Sturmabteilung was a highly organized Free Corps devoted to its brutal commander Gerhard Rossbach. The unit participated in the Kapp putsch of 1920 and the suppression of the Third Polish Uprising in East Upper Silesia in spring 1921. See Waite, *Vanguard,* pp. 191–196, and James M. Diehl, *Paramilitary Politics in Weimar Germany* (Bloomington: Indiana University Press, 1977), p. 326.

178. Lebenslauf des Regierungsrates Otto Hellwig, 1 July 35, in NARA, RG 242, BDC File of Otto Hellwig, A3343 SSO-083A, fr. 017.

179. Ibid., fr. 003.

180. Testimony of Otto Hellwig, 21 August 1947, in NARA, RG 238, Microfilm Series M1019, fr. 26.

181. Dienstleitungszeugnis, 25 January 1937, in NARA, RG 242, BDC File of Otto Hellwig, A3343 SSO-083A, fr. 037.

182. Lebenslauf, 15 September 1934, in NARA, RG 242, BDC File of Hans Trummler, A3343 SSO-191B, fr. 792.

183. Ibid.

184. Ibid.

185. Ibid.

186. Trummler an den Führer des Reichs SA-Hochschulenamtes Gruppenführer Dr. Bennecke, 8 July 1934, in ibid., fr. 919.

187. According to Fragebogen, 19 August 1937, in ibid., fr. 957, Trummler officially broke with his Lutheran religious faith in 1937.

188. Landesbauernschaft Braunschweig an den Landesbauernführer Giesecke, 23 September 1935, in ibid., fr. 880.

189. Bericht der Polizeipräsidium Leipzig, Abteilung IV, 20 February 1936, in ibid., fr. 855.

190. Ibid.

191. Geschäftsverteilungsplan des Geheimen Staatspolizeiamtes, Stand vom 1 July 1939, Gestapa, B.Nr 8/39 IAg, in USHMMA, RG 11.001M.01 (Select records from the "Osobyi" Archive in Moscow), r. 1, folder 38a, p. 16.

192. Banach, *Heydrichs Elite,* p. 43, reached this conclusion after a statistical survey of 1,885 members of the Gestapo, SD, and Kripo.

193. Ibid., p. 325.

194. Waite, *Vanguard,* chapter 10, made clear the deep connections between the Freikorps movement and the Third Reich.

195. Ibid., p. 326.

196. Ibid.

197. Schmer, Sens, Rasch, and Hellwig were in their forties by September 1939 and not counted among this younger group. Like their younger counterparts, however, all of them had joined the NSDAP by 1933, and all of them were in the SS by 1935. Only Rasch held a university degree.

198. Given Jakob Sporrenberg's ambivalent evaluation of Heinz Graefe, it appears that Graefe was an exception when it came to possessing the "revolutionary activism" of his colleagues in the SD.

199. Testimony of Hans Tesmer, 12 July 1967, in Generalstaatsanwalt bei dem Kammergericht, 1 Js 12/65 (RSHA) Ermittlungsvermerk vom 1 December 1968, Verfahren gegen Dr. Werner Best, u.a. (ASA 179), p. 61: "SS-Führer die national-sozialistischen Ziele hart und rücksichtlos durchsetzen worden."

200. George C. Browder, *Foundations of the Nazi Police State: The Formation of the Sipo and SD* (Lexington: University Press of Kentucky, 1990), p. 161.

201. See Generalstaatsanwalt bei dem Kammergericht, 1 Js 12/65 (RSHA) Ermittlungsvermerk vom 1 December 1968, Verfahren gegen Dr. Werner Best, u.a., p. 60.

202. Karl-Heinz Rux was the notable exception here, having never received any military training.

203. Heydrich's desire to use SS officers with military training was also clear in his selection of personnel for the Polish "attacks" on German border posts at the very end of August. As Runzheimer, "Die Grenzzwischenfälle," p. 115, notes, "Hellwig . . . Als ehemaliger Offizier schien er besonders geeignet, weil er militärische Vorbildung besass" ("Hellwig, as a former army officer, was particularly suited [for the task] because he had military training").

204. The militarization of the various branches of the German police during the Nazi period is explored in Edward B. Westermann in three articles: "'Friend and Helper': German Uniformed Police Operations in Poland and the General Government, 1939–1941," *Journal of Military History* 58, no. 4 (October 1994): 643–661; "Himmler's Uniformed Police on the Eastern Front: The Reich's Secret Soldiers, 1941–1942," *War in History* 3, no. 3 (1996): 309–329; and "'Ordinary Men' or 'Ideological Soldiers'? Police Battalion 310 in Russia, 1942," *German Studies Review* 21, no. 1 (February 1998): 41–68.

Chapter 3. The German Army and the
Opening Phase of Operation TANNENBERG

1. Włodzimierz Jastrzębski, *Der Bromberger Blutsonntag: Legende und Wirklichkeit* (Poznań: Westinstitut, 1990), pp. 19ff.

2. Robert M. Kennedy, *The German Campaign in Poland (1939)* (Washington, DC: Department of the Army, 1956), pp. 81ff.

3. Testimony of Kurt Glende, 13 November 1965, in ZStL, 211 AR-Z 13/63 (St.A. Berlin—3P[k] Js 198/61), Strafverfahren gegen Lothar Beutel, Helmut Bischoff, Dr. Walter Hammer, Erich Preckel, und andere Angehörige EG IV wegen Mordes, vol. 1, p. 762.

4. Glende recounted Meisinger's comments: "Ich erwarte von Ihnen unbedingten Gehorsam und Ausführung aller gegebenen Befehle. Was auf Feigheit und nicht befolgung von Befehle steht, das Wissen Sie ja?" ("I expect from all of you unconditional obedience and the fulfillment of all orders you are given. You are aware what will happen to you if you are cowards and do not carry out your orders, correct?" (ibid.).

5. Ibid. See also testimony of Kurt Donajkowski, 11 May 1967, and testimony of Walter Hammer, 13 January 1964, in ZStL, 211 AR-Z 13/63, vol. 1, p. 7.

6. Bischoff quoted in ibid., p. 103.

7. Ibid., p. 69.

8. Ibid., p. 67.

9. Ibid., p. 66.

10. Testimony of Kurt Vogel, 1 December 1964, in ibid., vol. 1, p. 6.

11. Ibid.

12. ZStL, Verfahren gegen Dr. Werner Best, u.a., Der Generalstaatsanwalt bei dem Kammergericht—1 Js 12/65 (RSHA) ASA 179—Ermittlungsvermerk vom 10 December 1968, p. 351.

13. Oberkriegsgerichtsrat an AOK 3 zur Bekanntgabe an alle unterstellten Truppen, 5 September 1939, NARA, RG 242, T-314, r. 33, fr. 350.

14. Schreiben des Bischoff an den Stadtbaurat Froese, 13 March 1943, in ZStL, 211 AR-Z 13/63, vol. 1, p. 221.

15. Ibid., p. 65.

16. Ibid., p. 107, and testimony of Walter Hammer, 13 January 1964, in ibid., p. 8.

17. Unternehmen Tannenberg—Tagesbericht, 6 September 1939, in USHMMA, RG 15.007M (Records of the RSHA), file 1, r. 2, p. 3.

18. Jastrzębski, *Bromberger Blutsonntag*, pp. 73ff. During her travels in interwar Poland, the English journalist Clare Hollingworth also noted how ethnic German political parties, like the Jungdeutschepartei, were "openly irredentist" (*The Three Weeks' War in Poland* [London: Duckworth, 1940], pp. 13ff).

19. Jastrzębski, *Bromberger Blutsonntag*, p. 185.

20. Ibid., p. 168. By February 1940, this estimate was raised tenfold in German newspapers to over 50,000 Volksdeutsche killed. The Schreiben des Führers des EK 16, Dr. Oebsger-Röder, 30 September 1939, in ZStL, 211 AR-Z 13/63, vol. 1, p. 8, put the total number of Volksdeutsche casualties at 1,300 (1,000 killed, 300 missing).

21. Jastrzębski, *Bromberger Blutsonntag*, p. 105.

22. Ibid., p. 112f.

23. Ibid., p. 112.

24. Schreiben des Bischoff an den Stadtbaurat Froese, 13 March 1943, in ZStL, 211 AR-Z 13/63, vol. 1, p. 36.

25. Ibid.

26. Jastrzębski, *Bromberger Blutsonntag*, p. 117.

27. Ibid.

28. Schreiben des Bischoff an den Stadtbaurat Froese, 13 March 1943, in ZStL, 211 AR-Z 13/63, vol. 1, Anlage B, p. 183f.

29. Jastrzębski, *Bromberger Blutsonntag*, p. 117.

30. Ibid., p. 118.

31. Ibid., p. 120.

32. Ibid.

33. Ibid., p. 118.

34. Testimony of Walther Nethe, 20 January 1967, in ZStL, 211 AR-Z 13/63, vol. 1, p. 151f.

35. Testimony of Franciszek Derezinski, 28 August 1948, in ibid., p. 180.

36. Testimonies of Edmund Sündermann and Gerhard Grams, 28 August 1948, in ibid., pp. 144ff.

37. Testimony of Walther Nethe, 20 January 1967, in ibid., p. 152.

38. Erlass der RFSS und Chefs der deutschen Polizei im Reichsministerium des Innerns vom 3 September 1939, *Betr.* Behandlung der polnischen Aufständischen (röm 2) Nr. 1537/39, in ZStL, Verfahren gegen Werner Best u.a., 1 Js 12/65 (RSHA) ASA 179, p. 360. Himmler seems to have repeated his 3 September instructions on 7 September. According to telegraphed orders sent by Kurt Daluege, "Der Reichsführer SS hat fernmündlich befohlen, dass die Exekutionen im besetzten Gebiet durch die Polizei selbst durchgeführt werden sollen, nicht durch die Armee" ("The RFSS has ordered via telephone that executions in the occupied territories should be carried out by the police alone, not by the army"). See Vermerk, Der Chef der Ordnungspolizei, 7 September 1939, in NARA, RG 242, T-580, BDC File of Kurt Daluege, r. 95. My thanks to Martin Dean for reference to this document.

39. See, for example, the work of Jürgen Förster, "Jewish Policies of the German Military, 1939–1942," in *The Shoah and the War*, ed. Asher Cohen, Yehoyakim Cochavi, and Yoav Gelber (New York: Peter Lang, 1992), p. 56, and Jürgen Förster, "Complicity or Entanglement? Wehrmacht, War, and Holocaust," in *The Holocaust and History: The Known, the Unknown, the Disputed, and the Reexamined*, ed. Michael Berenbaum and Abraham J. Peck (Bloomington: Indiana University Press, 1998), p. 271.

40. Fall Weiss—Sonderbestimmungen zu den Anordnungen für die Versorgung, OKW, 24 July 1939, in NARA, RG 242, T-78, r. 351, fr. 6310574ff.

41. Tätigkeitsbericht über den Einsatz im Osten (28 August 1939 to 27 September 1939) von der Gericht des Gen.Kdo.III, in NARA, RG 242, T-314, r. 182, fr. 4.

42. Tagebuch der Reichssicherheitshauptamt, 7–8 September 1939, in ZStL, 211 AR-Z 13/63, vol. 1, p. 70.

43. The Wehrmacht court pulled out of Bydgoszcz on 13 September only one week after it had arrived in the city. The SS fulfilled the task of "punishing" the Poles in particularly bloody fashion. For more on the activity of the SS Special Court in Bydgoszcz, see Christian Jansen and Arno Weckbecker, *Der "Volksdeutsche Selbstschutz" in Polen 1939/40* (Munich: Oldenbourg, 1992), pp. 56ff.

44. According to OKW Anweisungen, 14 June 1939, in NARA, RG 242, T-77, r. 978, fr. 4467814, "Geiselnehmen und Geiseltötung ist durch das Völkerrecht nicht verboten" ("The law does not prohibit the taking and shooting of hostages"), based upon the Hague Land Warfare Agreement of 1907.

45. Befehl zur Sicherung und Befriedung Brombergs, Anlage 1 zum Kriegstagebuch I, Korück 580, 9 September 1939, in NARA, RG 242, T-301, r. 36, fr. 1186.

46. Ibid., fr. 1190. These executions were also mentioned in the reports of Einsatzgruppe IV, although no numbers were offered. See Unternehmen Tannenberg—Tagesbericht, 9 September 1939, USHMMA, RG 15.007M, file 1, r. 2, p. 23.

47. Tagesbefehl der III.Armeekorps, 8 September 1939, in ZStL, 211 AR-Z 13/63, Schlussvermerk in dem Verfahren gegen Lothar Beutel u.a., p. 73.

48. Befehl zur Sicherung und Befriedung Brombergs, Anlage zum KTB 1 der Kommandant für das rückwärtige Armeegebietes 580, 9 September 1939, in NARA, RG 242, T-501, r. 36, fr. 1186.

49. Unternehmen Tannenberg—Tagesbericht, 7 September 1939, in USHMMA, RG 15.007M, file 1, r. 2, p. 11.

50. Ibid., p. 24.

51. Ibid., p. 22.

52. Ibid.

53. For Himmler's order, see Unternehmen Tannenberg—Tagesbericht, 11 September 1939, in ibid., p. 49.

54. ZStL, 211 AR-Z 13/63, vol. 1, p. 148.

55. Befehl zur Sicherung und Befriedung Brombergs, Anlage 1 zum Kriegstagebuch I, Korück 580, 9 September 1939, in NARA, RG 242, T-301, r. 36, fr. 1198.

56. Ibid., fr. 1197.

57. One raid had actually been carried out in Schwedenhöhe on 7 September. The number of Poles arrested is unknown. See Jastrzębski, *Bromberger Blutsonntag,* p. 120.

58. Testimony of Erich Müller, 30 November 1964; testimony of Erich Preckel, 19 July 1965; and testimony of Walter Hammer, 7 July 1965, all in ZStL, 211 AR-Z 13/63, vol. 1, pp. 222ff.

59. Testimony of Paul Fahnenstich, 15 July 1965, in ibid., p. 226. Also see Testimony of Bruno Griesche, 1 December 1964, in ibid., p. 229.

60. Schreiben des Bischoff an den Stadtbaurat Froese, 13 March 1943, in ibid., p. 221.

61. Testimony of Bruno Griesche, 1 December 1964, in ibid., p. 229.

62. Schreiben des Bischoff an den Stadtbaurat Froese, 13 March 1943, in ibid., p. 221.

63. Entry for 10 September 1939, in Kriegstagebuch I der Korück 580, in NARA, RG 242, T-301, r. 36, fr. 1197.

64. Schreiben des Walter Hammer, 28 July 1965 in ZStL, 211 AR-Z 13/63, vol. 1, p. 159f.

65. Strauss's order quoted in ZStL, Verfahren gegen Dr. Werner Best u.a., 1 Js 12/65 (RSHA) ASA 179, p. 74.

66. Colonel Gösch was the commander of Landesschützregiment 3 and was aided in his task by SS-Brigadeführer Henze, who arrived in Bydgoszcz on 11 September to begin his duties as Police president. See Anlage 1 zum Kriegstagebuch I der Korück 580, in NARA, RG 242, T-301, r. 36, fr. 1205.

67. Unternehmen Tannenberg—Tagesbericht, 13 September 1939, in USHMMA, RG 15.007M, file 1, r. 2, p. 60.

68. Jastrzębski, *Bromberger Blutsonntag,* p. 142. See also Jansen and Weckbecker, *Der "Volksdeutsche Selbstschutz,"* p. 155. A postwar report of West German investigators concluded that the SD and Selbstschutz had eliminated the greater part of the intelligentsia of Bydgoszcz by as early as the first week of November 1939. See ZStL, "Einsatzgruppen in Polen," vol. 2, pp. 29ff.

69. ZStL, 211 AR-Z 13/63, vol. 1, p. 104. See also Jastrzębski, *Bromberger Blutsonntag,* p. 121.

70. Jastrzębski, *Bromberger Blutsonntag,* p. 126.

71. Helmut Krausnick and Hans-Heinrich Wilhelm, *Die Truppe des Weltanschauungskrieges: Die Einsatzgruppen der Sicherheitspolizei und des SD, 1938–1942* (Stuttgart: Deutsche Verlags-Anstalt, 1981), pp. 55ff.

72. Bekanntmachung Oberbefehlshaber des Heeres an der Befehlshaber AOK III, 17 September 1939, in NARA, RG 242, T-312, r. 31, fr. 7538748.

73. Jastrzębski, *Bromberger Blutsonntag*, p. 120.

74. T. Hunt Tooley, *National Identity and Weimar Germany: Upper Silesia and the Eastern Border, 1918–1922* (Lincoln: University of Nebraska Press, 1997).

75. Andrzej Szefer, "Zbrodnie Hitlerowskie na Górnym Śląsku we Wrzesniu 1939R," in *Biuletyn Głównej Komisji Badania Zbrodni Hitlerowskich w Polsce*, 32 (Warsaw: Wydawnictwo Prawnicze, 1987), p. 164.

76. Teil II, Feindabgaben zu den Generalkommando VIII AK, Ia Nr. 72/39 Geh.Kdos. Chefsache in VIII AK, Ia Aufmarschanweisung (Einsatzbefehle), 26 June 1939–23 August 1939, in NARA, RG 242, T-314, r. 365, fr. 62.

77. Testimony of Bruno Streckenbach, 2 November 1961, in ZStL, 201 AR-Z 76/59, vol. 1 (StA Hamburg—141 Js 31/67), p. 128f. The Korfanty Brigades were named after Wojciech Korfanty, the leader of Polish nationalists who rose up against the Germans in Upper Silesia in 1921.

78. Kennedy, *The German Campaign in Poland*, pp. 83ff, and Pat McTaggart, "Poland '39," in *Hitler's Army: The Evolution and Structure of German Forces, 1939–1945*, ed. Command Magazine (Conshohocken, PA: Combined Books, 1996), pp. 210ff.

79. GAK 3, Ia. Abendmeldung an Gen.Kdo VIII AK, Gleiwitz, 1 September 1939, in NARA, RG 242, T-314, r. 365, fr. 241.

80. Gen.Kdo VIII AK, Abt. Ia, Nr. 20. An Inf. Rgt. 28, 2 September 1939, in ibid., fr. 290.

81. Bundesarchiv-Militärarchiv Freiburg (hereafter cited as BA/MA), RH 26-45/2, 45.I.D. KTB vom polnischen Feldzug, 2 September 1939, p. 10.

82. Gen.Kdo VIII AK, Abt. Ia, Nr. 21 An SS-Standarte Germania, 2 September 1939, in NARA, RG 242, T-314, r. 365, fr. 295.

83. Józef Fajkowski, *Wieś w Ogniu. Eksterminacja wsi Polskiej w Okresie Okupacji Hitlerowskiej* (Warsaw: Ludowa Spóldzielnia Wydawnicza, 1971), p. 45, and Szymon Datner, Janusz Gumkowski, and Kazimierz Leszczyński, *Genocide 1939–1945* (Warsaw: Wydawnictwo Zachodnie, 1962), p. 217.

84. Abwehrbericht, Ic/AO AOK 14 an der Ic/AO Heeresgruppe Süd, 2 September 1939, in NARA, RG 242, T-311, r. 255, fr. 142.

85. Ibid., fr. 143.

86. Gen.Kdo. VIII AK, Abt. Ia, an 239 Division, 3 September 1939, in NARA, RG 242, T-314, r. 365, fr. 331, and Gen.Kdo. VIII AK, Abt. Ia, Nr. 23, 3 September 1939, in NARA, RG 242, T-314, r. 365, fr. 337.

87. Word of the intensity of the battle being waged behind the lines by the Fourteenth Army also reached Berlin, as indicated by a note Halder made in his war diary on 3 September 1939: "14. Armee braucht Polizei für rückwärtiges Gebiet" ("The Fourteenth Army needs police for rear areas"). See Generaloberst Halder, *Kriegstagebuch, Band I: Vom Polenfeldzug bis zum Ende der Westoffensive (14.8.1939–30.6.1940)* (Stuttgart: W. Kohlhammer Verlag, 1962), p. 57.

88. Elisabeth Wagner, ed., *Der Generalquartiermeister: Briefe und Tagebuchaufzeichnungen des Generalquartiermeisters des Heeres General der Artillerie Eduard Wagner* (Munich: Günter Olzog Verlag, 1963), p. 123.

89. See note 38 of this chapter.

90. Fernschreiben Brauchitsch and der Ic AOK 14, 3 September 1939, in NARA, RG 242, T-312, r. 477, fr. 8067825.

91. GAK 3, Abt. Ia, an die Truppe, 4 September 1939, in NARA, RG 242, T-314, r. 840, fr. 43.

92. Testimony of Hubert Schwerhoff, 5 February 1971, in ZStL, 201 AR-Z 76/59 (StA. Hamburg—141 Js 31/67) Verfahren gegen Bruno Streckenbach, vol. 9, p. 148.

93. Testimony of Maria N., 19 May 1967, in ZStL, 205 AR-Z 302/67, vol. 3, p. 559.

94. Ibid., p. 560.

95. Testimony of Rafal K., 25 April 1967, in ibid., p. 568.

96. Ibid., p. 570.

97. Ibid.

98. Ibid., p. 571.

99. Ibid., pp. 571ff.

100. According to Entwurf des ZStL an das Bundesministerium des Inneren in Wien, 16 August 1978, in ibid., p. 597, men from EK 1/I took part in the killing of at least eighty of these victims. The estimate of the total number of people killed in the Zamkowa Street courtyard on 4 September comes from Datner, *Genocide,* p. 212.

101. Entwurf des ZStL an das Bundesministerium des Inneren in Wien, 16 August 1978, in ZStL, 205 AR-Z 302/67, p. 597.

102. Datner, *Genocide,* p. 212.

103. Szefer, "Zbrodnie Hitlerowskie," p. 165.

104. Polizeiregiment 3, Kommando Ia dem Generalkommando VIII Armeekorps, 5 September 1939, in NARA, RG 242, T-315, r. 1449, fr. 56.

105. Fernschreiben Himmlers an von Woyrsch, z.Zt. Pol. Präsidium Gleiwitz, 3 September 1939, Berlin, Nr. 189 617, reproduced in ZStL, "Einsatzgruppen in Polen," p. 200.

106. Unternehmen Tannenberg—Tagesbericht, 7 September 1939, in USHMMA, RG 15.007M, file 1, r. 2, p. 12.

107. Unternehmen Tannenberg—Tagesbericht, 8 September 1939, in ibid., p. 19.

108. GAK 3 (Brandt) an SS-Obergruppenführer von Woyrsch, 8 September 1939, in NARA, RG 242, T-314, r. 840, fr. 85.

109. Unternehmen Tannenberg—Tagesbericht, 9 September 1939, in USHMMA, RG 15.007M, file 1, r. 2, pp. 26, 39.

110. Czesław Madajczyk, *Die Okkupationspolitik Nazideutschlands in Polen 1939–1945* (Berlin: Akademie-Verlag, 1987), p. 17.

111. Ibid.

112. Ibid.

113. For example, a register compiled by the Main Commission for the Investigation of Nazi Crimes in Poland lists the execution of eighty former Silesian insurgents in Katowice by the Wehrmacht on 4 September 1939. This register is quoted in Szymon Datner, *Crimes Committed by the Wehrmacht during the September Campaign and the Period of Military Government* (Poznań: Instytut Zachodni, 1962), p. 12.

114. Unternehmen Tannenberg—Tagesbericht, 8 September 1939, in USHMMA, RG 15.007M, file 1, r. 2, p. 17.

115. Tätigkeitsbericht, GFP Gruppe 520 an die Verbindungsgruppe OKW/Ausl.-Abw. beim Oberbefehlshaber der Heeres, Berlin, 15 September 1939, in NARA, RG 242, T-311, r. 255, fr. 102.

116. Ibid.

117. Vortragsnotiz für den Herrn Oberbefehlshaber, O.Qu. IV, 17 September 1939, in NARA, RG 242, T-78, r. 296, fr. 6245626. Also quoted in ZStL, "Einsatzgruppen in Polen," p. 148f.

118. Vortragsnotiz für den Herrn Oberbefehlshaber, O.Qu. IV, 17 September 1939, in NARA, RG 242, T-78, r. 296, fr. 6245627.

119. Best claimed, "Es seien lediglich scharfe Verfügungen im Sinne des Führers erlassen worden, gegen Insurgenten vorzugehen" (ibid.).

120. Ibid.

121. Testimony of Rudolf Langhäuser, 30 April 1967, in ZStL, 201 AR-Z 76/59, vol. 3, p. 48.

122. Ibid.

123. Ibid., p. 48f.

124. According to the testimony of Dr. Günther Knobloch, 25 June 1961, in ZStL, 8 AR-Z 52/60 (StA. Würzburg—1 Js 2469/60—Verfahren gegen Alfred Hasselberg wegen Mordes), vol. 3, p. 514, the Security Police executed all 182 prisoners in Lubliniec.

125. Michael Geyer, "The Crisis of Military Leadership in the 1930s," *Journal of Strategic Studies* 14 (December 1991): 454.

126. Klaus-Jürgen Müller, *The Army, Politics, and Society in Germany, 1933–45* (New York: St. Martin's Press, 1987), pp. 33ff.

127. In some ways, this development was predated by the development of German reprisal doctrine in the years before World War I. When facing civilian resistance, the military theorist Julius von Hartmann argued, "terrorism becomes a principle of military necessity." Similarly, in 1902, the German General Staff warned officers to "guard against excessive humanitarian notions [because] certain severities are indispensable to war, nay more, that the only true humanity very often lies in a ruthless application of them." See John Horne and Alan Kramer, *German Atrocities 1914: A History of Denial* (New Haven, CT: Yale University Press, 2001), pp. 143, 148.

128. The notion of a partial identity of interests between the German army and the Nazi regime is an especially important element of Manfred Messerschmidt, *Die Wehrmacht im NS–Staat: Zeit der Indoktrination* (Hamburg: Decker, 1969).

129. The number of Poles killed in formal Wehrmacht executions is controversial. Madajczyk, *Die Okkupationspolitik*, p. 12, estimates the total number shot in September 1939 at 16,000, while Wolfgang Schumann and Ludwig Nestler, eds., *Europa unterm Hakenkreuz: Die faschistische Okkupationspolitik in Polen, 1939–1945* (Berlin: Deutscher Verlag der Wissenschaften, 1989), p. 80, places the figure at 27,000.

Chapter 4. Nazi Anti-Jewish Policy during the Polish Campaign

1. Saul Friedländer, *Nazi Germany and the Jews*, vol. 1, *The Years of Persecution, 1933–1939* (New York: HarperCollins, 1997), p. 18.

2. See Document No. 53, "Unsigned Memorandum," from the German Foreign Office, 12 October 1938, in *Documents on German Foreign Policy 1918–1945: From the Archives of the German Foreign Ministry*, vol. 4 (London: His Majesty's Stationery Office, 1951), p. 54

3. Emanuel Melzer, "Relations between Poland and Germany and Their Impact on the Jewish Problem in Poland (1935–1938)," *Yad Vashem Studies* 12 (1977): 216. The "problem" was exacerbated by the addition of another 20,000 Jews of Polish citizenship into the Reich by the incorporation of Austria in March 1938.

4. Karol Jonca, "The Expulsion of Polish Jews," in *Polin: Studies in Polish Jewry*, vol. 8, ed. A. Polonsky, E. Mendelsohn, and J. Tomaszewski (London: Littman Library of Jewish Civilization, 1994), p. 255. Also see Sybil Milton, "The Expulsion of Polish Jews from Germany, October 1938 to July 1939: A Documentation," in *Leo Baeck Institute: Yearbook 1984*, vol. 29 (London: Secker and Warburg, 1984), pp. 169–174, and Melzer, "Relations," pp. 193–229.

5. Ibid., p. 270. The SS originally intended to expel 10.000 Polish Jews.

6. Such is the conclusion also expressed in Michael Wildt, "Before the 'Final Solution': The Judenpolitik of the SD, 1935-1938," in *Leo Baeck Institute: Yearbook 1998*, vol. 43 (London: Secker and Warburg, 1998), pp. 241–269, and *Die Judenpolitik des SD 1935 bis 1938: Eine Dokumentation*, ed. M. Wildt (Munich: Oldenbourg, 1995).

7. Jonca, "The Expulsion of Polish Jews," p. 255.

8. Rosenberg stated, "Es ist zu wünschen, dass die Judenfreunde in der Welt, vor allem die westlichen Demokratien, die über soviel kaum in allen Erdteilen verfügen, den Juden ein Gebiet ausserhalb Palästinas zuweisen, allerdings nicht um einen jüdischen Staat, sondern um ein jüdisches Reservat einzurichten" ("It is our wish that the friends of Jews in the world, above all in the western democracies, which have so many places [in the world] at their disposal, would allocate a place for the Jews other than Palestine; not a Jewish state per se, but a Jewish reservation"). See Auswärtiges Amt, 83-26 19/1 "Die Judenfrage als Faktor der Aussenpolitik im Jahre 1938," 25 January 1939, in USHMMA, RG 11.001M.01, file 7-549, fr. 56. Jonny Moser, "Nisko: The First Experiment in Deportation," in *Simon Wiesenthal Center Annual*, vol. 2, ed. H. Friedlander and S. Milton (White Plains, NY: Kraus International Publications, 1985), p. 2f.

9. Schumburg wrote of Rosenberg's statement "Das ist das Programm der aussenpolitischen Haltung Deutschlands in der Judenfrage" in Auswärtiges Amt, 83-26 19/1 "Die Judenfrage als Faktor der Aussenpolitik im Jahre 1938," 25 January 1939, in USHMMA, RG 11.001M.01, file 7-549, fr. 56.

10. According to Walter Huppenkothen, the liaison officer of Einsatzgruppe I, Colonel Otto Wöhler of the Fourteenth Army told him von Woyrsch's orders were "Furcht und Schrecken in der Bevölkerung zu verbreiten, um Gewalttaten seitens der Bevölkerung zu verhindern" ("to spread fear and terror through the populace, in order to prevent civilians from perpetrating acts of violence [against German personnel]"). (Helmut Krausnick and Hans-Heinrich Wilhelm, *Die Truppe des Weltanschauungskrieges: Die Einsatzgruppen der Sicherheitspolizei und des SD, 1938–1942* [Stuttgart: Deutsche Verlags-Anstalt, 1981], p. 51). Testimony of Bruno Streckenbach, 2 November 1961, in ZStL, 201 AR-Z 76/59 (StA. Hamburg—141 Js

31/67), Verfahren gegen Bruno Streckenbach wegen Mordes, vol. 1, p. 133. See also Aktenvermerk, 6 July 1967, in ZStL, 205 AR-Z 302/67, vol. 2, p. 191, in which West German investigators concluded from the findings of a German army court-martial inquiry in September 1939 that von Woyrsch was given the "special task" *(Spezialauftrag)* of terrorizing the Jewish population into fleeing east. Von Woyrsch himself professed that Dr. Rasch had received "special tasks" *(besondere Aufträge)* without his knowledge in an attempt to shift blame to the already deceased Rasch. See Testimony of Udo von Woyrsch, 14 December 1967, in ZStL, 205 AR-Z 302/67 (GStA. Berlin—Js 12/65 [RSHA]), vol. 1, p. 238f. Last, according to Richard Breitman, *Official Secrets: What the Nazis Planned, What the British and Americans Knew* (New York: Hill and Wang, 1998), p. 32, on 25 August Himmler sent out official orders via Karl Wolff to police and Waffen-SS commanders who were to be deployed in Poland. The content of these orders is unknown, but given the similarity of Einsatzgruppen and SSTV operations against Polish Jews, it is likely that Himmler's instructions concerned terrorizing Jews in order to force their flight to the east.

    11. ZStL, "Einsatzgruppen in Polen," p. 88.

    12. Donald Grey Brownlow and John Eluthère Du Pont, *Hell Was My Home: Arnold Shay, Survivor of the Holocaust* (West Hanover, MA: Christopher Publishing House, 1983), p. 45. Von Woyrsch blamed the destruction of the synagogue on "unidentified perpetrators" in his report to Berlin. See Unternehmen Tannenberg—Tagesbericht, 8 September 1939, in USHMMA, RG 15.007M, file 1, r. 2, p. 26.

    13. Andrzej Szefer, "Zbrodnie Hitlerowskie na Górnym Śląsku we Wrześniu 1939R," in *Biuletyn Głównej Komisji Badania Zbrodni Hitlerowskich w Polsce*, vol. 32 (Warsaw: Wydawnictwo Prawnicze, 1987), p. 167. In the daily report filed on 10 September, events in Będzin were described as follows: "Nach dem Brande der Synagoge in Bedzin machten sich allgemeine Unruhen bemerkbar, bei denen auf die Polizei geschossen wurde. Es erfolgten mehrere standrechtliche Erschiessungen" ("Following the burning of the synagogue in Bedzin, there was considerable resistance [by the Jews], and some of these were shot. These executions were followed by other shootings that had been ordered by courts-martial") (Unternehmen Tannenberg—Tagesberichte, 10 September 1939, in USHMMA, RG 15.007M, file 1, r. 2, p. 42).

    14. Unternehmen Tannenberg—Tagesberichte, 9 September 1939, in ibid., p. 31: "In Kattowitz erfolgte ein Überfall auf eine Wehrmachtskolonne. Bei der Niederkämpfung durch die Schutz- und Sicherheitspolizei geriet eine Synagoge in Brand und brannte bis auf die Grundmauern nieder" ("In Katowice an army column was attacked. During the fight by the Protective and Security Police the synagogue caught fire and burned to its foundation").

    15. Testimony of Kurt J., 16 November 1961, in ZStL 205 AR-Z 302/67, vol. 4, p. 380.

    16. Kriegstagebuch I der GAK 3, 11 September 1939, in NARA, RG 242, T-314, r. 840, fr. 184.

    17. Fernschreiben, O.Qu. AOK 14 (Zellner) an der Oberbefehlshaber AOK 8 (Blaskowitz), 7 September 1939, in NARA, RG 242, T-312, r. 477, fr. 8067831.

    18. Fernschreiben Himmlers an der Befehlshaber Orpo und Sipo AOK 10, AOK 14, 9 September 1939, in NARA, RG 242, T-312, r. 477, fr. 8067851.

    19. Besonderen Anordnungen Nr. 14, O.Qu. (Zellner), AOK 14, 12 September 1939, in ibid., fr. 8067376.

20. See the testimony of Bruno Streckenbach, 25 November 1966, in ZStL, 201 AR-Z 76/59, vol. 2, p. 42, in which Streckenbach stated of Heydrich's visit to Kraków that the orders he received to force Jews east were "im Zusammenhang damit an den Befehl Himmlers . . . durch rigorose Massnahmen insbesondere das Judentum zur Flucht in die russisch besetzten Gebiete zu veranlassen" ("in connection with Himmler's orders . . . especially Jews were to be forced to flee into the Russian occupation zone using 'rigorous measures'").

21. In the testimony of Bruno Streckenbach, 2 November 1961, in ZStL, 201 AR-Z 76/59, vol. 1, p. 132, the former commander of EG I told German investigators, "Im Verlaufe des Feldzuges erging dann aber die Weisung, nach Möglichkeit die Juden in das Gebiet nach Osten abzuschieben, das bei Festlegung der späteren D-Linie werden würde" ("During the military campaign I received instructions to find a way of forcing Jews in the region [of East Upper Silesia and western Galicia] to the east, where the demarcation line was later to be established").

22. Testimony of Bruno Streckenbach, 16 June 1961, in ZStL, 8 AR-Z 52/60 (StA Würzburg—1 Js 2469/60—Verfahren gegen Dr. Alfred Hasselberg wegen Mordes, 6 April 1960), vol. 3, p. 482.

23. See Amtschefsbesprechung, 7 September 1939, Stabskanzlei I 11 (dated 8 September 1939), in USHMMA, RG 14.016M (Records of the RSHA from the Bundesarchiv Koblenz, R 58/825), microfiche 1, p. 2.

24. Copy of Heydrich telegram "an alle Stapoleitstellen, Berlin, Nr. 191 332, 7.9.1939, 2115" dated 8 September 1939 and reproduced in Tuvia Friedman, *15 Jahre Zuchthaus für Wolff* (Haifa: Institute of Documentation in Israel, 1990).

25. Heydrich approved Stahlecker and Eichmann's plans to deport Vienna's and Mährisch-Ostrau's Jews to a specially designated territory in occupied Poland on 12 September, although at that time Nisko still lay in territory intended for the Soviets. See Moser, "Nisko: The First Experiment in Deportation," p. 3, and Seev Goshen, "Eichmann und die Nisko-Aktion im Oktober 1939: Eine Fallstudie zur NS-Judenpolitik in der letzten Etappe vor der 'Endlösung,'" *Vierteljahrshefte für Zeitgeschichte* 29, no. 1 (1981): 75–96.

26. Testimony of Bruno Streckenbach, 2 November 1961, in ZStL, 201 AR-Z 76/59, vol. 1, p. 133. Steinbacher, *Musterstadt Auschwitz*, p. 56.

27. Amtschefsbesprechung, 14 September 1939, Stabskanzlei I 11 (dated 15 September 1939), in USHMMA, RG 14.016M, microfiche 1, p. 10.

28. Document 104, 20 September 1939, in *Documents on German Foreign Policy, 1918–1945*, Series D (1937–1945), vol. 8, *The War Years: September 4, 1939–March 18, 1940*, p. 105.

29. Walter Warlimont, *Inside Hitler's Headquarters, 1939–1945*, trans. R. H. Barry (Novato, CA: Presidio, 1964), p. 35.

30. Document 103, 20 September 1939, in *Documents on German Foreign Policy*, vol. 8, p. 104.

31. Amtschefsbesprechung, 21 September 1939, Stabskanzlei I 11 (dated 27 September 1939), USHMMA, RG 14.016M, microfiche 1, p. 26. According to one former member of Einsatzgruppe I, between the third week of September and the beginning of October, close to 18,000 Polish Jews were expelled into eastern Poland from the southern sector of the demarcation line alone. See Statement of Heinrich K., in Bericht der ZStL, 8 AR-Z 52/60, p. 3.

32. Christopher R. Browning, *Nazi Policy, Jewish Workers, German Killers* (New York: Cambridge University Press, 2000), p. 4.

33. Document 157, 28 September 1939, in *Documents on German Foreign Policy,* vol. 8, p. 164.

34. Götz Aly, *"Final Solution": Nazi Population Policy and the Murder of the European Jews,* trans. B. Cooper and A. Brown (New York: Arnold, 1999), p. 34.

35. Testimony of Fritz S., 30 October 1963, in ZStL, 205 AR-Z 302/67, vol. 1, p. 139. Also see Unternehmen Tannenberg—Tagesberichte, 16 September 1939, in USHMMA, RG 15.007M, file 1, r. 2, p. 98.

36. This Order Police unit was part of von Woyrsch's Police Group 1. See chapter 2, note 151.

37. Erschiessungen ohne gerichtliches Verfahren, Korpskommando XVIII an der Generalkommando XVIII AK, 28 September 1939, in NARA, RG 242, T-311, r. 254, fr. 758f.

38. Ibid., fr. 760, and ZStL, "Einsatzgruppen in Polen," p. 90.

39. Organisationsbefehl wegen der Zurücknahme hinter den San, Abt. Ia, Gen.Kdo., XXII AK, 22 September 1939, in NARA, RG 242, T-314, r. 665, fr. 510–512.

40. Korpsbefehl, Abt. Ia, Korpskommand XVIII, 24 September 1939, in NARA, RG 242, T-314, r. 594, fr. 542.

41. Besondere Anordnungen zum Korpsbefehl für des 28 September 1939, Abt. Ia, Gen.Kdo XVIII AK, in ibid., fr. 185.

42. ZStL, "Einsatzgruppen in Polen," p. 35.

43. Testimony of Rudolf Fritz Körner, 14 April 1964, in ZStL, 201 AR-Z 76/59 (StA Hamburg—141 Js 31/67), vol. 2, p. 271.

44. Testimony of Gerhard Kotzam, 25 October 1960, in ZStL, 8 AR-Z 52/60 (StA Würzburg—1 Js 2469/60—Verfahren gegen Dr. Alfred Hasselberg wegen Mordes), vol. 2, p. 333.

45. Korpsbefehl, Abt. Ia, Korpskommand XVIII, 24 September 1939, in NARA, RG 242, T-314, r. 594, fr. 542. The Einsatzkommandos of Bruno Müller (EK 2/I) and Karl Brunner (EK 4/I) were broken up into Teilkommandos and stationed from East Upper Silesia to Kraków and Tarnów.

46. According to the *Jaroslav Book: A Memorial to the Jewish Community of Jaroslav* (Tel-Aviv: Jaroslav Societies, 1978), p. 275, soon after they arrived, men with Einsatzkommando 3/I ordered Jews to gather on the town square and bring with them the keys to their homes and businesses. Those Jews who heeded the call were then searched for jewelry and other valuables before being pushed over the San River.

47. Testimony of Alfred Hasselberg, 2 December 1939, SS Disziplinar-Sache gegen Dr. Hasselberg wegen dienstlicher Verfehlungen in NARA, BDC File of Alfred Hasselberg, A3343 SSO-068A, fr. 1228.

48. Testimony of Bruno Streckenbach, 16 June 1961, in ZStL, 8 AR-Z 52/60, vol. 3, p. 482. Also see Aktenvermerk Heydrichs, Der Chef der Sipo und des SD, C.d.S. B.-Nr.: 533552/40, Berlin, 2 July 1940, reproduced in Helmut Krausnick, "Hitler und die Morde in Polen: Ein Beitrag zum Konflikt zwischen Heer und SS um die Verwaltung der besetzten Gebiete," *Vierteljahrshefte für Zeitgeschichte* 11, no. 2 (1963): 207, where Heydrich referred to "Weisungen des Führers sowie des

Generalfeldmarschalls durchgeführte politische Tätigkeit" ("the Führer's instructions as well as those of Field Marshal Göring concerning political activities that are to be carried out").

49. Testimony of Hans Block, 8 December 1939, SS Disziplinar-Sache gegen Dr. Hasselberg wegen dienstlicher Verfehlungen, in NARA, BDC File of Alfred Hasselberg, A3343 SSO-068A, fr. 1342.

50. Ibid., fr. 1343. The SS Honor Court tried Hasselberg in December 1939 for a variety of offenses, the most serious of which were plundering and mistreatment of his men. Hasselberg was found guilty of the charges and thrown out of the SS.

51. Testimony of Criminal Secretary Kubin, 6 December 1939, SS Disziplinar-Sache gegen Dr. Hasselberg wegen dienstlicher Verfehlungen, ibid., fr. 1312f.

52. Ibid., fr. 1312.

53. Testimony of Władysław T., 18 June 1968, in ZStL, 205 AR-Z 302/67, vol. 3, p. 515. See also Antoni Rachfal, "Eksterminacja Ludności Żydowskiej w Latach Wojny 1939–1944 Na Terenie Obecnego Woj. Przemyskiego," in *Studia nad okupacją hitlerowską południowo-wschodniej cze'sci Polski,* ed. T. Kowalski (Rzeszów: Tow.Nauk w Rzeszowie, 1985), p. 77.

54. Testimony of Stanisław T., 18 June 1939, in ZStL, 205 AR-Z 302/67, vol. 3, p. 512. According to one Polish historian, another ninety Jews were shot in Dynów several days later. See Stanisław Zabierowski, "Zbrodnie Wehrmachtu W Południowo-Wschodniej Części Polski," in *Biuletyn Głównej Komisji Badania Zbrodni Hitlerowskich W Polsce,* vol. 32 (Warsaw: Wydawnictwo Prawnicze, 1987), p. 186.

55. See the statements of several Polish witnesses collected in ZStL, 205 AR-Z 302/67, vol. 3, pp. 498–577.

56. See Arie Menczer, ed., *Sefer Przemyśl* (Tel Aviv: Former Residents of Przemyśl in Israel, 1964).

57. Testimony of Georg R. in Aktenvermerk, 7 November 1963, in ZStL, 205 AR-Z 302/67, vol. 1, p. 138. The witness recalled specifically that one of these lists was in the hands of SS First Lieutenant Eugen Huck, a member of the command staff from the Sipo Border Police School in Pretzsch. See also Zabierowski, "Zbrodnie Wehrmachtu," p. 187.

58. Zwischenbericht Nr. 1 der Untersuchungsstelle der NS-Gewaltverbrechen beim Landestab der Polizei Israel, 21 August 1962, in ZStL, 206 AR-Z 28/60 (Verfahren gegen Martin Fellenz), vol. 13, p. 104.

59. This figure was the total decided by Israeli authorities during an investigation into events in Przemyśl conducted in 1962.

60. Armeetagesbefehl, 19 September 1939, A.H.Qu. AOK 14, Abt. IIa in Anlagen zum KTB I der 7.Infanterie Division, in BA/MA, RH 26-7/120, part 2.

61. ZStL, "Einsatzgruppen in Polen," p. 90.

62. Helmuth Groscurth, *Tagebücher eines Abwehroffiziers, 1938–1940: Mit weiteren Dokumenten zur Militäropposition gegen Hitler,* ed. Helmut Krausnick and Harold C. Deutsch (Stuttgart: Deutsche Verlags-Anstalt, 1970), p. 209 n. 509.

63. Ibid. See also Martin Broszat, *Nationalsozialistische Polenpolitik, 1939–1945* (Stuttgart: Deutsche Verlags-Anstalt, 1961), p. 28, and Klaus-Jürgen Müller, *Das Heer und Hitler: Armee und nationalsozialistisches Regime, 1933–1940* (Stuttgart: Deutsche Verlags-Anstalt, 1969), p. 426.

64. Groscurth, *Tagebücher,* p. 209 n. 509.

65. Abschrift, AOK 14, Abt. Ic/AO Nr. 39. A.H.Qu. Rzeszów, 19 September 1939, in NARA, RG 242, T-312, r. 477, fr. 8067862.

66. Groscurth, *Tagebücher,* p. 209 n. 509. See also Krausnick and Wilhelm, *Die Truppe,* p. 36, for details on the negotiations between Wagner and Heydrich. Groscurth noted in his diary on 23 September that Wagner requested the withdrawal of von Woyrsch's unit because "die Einsatzkommandos (Woyrsch) verheerend wirkten" ("the EKs of von Woyrsch were wreaking havoc") (*Tagebücher,* p. 209).

67. Kriegstagebuch I, GAK 3, 21 September 1939, in NARA, RG 242, T-314, r. 840, fr. 194. Udo von Woyrsch was never court-martialed. See Testimony of Udo von Woyrsch, 14 December 1967, in ZStL, 205 AR-Z 302/67, vol. 1, p. 238.

68. Unternehmen Tannenberg—Tagesberichte, 23 September 1939, in USHMMA, RG 15.007M, file 2, r. 2, p. 27.

69. My emphasis. Befehl an die Kommandeure, AOK 14, 1 October 1939, reproduced in ZStL, "Einsatzgruppen in Polen," p. 204.

70. Testimony of Gerhard K., 25 October 1960, in ZStL, 8 AR-Z 52/60, vol. 1, p. 333. Dr. Hasselberg, the commander of the local Einsatzkommando, accompanied by an unidentified Wehrmacht officer, carried out negotiations with the Soviets for the transfer of Jews from Jarosław over the San. See also Czesław Madajczyk, *Die Okkupationspolitik Nazideutschlands in Polen, 1939–1945* (East Berlin: Akademie Verlag, 1987), p. 18.

71. Ibid.

72. Besondere Anordnungen für die rückwärtige Dienste zum Einsatz der 4. Armee in Kongresspolen Nr. 1, O.Qu. (Richter), AOK 4, 17 September 1939, in NARA, RG 242, T-312, r. 1332, fr. 000306.

73. According to Unternehmen Tannenberg—Tagesbericht, 17 September 1939, in USHMMA, RG 15.007M, file 1, r. 2, p. 114, SD Headquarters in Berlin also concluded that the demarcation line would run from Eydtkuhnen and Suwalki in the north, through Białystok, and on to Stryj in the south.

74. Testimony of Ernst Mielke, 26 March 1966, in ZStL, 211 AR-Z 13/63, vol. 5, p. 1013.

75. "The Suffering Commences," in *The Bialystoker Memorial Book* (New York: Bialystoker Center, 1982), p. 51.

76. Ibid.

77. Testimony of Erich Laubnis, 4 March 1965, in ZStL, 211 AR-Z 13/63, vol. 5, p. 981. Others in EG IV corroborated Laubnis's story. See testimony of Fritz Kruttke, 15 May 1967, in ZStL, 211 AR-Z 13/63, vol. 7, p. 1478, and testimony of Reinhold Meyer, 21 September 1965, in ZStL, 211 AR-Z 13/63, vol. 3, p. 617. One of the thieves spent two years in the Dachau concentration camp.

78. Testimony of Emil Greil, 13 October 1964, in ZStL, 211 AR-Z 13/62, vol. 1, p. 39.

79. Testimony of Kurt Glende, 13 November 1965, in ZStL, 211 AR-Z 13/63, vol. 4, p. 762. Army Group North also issued instructions for Jews and Poles to be prevented from crossing the demarcation line, but EG IV was not detailed to this duty. See Tagesbericht, Anlagen zum Kriegstagebuch, Teil 3, der 206.I.D, 27 September 1939, in NARA, RG 242, T-315, r. 1594, fr. 83.

80. ZStL, "Einsatzgruppen in Polen," p. 64.

81. Unternehmen Tannenberg—Tagesbericht, 6 September 1939, in USH-MMA, RG 15.007M, file 1, r. 2, p. 7.

82. Unternehmen Tannenberg—Tagesbericht, 7 September 1939, in ibid., p. 14.

83. Ibid.

84. Unternehmen Tannenberg—Tagesbericht, 10 September 1939, in USH-MMA, RG 15.007M, file 1, r. 2, p. 40.

85. Ibid.

86. Ibid., p. 41. No details on the content of the regulations were offered.

87. Testimony of Wilhelm [sic] von Küchler, 29 April 1948, in NARA, RG 232, M 898 (High Command Case), r. 37, fr. 396f.

88. Dokument von Küchler Nr. 11: "Eidesstattliche Erklärung von General a.D. Martin Grase, Adjutant von Küchler," 6 April 1948, Nachlass von Küchler, in BA/MA, N 184/3, vol. 1.

89. Dokument von Küchler Nr. 13: "Eidesstattliche Erklärung von Dr. Jur. Franz Hinz," 23 March 1948, Nachlass von Küchler, in BA/MA, N 184/3, vol. 1.

90. General Franz Halder entered in his diary on 10 September that "SS artillery of the Panzer Corps has herded Jews together into a church and murdered them." See document submitted during the Nuremberg testimony of Halder on 14 April 1948, in NARA, RG 238, M 898 (High Command Case), r. 3, fr. 689.

91. Rachel Weiser-Nagel, "I Was Just Thirteen," in *Rozhan Memorial Book,* ed. B. Halevy (Tel-Aviv: Sigalit, 1977), p. 41f.

92. Minna Mlinek-Magnushever, "Troubles and Horrors at the Beginning of the War," in ibid., p. 61. Another witness, young Yitzchak Magnushever, also recalled the officer saying, "We shall exterminate all the Jews anyhow" (p. 31).

93. Dokument von Küchler Nr. 13: "Eidesstattliche Erklärung von Dr. Jur. Franz Hinz," 23 March 1948, Nachlass von Küchler, in BA/MA, N 184/3, vol. 1.

94. Dokument von Küchler Nr. 15: "Eidesstattliche Versicherung von Werner Kempf," 6 April 1948, Nachlass von Küchler, in BA/MA, N 184/3, vol. 1.

95. Aktennotiz, OKH, Chef des Heeresjustiz, 14 September 1939, in NARA, RG 242, T-78, r. 296, fr. 6245625. General Halder entered a different sentence into his diary: a "military court has decreed one year penitentiary. Küchler has not yet confirmed the verdict because a harsher sentence was due." See Testimony of General Franz Halder, 14 April 1948, in NARA, RG 238, M 898 (High Command Case), r. 3, fr. 689f.

96. Copy of SS court-martial judgment quoted in Krausnick and Wilhelm, *Die Truppe,* p. 66.

97. Dokument von Küchler Nr. 15: "Eidesstattliche Versicherung von Werner Kempf," 6 April 1948, Nachlass von Küchler, in BA/MA, N 184/3, vol. 1.

98. Testimony of Wilhelm [sic] von Küchler, 27 April 1948, in NARA, RG 232, M 898 (High Command Case), r. 4, fr. 244f. Koch was likely the official who ordered the initiation of anti-Jewish measures along the East Prussian–Polish frontier.

99. Ibid.

100. According to Krausnick and Wilhelm, *Die Truppe,* p. 82, Hitler declared the 4 October 1939 general amnesty in response to efforts by German commanders to punish SS and army personnel for crimes they committed against civilians in

Poland, crimes that Hitler rationalized as resulting from "embitterment caused by Polish atrocities," such as the Bromberg Bloody Sunday.

101. Anlagen zu Operationsbefehl Nr. 16, AOK 3, Ia, Nr. 106/39 geh. an I.A.K., 14 September 1939, in NARA, RG 242, T-314, r. 33, fr. 175.

102. Unternehmen Tannenberg—Tagesbericht, 19 September 1939, in USH-MMA, RG 15.007M, file 1, r. 2, p. 121.

103. Ibid.

104. Kriegstagebuch der I.A.K., 27 September 1939, in NARA, RG 242, T-314, r. 33, fr. 57.

105. An SD report three days later mentioned that "the guarding of bridges over the Narew is being coordinated with the Order Police. Jews and Poles who have streamed over to this side of the Narew are being forced back. To prevent crossing of the Narew in different places during the night, special patrols were begun." See Unternehmen Tannenberg—Tagesbericht, 27 September 1939, in USHMMA, RG 15.007M, file 2, r. 2, p. 50.

106. Unternehmen Tannenberg—Tagesbericht, 29 September 1939, in USH-MMA, RG 15.007M, file 2, r. 2, p. 55.

107. Copy of von Küchler's order published in *TWC*, vol. 10 (High Command Case), p. 155.

108. Wilhelm Keitel, "Lebenserrinnerungen aus der Zeitperiode vom 4.2.1938–10.8.1940," vol. 5, 1946, Nachlass Keitel, in BA/MA, N 54/5, p. 51. Note Keitel's selective memory concerning the army's willingness to use SS security formations behind the lines.

109. Fritsch purposefully sought death in combat by leading a regiment from the 12th Infantry Division against the defenses of Warsaw on 22 September. Hitler had removed Fritsch from his post after he was falsely accused of being a homosexual. The best scholarly treatment of the Blomberg-Fritsch Crisis is Karl-Heinz Janssen and Fritz Tobias, *Der Sturz der Generäle; Hitler und die Blomberg-Fritsch-Krise 1938* (Munich: Beck, 1994).

110. Dokument von Küchler Nr. 18: "Eidesstattliche Versicherung von Karl Wilhelm Melior," 20 April 1948, in NARA, RG 238, M 898 (High Command Case), r. 44, fr. 535.

111. Testimony of Wilhelm [*sic*] von Küchler, 27 April 1948, in NARA, RG 232, M 898 (High Command Case), r. 4, fr. 246.

112. Samuel W. Mitcham Jr. and Gene Mueller, *Hitler's Commanders: Officers of the Wehrmacht, the Luftwaffe, the Kriegsmarine, and the Waffen-SS* (New York: Cooper Square Press, 2000), p. 53.

113. Erschiessung von Juden durch Obermusikmeister der Leibstandarte, Schreiben Reichenau an die Heeresgruppe Süd, 19 September 1939, in NARA, RG 242, T-311, r. 254, fr. 769.

114. Ibid. The other officer referred to by Reichenau was probably Reserve Lieutenant Bruno Kleinmischel, who was court-martialed by a Tenth Army war court on 19 September for his role in the killing of twenty-two Jews in Konskie. See Alexander B. Rossino, "Destructive Impulses: German Soldiers and the Conquest of Poland," *Holocaust and Genocide Studies* 11, no. 3 (Winter 1997): 358f.

115. Fernschreiben, HGr Süd an der AOK 10 (Reichenau), 20 September 1939, in NARA, RG 242, T-311, r. 254, fr. 270.

116. Dokument Hoth Nr. 39, "Eidesstattliche Versicherung von Smilo Freiherr von Lüttwitz (General der Panzertruppe)," 26 February 1948, in NARA, RG 238, M 898 (High Command Case), r. 44, fr. 145. Von Lüttwitz was at that time a lieutenant colonel and Hoth's adjutant.

117. Ibid.

118. A copy of Himmler's telegram can be found in ZStL, "Einsatzgruppen in Polen," vol. 2 (20 May 1963), p. 38. For an interesting interpretation of events in Włocławek as a "training exercise" for later killing operations by the SS, see Konrad Kwiet, "Erziehung zum Mord—Zwei Beispiele zur Kontinuität der deutschen 'Endlösung der Judenfrage,'" in *Geschichte und Emanzipation: Festschrift für Reinhard Rürup*, ed. M. Grüttner, R. Hachtmann, and Heinz-Gerhard Haupt (Frankfurt/Main: Campus Verlag, 1999), pp. 435–457.

119. Tätigkeitsbericht während des Einsatzes vom 13. bis 26.9.1939, SS Standartenführer Nostitz an den Generalinspekteur der verstärkten SS Totenkopfstandarten, 28 September 1939, in USHMMA, RG 48.004M (Records of the Military Historical Institute, Prague), r. 3, fr. 300040. The same document is held at the Military Historical Institute in Prague, box 8, folder 34 (3rd SS–Pz.Div. "Totenkopf").

120. Besondere Anordnungen Nr. 22 für die Versorgung der 8.Armee, AOK 8, 15 September 1939, in NARA, RG 242, T-312, r. 38, fr. 7547369.

121. ZStL, "Einsatzgruppen in Polen," vol. 2, p. 37. Pancke apparently also served as Eicke's personal deputy and as such was responsible for transmitting topsecret instructions from Eicke to SS units in the field. See Charles W. Sydnor Jr., *Soldiers of Destruction: The SS Death's Head Division, 1939–1945,* rev. ed. (Princeton, NJ: Princeton University Press, 1990), p. 40.

122. Korück 581 (Qu. Nr. 14/39) an AOK 8, 25 September 1939, in NARA, RG 242, T-312, r. 45, fr. 7557539, and ZStL, "Einsatzgruppen in Polen," vol. 2, p. 161f.

123. Besondere Anordnung Nr. 28 für die rückwärtigen Dienste, AOK 8, 21 September 1939, in NARA, RG 242, T-312, r. 39, fr. 7548888. See also ZStL, "Einsatzgruppen in Polen," vol. 1, p. 93.

124. Korück 581 (Qu. Nr. 14/39) an AOK 8, 25 September 1939, in NARA, RG 242, T-312, r. 45, fr. 7557540.

125. Ibid., fr. 7557538.

126. Ibid.

127. Bericht über den Einsatz des I. Bataillons der 2. SS Totenkopfstandarte in Włocławek, 20 October 1939, in USHMMA, RG 48.004M, r. 3, fr. 300041. Pancke may have also reminded Nostitz at this point of Himmler's anti-Jewish "terror order" from 25 August, if indeed the order to terrorize Polish Jews was passed down on that date. See note 10 of this chapter.

128. Ibid.

129. Ibid.

130. Korück 581 (Qu. Nr. 14/39) an AOK 8, 25 September 1939, in NARA, RG 242, T-312, r. 45, fr. 7557539.

131. Ibid., and Fernschreiben, Korück 581 an dem AOK 8 über Korück 530, 24 September 1939, in NARA, RG 242, T-312, r. 45, fr. 7557537.

132. Korück 581 (Qu. Nr. 14/39) an AOK 8, 25 September 1939, in NARA, RG 242, T-312, r. 45, fr. 7557540.

133. Ibid.

134. SS Standartenführer Nostitz an der Korück 581, 22 September 1939, in NARA, RG 242, T-312, r. 45, fr. 7557538. The Jews of Włocławek were not engaged in any clandestine anti-German activity but had come together to celebrate Sukkoth. As Böhm-Tettelbach reported to the Eighth Army, an investigation yielded the conclusion that "the Jews gathered for their Sukkoth. The assembly of a malicious mob is not to be feared." See Fernschreiben, Korück 581 an dem AOK 8 über Korück 530, 24 September 1939, in NARA, RG 242, T-312, r. 45, fr. 7557537.

135. Müller an den Generalinspekteur der verstärkten SS-Totenkopfstandarten SS Gruppenführer Eicke, Geheime Staatspolizei, B.-Nr. o 14 87/39 g., 10 October 1939, in USHMMA, RG 48.004M, r. 3, fr. 300037.

136. Ibid., fr. 300038.

137. Eicke an den Kommandeur SS Totenkopf–Inf. Rgt. 2, SS Standartenführer Nostitz, 18 October 1939, in USHMMA, RG 48.004M, r. 3, fr. 300039.

138. Bericht über den Einsatz des I. Bataillons der 2. SS Totenkopfstandarte in Włocławek, 20 October 1939, in USHMMA, RG 48.004M, r. 3, fr. 300041.

139. Fernschreiben, Korück 581 (Qu. Nr. 14/39) an AOK 8, 25 September 1939, in NARA, RG 242, T-312, r. 45, fr. 7557540.

140. Ibid.

141. Ibid. Incidentally, in Schlussbericht des Sonderbefehlshabers der Polizei beim AOK 8, 30 September 1939, in ZStL, "Einsatzgruppen in Polen," vol. 2, p. 39, Nostitz's superior, Günther Pancke, stressed that his work with all of the commanders in the Eighth Army had gone well. Pancke recalled that even General Wilhelm Ulex, the commander of the X Corps, and later a vocal critic of the SS, had "greeted the activities of the Special Commander of Police with particular warmth."

142. See Sydnor, *Soldiers*, chap. 9; George H. Stein, *The Waffen SS: Hitler's Elite Guard at War, 1939–1945* (Ithaca, NY: Cornell University Press, 1966); and Bernd Wegner, *Hitlers Politische Soldaten: Die Waffen-SS, 1933–1945* (Paderborn: Schöningh, 1982), for a complete description of the racial-political ethos of the Waffen-SS.

143. RSHA Protokol, 7 September 1939, in ZStL, 211 AR-Z 13/63 Schlussvermerk in dem Strafverfahren gegen Lothar Beutel et al., p. 16.

144. Groscurth, *Tagebücher*, p. 201.

145. Ibid., p. 202. See also Müller, *Das Heer und Hitler*, p. 428, and Richard Breitman, *The Architect of Genocide: Himmler and the Final Solution* (New York: Knopf, 1991), p. 70.

146. Groscurth, *Tagebücher*, p. 202.

147. ZStL, "Einsatzgruppen in Polen," vol. 1, p. 122f.

148. Ibid., p. 124f. See also the Testimony of Erwin Lahousen, 11 February 1948, in NARA, RG 238, M 898 (High Command Case), r. 2, fr. 446.

149. An entry in Franz Halder's diary of 19 September 1939 noted: "Heydrich (through Wagner), A. army must be notified of any operations assigned to them. Liaison officers, Himmler–Commander-in-Chief of the army. B. Clean up once and for all: Jews, Intelligentsia, clergy, [and] nobility. C. army demands: Clean up after withdrawal of Army and transfer to civil administration in early December." Quoted during the Testimony of General Franz Halder, 15 April 1948, in NARA, RG 238, M 898 (High Command Case), r. 3, fr. 853. Also see Müller, *Das Heer und*

Hitler, p. 430, and Hans Umbreit, *Deutsche Militärverwaltungen 1938/39: Die militärische Besetzung der Tschechoslowakei und Polens* (Stuttgart: Deutsche Verlags-Anstalt, 1977), p. 168f.

150. Müller, *Das Heer und Hitler,* p. 668.

151. Tätigkeit und Aufgaben der Polizei Einsatzgruppen im Operationsgebiet, Der Oberbefehlshaber des Heeres, OKH, 21 September 1939, reproduced in Müller, *Das Heer und Hitler,* p. 667f.

152. Müller, *Das Heer und Hitler,* p. 432.

153. ZStL, "Einsatzgruppen in Polen," vol. 1, p. 129.

154. Ibid., p.132f.

155. Vorschlag für Führung der Sperrlinie, Anlage I zu Kriegstagebuch, GAK 3, 28 September 1939, in NARA, RG 242, T-314, r. 840, fr. 113.

156. Ibid., fr. 114.

157. Fernschreiben, GAK 3 an AOK 10; AOK 14, 23 September 1939, in NARA, RG 242, T-311, r. 242, fr. 402.

158. Aktenvermerk Heydrichs, Der Chef der Sipo und des SD, C.d.S. B.-Nr.: 533552/40, Berlin, 2 July 1940, reproduced in Krausnick, "Hitler und die Morde," p. 206f.

Chapter 5. Institutional Brutality and German Army Reprisal Policy

1. See, for example, Mark Mazower, *Inside Hitler's Greece: The Experience of Occupation, 1941–44* (New Haven, CT: Yale University Press, 1993), chap. 15, for evidence of German violence against Greeks.

2. Jürgen Förster, "Jewish Policies of the German Military, 1939–1942," in *The Shoah and the War,* ed. Asher Cohen, Yehoyakim Cochavi, and Yoav Gelber (New York: Peter Lang, 1992), p. 56; Jürgen Förster, "Complicity or Entanglement? Wehrmacht, War, and Holocaust," in *The Holocaust and History: The Known, the Unknown, the Disputed, and the Reexamined,* ed. Michael Berenbaum and Abraham J. Peck (Bloomington: Indiana University Press, 1998), p. 271; Hans Umbreit, *Deutsche Militärverwaltungen 1938/39: Die militärische Besetzung der Tschechoslowakei und Polens* (Stuttgart: Deutsche Verlags-Anstalt, 1977), pp. 137 and 273. Exceptions in the west are Richard C. Lukas, *The Forgotten Holocaust: The Poles under German Occupation, 1939–1944* (Lexington: University Press of Kentucky, 1986), and Tadeusz Piotrowski, *Poland's Holocaust: Ethnic Strife, Collaboration with Occupying Forces, and Genocide in the Second Republic, 1918–1947* (Jefferson, NC: McFarland, 1998).

3. Omer Bartov, *Hitler's Army: Soldiers, Nazis, and War in the Third Reich* (New York: Oxford University Press, 1991), p. 61.

4. Merkblatt über Eigenarten der polnischen Kriegsführung, 1 July 1939, 12 Abt. (III), OKH—Gen.St.d.H., Nr. 1343/39g, Berlin, in NARA, RG 242, T-79, r. 131, fr. 000525.

5. Richard C. Fattig, "Reprisal: The German Army and the Execution of Hostages during the Second World War" (Ph.D. Thesis, University of California, San Diego, 1980), pp. 7ff.

6. According to the Armed Forces High Command (OKW), "Geiselnehmen

und Geiseltötung ist durch das Völkerrecht nicht verboten" ("The taking and shooting of hostages is not prohibited by the law"). See OKW Anweisungen, 14 June 1939, in NARA, RG 242, T-77, r. 978, fr. 4467814.

7. Fall Weiss—Sonderbestimmungen zu den Anordnungen für die Versorgung, 24 July 1939, OKW, in NARA, RG 242, T-78, r. 351, fr. 6310574ff.

8. See, for example, a series of hypothetical situations concerning conflicts with civilians set out by OKW in an unnumbered document dated 15 July 1939, in NARA, RG 242, T-77, r. 978, fr. 4467798–822.

9. For explanations of the later impact of reprisal policies in the occupied USSR and Serbia, see the controversial essays by Hannes Heer, "Killing Fields: Die Wehrmacht und der Holocaust" (pp. 57–77), and "Die Logik des Vernicht-ungskrieges: Wehrmacht und Partisanenkampf" (pp. 104–138), in *Vernichtungs-krieg: Verbrechen der Wehrmacht 1941–1944,* ed. Hannes Heer and Klaus Naumann (Hamburg: HIS Verlagsges, 1995), as well as Walter Manoschek, *"Ser-bien ist Judenfrei!": Militärische Besatzungspolitik und Judenvernichtung in Ser-bien 1941/42* (Munich: Oldenbourg, 1993). Also see Fattig, "Reprisal," and for the impact of reprisal policy on military discipline, see Bartov, *Hitler's Army,* chap. 3.

10. Kriegstagebuch der 19.I.D. vom Einsatz im Polenfeldzug, 25 August–30 September 1939, in BA/MA, RH 26-19/2.

11. Ibid.

12. "Die 10.Division im polnischen Feldzug," 31 October 1939, in BA/MA, RH 26-10/544, p. 6.

13. Ibid.

14. Ibid., pp. 6ff.

15. Kriegstagebuch mit Karten, 21 June–20 October 1939, 3.I, in BA/MA, RH 26-3/1.

16. Kriegstagebuch des Generalkommando XIX AK, 3 September 1939, in NARA, RG 242, T-314, r. 611, fr. 622. Later in the war, German personnel in-creasingly used these adjectives as coded euphemisms denoting enemies who were to be summarily eliminated. See Mazower, *Hitler's Greece,* p. 191, and Heer, "Die Logik," p. 106. For other examples of coded language used by the Wehrmacht, see Hamburger Institut für Sozialforschung, *Vernichtungskrieg: Verbrechen der Wehrmacht 1941 bis 1944 Ausstellungskatalog* (Hamburg: HIS Verlagsges, 1996), p. 140.

17. Kriegstagebuch der 19.I.D., 4 September 1939, in BA/MA, RH 26-19/2.

18. Anlagen zum Kriegstagebuch 1 der Ia, 337.Infanterie Regiment, 8 September 1939, in NARA, RG 242, T-315, r. 1609, fr. 147.

19. Unternehmen Tannenberg—Tagesbericht für die Zeit vom 12 September 1939 bis 13 September 1939, in USHMMA, RG 15.007M (Records of the Reich Security Main Office—RSHA), file 1, r. 2, p. 59.

20. Unternehmen Tannenberg—Tagesbericht, 6 September 1939, in USHMMA, RG 15.007M, file 1, r. 2, p. 5.

21. Korpsbefehl für den 3 September 1939, Abt. Ia, Generalkommando VIII (Busch), 2 September 1939, in NARA, RG 242, T-314, r. 840, fr. 32.

22. Divisionsbefehl für den Vormarsch am 8 September 1939, Abt. Ia, 252.I.D., Nr. 3/39, in NARA, RG 242, T-315, r. 1740, fr. 85.

23. Kriegstagebuch der 19.I.D. vom Einsatz im Polenfeldzug, 25 August–30 September 1939, in BA/MA, RH 26-19/2.

24. Heeresgruppe Nord an der XIX.A.K., 9 September 1939, in NARA, RG 242, T-314, r. 613, fr. 274.

25. Kriegstagebuch I der 3.I.D., 21 June–20 October 1939, in BA/MA, RH 26-3/1.

26. Divisionsbefehl für den 18 September 1939 aus dem Kriegstagebuch Ia des 208.I.D., in NARA, RG 242, T-315, r. 1609, fr. 240.

27. Gefechtsbericht, 16 September 1939, Kriegstagebuch Teile 1–2 der 206.I.D., in NARA, RG 242, T-315, r. 1594, fr. 48.

28. Besondere Anordnungen Nr. 11 für die Versorgung der 8.Armee, 4 September 1939, AOK 8, in NARA, RG 242, T-312, r. 38, fr. 7547023.

29. Lagebericht der Landrat Neu-Sandez an der CdZ Krakau, 21 September 1939, in NARA, RG 242, T-501, r. 229, fr. 660.

30. Befehle AOK 8 an der Gruppe Schenckendorff, 3 September 1939, AOK 8, in NARA, RG 242, T-314, r. 870, fr. 79.

31. Documents illustrating Schenckendorff's disillusionment with collective punishment policy can be found in Reinhard Rürup, ed., *Der Krieg gegen die Sowjetunion 1941–1945: Eine Dokumentation* (Berlin: Argon, 1991), pp. 132ff. The frustration of other officers with standard Wehrmacht reprisal measures is discussed in chapters six and seven of Theo Schulte, *The German Army and Nazi Policies in Occupied Russia* (Oxford: Berg, 1989), and attempts to change the policies are documented in Timothy P. Mulligan, *The Politics of Illusion and Empire: German Occupation Policy in the Soviet Union, 1942–1943* (New York: Praeger, 1988).

32. Besondere Anordnungen für die rückwärtigen Dienst Nr. 1, Anlage 1, Merkblatt zur Bekanntgabe an die gegen Polen eingesetzten Truppen, 24 August 1939, in NARA, RG 242, T-312, r. 39, fr. 7548860.

33. Besondere Anordnungen Nr. 7 für die Versorgung der 8.Armee, 31 August 1939, AOK 8, in ibid., fr. 7548779.

34. KTB 2 der Gruppe Schenckendorff, 7 September 1939, in NARA, RG 242, T-312, r. 852, fr. 317.

35. KTB 2 der Gruppe Schenckendorff, 8 September 1939, in ibid., fr. 322.

36. Bekanntmachung, Gruppe Schenckendorff, 11 September 1939, in ibid., fr. 588.

37. Befehle, 4 September 1939, AOK 10, in NARA, RG 242, T-312, r. 75, fr. 7595346.

38. Besondere Anordnungen Nr. 11 für die Versorgung der 8.Armee, 4 September 1939, AOK 8, in NARA, RG 242, T-312, r. 38, fr. 7547023. The Security Police referred to were likely elements of Einsatzgruppe III, which was active in support of the Eighth Army in the Poznań region.

39. Ibid.

40. Ic/AO (Schniewind) an O.Qu. (Jaenecke), 7 September 1939, AOK 8, in NARA, RG 242, T-312, r. 45, fr. 7557385.

41. The use of the term "field court martial" in this impromptu case should not be confused with the German term *Feldkriegsgericht,* or Field War Court, which was a formally established, mobile court-martial.

42. Korpsbefehl für die Säuberung von Otwock, 16 September 1939, Gen.Kdo. I.A.K., in NARA, RG 242, T-314, r. 33, fr. 279f.

43. Tagesbericht, 11 September 1939, Gruppe Schenckendorff, in NARA, RG 242, T-312, r. 852, fr. 595.

44. Tagesbefehl, 15 September 1939, Gruppe Schenckendorff, in ibid., fr. 45.

45. Befehl für die Besetzung der Stadt Graudenz, 4 September 1939, Anlage 28, Kriegstagebuch der 21.I.D., in BA/MA, RH 26-21/2.

46. Gefechtsbericht, 16 September 1939, Kriegstagebuch Teile 1–2 der 206.I.D., in NARA, RG 242, T- 315, r. 1594, fr. 48.

47. Kriegstagebuch der 19.I.D. vom Einsatz im Polenfeldzug, 25 August 1939–26 September 1939, in BA/MA, RH 26-19/2.

48. Besondere Anordnungen für die Versorgung, Korpsbefehle, usw., August–September 1939, Teil 2, Anlagen zum Kriegstagebuch I der 7.I.D., in BA/MA, RH 26-7/120.

49. The term "Congress-Poles" refers to Congress Poland, the historical Polish heartland centered south of Warsaw. It meant in this case those persons of pure Polish stock who immigrated into areas of western Poland that Germany had ceded in 1919. Reference to "the Protectorate of Lodz" at this point in the campaign indicates that some in the Wehrmacht knew of SS plans for the mass resettlement of Poles and Jews from areas considered historically German. These areas, including the province of Poznań, West Prussia, and East Upper Silesia, were formally incorporated into Germany in October 1939. For more on subsequent resettlement operations, see Richard Breitman, *The Architect of Genocide: Himmler and the Final Solution* (New York: Knopf, 1991), Czesław Madajczyk, *Die Okkupationspolitik Nazideutschlands in Polen 1939–1945* (East Berlin: Akademie-Verlag, 1987), and Götz Aly, *"Final Solution": Nazi Population Policy and the Murder of the European Jews,* trans. B. Cooper and A. Brown (New York: Arnold, 1999).

50. Befriedung des Militärbezirks Posen, 23 September 1939, Ia/Ic Aktennotiz 1, 252.I.D., in NARA, RG 242, T-315, r. 1740, fr. 56–59.

51. Merkblatt über Eigenarten der polnischen Kriegsführung, 1 July 1939, 12. Abt. (III), OKH—Gen.St.d.H., Nr. 1343/39g, Berlin, in NARA, RG 242, T-79, r. 131, fr. 000525.

52. Polnische Sabotageorganisation, 31 August 1939, Ic/AO, AOK 10, Nr. 206/39 Abw. III, Oppeln, in NARA, RG 242, T-79, r. 8, fr. 001223.

53. Madajczyk, *Die Okkupationspolitik,* p. 28.

54. Wolfgang Schumann and Ludwig Nestler, eds., *Europa unterm Hakenkreuz: Die faschistische Okkupationspolitik in Polen, 1939–1945* (Berlin: Deutscher Verlag der Wissenschaften, 1989), pp. 346–353.

55. Robert G.L. Waite, *Vanguard of Nazism: The Free Corps Movement in Postwar Germany, 1918–1923* (New York: W. W. Norton, 1952), p. 96, and T. Hunt Tooley, *National Identity and Weimar Germany: Upper Silesia and the Eastern Border, 1918–1922* (Lincoln: University of Nebraska Press, 1997), p. 78.

56. Nigel H. Jones, *Hitler's Heralds: The Story of the Freikorps, 1918–1923* (New York: Dorset Press, 1987), p. 119.

57. John Horne and Alan Kramer, *German Atrocities 1914: A History of Denial* (New Haven, CT: Yale University Press, 2001), pp. 38ff. See also Horne and Kramer, "German 'Atrocities' and Franco-German Opinion, 1914: The Evidence of

German Soldiers' Diaries," *Journal of Modern History* 66 (1994): 1–33; Alan Kramer, "'Grueltaten,' Zum Problem der deutschen Kriegsverbrechen in Belgien und Frankreich 1914," in *"Keiner fühlt sich hier als Mensch": Erlebnis und Wirkung des Ersten Weltkriegs,* ed. G. Hirschfeld, G. Krumreich, and I. Renz (Essen: Klartext, 1993), pp. 83–112; Lothar Wieland, *Belgien 1914: Die Frage des belgischen "Franktireurkrieges" und die deutsche öffentliche Meinung von 1914 bis 1936* (Frankfurt/Main: Peter Lang, 1984).

58. Horne and Kramer, *German Atrocities,* pp. 139ff.

59. Ibid., p. 167.

60. Ibid., p. 168.

61. Ibid.

62. Ibid., p. 170.

63. Ibid.

64. Ibid.

65. Kramer, "'Grueltaten,'" p. 92.

66. Horne and Kramer, "German 'Atrocities,'" pp. 28–29. See also David Schoenbaum, *Zabern 1913: Consensus Politics in Imperial Germany* (London: George Allen and Unwin, 1982).

67. See Kramer, "'Grueltaten,'" p. 103, and Roger Chickering, "Die Alldeutschen erwarten den Krieg," in *Bereit zum Krieg: Kriegsmentalität im wilhelminischen Deutschland, 1890–1914,* ed. J. Dülffer and K. Holl (Göttingen: Vandenhoeck and Ruprecht, 1986), pp. 20–32.

68. Hitler quoted from Canaris's diary in Winfried Baumgart, "Zur Ansprache Hitlers vor den Führern der Wehrmacht am 22 August 1939," *Vierteljahrshefte für Zeitgeschichte* 19 (1971): 303.

69. Bekanntmachung, 17 September 1939, Oberbefehlshaber des Heeres (von Brauchitsch) an der Befehlshaber AOK III (von Küchler), in NARA, RG 242, T-312, r. 31, fr. 7538748.

70. Statement of Władysława Bera (Protokół Przesłuchania Świadka; hereafter cited as PPS), Syn.Akt. 85/68, 16 September 1968 in USHMMA, RG 15.042M (Records of the Main Crimes Commission for the Investigation of Nazi War Crimes, Poznań; hereafter cited as MCC), r. 77, file Ds 259/67.

71. Statement of Władysław Wolda, PPS, Syn.Akt. 85/68, 16 September 1968, in ibid.

72. Statement of Sofia Barska, PPS, Syn.Akt. 85/68, 16 September 1968, in ibid.

73. Statement of Regina Jakubiak, PPS, 8 October 1968, in USHMMA, RG 15.042M, r. 17, file Ds 28/71.

74. Statement of Branisław Ganek, PPS, 15 October 1968, in ibid.

75. Ibid.

76. Statement of Josef Bałata, PPS, 7 October 1968, in ibid.

77. Ibid.

78. OKL S 28/71, Sprawozdanie, 19 August 1981, Piotrków Trybunalski, in ibid.

79. Ibid.

80. Ibid. See also the Statement of Henryk Marian Gemel, PPS, 8 October 1968, in ibid.

81. OKL Ds 28/71, Informacja o Pacyfikacji wsi Milejowiec, in ibid.

82. OKL Ds 30/71, Informacja o Pacyfikacji wsi Krezna, in USHMMA, RG 15.042M, r. 17, file Ds 30/71.

83. OKL Ds 30/71, Sprawozdanie, 28 January 1975, Łódź, in ibid.

84. Militärbefehlshaber Posen an der Gruppe Schenckendorff, 24 September 1939, in NARA, RG 242, T-314, r. 852, fr. 175.

85. Fattig, "Reprisal," p. 7.

86. Fattig, "Reprisal," p. 7f.

87. Datner, *Crimes,* p. 7.

88. Fattig, "Reprisal," p. 8.

89. Fattig, "Reprisal," offers an excellent overview of the origins and development of German reprisal policy from the Franco-Prussian War onward.

Chapter 6. From Retaliation to Atrocity

1. Detailed information about the formation and history of the SS *Leibstandarte* "Adolf Hitler" can be found in Charles Messenger, *Hitler's Gladiator: The Life and Times of Oberstgruppenführer and Panzergeneral-Oberst der Waffen-SS Sepp Dietrich* (London: Brassey's, 1988).

2. "Die 10.Division im polnischen Feldzug," 31 October 1939, p. 6, in BA/MA, RH 26-10/544.

3. Ibid. The 10th Infantry Division was composed of the 20th, 41st, and 85th Infantry Regiments.

4. Copy of Ermittlungen gegen Unbekannt wegen NS-Verbrechen, Staatsanwaltschaft bei dem Landgericht München I, Nr. 320 UJs 206362/83 (Tötungen an polnischen Zivilisten am 1 und 2 September 1939 in Wyszanow und Torzeniec, Kreis Kepno), pp. 4–5, in USHMMA, RG 15.042M, r. 50, file Ds 29/70, vol. 1.

5. Statement of Aniela Hes, née Góralski, PPS, OKWr.KPP.13/79, 27 April 1979, in ibid.

6. "Die 10.Division im polnischen Feldzug," 31 October 1939, p. 7, in BA/MA, RH 26-10/544.

7. Ibid.

8. Statement of Janina Rózanska, née Tomala, PPS, OKWr. KPP 2/81, 28 January 1981, in USHMMA, RG 15.042M, r. 50, file Ds 29/70, vol. 1.

9. Statement of Anna Wolna, PPS, OKL S 2/86, 23 September 1986, in USHMMA, RG 15.042M, r. 52, file S 2/86.

10. Ibid.

11. Statement of Zofia Monka, PPS, OKL S 2/86, 28 August 1986, in ibid.

12. Statement of Mieczysław Kaczmarek, PPS, OKL S 2/86, 17 September 1986, and Ludwik Monka, PPS, OKL S 2/86, 28 August 1986, both in ibid.

13. Statement of Krystyna Grzesiak, PPS, OKL S 2/86, 20 October 1986, in ibid.

14. See statements of Zofia Monka, Mieczysław Kaczmarek, and Ludwik Monka above.

15. Statement of Karol Musialek, PPS, 24 February 1981, in USHMMA, RG 15.042M, r. 50, file Ds 29/70, vol. 1.

16. Statement of Franciszek Lizon, PPS, 24 February 1981, in ibid.

17. Statement of Tadeusz Kik, PPS, 27 February 1981, in ibid.

18. Statement of Franciszek Lizon, PPS, 24 February 1981, in ibid.

19. Ibid.

20. Statement of Karol Musialek, PPS, 24 February 1981, in ibid.

21. Statement of Franciszek Klimas, PPS, KPP1/81, 13 February 1981, in ibid.

22. Statement of Henryk Okon, PPS, KPP8/72, 7 February 1972, in ibid.

23. Ibid.

24. Statement of Jan Polak, PPS, 24 June 1949, in ibid.

25. Ermittlungsverfahren gegen Soldaten der SS-Leibstandarte "Adolf Hitler," ZStL, Nr. 7b Js 2679/82, 12 March 1986, p. 7, in USHMMA, RG 15.042M, r. 36, file Ds 424/67.

26. Ibid., p. 8.

27. Ibid., p. 10.

28. Ibid., p. 12.

29. Ibid.

30. Ibid., p. 12f.

31. Ibid., p. 14.

32. Ibid., p. 17f.

33. Ibid., p. 19.

34. Ibid., pp. 22ff, 28.

35. Ibid., p. 15.

36. Ibid., p. 20.

37. Ermittlungsverfahren gegen Generalmajor a.D. Herbert Loch und unbekannte Soldaten wegen Mordes u.a. (Kriegsverbrechen), ZStL, 7 Js 9/73, 20 July 1973, p. 5, in USHMMA, RG 15.042M, r. 41, file Ds 252/67. Polish witnesses to the event misidentified the perpetrators as SS men. German investigators concluded in another case that the *Leibstandarte* moved east after occupying Złoczew and not northwest toward Stanisławów. See Ermittlungsverfahren gegen unbekannte Angehörige der 17. und 10. Infanteriedivision wegen Kriegsverbrechen (Mordes u.a.), ZStL, 7 Js 5445/80, 25 February 1988, p. 13, in USHMMA, RG 15.042M, r. 40, file S 17/75.

38. Statement of Stanisław Laskowski, PPS, OKL.Ds.17/70, 29 November 1974, in USHMMA, RG 15.042M, r. 41, file Ds 17/70.

39. Statement of Stanisława Podsiadła, PPS, OKL Ds 13/69, 11 February 1970, in USHMMA, RG 15.042M, r. 41, file Ds 13/69.

40. Statement of Stanisław Jaworski, PPS, OKL Ds 13/69, 10 February 1969, in ibid.

41. Ibid.

42. Statements of Michalina Lewinska and Eleonara Mizerska cited in Ermittlungsverfahren gegen unbekannte Angehörige der 17. und 10. Infanteriedivision wegen Kriegsverbrechen (Mordes u.a.), ZStL, 7 Js 5445/80, 25 February 1988, p. 3, in USHMMA, RG 15.042M, r. 40, file S 17/75, and r. 41, file Ds 13/69.

43. Samuel J. Lewis, *Forgotten Lessons: German Army Infantry Policy, 1918–1941* (New York: Praeger, 1985), p. 86.

44. Statement of Antoni Paszkowski, PPS, OKP KPP 48/75, 24 September 1975, in USHMMA, RG 15.042M, r. 40, file S 17/75, and Statement of Janina Matuszewska, née Paszkowski, PPS, OKWr.KPP 50/75, 30 September 1975, in ibid. See also Ermittlungsverfahren gegen unbekannte Angehörige der 17. und 10. In-

fanteriedivision wegen Kriegsverbrechen (Mordes u.a.), ZStL, 7 Js 5445/80, 25 February 1988, p. 4, in ibid.

45. Ermittlungsverfahren gegen unbekannte Angehörige der 17. und 10. Infanteriedivision wegen Kriegsverbrechen (Mordes u.a.), ZStL, 7 Js 5445/80, 25 February 1988, p. 5, in ibid. See also Notatka Służbowa, Okregowa Komisja Badania Zbrodni Hitlerowskich w Łódźi, Lask, 15 May 1975, in ibid.

46. Ermittlungsverfahren gegen unbekannte Angehörige der 17. und 10. Infanteriedivision wegen Kriegsverbrechen (Mordes u.a.), ZStL, 7 Js 5445/80, 25 February 1988, pp. 10–11, in ibid.

47. Ibid., p. 7, and Statement of Zygmunt Urbaniak, PPS, OKL S 17/75, 21 May 1975, in ibid.

48. Statement of Józef Kuławiak, PPS, Sygn.akt. Ko 44/67, 21 April 1967, in ibid. See also Ermittlungsverfahren, p. 9, in ibid.

49. Ibid.

50. Messenger, *Hitler's Gladiator*, p. 74, and James Weingartner, "Joseph 'Sepp' Dietrich—Hitlers Volksgeneral," in *Die Militärelite des Dritten Reiches*, ed. R. Smelser and E. Syring (Berlin: Ullstein, 1995), p. 118, and George H. Stein, *The Waffen SS: Hitler's Elite Guard at War, 1939–1945* (Ithaca, NY: Cornell University Press, 1966), p. 28.

51. Messenger, *Hitler's Gladiator*, p. 120f.

52. For information on SS killings in Dobron, Mogilno Male, and Dobron Duzy, see USHMMA, RG 15.042M, r. 40, file S 12/75. For more on the killing of Polish boy scouts in Chechło and other murders in the vicinity of Pabianice, see USHMMA, RG 15.042M, r. 39, file S 58/72.

53. Rolf Elble, *Die Schlacht an der Bzura im September 1939 aus deutscher und polnischer Sicht* (Freiburg: Verlag Rombach, 1975), p. 120.

54. Statement of Jan Nowicki, PPS, OKL S 31/70, 22 March 1973, in USHMMA, RG 15.042M, r. 43, file Ds 31/70.

55. Ibid. Witnesses corroborated Nowicki's story. See Second Statement of Bolesław Cieslinski, PPS, OKL S 31/70, 4 June 1973, in ibid.

56. First Statement of Bolesław Cieslinski, PPS, OKL S 31/70, 23 March 1973, and Statement of Konstanty Wesoly, PPS, OKL S 31/70, 15 November 1974, both in ibid.

57. Statement of Marcjanna Anyszka, née Okraska, PPS, OKL S 31/70, 23 March 1973, in ibid.

58. Statement of Marianna Dratek, PPS, OKL S 31/70, 7 April 1973, in ibid.

59. The 20th Infantry Regiment was no longer in the area, having been ordered north to reinforce the 24th Infantry Division. See Elble, *Die Schlacht an der Bzura*, p. 139.

60. Statement of Jan Kozlowski, PPS, OKWr. Ds.280/67, 3 February 1969, in USHMMA, RG 15.042M, r. 71, file Ds 280/67.

61. Statement of Stefan Kozlowski, PPS, OKWr. Ds.280/67, 4 February 1969, in ibid.

62. OKL Ds 280/67, Sprawozdanie, Łódź, 10 March 1970, in ibid.

63. Statement of Ewa Duda, PPS, OKL Ds 280/67, 9 November 1967, in ibid.

64. Statement of Henryk Pniewski, PPS, Sygn.akt. KPP 8/81, 21 October 1981, in USHMMA, RG 15.042M, r. 42, file Ds 179/62.

65. Ibid.

66. Ibid.

67. Statement of Antoni Antosik, PPS, Sygn.akt. Ko18/68, 29 March 1968, in ibid.

68. OKL Ds 163/67, Sprawozdanie, 1978, Poznań, in USHMMA, RG 15.042M, r. 57, file Ds 163/67.

69. Statement of Stanisław Jaros, PPS, Sygn.akt. Ko 101/68, 6 December 1968, in ibid.

70. Statement of Wacław Walczak, PPS, Sygn.akt. Ko 31/69, 7 October 1969, in ibid.

71. Ibid.

72. See OKL Ds 163/67, Sprawozdanie, 1978, Poznań, in ibid.

73. Statement of Józef Smiałek, PPS, OKL Ds 163/67, 17 March 1970, in ibid.

74. For details on these incidents see USHMMA, RG 15.042M, r. 44, file S 10/77-A/I.

75. See USHMMA, RG 15.042M, r. 24, file Ds 115/67, and USHMMA, RG 15.042M, r. 24, file Ds 185/67.

76. Statement of Jan Swiderski, PPS, OKL Ds 115/67, 21 September 1967, in USHMMA, RG 15.042M, r. 24, file Ds 115/67. See also the statements of Apolonia Bernat, Teodor Bodnarski, and Stanisław Pabianczyk in the same file. See also the Statement of Jerzy Bernaciak, PPS, OKL Ds 149/67, 14 September 1967, in USHMMA, RG 15.042M, r. 24, file Ds 149/67, vol. 2.

77. Statement of Jan Skrocki, PPS, OKL S 16/73, 4 June 1973, in USHMMA, RG 15.042M, r. 43, file S 16/73. Skrocki recalled the number of priests incorrectly. Ignacy Sankowski participated in exhuming the bodies in September 1939 and remembered finding five bodies wearing long, black clerical garb. See Statement of Ignacy Sankowski, PPS, OKL S 16/73, 4 June 1973, in ibid.

78. Elble, *Die Schlacht an der Bzura*, p. 172.

79. Ibid., p. 104.

80. OKL S 108/67, Sprawozdanie, no date, Łowicz in USHMMA, RG 15.042M, r. 8, file Ds 108/67. Also see Statement of Edward-Joachim Pelka, PPS, OKL Ds 108/67, 12 June 1973, in ibid.

81. OKL S 108/67, Sprawozdanie, no date, Łowicz, and Statement of Edward-Joachim Pelka in ibid.

82. Statement of Stefania Wolski, PPS, OKL Ds 108/67, 10 March 1973, in ibid.

83. Statement of Edward Wróbel, PPS, OKL Ds 108/67, 2 June 1973, in ibid.

84. Protokół, 18 January 1974, Lutomiersk, in USHMMA, RG 15.042M, r. 32, file Ds 94/67.

85. Ibid.

86. Ibid.

87. Ibid.

88. Ibid.

89. The first German units in Rawa Mazowiecka were the 1st and 4th Panzer Divisions, which passed through the city on 7 September.

90. Notatka Urzedowa, OKL S 223/67, 20 September 1977, Rawa Mazowiecka, in USHMMA, RG 15.042M, r. 9, file Ds 223/67.

91. Ibid.

92. Statement of Ewa Sadzik, PPS, OKL Ds 8/69, in ibid.

93. Ibid.

94. Statement of Stefan Biskupski, PPS, OKL S 223/67, 7 November 1967, and Statement of Wiktor Galinski, PPS, OKL S 223/67, 7 November 1968, both in ibid.

95. Statement of Jozef Luczynski, PPS, Ko 28/67, 1 December 1967, in ibid.

96. Statement of Jan Pawlewski, PPS, OKL S 223/67, 8 January 1969, in ibid.

97. Notatka Urzedowa, OKL S 223/67, 20 September 1977, Rawa Mazowiecka, in ibid.

98. Ibid.

99. It has been impossible to determine the exact unit that was in the area. Chances are it was either the 30th Infantry Division or the 14th Infantry Division, which brought up the rear of the XVI Corps following the 1st and 4th Panzer Divisions. See Tagesmeldungen vom 4 September 1939, in Kurt Mehner, ed., *Die Geheimen Tagesberichte der Deutschen Wehrmachtführung im Zweiten Weltkrieg 1939–1945*, vol. 1 (Osnabrück: Biblio Verlag, 1995), pp. 9ff. As it later turned out, the infantryman was killed by trigger-happy comrades who shot him through the window of a house he had ducked into to quickly wash and shave. The man had taken off his tunic and stood in the window for light. While shaving he drew the attention of passing troops who mistook him for a Pole and shot him, indicating once again the readiness of German military personnel to summarily kill Polish civilians. See Statement of Bronisława Kleket, PPS, OKL Ds 291/67, 20 April 1968, in USHMMA, RG 15.042M, r. 77, file S 291/67.

100. Statement of Józef Włodarek, PPS, OKL Ds 291/67, 12 March 1970, in ibid.

101. Ibid.

102. An addendum to Włodarek's statement mentioned fifteen Jews, but other witnesses recalled that the number shot was twelve. See Statement of Józef Płomnik, PPS, OKL Ds 291/67, 20 April 1968, in ibid.

103. Addendum to Statement of Józef Włodarek, PPS, OKL Ds 291/67, 12 March 1970, in ibid.

104. Jacob Apenszlak, ed., *The Black Book of Polish Jewry* (New York: American Federation for Polish Jews, 1943), p. 5.

105. Ibid., p. 7. These soldiers probably belonged to the 10th Infantry Division, which was in the area at the time.

106. Ibid., p. 9. The men of the 10th Infantry Division were also the likely perpetrators of these acts.

107. Ibid., pp. 5–15.

108. Omer Bartov, *Hitler's Army: Soldiers, Nazis, and War in the Third Reich* (New York: Oxford University Press, 1991), p. 61.

109. Jürgen Förster, "Complicity or Entanglement? Wehrmacht, War, and Holocaust," in *The Holocaust and History: The Known, the Unknown, the Disputed, and the Reexamined*, ed. M. Berenbaum and A. J. Peck (Bloomington: Indiana University Press, 1998), p. 271.

110. These incidents are described in detail in Alexander B. Rossino, "Destructive Impulses: German Soldiers and the Conquest of Poland," *Holocaust and Genocide Studies* 11, no. 3 (Winter 1997): 351–365.

111. Entry of 5 September 1939, Sammelmappe Ic (Polen), 19 August–11 October 1939, AOK 8, Ic/AO, Nr. 643/39g., in BA/MA, RH 26-10/540.

112. Besondere Anordnungen auf dem Ic-Gebiet, 14 September 1939, Teil 2, 7.I.D. Anlagen zum Kriegstagebuch I. Besondere Anordnungen für die Versorgung, Korpsbefehle, usw. Aug.–Sept. 1939, in BA/MA, RH 26-7/120.

113. War diary entry of 3 September 1939, in Feldzug in Polen Kriegstagebuch Ia, 25 August–20 October 1939, 31.Division, in BA/MA, 26-31/1.

114. Tagesbefehl, 5 September 1939, Ia, Grenzschutz-Abschnittskommando 3, in NARA, RG 242, T-314, r. 840, fr. 75.

115. Armeetagesbefehl, 18 September 1939, AOK 14, in NARA, RG 242, T-314, r. 665, fr. 442.

116. Übersicht die durch die Wehrmacht gerichte in der Zeit vom 26 August bis 18 November 1939 zum Tode verurteilten Personen, in BA/MA, "Der Bestand 'Reichskriegsgericht' im Prager Militärhistorischen Archiv," r. M1001/2, A36, fr. 2. The figure for murder and self-inflicted wounds was a combined total of five.

117. Robert M. Kennedy, *The German Campaign in Poland (1939)* (Washington, DC: Department of the Army, 1956), p. 77, lists the operational strength of German forces in Poland at 630,000 men for Army Group North and 886,000 for Army Group South.

118. See Aussetzung der Strafvollstreckung zum Zwecke der Bewährung, 18 September 1940, in BA/MA, "Der Bestand 'Reichskriegsgericht' im Prager Militärhistorischen Archiv," r. M1001/2, A36, fr. 51.

119. See chapter three on the "Perversion of Discipline" in Bartov, *Hitler's Army,* pp. 59–105.

120. Merkblatt für das Verhalten deutschen Soldaten im besetzten Gebiet in Polen, 20 September 1939, Anlage zu AOK, Abt. Ia/Ic in USHMMA, RG 48.004M (Records of the Military Historical Institute, Prague), r. 3, fr. 300018.

121. Halder diary quoted in Klaus-Jürgen Müller, *Das Heer und Hitler. Armee und nationalsozialistisches Regime, 1933–1940* (Stuttgart: Deutsche Verlags-Anstalt, 1969), p. 435.

122. Entry of 6 September 1939, Anlagen Band 2 zum Kriegstagebuch, Abt. Ia, 4. Division, in BA/MA, RH 26-4/3.

123. Entry of 4 September 1939, Kriegstagebuch 1 der Grenzschutz-Abschnittskommando 3, in NARA, RG 242, T-314, r. 840, fr. 176.

124. Ia, GAK 3 (von Knobelsdorff) an die Truppe, 4 September 1939, in NARA, RG 242, T-314, r. 840, fr. 43.

125. Entry of 4 September 1939, Kriegstagebuch 1 der GAK 3, in NARA, RG 242, T-314, r. 840, fr. 176.

126. Befriedung der Militärbezirks Posen, 23 September 1939, Generalleutnant Böhm-Bezing, Ia/Ic Aktennotiz 1, in NARA, RG 242, T-315, r. 1740, fr. 56.

127. Merkblatt für das Verhalten deutschen Soldaten im besetzten Gebiet in Polen, 20 September 1939, Anlage zu AOK, Abt. Ia/Ic, in USHMMA, RG 48.004M, r. 3, fr. 300018.

128. Statement of Jan Szuminski, PPS, Ko 59/72, 4 March 1972, in USHMMA, RG 15.042M, r. 13, file Ds 321/67.

129. Statement of Bronisław Panek, PPS, Ko 64/68, 15 October 1968, in USHMMA, RG 15.042M, r. 17, file S 28/71, vol. 1.

130. Statement of Marianna Wolski, PPS, Ko 79/68, 30 September 1968, in USHMMA, RG 15.042M, r. 8, File Ds 108/67.

131. Statement of Stefania Wolski, PPS, Ko 79/68, 10 March 1973, in ibid.

132. Statement of Władysław Pegiel, PPS, 18 March 1975, in USHMMA, RG 15.042M (Records of the MCC), r. 16, file DS 4/71.

133. Statement of Stanisława Mularczyk, PPS, Ko 23/68, 4 June 1968, in USHMMA, RG 15.042M, r. 15, file Ds 477/67.

134. Statement of Helena Stefanek, PPS, Ko. 57/70, 17 April 1979, in USHMMA, RG 15.042M, r. 14, file Ds 417/67.

135. Of the overall German attitude toward Polish POWs, Szymon Datner, *Crimes Committed by the Wehrmacht during the September Campaign and the Period of Military Government* (Poznań: Institute for Western Affairs, 1962), p. 8, writes that it "was not everywhere uniform. The front-line troops made efforts to behave decently to the prisoners they took and to keep up the appearance of respecting the customs of war of civilized countries." The best volumes on the treatment of Soviet prisoners remain Alfred Streim, *Die Behandlung sowjetischer Kriegsgefangener im "Fall Barbarossa"* (Heidelberg: Juristischer Verlag, 1981), and Christian Streit, *Keine Kameraden: Die Wehrmacht und die sowjetischen Kriegsgefangenen, 1941–1945* (Stuttgart: Deutsche Verlags-Anstalt, 1978). Christian Gerlach, *Kalkulierte Morde: Die deutsche Wirtschafts- und Vernichtungspolitik in Weissrussland 1941 bis 1944* (Hamburg: HIS Verlagsges, 1999), and Reinhard Otto, *Wehrmacht, Gestapo, und sowjetische Kriegsgefangene im deutschen Reichsgebiet, 1941–42* (Munich: Oldenbourg, 1998), are the two most recent works to deal with this subject.

136. Kennedy, *The German Campaign*, p. 120.

137. Joan Beaumont, "Protecting Prisoners of War, 1939–95," in *Prisoners of War and Their Captors in World War II,* ed. B. Moore and K. Fedorowich (Oxford: Berg Publishers, 1996).

138. Ibid.

139. Statement of Stanisław Smiałkowski recorded in OKL Ds 295/67, Postanowienie, 21 February 1976, Łódź, in USHMMA, RG 15.042M, r. 10, file Ds 295/67.

140. Statement of Franciszek Michalski, PPS, 5 November 1974, in ibid.

141. Ryszard Mik, "Zbrodnie Wehrmachtu na Jeńcach Polskich w Rejonie Bitwy nad Bzura," in *Biuletyn Głównej Komisji Badania Zbrodni Hitlerowskich w Polsce,* vol. 32 (Warsaw: Wydawnictwo Prawnicze, 1987), p. 124.

142. Statement of Jozef Maj, PPS, 21 December 1976, in USHMMA, RG 15.042M, r. 46, file Ds 25/75.

143. Mik, "Zbrodnie Wehrmachtu," p. 126.

144. Statement of Stanislaw Kepinski, PPS, 28 December 1976, in USHMMA, RG 15.042M, r. 46, file Ds 25/75.

145. Notatka Służbowa, Delegatura Terenowa KBZH w Sochaczewie, 14 December 1978, in USHMMA, RG 15.042M, r. 44, file Ds 10/77-B.

146. Statement of Tadeusz Starzynski, PPS, 3 May 1982, in USHMMA, RG 15.042M, r. 44, file Ds 10/77. The German tanks were part of either the 4th or 1st Panzer Divisions, both of which were in the area at the time.

147. The entire account of the Ciepielów massacre is reprinted in Janusz Gumkowski and Kazimierz Leszczynski, *Poland under Nazi Occupation* (Warsaw: Polonia, 1961), pp. 53ff.

148. Datner, *Crimes,* pp. 11ff.

149. Tadeusz Cyprian, "Zbrodnie Wehrmachtu na Polskich Jeńcach Wojennych," in *Biuletyn*, p. 115.

Chapter 7. Explaining German Brutality

1. From the experience report of Gefreiter Tumpold, 137th Mountain Rifle Regiment, "Es geht um den Wald von Stronjowice!" in Ic/WPr. (Wehrmacht Propaganda Office), XVIII AK, VII-B24-220, Krieg 1939/40, Feldzug in Polen, in NARA, RG 242, T-314, r. 1643, fr. 153. The poem translates as "We soldiers are true to you our Führer / We are creating through you a new East! / A word from you and we are ready to storm the West at any time. / Because you gave us the strength to believe, / you have created a new Germany / that is strong enough at any time / to strike at those who insult her honor!"

2. Omer Bartov, *Hitler's Army: Soldiers, Nazis, and War in the Third Reich* (New York: Oxford University Press, 1991), and *The Eastern Front, 1941–45: German Troops and the Barbarisation of Warfare* (New York: Macmillan, 1986).

3. The examination of German soldiers' letters and diaries is a rapidly growing area of historical inquiry too extensive to fully recount here. Those interested in Feldpostbriefe should consult Klaus Latzel, "Tourismus und Gewalt: Kriegswahrnehmungen in Feldpostbriefen," in *Vernichtungskrieg. Verbrechen der Wehrmacht 1941 bis 1944,* ed. H. Heer and K. Naumann (Hamburg: HIS Verlagsges, 1995), pp. 447–459; Klaus Latzel, *Deutsche Soldaten—nationalsozialistischer Krieg? Kriegserlebnis—Kriegserfahrung, 1939–1945* (Paderborn: Schöningh, 1998); Otto Buchbender and Reinhold Sterz, eds., *Das Andere Gesicht des Krieges: Deutsche Feldpostbriefe, 1939–1945* (Munich: C. H. Beck, 1982); Hans Dollinger, ed., *Kain, Wo ist dein Bruder? Was der Mensch im Zweiten Weltkrieg erleiden musste—dokumentiert in Tagebüchern und Briefen* (Frankfurt/Main: List, 1992); Detlef Vogel, "Der Kriegsalltag im Spiegel von Feldpostbriefen (1939–1945)," in *Der Krieg des kleinen Mannes: Eine Militärgeschichte von unten,* ed. W. Wette (Munich: Piper, 1992), pp. 199–212; and Walter Manoschek, ed., *"Es gibt nur eines für das Judentum: Vernichtung": Das Judenbild in deutschen Soldatenbriefen, 1939–1941* (Hamburg: HIS Verlagsges, 1995). Among the few offerings in English are Bartov, *Hitler's Army;* Stephen G. Fritz, *Frontsoldaten* (Lexington: University Press of Kentucky, 1995); Alexander B. Rossino, "Destructive Impulses: German Soldiers and the Conquest of Poland," in *Holocaust and Genocide Studies* 11, no. 3 (Winter 1997): 351–365; and Horst Fuchs Richardson, ed. and trans., *Sieg Heil! War Letters of Tank Gunner Karl Fuchs, 1937–1941* (Hamden, CT: Archon, 1987).

4. This is a conclusion expressed in Vogel, "Der Kriegsalltag," p. 200, and Martin Joseph, "NS-Propaganda und Feldpost, Anspruch und Wirklichkeit" (1987), pp. 140ff, in BA/MA, Library Collection Nr. M VII O 21.

5. As Halder put it in his original instructions dated 7 October 1939: "The first armed action of the young National Socialist army, the war in Poland, had been brought to a victorious conclusion. It follows that this campaign can possibly be preserved for posterity. Therefore, the deeds of the army, in particular the efforts of individual squads of troops and of individual leaders and soldiers of the armed forces should be conveyed by us to the farthest circles of the German people. For

this purpose it is desired that documents from war diaries be expanded and vividly refashioned, using the fresh impressions of the war experience, from reports prepared by command authorities, officers, non-commissioned officers, and the men." See Army High Command (OKH), Gen.St.d.H., Ausb.Abt. (III), Nr. 409/39, Hauptquartier, 7 October 1939, in NARA, RG 242, T-315, r. 2322, fr. 001133.

6. A good example of these unit histories is Generalkommando VII, ed., *Wir zogen gegen Polen: Kriegserinnerungswerk des VII. Armeekorps* (Munich: F. Eher, 1940).

7. Generalkommando II.AK., Abt. Ic. K.H.Qu. Königswinter, 21 October 1939, in NARA, RG 242, T-315, r. 2322, fr. 001130, in which the II Corps requests "portrayals of skirmishes in Poland, possibly with an eye towards the tactical connection with lesser or greater operations; experience reports of individual soldiers; and photographs to supplement the reports, or to be presented as individual pictures."

8. OKH, Gen.St.d.H., Ausb.Abt. (III), Nr. 409/39. Hauptquartier, 7 October 1939, in NARA, RG 242, T-315, r. 2322, fr. 001133.

9. Regarding the use of experience reports in newspapers on the home front, see Berichterstattung für Heimatzeitungen über den Feldzug in Polen, 20 October 1939, OKW 3191/39, WFA/WPr., IId, in BA/MA, RH 1/v.81. Orders for their use in military newspapers came earlier in Merkblatt für Feldzeitungen, Anlage I, 11 September 1939, OKW 2270/39, WFA/WPr., IId, in BA/MA, RH 1/v.81.

10. For typical editorial comments, see "Aufsätze über Polenfeldzug," 11 December 1939, 2.Geb.Div. Ic an der Stellvertreter Generalkommando XVIII.A.K. (Presse Offizier), in NARA, RG 242, T-314, r. 1643, fr. 524.

11. This collection is held in the records of Generalkommando XVIII Corps, Ic (Intelligence Officer), Wehrpropaganda activity, in NARA, RG 242, T-314, VII-B20 through VII-B29, reels 1640–44.

12. The measures taken by the SS and Abwehr in contriving the "Polish attack" are well documented in Alfred Spiess and Heiner Lichtenstein, *Das Unternehmen Tannenberg* (Wiesbaden: Limes-Verlag, 1979).

13. Hitler quoted in *Das Gebirgsjägerregiment 99 im polnischen Feldzug* (Bonn: n.p., 1939), p. 4, in BA/MA, Library Collection Nr. O IIIa 99.

14. Leutnant Kleeberg, *Regiments—Nachrichtenzug I.R. 94 im Polenfeldzug* (Bonn: n.p., 1940), entry of 31 August 1939, in BA/MA, MSg 2/2924.

15. *Pioniere im Kampf: Erlebnisberichte aus dem Polenfeldzug 1939*, ed. Oberstleutnant Liere (Berlin: n.p., 1940), p. 5 in BA/MA, Library Collection Nr. M VII b 23.

16. Experience report of Gefreiter Mathias Strehn, "Stockerauer Kavallerie im polnischen Krieg," Ic/WPr., XVIII AK, VII-B25, Krieg 1939/40, Feldzug in Polen, in NARA, RG 242, T-314, r. 1643, fr. 535.

17. Ibid., fr. 536.

18. Experience report of Gefreiter Willi Romer, "Meine Erlebnisse beim Polenfeldzug," Ic/WPr., XVIII AK, VII-B26-305, Krieg 1939/40, Feldzug in Polen, in NARA, RG 242, T-314, r. 1644, fr. 26.

19. Experience report of Jozef Heront, "Die letzten 24 Stunden vor Kriegsbeginn," Ic/WPr., XVIII AK, VII-B29-2, Krieg 1939/40, Feldzug in Polen, in ibid., fr. 562.

20. Feldpostbrief of Soldat W.B, 1 September 1939, in Sammlung Sterz, Bibliothek für Zeitgeschichte, Stuttgart (hereafter cited as BfZ).

21. Propaganda report of Dr. Franz Pesendorfer, "Im Kampf um deutsches Recht," September 1939, Ic/WPr., XVIII AK, VII-B22-102, Krieg 1939/40, Feldzug in Polen, in NARA, RG 242, T-314, r. 1642, fr. 558.

22. Goebbels quoted in Tomasz Szarota, "Poland and Poles in German Eyes during World War II," *Polish Western Affairs* 19, no. 2 (1978): 232.

23. Hans Freiherr von Rosen, *Dokumentation: Der Verschleppung der Deutschen aus Posen und Pommerellen in September 1939* (Berlin: Westkreuz, 1990).

24. Some of these measures are described in Louis De Jong, *The German Fifth Column in the Second World War,* trans. C. M. Geyl (Chicago: University of Chicago Press, 1956), p. 38.

25. For more on the tensions and measures implemented by Polish authorities leading up to the so-called "Bromberg Bloody Sunday," see Włodzimierz Jastrzębski, *Der Bromberger Blutsonntag: Legende und Wirklichkeit* (Poznań: Westinstitut, 1990).

26. Experience report of Leutnant Alexander Lernet-Holenia in *Die 7.Schwadron Kavallerieschützenregiment 10 im Polenfeldzug* (N.p., 1940), p. 2, in BA/MA, Library Collection Nr. O IIIb 159.

27. Experience report of Leutnant Schumann in *Das Gebirgsjägerregiment 99 im polnischen Feldzug,* p. 159, in BA/MA, Library Collection Nr. O IIIa 99.

28. Hitler incorrectly stated the time of the German assault, which started at 4:45 A.M. See experience report of Gefreiter Wilhelm Bechholds, "Der Führer spricht!" in *Wir marschieren gegen Polen. Ein Erinnerungsbuch an den polnischen Feldzug vom Infanterie-Regiment 179* (Munich: Oldenbourg, 1940), in BA/MA, Library Collection Nr. O IIIa 179a.

29. Experience report of Gefreiter Erich Müller, "Abschied des II. Bataillon von seiner Garnison," in *Infanterie-Regiment 309 marschiert an den Feind, Erlebnisberichte aus dem Polenfeldzug 1939* (Berlin: n.p., 1940), p. 30, in BA/MA, Library Collection Nr. O IIIa 309.

30. Experience report of an unidentified soldier in *Wir marschieren für das Reich: Deutsche Jugend im Kampferlebnis des polnischen Feldzugs* (Munich: Oldenbourg, 1940), p. 22f, in BA/MA, Library Collection Nr. M VIIIb 33.

31. Experience report of Unteroffizier Kurt Schmoll, "Die Kriegsfackel loht über polnischem Land," in *Infanterie-Regiment 309 marschiert,* p. 31, in BA/MA, Library Collection Nr. O IIIa 309.

32. Experience report of Gefreiter Wallner (no unit given), "Vorbereitungen," Ic/WPr., XVIII AK, VII-B28-398, Krieg 1939/40, Feldzug in Polen, in NARA, RG 242, T-314, r. 1644, fr. 541.

33. Experience report of Unteroffizier Bürckhardt (no unit given), "Soldaten der Ostfront berichten!" Ic/WPr., XVIII AK, VII-B28-365, Krieg 1939/40, Feldzug in Polen, in ibid., fr. 437.

34. Experience report of an unidentified soldier in *Das Infanterieregiment 151, 1939–1942. Geschichte des Regiments in den Feldzügen in Polen, Holland, Belgien, Frankreich, Baltenland und Russland. Auf Grund der amtlichen Kriegstagebücher unter Verwendung von Gefechtsberichten, Regiments-Akten, Erlebnisse von*

Mitkämpfern und anderen Quellen (1944), p. 10, in BA/MA, Library Collection Nr. O IIIa 151.

35. Kriegstagebuch I.R. 13, September 1939, in NARA, RG 242, T-315, r. 622, fr. 000263.

36. Hitler quoted in *Das Gebirgsjägerregiment 99 im polnischen Feldzug*, p. 5, in BA/MA, Library Collection Nr. O IIIa 99.

37. Experience report of Oberleutnant Hans Eichhorn, "Wie es war," in *Wir marschieren gegen Polen*, p. 11, in BA/MA, Library Collection Nr. O IIIa 179a.

38. Feldpostbrief of Werner ?, im Felde, 8 September 1939, reprinted in *Kurhessen kämpften in Polen. Einsatz und Erlebnisse des I.R. 15 (Mot.)* (Kassel: n.p., 1940), p. 29, in BA/MA, Library Collection Nr. O IIIa 15.

39. Experience report of Rifleman Otto Eder, "Winniki," Ic/WPr., XVIII AK, VII-B24-209, Krieg 1939/40, Feldzug in Polen, in NARA, RG 242, T-314, r. 1643, fr. 79.

40. Ibid.

41. Feldpostbrief of H. H., 12 September 1939, in BA/MA, MSg 2/5275.

42. Diary excerpt of an anonymous member of the 59th Infantry Regiment in *Mit 9/59 in Polen. Tagebuchblätter entstanden auf kurzer Rast in Feindesland* (N.p., 1939), in BA/MA, Library Collection.

43. Experience report of Schütze Ludwig Plawitzki, "Kameraden, der Tanz geht los. In einer Woche von Hildesheim nach Napoleon," in ibid.

44. Experience report of Oberleutnant Edgar Alker, "Steirische Gebirgsjäger—allzeit voran! Das Löben-Brucker Gebirgsjäger Bataillon im polnischen Feldzug," in Ic/WPr., XVIII AK, VII-B20-46, Krieg 1939/40, Feldzug in Polen, in NARA, RG 242, T-314, r. 1641, fr. 1045.

45. Experience report of Kübler, Gefechtsbericht des Gebirgsjägerregiment 98, Polnischer Feldzug 25 August bis 21 September 1939, Ic/WPr., XVIII AK, VII-B26-314, Krieg 1939/40, Feldzug in Polen, in NARA, RG 242, T-314, r. 1644, fr. 59.

46. Experience report of Rifleman Ernst Bruzek, "Meine Erlebnisse im Polenfeldzug als Gebirgsjäger in einem Gebirgsjägerregiment," Ic/WPr., XVIII AK, VII-B20-14, Krieg 1939/40, Feldzug in Polen, in NARA, RG 242, T-314, r. 1641, fr. 821.

47. Experience report of Hauptmann Heinz Winter, "Niederbarnims Mannschaft tritt an," in *Infanterie-Regiment 309 marschiert an den Feind*, p. 19, in BA/MA, Library Collection Nr. O IIIa 309.

48. Experience report of Soldat Stachelhaus, "Berichte vom Feldzug in Polen: Aus den Kämpfen einer Gebirgs-Division. Der Weg nach Lemberg," Ic/WPr., XVIII AK, VII-B23-174, Krieg 1939/40, Feldzug in Polen, in NARA, RG 242, T-314, r. 1642, fr. 1011.

49. Experience report of Leutnant Faber, "Von Zohatyn nach Lodzinka," Ic/WPr., XVIII AK, VII-B24-204, Krieg 1939/40, Feldzug in Polen, in NARA, RG 242, T-314, r. 1643, fr. 55.

50. Experience report of Gefreiter Peter Infeld, "Wie ich Galizien erlebte," Ic/WPr., XVIII AK, VII-B25-267, Krieg 1939/40, Feldzug in Polen, in ibid., fr. 553.

51. Experience report of Gefreiter Josef Heront, "Die letzten 24 Stunden vor Kriegsbeginn," Ic/WPr., XVIII AK, VII-B29-2, Krieg 1939/40, Feldzug in Polen, in NARA, RG 242, T-314, r. 1644, fr. 562.

52. Christian Jansen and Arno Weckbecker, *Der "Volksdeutsche Selbstschutz" in Polen 1939/40* (Munich: Oldenbourg, 1992), p. 27.

53. De Jong, *The German Fifth Column*, p. 46.

54. Experience report of Unteroffizier Siebenpfund, "Der Polenfeldzug bei der 11/199," Ic/WPr., XVIII AK, VII-B26-297, Krieg 1939/40, Feldzug in Polen, in NARA, RG 242, T-314, r. 1644, fr. 161.

55. Experience report of Unteroffizier Franz Ortner, "Erlebnis im polnischen Feldzug," Ic/WPr., XVIII AK, VII-B27-320, Krieg 1939/40, Feldzug in Polen, in ibid., fr. 205.

56. Excerpt from the diary of Leutnant S., 7 September 1939, in BA/MA, MSg 2/3232.

57. Feldpostbrief of Gefreiter W.K., 10 September 1939, in Sammlung Sterz, BfZ.

58. Experience report of Gefreiter Müller, "In Rudki," in *Wir marschieren gegen Polen*, in BA/MA, Library Collection Nr. O IIIa 179a. Rifleman Justus Erhardt, whose unit captured three prisoners near a site where ethnic German women and children had been killed, shared Müller's sentiments. After a perfunctory trial, the prisoners were shot. See Erhardt's experience report, "Der grosse Marsch," in *Infanterie-Regiment 309 marschiert an den Feind,* p. 8, in BA/MA, Library Collection Nr. O IIIa 309.

59. Experience report of Feldwebel Wilhelm Hössmer, "Angriff auf Neu-Sandec," Ic/WPr., XVIII AK, VII-B20-7, Krieg 1939/40, Feldzug in Polen, in NARA, RG 242, T-314, r. 1641, fr. 758, and experience report of Unteroffizier Herbert Franke, "Mit einer Gebirgs-Nachricht-Abteilung nach Polen," Ic/WPr., XVIII AK, VII-B21-89, Krieg 1939/40, Feldzug in Polen, in NARA, RG 242, T-314, r. 1642, fr. 370.

60. Excerpt from the diary of Leutnant S., 30 August 1939, in BA/MA, MSg 2/3232.

61. Experience report of Gefreiter Josef Loipführer, "Der Marsch durch Polen," Ic/WPr., XVIII AK, VII-B28-378, Krieg 1939/40, Feldzug in Polen, in NARA, RG 242, T-314, r. 1644, fr. 466.

62. *Die 10.Division im polnischen Feldzug,* in BA/MA, RH 26-10/544.

63. Abendmeldung, 16 September 1939, GFP Gruppe 580 an der Ic, Heeresgruppe Süd, in NARA, RG 242, T-311, r. 255, fr. 86.

64. Experience report of Oberleutnant Artmann, "Neun Tage vor Lemberg," Ic/WPr., XVIII AK, VII-B21-95, Krieg 1939/40, Feldzug in Polen, in NARA, RG 242, T-314, r. 1642, fr. 475.

65. Experience report of Gefreiter Wilhelm Jahoda, "Eine Nachfahrt," Ic/WPr., XVIII AK, VII-B27-336, Krieg 1939/40, Feldzug in Polen, in NARA, RG 242, T-314, r. 1644, fr. 272, and experience report of Gefreiter Karl Patterer, "Eine Gebirgsbatterie im Polen-Feldzug," Ic/WPr., XVIII AK, VII-B25-283, Krieg 1939/40, Feldzug in Polen, in NARA, RG 242, T-314, r. 1643, fr. 661.

66. See the experience report of an anonymous trooper with the 136th Mountain Regiment, "Der Vormarsch auf Lemberg," Ic/WPr., XVIII AK, VII-B26-311, Krieg 1939/40, Feldzug in Polen, in NARA, RG 242, T-314, r. 1644, fr. 48, and that of Unteroffizier Richard Bremer, "Pioniere beim Strassenkampf," in *Mit dem XIII Armeekorps in Polen, Ein Erinnerungsbuch* (Munich: n.p., 1940), p. 53.

67. See the experience report of Feldwebel Wilhelm Hössmer, "Angriff auf Neu-Sandec," Ic/WPr., XVIII AK, VII-B20-7, Krieg 1939/40, Feldzug in Polen, in NARA, RG 242, T-314, r. 1641, fr. 758, and that of Rifleman Herbert Nagl, "Sanwache," Ic/WPr., XVIII AK, VII-B24-225, Krieg 1939/40, Feldzug in Polen, in NARA, RG 242, T-314, r. 1643, fr. 180.

68. Experience report of Wilhelm Jahoda, "Eine Nachfahrt," Ic/WPr., XVIII AK, VII-B27-336, Krieg 1939/40, Feldzug in Polen, in NARA, RG 242, T-314, r. 1644, fr. 272.

69. See, for example, the experience report of Unteroffizier M. Holzhey of the 217th Infantry Regiment, "Als Verbindungsoffizier beim Einsatz Polen," Ic/WPr., XVIII AK, VII-B28-383, Krieg 1939/40, Feldzug in Polen, in NARA, RG 242, T-314, r. 1644, fr. 501.

70. Feldpostbrief of Soldat R. F., 16 September 1939, in Sammlung Sterz, BfZ.

71. Experience report of Gefreiter Potesegger, "Streiflichter aus dem Polenfeldzug," Ic/WPr., XVIII AK, VII-B27-321, Krieg 1939/40, Feldzug in Polen, in NARA, RG 242, T-314, r. 1644, fr. 213.

72. Experience report of Soldat Hans Oberheuer, "Als Tragtierführer Quer durch Polen," Ic/WPr., XVIII AK, VII-B27-323, Krieg 1939/40, Feldzug in Polen, in ibid., fr. 225.

73. Experience report of Hauptmann Koerner, "Polnische Kultur," in *Wir marschieren gegen Polen* in BA/MA, Library Collection Nr. O IIIa 179a.

74. Feldpostbrief of Unteroffizier K. A., 8 September 1939, Sammlung Sterz, BfZ.

75. Experience report of Unteroffizier Franz Anderl, "Auf deutschen Spuren im Osten," Ic/WPr., XVIII AK, VII-B24-253, Krieg 1939/40, Feldzug in Polen, in NARA, RG 242, T-314, r. 1643, fr. 454.

76. Ibid.

77. Experience report of Unteroffizier Hermann Ritter, "Marschunterkünfte," in *Infanterie-Regiment 309 marschiert an den Feind*, p. 48, in BA/MA, Library Collection Nr. O IIIa 309.

78. Latzel, "Tourismus und Gewalt," and *Deutsche Soldaten,* pp. 172ff.

79. For an interesting discussion of the similarity and differences of German reactions to Eastern Europe in World War I, see Dennis E. Showalter, "'The East Gives Nothing Back': The Great War and the German Army in Russia," *Journal of the Historical Society* 2, no. 1 (Winter 2002): 1–19. Also see Vejas G. Liulevicius, *War Land on the Eastern Front: Culture, National Identity, and German Occupation in World War I* (New York: Cambridge University Press, 2000).

80. Experience report of Feldwebel Erich Hildebrand, "Polnischer Dreck und deutsche Sauberkeit," in *Infanterie-Regiment 309 marschiert an den Feind*, p. 157, in BA/MA, Library Collection Nr. O IIIa 309.

81. Excerpt from the diary of Leutnant Kleeberg, 8 September 1939, reprinted in *Regiments-Nachrichtenzug I.R. 94 im Polenfeldzug*, in BA/MA, MSg 2/2924. Incidentally, it was not only Germans who felt as if they had crossed a cultural frontier when moving eastward through Poland. As she fled advancing German troops in September 1939, English journalist Clare Hollingworth also noted how "beyond Sosnowiec we passed that point where the empires of Germany, Austria and Russia touched before 1914. In daylight you can see the architectural change: from ugly

German solidity to the wood huts of the Russian village" (*The Three Weeks' War in Poland* [London: Duckworth, 1940], p. 20).

82. Excerpt from the diary of Leutnant Alexander Lernet-Holenia, 12 September 1939, reprinted in *Die 7. Schwadron Kavallerieschützenregiment 10 im Polenfeldzug*, p. 18, in BA/MA, Library Collection Nr. O IIIb 159.

83. Experience report of Unteroffizier Kurt Schmoll, "Die Kriegsfackel loht über polnischem Land," in *Infanterie-Regiment 309 marschiert an den Feind*, p. 31, in BA/MA, Library Collection Nr. O IIIa 309.

84. Experience report of Feldwebel Erich Hildebrand, "Polnischer Dreck und deutsche Sauberkeit," in ibid., p. 156.

85. See the experience report of Gefreiter Alfons Kienle, "Das deutsche Dorf," Ic/WPr., XVIII AK, VII-B21-65, Krieg 1939/40, Feldzug in Polen, in NARA, RG 242, T-314, r. 1642, fr. 110.

86. Experience report of Unteroffizier Siebenpfund, "Der Polenfeldzug bei der 11./199," Ic/WPr., XVIII AK, VII-B26-297, Krieg 1939/40, Feldzug in Polen, in NARA, RG 242, T-314, r. 1644, fr. 157.

87. Raul Hilberg, *The Destruction of the European Jews*, vol. 3 (New York: Holmes and Meier, 1985), p. 1048.

88. The literature surrounding the pervasive influence of anti-Semitism in German society is far too extensive to discuss here. Opinions of its impact on the German mentality are also controversial, ranging from the highly polemical writings of Daniel J. Goldhagen, *Hitler's Willing Executioners: Ordinary Germans and the Holocaust* (New York: Knopf, 1996), and John Weiss, *Ideology of Death: Why the Holocaust Happened in Germany* (Chicago: Ivan R. Dee, 1996), to the more measured work of Christopher R. Browning, *Ordinary Men: Reserve Police Battalion 101 and the Final Solution in Poland* (New York: HarperCollins, 1992), and the multifaceted interpretation of Raul Hilberg, *Perpetrators, Victims, Bystanders: The Jewish Catastrophe, 1939–1945* (New York: HarperCollins, 1992).

89. Excerpt from the diary of Leutnant H. A., 29 August 1939, in BA/MA, MSg 2/5690.

90. Feldpostbrief of Soldat H.B., 7 October 1939, in Sammlung Sterz, BfZ.

91. Feldpostbrief of Unteroffizier K.S., 15 October 1939, in Sammlung Sterz, BfZ.

92. Experience report of Gefreiter Potesegger, "Streiflichter aus dem Polenfeldzug," Ic/WPr., XVIII AK, VII-B27-317, Krieg 1939/40, Feldzug in Polen, in NARA, RG 242, T-314, r. 1644, fr. 193.

93. Feldpostbrief of Unteroffizier A. K., 12 October 1939, in Sammlung Sterz, BfZ.

94. Experience report of Gefreiter Müller, "In Rudki," in *Wir Marschieren gegen Polen*, in BA/MA, Library Collection Nr. O IIIa 179a.

95. See the experience reports of Leutnant Alfred Detig, "Deutschland, wie bist du schön! Bekenntnisse in Polen," Ic/WPr., XVIII AK, VII-B22-107, Krieg 1939/40, Feldzug in Polen, in NARA, RG 242, T-314, r. 1642, fr. 609, and Gefreiter Sepp Ritter, "Die Gebirgspioniere in Polen," Ic/WPr., XVIII AK, VII-B27-341, Krieg 1939/40, Feldzug in Polen, in NARA, RG 242, T-314, r. 1644, fr. 307.

96. Experience report of Hauptmann Koerner, "Polnische Kultur," in *Wir marschieren gegen Polen*, in BA/MA, Library Collection Nr. O IIIa 179a.

97. Experience report of an anonymous soldier in *Wir marschieren für das Reich,* p. 129.

98. Excerpt from the diary of Oberjäger Hans Peinitisch, 6 September 1939, Ic/WPr., XVIII AK, VII-B24-231, Krieg 1939/40, Feldzug in Polen, in NARA, RG 242, T-314, r. 1643, fr. 220.

99. Experience report of Grenadier Dreyer, "General Warschau," in NARA, RG 242, T-315, r. 622, fr. 000423.

100. Experience report of Gefreiter Potesegger, "Streiflichter aus dem Polenfeldzug," Ic/WPr., XVIII AK, VII-B27-317, Krieg 1939/40, Feldzug in Polen, in NARA, RG 242, T-314, r. 1644, fr. 192.

101. Excerpt from the diary of Leutnant Kleeberg, 10 September 1939, reprinted in *Regiments-Nachrichtenzug I.R. 94 im Polenfeldzug,* in BA/MA, MSg 2/2924, and the experience report of Gefreiter Mathias Strehn, "Stockerauer Kavallerie im polnischen Krieg," Ic/WPr., XVIII AK, VII-B25, Krieg 1939/40, Feldzug in Polen, in NARA, RG 242, T-314, r. 1643, fr. 538.

102. Experience report of Dr. Brachetka, "Polnische Beutepferde," Ic/WPr., XVIII AK, VII-B20-11, Krieg 1939/40, Feldzug in Polen, in NARA, RG 242, T-314, r. 1641, fr. 799.

103. Experience report of Rifleman Hans Geissler, "Fünf Tage in polnischer Gefangenschaft," Ic/WPr., XVIII AK, VII-B21-63, Krieg 1939/40, Feldzug in Polen, in NARA, RG 242, T-314, r. 1642, fr. 97.

104. Feldpostbrief of Obergefreiter J. E., 30 December 1939, Sammlung Sterz, BfZ.

105. Experience report of Gefreiter Müller, "In Rudki," in *Wir Marschieren gegen Polen,* in BA/MA, Library Collection Nr. O IIIa 179a.

106. Experience report of Rifleman Herbert Nagl, "Sanwache," Ic/WPr., XVIII AK, VII-B24-225, Krieg 1939/40, Feldzug in Polen, in NARA, RG 242, T-314, r. 1643, fr. 180.

107. Experience report of Gefreiter Grömmer, "Erinnerungen an den Polenfeldzug," Ic/WPr., XVIII AK, VII-B25-275, Krieg 1939/40, Feldzug in Polen, in ibid., fr. 619.

108. Feldpostbrief of Gefreiter W. K., 10 September 1939, in Sammlung Sterz, BfZ, and experience report of Unteroffizier Richard Bremer, "Pioniere beim Strassenkampf," in *Mit dem XIII Armeekorps in Polen,* p. 53.

109. Excerpt from the diary of Leutnant H. A., 3 September 1939, in BA/MA, MSg 2/5690.

110. Quoted from a copy of orders found in the diary of Leutnant S., 30 August 1939, in BA/MA, MSg 2/3232.

111. See the feldpostbrief of Soldat P. S., 16 September, in Sammlung Sterz, BfZ, in which he wrote: "We push on past razed villages and houses, some of which are still smoking. Any village from which the civilian population fires at the troops is burned to the ground, the inhabitants shot."

112. For example, Colonel Erwin Jaenecke issued orders on 4 September for troops in the Eighth Army to avoid burning houses because Polish defenders were using the homes of ethnic Germans who had fled. See Besondere Anordnungen Nr. 11 für die Versorgung der 8.Armee, 4 September 1939, AOK 8, in NARA, RG 242, T-312, r. 38, fr. 7547023.

113. Quoted from a copy of orders found in the diary of Leutnant S., 30 August 1939, in BA/MA, MSg 2/3232.

114. Bartov, *Hitler's Army*, p. 106.

115. Excerpt from the diary of Regimentsarzt R. J. K., 12 September 1939, in BA/MA, MSg 2/3943.

116. Feldpostbrief of H. H., 10 September 1939, reprinted in *Kurhessen kämpften in Polen*, p. 26, in BA/MA, Nr. O IIIa 15.

117. See, for example, the experience report of an anonymous member of the 136th Mountain Rifle Regiment, "Der Vormarsch auf Lemberg, Erlebnisse der 2. Gebirgsdivision im polnischen Feldzug," Ic/WPr., XVIII AK, VII-B26-311, Krieg 1939/40, Feldzug in Polen, in NARA, RG 242, T-314, r. 1644, fr. 48.

118. Experience report of Leutnant Alfred Detig, "Mit Panzerwagen nach Galizien," Ic/WPr., XVIII AK, VII-B22-108, Krieg 1939/40, Feldzug in Polen, in NARA, RG 242, T-314, r. 1642, fr. 623.

119. William L. Shirer, *Berlin Diary: The Journal of a Foreign Correspondent, 1934–1941* (New York: Alfred Knopf, 1941), p. 209.

120. For a discussion of the specific application of racial-biological instruction in the schools of Göttingen, see Berthold Michael, *Schule und Erziehung im Griff des Totalitären Staates. Die Göttinger Schulen in der nationalsozialistischen Zeit von 1933 bis 1945* (Göttingen: Vandenhoeck and Ruprecht, 1994), pp. 30ff.

121. Bartov, *Hitler's Army*, p. 107.

122. This author was unable to find a single incident during the German campaign in France in which regular German troops treated the French people as callously and cruelly as they did Poles and Jews in Poland. One exception, if it can be considered such, would be the summary machine-gunning of 100 British prisoners of war by members of Theodor Eicke's SS Death's Head Division at Le Paradis on 27 May 1940. See Charles W. Sydnor Jr., *Soldiers of Destruction: The SS Death's Head Division 1939–1945*, rev. ed. (Princeton, NJ: Princeton University Press, 1990), pp. 106–109, and George H. Stein, *The Waffen SS: Hitler's Elite Guard at War, 1939–1945* (Ithaca, NY: Cornell University Press, 1966), p. 92. The Wehrmacht threatened French civilians with death for acts that were perceived to be hostile to the occupation forces, but the commander of occupied France, General Otto von Stülpnagel, tried to limit the number of hostages shot, even when faced with Hitler's demands that the army escalate the number of Frenchmen executed in reprisals. See Hans Umbreit, *Der Militärbefehlshaber in Frankreich, 1940–1944* (Boppard am Rhein: H. Boldt, 1968), p. 127f.

123. Bartov, *Hitler's Army*, pp. 106ff, and *The Eastern Front*, pp. 100ff. For more on the impact of Nazism on the formation of "enemy stereotypes," see Peter Jahn, "'Russenfurcht' und Antibolschewismus: Zur Entstehung und Wirkung von Feindbildern," in *Erobern und Vernichten. Der Krieg gegen die Sowjetunion, 1941–1945*, ed. P. Jahn and R. Rürup (Berlin: Argon, 1991), pp. 47–61, and Walter Manoschek, "'Gehst mit Juden erschiessen?' Die Vernichtung der Juden in Serbien," in *Vernichtungskrieg. Verbrechen der Wehrmacht 1941 bis 1944*, ed. H. Heer and K. Naumann (Hamburg: HIS Verlagsges, 1995), pp. 39–56.

124. Übersicht über die Geburtsjahrgangsstärken der Unteroffizier und Mannschaften nach dem Stande vom 31.1.1939, 24 February 1939, 10.Division, Nr. 268 geheim, in NARA, RG 242, T-79, r. 210, fr. 758.

125. All of the statistics for the 20th, 41st, and 85th Regiments can be found in ibid. These general conclusions about the age of German frontline troops in September 1939 are confirmed by statistics in Bernhard R. Kroener, "Die personellen Ressourcen des Dritten Reiches im Spannungsfeld zwischen Wehrmacht, Bürokratie und Kriegswirtschaft, 1939–1942," in *Organisation und Mobilisierung des Deutschen Machtbereichs. Erster Halbband: Kriegsverwaltung, Wirtschaft und Personnelle Ressourcen, 1939–1941,* ed. Bernhard R. Kroener, Rolf-Dieter Müller, and Hans Umbreit (Stuttgart: Deutsche Verlags-Anstalt, 1988), pp. 730ff.

126. The birth dates for seven men were not listed, but it can be assumed from the birth dates of their comrades that they were probably not born after 1915. See "Aufstellung der neuen 13.Kp. Inf.Rgt.41," 24 August 1936, in NARA, RG 242, T-79, r. 217, fr. 129.

127. The ages of nine men were not indicated. See ibid., fr. 132.

128. Of these, Detlev J. K. Peukert, *Inside Nazi Germany: Conformity, Opposition, and Racism in Everyday Life* (New Haven, CT: Yale University Press, 1987), p. 150, concludes that by the end of 1933, the *Hitlerjugend* had already incorporated 47 percent of boys between the ages of ten and fourteen.

129. Helga Gotschlich, *Reifezeugnis für den Krieg: Abituren des Jahrgangs 39 erinnern sich* (Berlin: Verlag der Nation, 1990), p. 188.

130. Zusammenarbeit der Dienststellen des Heeres mit den Stellen der Reichsjugendführung, 26 April 1937, Oberbefehlshaber des Heeres, Nr. 730/37g. 4, Abt. (Ic), Gen.St.d.H., Berlin, in NARA, RG 242, T-79, r. 42, fr. 000019.

131. See ibid. in which the General Staff spells out agreement between General von Blomberg and Reich Youth leader Baldur von Schirach: "In its training and instruction, the Hitler Youth will bear in mind the interests of the army and the commanders—each within his area—in close consultation with the HJ can and should aid the work of the Hitler Youth . . . as far as it is possible."

132. Hitlerjugend, 23 June 1938, Gen.Kdo XIII (Wehrkreiskommando XIII), Ia, Nr. 3795 geh., Nürnberg, in NARA, RG 242, T-79, r. 127, fr. 000547.

133. According to the General Staff, "Die Erziehung der Jungen zu einer kämpferischen Haltung und die vernünftige planmässige Steigerung der körperlichen Leistungsfähigkeit legt die Grundlage, auf der die Wehrmacht weiterbaut" ("Developing a soldierly bearing in the youth [of our nation] and systematically improving their physical capabilities lays the foundation upon which our armed forces can be further built"). See Zusammenarbeit der Dienststellen des Heeres mit den Stellen der Reichsjugendführung, 26 June 1937, Ob.d.H, Nr. 730/37g. 4, Abt. (Ic), Gen.St.d.H., Berlin, in NARA, RG 242, T-79, r. 42, fr. 000019.

134. The array of Hitler Youth subgroups and specialized training organizations, including those for glider pilots, was massive. For more information, see Richard E. Schroeder, "The Hitler Youth as a Paramilitary Organization" (Ph.D. diss., University of Chicago, 1975).

135. Bartov, *Hitler's Army,* p. 109.

136. Übersicht über die Geburtsjahrgangsstärken der Unteroffizier und Mannschaften nach dem Stande vom 31.1.1939, 24 February 1939, 10.Division, Nr. 268 geheim, in NARA, RG 242, T-79, r. 210, fr. 758.

137. Ibid.

138. A detailed description of the training provided by the Reich Labor Service

can be found in Siegfried Knappe and Ted Brusaw, *Soldat: Reflections of a German Soldier, 1936–1949* (New York: Dell, 1992), pp. 88–98.

139. Übersicht über die Geburtsjahrgangsstärken der Unteroffizier und Mannschaften nach dem Stande vom 31.1.1939, 24 February 1939, 10.Division, Nr. 268 geheim, in NARA, RG 242, T-79, r. 210, fr. 758.

140. Ibid.

141. See Conan Fischer, *Stormtroopers: A Social, Economic, and Ideological Analysis, 1929–1935* (London: George Allen and Unwin, 1983), p. 91.

142. Ibid.

143. It seems, however, that the 10th Infantry Division was remarkably well manned by early 1939. Its actual strength in January 1939 was 14,330 men and officers, while in April 1939 its actual strength declined to 13,850. See Übersicht über die Geburtsjahrgangsstärken der Unteroffizier und Mannschaften nach dem Stande vom 31.1.1939, 24 February 1939, 10.Division, Nr. 268 geheim, in NARA, RG 242, T-79, r. 210, fr. 758, and Nachweisung der Soll und Iststärken an Offizieren, Unteroffizieren, Gefreiten, Mannschaften und Pferden nach dem Stande vom 30.4.1939, 13 May 1939, 10.Division, Nr. 1030 geheim, in ibid., fr. 713.

144. Bartov, *The Eastern Front,* p. 41.

145. Ibid., p. 65.

146. See p. 678 of Bernhard R. Kroener, "Auf dem Weg zu einer 'national-sozialistischen Volksarmee,'" in *Von Stalingrad zur Währungsreform,* ed. Martin Broszat, Klaus-Dietmar Henke, and Hans Woller (Munich: Oldenbourg, 1988), pp. 651–682.

147. Wilhelm Deist, "The Rearmament of the Wehrmacht," in *Germany and the Second World War,* vol. 1, *The Buildup of German Aggression,* trans. P. S. Falla, D. S. McMurry, E. Osers, and L. Wilmot (New York: Oxford University Press, 1990), pp. 373–540, concludes that the composition of personnel in frontline divisions was generally similar. Much like the 10th Infantry Division, therefore, 78 percent of the men of these units were active duty personnel of similar age distribution, while 22 percent were reservists (p. 455).

148. Such is the opinion of Alfons Heck, a onetime member of the Hitler Youth: "Far from being forced, my peers and I could hardly wait to join the Hitler Youth. We craved action, which was offered in abundance" (*The Burden of Hitler's Legacy* [Frederick, CO: Renaissance House, 1988], p. 56).

149. Latzel, *Deutsche Soldaten,* p. 371.

150. For more on the historical enmity between Germans and Poles, see William W. Hagen, *Germans, Poles, and Jews: The Nationality Conflict in the Prussian East, 1772–1914* (Chicago: University of Chicago Press, 1980).

151. Ibid., p. 321.

152. Tomasz Szarota, "Polen unter deutscher Besatzung, 1939–1941: Vergleichende Betrachtungen," in *Zwei Wege nach Moskau: Vom Hitler-Stalin-Pakt bis zum "Unternehmen Barbarossa,"* ed. B. Wegner (Munich: Piper, 1991), p. 46.

153. Right-wingers would later exact revenge on Mathias Erzberger, a member of the Catholic Center Party and the man who signed the Trier Armistice. Two members of the Erhardt Brigade, a Freikorps formation, assassinated him in June 1920. See Hans Mommsen, *The Rise and Fall of Weimar Democracy,* trans. E. Forster and L. E. Jones (Chapel Hill: University of North Carolina Press, 1996), p. 77.

154. Harald von Riekhoff, *German-Polish Relations, 1918–1933* (Baltimore: Johns Hopkins University Press, 1971), pp. 13ff, 20.

155. Ibid., p. 46f. See also T. Hunt Tooley, *National Identity and Weimar Germany: Upper Silesia and the Eastern Border, 1918–1922* (Lincoln: University of Nebraska Press, 1997), pp. 229ff.

156. Karol Fiedor, "The Attitude of German Right-Wing Organizations to Poland in the Years 1918–1933," *Polish Western Affairs* 14, no. 1 (1973): 247.

157. Ibid., p. 260.

158. Karol Fiedor, Janusz Sobczak, and Wojciech Wrzesinski, "The Image of Poles in Germany and of the German in Poland in Inter-War Years and Its Role in Shaping the Relations between the Two States," *Polish Western Affairs* 19, no. 2 (1978): 203–228.

159. Penck quoted in Michael Burleigh, *Germany Turns Eastwards: A Study of Ostforschung in the Third Reich* (New York: Cambridge University Press, 1988), p. 25f.

160. Romuald Gelles, "Polish Issues in German Schoolbooks in the 1930s in the Evaluation of Polish Historians," *Polish Western Affairs* 16, no. 2 (1975): 206.

161. Ibid., p. 209.

162. Ibid., p. 214f.

163. According to George L. Mosse, "No other movement produced such spontaneity, filled the young people with such enthusiasm, or enrolled so many in its ranks" (*The Crisis of German Ideology: Intellectual Origins of the Third Reich* [New York: Schocken Books, 1964], pp. 164, 171).

164. On the anti-Semitic nature of many of these groups, see ibid., pp. 267–272, and Fiedor, "The Attitude of German Right-Wing Organizations," p. 258f.

165. Quoted in Gotschlich, *Reifezeugnis für den Krieg*, p. 23.

166. Ibid., p. 82.

167. Ibid.

168. Ibid., p. 157. For his part, Alfons Heck, a member of the Hitler Youth in September 1939, professed to have "let out a whoop" of approval upon hearing news that Germany and Poland were at war. His mother immediately scolded him, thus indicating some of the differences in attitude between older and younger German generations. See Heck, *The Burden*, p. 65.

169. Gotschlich, *Reifezeugnis für den Krieg*, p. 82.

170. The variety of these groups is discussed in Fiedor, "The Attitude of German Right-Wing Organizations." The only exception to this trend was the German Communist Party. See Richard Bessel, *Political Violence and the Rise of Nazism: The Stormtroopers in Eastern Germany, 1925–1934* (New Haven, CT: Yale University Press, 1984), p. 9.

171. Bessel, *Political Violence*, p. 6.

172. The Polish national census listed 1,036,000 ethnic Germans in 1921 and 1,122,000 in 1928. See Stephan Horak, *Poland and Her National Minorities, 1919–1939* (New York: Vantage Press, 1961), p. 95.

173. Bessel, *Political Violence*, pp. 72, 80, 109, and 110, and Fischer, *Stormtroopers*, p. 159.

174. Bessel, *Political Violence*, p. 109.

175. Fischer, *Stormtroopers*, p. 159.

176. For more on this topic see Anton Czubinski, "Poland's Place in Nazi Plans for a New Order in Europe in the Years 1934–1940," *Polish Western Affairs* 21, no. 1 (1980): 19–46, in particular p. 26f.

177. Fiedor, Sobczak, and Wrzesinski, "The Image of Poles," p. 219.

178. Tomasz Szarota, "Poland and Poles in German Eyes during World War II," *Polish Western Affairs* 19, no. 2 (1978): 230.

179. Ibid., pp. 231ff.

180. Detlev J. K. Peukert, "The Genesis of the 'Final Solution' from the Spirit of Science," in *Reevaluating the Third Reich*, ed. T. Childers and J. Caplan (New York: Holmes and Meier, 1993), p. 244.

181. Peukert, "The Genesis," p. 244, mentions, for example, the reform of the Reich Youth Welfare Law in November 1932, which prevented children considered "uneducable" from receiving instruction in the reform school system. Consider also a survey taken in 1925 by Dr. Ewald Melzer, the director of the Katherinenhof asylum, who asked the parents of 162 patients if they supported euthanasia. Only twenty rejected mercy killing under any circumstance, while the rest thought it justified under various circumstances. See Michael Burleigh, *Ethics and Extermination: Reflections on Nazi Genocide* (New York: Cambridge University Press, 1997), p. 121.

182. Robert Gellately, *Backing Hitler: Consent and Coercion in Nazi Germany* (New York: Oxford University Press, 2001), p. 91.

183. Claudia Koonz, "Eugenics, Gender, and Ethics in Nazi Germany: The Debate about Involuntary Sterilization, 1933–1936," in *Reevaluating the Third Reich*, ed. T. Childers and J. Caplan (New York: Holmes and Meier, 1993), p. 81.

184. Gellately, *Backing Hitler*, p. 94.

185. Peukert, "The Genesis," p. 244.

186. Michael Geyer, "The Stigma of Violence, Nationalism, and War in Twentieth-Century Germany," *German Studies Review* (Special issue, Winter 1992): 80.

Conclusion

1. According to Polish scholar Czesław Madajczyk, *Die Okkupationspolitik Nazideutschlands in Polen 1939–1945* (Berlin: Akademie-Verlag, 1987), p. 617, the official 1945 report of the Polish government's Biuro Odszkodowań Wojennych (Office of War Losses) placed civilian deaths during the German occupation at 6,028,000. This figure remains extremely controversial, however, because it does not differentiate between Polish Jews and Polish Gentiles. The commonly accepted figure for Polish (non-Jewish) losses is roughly 3 million. See Donald Niewyk and Francis Nicosia, *The Columbia Guide to the Holocaust* (New York: Columbia University Press, 2000), p. 49.

2. Frank Golczewski, "Polen," in *Dimension des Völkermords: Die Zahl der jüdischen Opfer des Nationalsozialismus*, ed. W. Benz (Munich: Oldenbourg, 1991), p. 495, contends that the Nazis murdered 2.7 million Polish Jews between 1939 and 1944, while Niewyk and Nicosia, *The Columbia Guide*, p. 421, consider this the low estimate, noting that 3 million is the high estimate.

3. Antony Polonsky, "Polish Jewry," in *The Holocaust Encyclopedia*, ed. W. Laqueur (New Haven, CT: Yale University Press, 2001), p. 488.

4. See Aktenvermerk Heydrichs, 2 July 1940, reproduced in Helmut Krausnick, "Hitler und die Morde in Polen: Ein Beitrag zum Konflikt zwischen Heer und SS um die Verwaltung der besetzten Gebiete," *Vierteljahrshefte für Zeitgeschichte* 11, no. 2 (1963): 207.

5. The phrase used by Brauchitsch in his memorandum of 21 September 1939 was "Die Einsatzgruppen der Polizei haben im Auftrage und nach Weisung des Führers gewisse volkspolitische Aufgaben im besetzten Gebiet durchzuführen" ("The Police Einsatzgruppen have been assigned by the Führer the task of implementing certain 'racial-political' tasks in the occupied territory"). See Klaus-Jürgen Müller, *Das Heer und Hitler: Armee und nationalsozialistisches Regime, 1933–1940* (Stuttgart: Deutsche Verlags Anstalt, 1969), p. 667f.

6. Heydrich's naval career came to an end in April 1931. See Günther Deschner, *Reinhard Heydrich: A Biography* (New York: Stein and Day, 1981), pp. 32ff.

7. Heydrich was equally strict in demanding that Sipo personnel be punished for property crimes, recommending that SS men found guilty of illegally "enriching themselves" (i.e., stealing) be severely punished. SS commanders found guilty of the same offense were to be shot. See Vermerk, RSHA Amt I/I11, 16 October 1939, in USHMMA, RG 14.016M (Records of the RSHA, Bundesarchiv Koblenz, R 58/825), fiche 1, p. 39.

8. The use of militarized police units for killing civilians is further explored in Edward B. Westermann, "'Friend and Helper': German Uniformed Police Operations in Poland and the General Government, 1939–1941," *Journal of Military History* 58, no. 4 (October 1994): 643–661, "Himmler's Uniformed Police on the Eastern Front: The Reich's Secret Soldiers, 1941–1942," *War in History* 3, no. 3 (1996): 309–329, and "'Ordinary Men' or 'Ideological Soldiers'? Police Battalion 310 in Russia, 1942," *German Studies Review* 21, no. 1 (February 1998): 41–68.

9. This method of minimizing individual responsibility for the murder of Jews in the USSR also came through clearly in testimony delivered during the trial of Einsatzgruppen personnel at Nuremberg. As Heinz Schubert, a former member of Einsatzgruppe D swore in his affidavit of 24 February 1947, "The actual shooting . . . was carried out in strictest conformity with [Otto] Ohlendorf's order, [meaning] in a military and in the most human[e] manner possible. Otherwise . . . the moral strain would have been too great for the execution squad" (Document NO-3055, Prosecution Exhibit 28, in *TWC*, vol. 4, "The Einsatzgruppen Case," p. 208).

10. The handing down of criminal orders before Germany's invasion of the Soviet Union is covered exceptionally well in Jürgen Förster, "Operation Barbarossa as a War of Conquest and Annihilation," in *Germany and the Second World War*, vol. 4, *The Attack on the Soviet Union*, ed. H. Boog et al., trans. E. Osers (New York: Oxford University Press, 1998), pp. 481–521.

11. See Klaus-Jürgen Müller, "Zu Vorgeschichte und Inhalt der Rede Himmlers vor der Höheren Generalität am 15. März 1940 in Koblenz," *Vierteljahrshefte für Zeitgeschichte* 18, no. 1 (1970): 95–120; Richard Breitman, *The Architect of Genocide: Himmler and the Final Solution* (New York: Alfred Knopf, 1991), chap. 5; and Krausnick, "Hitler und die Morde," pp. 197ff.

12. The cultural notion of "the East" and its impact on German behavior is also explored in Alexander B. Rossino, "Destructive Impulses: German Soldiers and the

Conquest of Poland," *Holocaust and Genocide Studies* 11, no. 3 (Winter 1997): 351–365; Rossino, "Eastern Europe through German Eyes: Soldiers' Photographs, 1939–1942," in *History of Photography: Photography of the Holocaust* 23, no. 4 (Winter 1999): 313–321; and Omer Bartov, *Hitler's Army: Soldiers, Nazis, and War in the Third Reich* (New York: Oxford University Press, 1991), chap. 4.

13. Förster, "Operation Barbarossa," p. 496f.

14. For studies on the evolution of Nazi anti-Jewish policy from resettlement to physical elimination, see Götz Aly, *"Final Solution": Nazi Population Policy and the Murder of the European Jews,* trans. B. Cooper and A. Brown (New York: Arnold, 1999); Christopher R. Browning, *Nazi Policy, Jewish Workers, German Killers* (New York: Cambridge University Press, 2000); and Peter Longerich, *Politik der Vernichtung: Eine Gesamtdarstellung der nationalsozialistischen Judenverfolgung* (Munich: Piper, 1998).

15. Christian Jansen and Arno Weckbecker, *Der "Volksdeutsche Selbstschutz" in Polen 1939/40* (Munich: Oldenbourg, 1992), p. 35.

16. Vermerk, RSHA Amt I/I11, 16 October 1939, in USHMMA, RG 14.016M (Records of the RSHA, BAK, R 58/825), fiche 1, p. 40.

17. Estimates vary of the number of people killed by the Germans in occupied Poland between September and December 1939. The high figure of 50,000 is offered in Madajczyk, *Die Okkupationspolitik,* p. 15, and Włodzimierz Borodziej, *Terror und Politik: Die deutsche Polizei und die polnische Widerstandsbewegung im Generalgouvernement, 1939–1944* (Mainz: P. von Zabern, 1999), p. 25, while Tadeusz Piotrowski, *Poland's Holocaust: Ethnic Strife, Collaboration with Occupying Forces, and Genocide in the Second Republic, 1918–1947* (Jefferson, NC: McFarland, 1998), p. 23, cites the figure of 45,000 killed. The lowest estimate is 42,000, offered in Wolfgang Schumann and Ludwig Nestler, eds., *Europa Unterm Hakenkreuz: Die faschistische Okkupationspolitik in Polen, 1939–1945* (Berlin: Deutscher Verlag der Wissenschaften, 1989), p. 80f. Concerning Polish Jewish losses specifically, Schumann and Nestler, *Europa,* p. 86, estimate that over 7,000 had been killed by December 1939; Piotrowski, *Poland's Holocaust,* p. 29, corroborates this figure.

18. The notion of a "transitional phase" from the murder of some segments to all of Soviet Jewry is raised in Browning, *Nazi Policy,* pp. 29ff. Furthermore, similar to the Polish campaign, the Einsatzgruppen entered the USSR in June 1941 with ledgers in their possession naming 4,508 individuals who were to be immediately eliminated upon apprehension. Taken together, the existence of these Fahndungslisten, the relatively small size of the Einsatzgruppen (ca. 3,000 men), and Heydrich's orders outlining specific target groups strongly suggest that the pacification of conquered Soviet territory through the selective use of executions was official SS policy at the outset of Operation BARBAROSSA rather than the total annihilation of Soviet Jewry. See Fahndungslisten für die UdSSR in USHMMA, RG 14.016M (Bundesarchiv, Records of the RSHA, R58/574), fiche 2. For scholarly discussion of the initial killing phase in the Soviet Union, see Klaus-Michael Mallmann, "Die Türöffner der 'Endlösung': Zur Genesis des Genozids," in *Die Gestapo im Zweiten Weltkrieg: "Heimatfront" und besetztes Europa,* ed. G. Paul and K. Mallmann (Darmstadt: Primus, 2000), p. 445; P. Klein, ed., *Die Einsatzgruppen in der besetzten Sowjetunion 1941/42: Die Tätigkeits- und Lageberichte des Chefs der*

Sicherheitspolizei und des SD (Berlin: Edition Hentrich, 1997); Ralf Ogorreck, *Die Einsatzgruppen und die "Genesis der Endlösung"* (Berlin: Metropol Verlag, 1996); and Dieter Pohl, *Nationalsozialistische Judenverfolgung in Ostgalizien, 1941–1944: Organisation und Durchführung eines staatlichen Massenverbrechens* (Munich: Oldenbourg, 1997).

19. For example, Otto Rasch of the Special Purpose Einsatzgruppe in Poland later went on to command Einsatzgruppe C in the USSR, and Erich Naumann of Einsatzgruppe VI in Poland succeeded Arthur Nebe as the commander of Einsatzgruppe B. Also, a number of Security Police and Gestapo personnel organized into Sonderkommandos and deployed in the Białystok district and eastern Galicia in July 1941 were veterans of the Polish campaign, including Wolfgang Birkner (EG IV), Adolf Böhm (EG IV), and Edmund Schöne (EG IV). See Alexander B. Rossino, "Polish 'Neighbors' and German Invaders: Contextualizing Anti-Jewish Violence in the Białystok District during the Opening Weeks of Operation Barbarossa," in *Polin: Studies in Polish Jewry,* vol. 16, ed. A. Polonsky (London: Littman Library, 2003).

20. Henry Friedlander, *The Origins of Nazi Genocide: From Euthanasia to the Final Solution* (Chapel Hill: University of North Carolina Press, 1995), argues convincingly about the links between the gassing of the mentally ill and the later use of similar killing techniques in the death camps of occupied Poland.

GLOSSARY

Amt	Office
Abteilung	Section
Abwehr	Counterintelligence Office
A-Kartei	Catalog of State Enemies
Chefs der Zivilverwaltung (CdZs)	Chiefs of civil administration
Einsatzgruppen (EG)	Operational groups
Einsatzkommandos (EK)	Subcommands
Erlebnisberichte	Experience reports
Feldgendarmerie	Military Police
Feldpolizeibeamten	Field Police officers
Feldpostbriefe	Soldiers' letters
Freikorps	Volunteer corps
Freischärler	Insurgents
Geheime Feldpolizei (GFP)	Secret Field Police
Gruppenstab	Command staff
Hauptamt Sicherheitspolizei (HA-Sipo)	Security Police headquarters
Heckenschutzen	Snipers
Hitlerjugend	Hitler Youth
Kämpfer	Fighter
Kriminalpolizei (Kripo)	Criminal Police
Oberkommando der Wehrmacht (OKW)	Armed Forces High Command
Oberkommando des Heeres (OKH)	Army High Command
Ordnungspolizei (Orpo)	Order Police
Ostjuden	Eastern Jews
Polizeigruppe 1	Police Group 1
Reichsarbeitsdienst	Reich Labor Service
Reichssicherheitshauptamt (RSHA)	Reich Security Main Office
Rollkommando	Small unit
Schutzpolizei	Uniformed Police
Selbstschutz	Ethnic German civilian militia
Sicherheitsdienst (SD)	Security Service
Sicherheitspolizei (Sipo)	Security Police
Sonderfahndungslisten	Wanted persons lists
Sonderrefferat	Special administrative section
SS Totenkopfverbände (SSTV)	SS Death's Head units
Stadtkommandant	City commander

Sturmabteilung (SA)	Storm troopers
Truppenamt	Troop's office
Vergeltungsmassnahmen	Reprisal measures
Vernichtungskrieg	War of annihilation
Volksdeutsche	Ethnic Germans
Zentralstelle II P	Central office II P (Poland)

BIBLIOGRAPHY

Primary Source Collections

BERLIN DOCUMENT CENTER FILES, U.S. NATIONAL ARCHIVES, COLLEGE PARK, MARYLAND

A3343 SSO-007B (Emil Otto Rasch); A3342 SSO-013C (Udo von Woyrsch); A3343 SSO-026A (Heinz Graefe); A3343 SSO-053A (Ludwig Hahn); A3343 SSO-057B (Karl-Heinz Rux); A3343 SSO-058A (Walter Hammer); A3343 SSO-066 (Lothar Beutel); A3343 SSO-066B (Emanuel Schaefer); A3343 SSO-068A (Alfred Hasselberg); A3343 SSO-071B (Wilhelm Scharpwinkel); A3343 SSO-072B (Robert Schefe); A3343 SSO-073 (Helmut Bischoff); A3343 SSO-083A (Otto Hellwig); A3343 SSO-083B (Johann Schmer); A3343 SSO-112 (Karl Brunner); A3343 SSO-133B (Otto Sens); A3343 SSO-135 (Ernst Damzog); A3343 SSO-165B (Bruno Streckenbach); A3343 SSO-191B (Hans Trummler); A3343 SSO-208 (Hans Fischer); A3343 SSO-268A (Fritz Liphardt); A3343 SSO-327A (Bruno Müller)

BIBLIOTHEK FÜR ZEITGESCHICHTE, STUTTGART, GERMANY

Sammlung Sterz

BUNDESARCHIV-MILITÄRARCHIV, FREIBURG IM BREISGAU, GERMANY

Militärgeschichtliche Sammlungen (Military History Collections)
M1001/2 Bestand "Reichskriegsgericht" im Prager Militärhistorischen Archiv
MSg 2/2924 Leutnant Kleeberg, *Regiments–Nachrichtenzug I.R. 94 im Polenfeldzug* (Bonn, 1940)
MSg 2/3232 Tagebuch der Leutnant S.
MSg 2/3943 Tagebuch der Regimentsarzt R. J. K.
MSg 2/5275 Feldpostbriefe, Soldat H. H.
MSg 2/5690 Tagebuch der Leutnant H. A.

Nachlässe (Private Papers)
  N 184/3 Georg von Küchler
  N 54/5 Wilhelm Keitel

Kommandobehörden, Divisionen und sonstige Dienststellen des Heeres und der Waffen-SS (Command Authorities, Divisions, and other Agencies of the Army and the Waffen-SS)
  Oberkommando des Heeres (OKH) (Army High Command)
  RH 1/81
  3. Infanteriedivision
  RH 26-3/1
  4. Infanteriedivision
  RH 26-4/3
  7. Infanteriedivision
  RH 26-7/120
  10. Infanteriedivision
  RH 26-10/540, 544
  19. Infanteriedivision
  RH 26-19/2
  21. Infanteriedivision
  RH 26-21/2
  45. Infanteriedivision
  RH 26-45/2
  Wehrmachtführungsstab (Wehrmacht Operations Staff)
  RW 4/261

U.S. HOLOCAUST MEMORIAL MUSEUM ARCHIVE

11.001M.01 (Records from the "Osobyi" Archive in Moscow)

15.007M (Records of the Reichssicherheitshauptamt)

15.042M (Records of the Main Crimes Commission for the Investigation of Nazi War Crimes, Poznań)

14.016M (Records of the RSHA from the Bundesarchiv Koblenz, R 58/825)

48.004M (Records of the Military Historical Institute, Prague)

U.S. NATIONAL ARCHIVES AND RECORDS ADMINISTRATION, COLLEGE PARK, MARYLAND

RG 238

M 893 Records of the U.S. Nürnberg War Crimes Trials, *United States of America v. Wilhelm List et al.*, May 10, 1947–February 19, 1948

M 898 Records of the U.S. Nürnberg War Crimes Trials, *United States of America v. Wilhelm von Leeb et al.*, November 28, 1947–October 28, 1948

T-301 Records of the U.S. Nürnberg War Crimes Trials. NI Series, 1933–1948

RG 242

T-77 Records of the German Armed Forces High Command (Oberkommando der Wehrmacht/OKW)

T-78 Records of the Headquarters of the German Army High Command (Oberkommando des Heeres/OKH)

T-79 Records of the German Army Areas

T-311 Records of German Field Commands, Army Groups

T-312 Records of German Field Commands, Armies

T-314 Records of German Field Commands, Corps

T-315 Records of German Field Commands, Divisions

T-501 Records of German Field Commands, Rear Areas, Occupied Territories, and Others

ZENTRALE STELLE FÜR LANDESJUSTIZVERWALTUNGEN, LUDWIGSBURG, GERMANY (NOW BUNDESARCHIV-LUDWIGSBURG)

VI 415 AR 1310/65 E16 ASA 179 (Generalstaatsanwalt bei dem Kammergericht Berlin—1 Js 12/65 RSHA—Ermittlungsvermerk vom 1.12.1968). Verfahren gegen Dr. Werner Best und andere.

VI 415 AR 1310/65 E16 ASA 179 (Staatsanwaltschaft Berlin—1 Js 12/65 RSHA). Anklageschrift vom 10.2.1972 in der Strafsache gegen Dr. Werner Best wegen Mordes.

8 AR-Z 52/60 (Staatsanwaltschaft Würzburg—1 Js 2469/60). Verfahren gegen Alfred Hasselberg wegen Mordes.

201 AR-Z 76/59 (Staatsanwaltschaft Hamburg—141 Js 31/67). Verfahren gegen Bruno Streckenbach wegen Mordes.

205 AR-Z 302/67 (Staatsanwaltschaft Stuttgart—85 Js 49–53/74). Verfahren gegen Udo von Woyrsch wegen Mordes.

206 AR-Z 28/60. Verfahren gegen Martin Fellenz wegen Mordes.

211 AR-Z 13/63 (Staatsanwaltschaft Berlin—3P[K] Js 198/61). Schlussvermerk in dem Strafverfahren gegen Lothar Beutel, Helmut Bischoff, Walter Hammer, Erich Preckel, und andere Angehörige der Einsatzgruppe IV wegen Mordes vom 29.1.1971.

Primary Sources

Akten zur deutschen auswärtigen Politik, 1918–1945. Series D, 1937–1945. Baden-Baden: Impremerie Nationale, 1950.

Alperowitz, Yitzhak, ed. *Sefer Yaroslav.* Tel-Aviv: Irgun Yots'e Yaroslav be-Yisra'el, 1978.

American Council on Public Affairs. *Hitler's Words.* Edited by Gordon W. Prange. Washington, DC: Monumental Printing, 1944.

Apenszlak, Jacob, ed. *The Black Book of Polish Jewry.* New York: American Federation for Polish Jews, 1943.

Arad, Yitzhak, Shmuel Krakowski, and Shmuel Spector, eds. *The Einsatzgruppen Reports: Selections from the Dispatches of the Nazi Death Squads' Campaign against the Jews, July 1941–January 1943.* Translated by S. Schossberger. New York: Holocaust Library, 1989.

Bachrach, Shlomo, ed. *Memorial Book to the Community of Proshnitz.* Tel Aviv: Irgun Yots'e Proshnits be-Yisra'el, 1974.

Bähr, Walter, and Hans W. Bähr, eds. *Kriegsbriefe Gefallener Studenten, 1939–1945.* Tübingen: Rainer Wunderlich Verlag, 1952.

Bialystoker Center, ed. *The Bialystoker Memorial Book.* New York: Bialystoker Center, 1982.

Biderman, I. M., ed. *Wloclawek and Kujawy: Memorial Book.* New York: Wloclawek Memorial Book Committee, 1969.

Bock, Fedor von. *Zwischen Pflicht und Verweigerung: Das Kriegstagebuch.* Edited by Klaus Gerbet. Munich: Herbig, 1995.

Das Infanterieregiment 151, 1939–1942. Geschichte des Regiments in den Feldzügen in Polen, Holland, Belgien, Frankreich, Baltenland, und Russland. Auf Grund der amtlichen Kriegstagebücher unter Verwendung von Gefechtsberichten, Regiments-Akten, Erlebnisse von Mitkämpfern, und anderen Quellen (1944).

Das Gebirgsjägerregiment 99 im polnischen Feldzug. Bonn: N.p., 1939.

Die 7. Schwadron Kavallerieschützenregiment 10 im Polenfeldzug. N.p., 1940.

Documents and Materials Relating to the Eve of the Second World War. 2 vols. New York: International Publishers, 1948.

Domarus, Max. *Hitler: Reden und Proklamationen, 1932–1945.* 4 vols. Würzburg: Schmidt, 1962–1973.

Engel, Gerhard. *Heeresadjutant bei Hitler, 1938–1945: Aufzeichnungen des Majors Engel.* Edited by Hildegard von Kotze. Stuttgart: Deutsche Verlags-Anstalt, 1974.

Friedman, Tuvia, ed. *15 Jahre Zuchthaus für Wolff.* Haifa: Institute of Documentation in Israel, 1990.

Generalkommando VII, ed. *Wir zogen gegen Polen: Kriegserinnerungswerk des VII. Armeekorps.* Munich: F. Eher, 1940.

Gisevius, Hans Bernd. *Bis zum bitteren Ende: Vom Reichstagsbrand bis zum 20 July 1944.* Hamburg: Rütten and Loening, 1961.

Görlitz, Walter, ed. *Generalfeldmarshall Keitel: Verbrecher oder Offizier? Erinnerungen, Briefe, Dokumente des Chefs OKW.* Göttingen: Müsterschmidt Verlag, 1961.

Groscurth, Helmuth. *Tagebücher eines Abwehroffiziers 1938–1940: Mit weiteren Dokumenten zur Militäropposition gegen Hitler.* Edited by Helmut Krausnick and Harold C. Deutsch. Stuttgart: Deutsche Verlags-Anstalt, 1970.

Guderian, Heinz. *Panzer Leader.* Translated by C. Fitzgibbon. Costa Mesa, CA: Noontide Press, 1990.

Halder, Franz. *Kriegstagebuch,* vol. 1, *Vom Polenfeldzug bis zum Ende der Westoffensiv (14.8.1939–30.6.1940).* 3 vols. Stuttgart: W. Kohlhammer Verlag, 1962.

Halevy, Benjamin, ed. *Rozhan Memorial Book.* Tel-Aviv: Sigalit, 1977.

Hassell, Ulrich von. *Die Hassell-Tagebücher, 1938–1944: Aufzeichnungen vom Andern Deutschland.* Edited by Freiherr Hiller von Gätringen. Berlin: Siedler, 1988.

Heck, Alfons. *The Burden of Hitler's Legacy.* Frederick, CO: Renaissance House, 1988.

Hitler, Adolf. *Hitlers zweites Buch: Ein Dokument aus dem Jahr 1928.* Stuttgart: Deutsche Verlags-Anstalt, 1961.

———. *Mein Kampf.* Translated by R. Manheim. London: Pimlico Edition, 1992.

Hollingworth, Clare. *The Three Weeks' War in Poland.* London: Duckworth, 1940.

Höss, Rudolf. *Kommandant in Auschwitz: Autobiographische Aufzeichnungen von Rudolf Höss.* Edited by Martin Broszat. Stuttgart: Deutsche Verlags-Anstalt, 1958.

Hubatsch, Walther. *Hitlers Weisungen für die Kriegsführung, 1939–1945: Dokumente des Oberkommandos der Wehrmacht.* Frankfurt/Main: Bernard and Gräfe, 1962.

Infanterie-Regiment 309 marschiert an den Feind, Erlebnisberichte aus dem Polenfeldzug 1939. Berlin: N.p., 1940.

International Military Tribunal. *Trial of the Major War Criminals before the International Military Tribunal, Nuremberg, 14 November–1 October 1946*. 42 vols. Nuremberg: International Military Tribunal, 1947.

Klein, Harry, ed. *Czenstochov: Our Legacy*. Montreal: Klein, 1993.

Klein, Peter, ed. *Die Einsatzgruppen in der besetzten Sowjetunion 1941/42: Die Tätigkeits- und Lageberichte des Chefs der Sicherheitspolizei und des SD*. Berlin: Edition Hentrich, 1997.

Kleist, Peter. *Zwischen Hitler und Stalin, 1939–1945*. Bonn: Athenaeum-Verlag, 1950.

Knappe, Siegfried, and Ted Brusaw. *Soldat: Reflections of a German Soldier, 1936–1949*. New York: Dell, 1992.

Kordt, Erich. *Nicht aus den Akten . . . Die Wilhelmstrasse in Frieden und Krieg: Erlebnisse, Begegnungen, und Eindrücke, 1928–1945*. Stuttgart: Union Deutsche Verlagsgesellschaft, 1950.

Kurhessen kämpften in Polen: Einsatz und Erlebnisse des I.R. 15 (Mot.). Kassel: N.p., 1940.

Manoschek, Walter. *"Es gibt nur eines für das Judentum: Vernichtung": Das Judenbild in deutschen Soldatenbriefen, 1939–1941*. Hamburg: HIS Verlagsges, 1995.

Manstein, Erich von. *Lost Victories*. Edited and translated by A. G. Powell. London: Arms and Armour Press, 1982.

Mehner, Kurt, ed. *Die geheimen Tagesberichte der deutschen Wehrmachtführung im Zweiten Weltkrieg, 1939–1945*. Vol. 1. Osnabrück: Biblio Verlag, 1995.

Meiri, Shmuel, ed. *Wieliczka: A Memorial Book*. Tel-Aviv: Stern Press, 1980.

Menczer, Arie, ed. *Sefer Przemyśl*. Tel Aviv: Former Residents of Przemyśl in Israel, 1964.

Mit dem XIII Armeekorps in Polen, Ein Erinnerungsbuch. Munich: N.p., 1940.

Mit 9/59 in Polen, Tagebuchblätter entstanden auf kurzer Rast in Feindesland. N.p., 1939.

Nuremberg Military Tribunals. *Trials of War Criminals before the Nuremberg Military Tribunals under Control Council Law No. 10, Nuremberg, October 1946–April 1949*. 15 vols. Washington, DC: U.S. Government Printing Office, 1949–1953.

Oberstleutnant Liere, ed. *Pioniere im Kampf: Erlebnisberichte aus dem Polenfeldzug, 1939*. Berlin: N.p., 1940.

Office of the U.S. Chief Counsel for Prosecution of Axis Criminality. *Nazi Conspiracy and Aggression*. Washington, DC: U.S. Government Printing Office, 1946.

Orenstein, Benjamin, ed. *Churban Czenstochow: The Destruction of Czen-*

stokov. American Zone of Germany: Central Administration of Czenstochow Jews, 1948.

Polish Ministry of Information. *The Black Book of Poland*. New York: G. P. Putnam's Sons, 1942.

Rauschning, Hermann. *Hitler Speaks: A Series of Political Conversations with Adolf Hitler on His Real Aims*. London: Thornton Butterworth, 1939.

Regiments–Nachrichtenzug I.R. 94 im Polenfeldzug. Bonn: N.p., 1940.

Republic of Poland, Ministry of Foreign Affairs, ed. *German Occupation of Poland: Polish White Book*. New York: Greystone Press, 1942.

Ribbentrop, Joachim von. *The Ribbentrop Memoirs*. Translated by O. Watson. London: Weidenfeld and Nicolson, 1954.

Schlabrendorff, Fabian von. *Offiziere gegen Hitler*. Berlin: Siedler, 1984.

Shirer, William L. *Berlin Diary: The Journal of a Foreign Correspondent, 1934–1941*. New York: Alfred Knopf, 1941.

State of Israel Ministry of Justice. *The Trial of Adolf Eichmann: Record of Proceedings in the District Court of Jerusalem*. Vol. 1. Jerusalem: Keter, 1992.

Vogelsang, Thilo. "Neue Dokumente zur Geschichte der Reichswehr 1930–1933." *Vierteljahrshefte für Zeitgeschichte* 2, no. 4 (October 1954).

Wagner, Elisabeth, ed. *Der Generalquartiermeister: Briefe und Tagebuchaufzeichnungen des Generalquartiermeisters des Heeres General der Artillerie Eduard Wagner*. Munich and Vienna: Olzog Verlag, 1963.

Wald, Moshe Y., ed. *Rzeszów Jews Memorial Book*. Tel-Aviv: Ahdut Cooperative Press, 1967.

Warlimont, Walter. *Inside Hitler's Headquarters, 1939–1945*. Translated by R. H. Barry. Novato, CA: Presidio, 1964.

Wedel, Hasso von. *Die Propagandatruppen der Deutschen Wehrmacht*. Neckargemünd: Kurt Vowinckel Verlag, 1962.

Wir Marschieren für das Reich: Deutsche Jugend im Kampferlebnis des polnischen Feldzugs. Munich: Oldenbourg, 1940.

Wir marschieren gegen Polen: Ein Erinnerungsbuch an den polnischen Feldzug vom Infanterie Regiment 179. Munich: Oldenbourg, 1940.

Secondary Sources

Altrichter, Helmut, and Josef Becker, eds. *Kriegsausbruch 1939: Beteiligte, Betroffene, Neutrale*. Munich: C. H. Beck, 1989.

Aly, Götz. *"Final Solution": Nazi Population Policy and the Murder of the*

European Jews. Translated by B. Cooper and A. Brown. New York: Arnold, 1999.

Aly, Götz, and Suzanne Heim. *Vordenker der Vernichtung. Auschwitz und die deutsche Pläne für eine neue europäische Ordnung*. Frankfurt/Main: Fischer Taschenbuch, 1993.

Anderson, Truman O. "Die 62 Infanterie-Division: Repressalien im Heeresgebiet Süd, Oktober bis Dezember 1941." In *Vernichtungskrieg. Verbrechen der Wehrmacht 1941–1944*, edited by Hannes Heer and Klaus Naumann. Hamburg: HIS Verlagsges, 1995.

Aronson, Shlomo. *Reinhard Heydrich und die Frühgeschichte von Gestapo und SD*. Stuttgart: Deutsche Verlags-Anstalt, 1971.

Aschheim, Steven E. *Brothers and Strangers: The East European Jew in German and German Jewish Consciousness, 1800–1923*. Madison: University of Wisconsin Press, 1982.

August, Jochen. *"Sonderaktion Krakau" Die Verhaftung der Krakauer Wissenschaftler am 6. November 1939*. Hamburg: HIS Verlagsges, 1997.

Ausländer, Fietje, ed. *Verräter oder Vorbilder: Deserteure und ungehorsame Soldaten im Nationalsozialismus*. Bremen: Edition Temmer, 1990.

Baird, Jay W. *The Mythical World of Nazi War Propaganda, 1939–1945*. Minneapolis: University of Minnesota Press, 1974.

Banach, Jens. *Heydrichs Elite: Das Führerkorps der Sicherheitspolizei und des SD, 1936–1945*. Paderborn: Schöningh, 1998.

Bankier, David. *The Germans and the Final Solution: Public Opinion under Nazism*. Oxford: Blackwell, 1992.

Bartov, Omer. "The Conduct of War: Soldiers and the Barbarization of Warfare." In *Resistance against the Third Reich, 1933–1990*, edited by Michael Geyer and John W. Boyer. Chicago: University of Chicago Press, 1994.

———. *The Eastern Front, 1941–45: German Troops and the Barbarisation of Warfare*. New York: Macmillan, 1986.

———. "German Soldiers and the Holocaust: Historiography, Research, and Implications." In *The Holocaust: Origins, Implementation, Aftermath*, edited by Omer Bartov. London: Routledge, 2000.

———. *Hitler's Army: Soldiers, Nazis, and War in the Third Reich*. New York: Oxford University Press, 1991.

———. *Mirrors of Destruction: War, Genocide, and Modern Identity*. New York: Oxford University Press, 2000.

Basler, Werner. *Deutschlands Annexionspolitik in Polen und im Baltikum, 1914–1918*. Berlin: Rütten and Loening, 1962.

Baumgart, Winfried, and Hermann Boehm. "Zur Ansprache Hitlers vor den Führern der Wehrmacht am 22. August 1939." *Vierteljahrshefte für Zeitgeschichte* 19, no. 2 (April 1971): 303.

Beaumont, Joan. "Protecting Prisoners of War, 1939–95." In *Prisoners of War and Their Captors in World War II,* edited by Bob Moore and Kent Fedorowich. Oxford: Berg, 1996.

Berenbaum, Michael, ed. *A Mosaic of Victims: Non-Jews Persecuted and Murdered by the Nazis.* New York: New York University Press, 1990.

Berghahn, Volker R. "NSDAP und 'Geistige Führung' der Wehrmacht 1939–1945." *Vierteljahrshefte für Zeitgeschichte* 17, no. 1 (1969).

Bessel, Richard. *Political Violence and the Rise of Nazism: The Stormtroopers in Eastern Germany, 1925–1934.* New Haven, CT: Yale University Press, 1984.

Best, Geoffrey. *Humanity in Warfare.* New York: Columbia University Press, 1980.

Birn, Ruth Bettina. "Guilty Conscience, Antisemitism, and the Personal Development of Some SS Leaders." In *Remembering for the Future: The Impact of the Holocaust on the Contemporary World.* Oxford: Pergamon Press, 1988.

———. *Die Höheren SS- und Polizeiführer.* Düsseldorf: Droste, 1986.

Bloch, Charles. *Hitler und die europäischen Mächte 1933/1934: Kontinuität oder Bruch.* Frankfurt/Main: Europäische Verlagsanstalt, 1966.

Booms, Hans. "Der Ursprung des Zweiten Weltkrieges—Revision oder Expansion?" In *Kriegsbeginn 1939,* edited by Gottfried Niedhart. Darmstadt: Wissenschaftliche Buchgesellschaft, 1976.

Borodziej, Włodzimierz. *Terror und Politik: Die Deutsche Polizei und die polnische Widerstandsbewegung im Generalgouvernement, 1939–1944.* Mainz: P. von Zabern, 1999.

Borodziej, Włodzimierz, and Klaus Ziemer, eds. *Deutsch-polnische Beziehungen, 1939–1945–1949: Eine Einführung.* Osnabrück: Fibre Verlag, 2000.

Bracher, Karl Dietrich. *Die Deutsche Diktatur: Entstehung, Struktur, Folgen des Nationalsozialismus.* Cologne: Kiepenheuer and Witsch, 1969.

Breitman, Richard. *The Architect of Genocide: Himmler and the Final Solution.* New York: Alfred Knopf, 1991.

———. *Official Secrets: What the Nazis Planned, What the British and Americans Knew.* New York: Hill and Wang, 1998.

Broszat, Martin. *Nationalsozialistische Polenpolitik, 1939–1945.* Stuttgart: Deutsche Verlags-Anstalt, 1961.

———. *Zweihundert Jahre deutsche Polenpolitik.* Frankfurt/Main: Suhrkamp Taschenbuch, 1972.

Browder, George C. *Foundations of the Nazi Police State: The Formation of the Sipo and SD.* Lexington: University Press of Kentucky, 1990.

———. *Hitler's Enforcers: The Gestapo and the SS Security Service in the Nazi Revolution.* New York: Oxford University Press, 1996.

Brown, Paul. "Forester to *Feldpolizeichef:* The Life and Counterintelligence Career of Wilhelm Krichbaum." Master's thesis, Southern Illinois University, 1999.

Browning, Christopher R. *Fateful Months: Essays on the Emergence of the Final Solution.* New York: Holmes and Meier, 1985.

———. *The Final Solution and the German Foreign Office: A Study of Referat D III of Abteilung Deutschland, 1940–1943.* New York: Holmes and Meier, 1978.

———. *Nazi Policy, Jewish Workers, German Killers.* New York: Cambridge University Press, 2000.

———. *Ordinary Men: Reserve Police Battalion 101 and the Final Solution in Poland.* New York: HarperCollins, 1992.

———. *The Path to Genocide: Essays on Launching the Final Solution.* New York: Cambridge University Press, 1992.

Brownlow, Donald Grey, and John Eluthère Du Pont. *Hell Was My Home: Arnold Shay, Survivor of the Holocaust.* West Hanover, MA: Christopher, 1983.

Buchbender, Otto, and Reinhold Sterz, eds. *Das andere Gesicht des Krieges: Deutsche Feldpostbriefe, 1939–1945.* Munich: C. H. Beck, 1982.

Burleigh, Michael. *Germany Turns Eastwards: A Study of Ostforschung in the Third Reich.* New York: Cambridge University Press, 1988.

———. "Psychiatry, German Society and Nazi 'Euthanasia.'" In *Ethics and Extermination: Reflections on Nazi Genocide,* edited by Michael Burleigh. New York: Cambridge University Press, 1997.

Burleigh, Michael, ed. *Confronting the Nazi Past: New Debates on Modern German History.* New York: St. Martin's Press, 1996.

Buttlar, Florian von, Stefanie Endlich, and Annette Leo, eds. *Fürstenberg–Drögens: Schichten eines Verlassenen Ortes.* Berlin: Hentrich, 1994.

Chickering, Roger. "Die Alldeutschen erwarten den Krieg." In *Bereit zum Krieg: Kriegsmentalität im wilhelminischen Deutschland, 1890–1914,* edited by Jost Dülffer and Karl Holl. Göttingen: Vandenhoeck and Ruprecht, 1986.

Chickering, Roger, and Stig Förster, eds. *In the Shadows of Total War: Europe, East Asia, and the United States, 1919–1939.* New York: Cambridge University Press, 2002.

Chrobaczyński, Jacek. "Rassenkrieg gegen Polen." In *Anpassung, Kollabo-*

ration, *Widerstand: Kollektive Reaktionen auf die Okkupation,* edited by Wolfgang Benz, Johannes Houwink ten Cate, and Gerhard Otto. Berlin: Metropol, 1996.

Citino, Robert M. *The Path to Blitzkrieg: Doctrine and Training in the German Army, 1920–1939.* Boulder, CO: Lynne Rienner, 1999.

Connelly, John. "Nazis and Slavs: From Racial Theory to Racist Practice." *Central European History* 32, no. 1 (1999).

Conze, Werner. *Polnische Nation und deutsche Politik im Ersten Weltkrieg.* Graz: Böhlau Verlag, 1958.

Corni, Gustavo, and Horst Gies. *Blut und Boden: Rassenideologie und Agrarpolitik im Staat Hitlers.* Idstein: Schulz-Kirchner Verlag, 1994.

Craig, Gordon A., and Felix Gilbert, eds. *The Diplomats, 1919–1939.* Vol. 2, *The Thirties.* New York: Atheneum, 1965.

Cygański, Mirosław. "Nazi Persecutions of Polish National Minorities in the Rhineland-Westphalia Provinces in the Years 1933–1945." *Polish Western Affairs* 17, no. 1–2 (1976).

Cyprian, Tadeusz. "Zbrodnie Wehrmachtu na Polskich Jeńcach Wojennych." In *Biuletyn Głównej Komisji Badania Zbrodni Hitlerowskich w Polsce.* Vol. 32. Warsaw: Wydawnictwo Prawnicze, 1987.

Czubiński, Anton. "Poland's Place in Nazi Plans for a New Order in Europe in the Years 1934–1940." *Polish Western Affairs* 21, no. 1 (1980).

Dahlmann, Dittmar, and Gerhard Hirschfeld, eds. *Lager, Zwangsarbeit, Vertreibung, und Deportation: Dimensionen der Massenverbrechen in der Sowjetunion und in Deutschland, 1933 bis 1945.* Essen: Klartext, 1999.

Datner, Szymon. *Crimes Committed by the Wehrmacht during the September Campaign and the Period of Military Government.* Poznań: Institute for Western Affairs, 1962.

Datner, Szymon, Janusz Gumkowski, and Kazimierz Leszczyński. *Genocide, 1939–1945.* Warsaw: Wydawnictwo Zachodnie, 1962.

Deist, Wilhelm. "The Rearmament of the Wehrmacht." In *Germany and the Second World War,* vol. 1, *The Buildup of German Aggression,* edited by the Militärgeschichtliches Forschungsamt and translated by P. S. Falla, D. S. McMurry, E. Osers, and L. Wilmot. 5 vols. New York: Oxford University Press, 1990.

——. "The Wehrmacht at War." Paper presented at Georgetown University, Washington, DC, April 11, 1996.

De Jong, Louis. *The German Fifth Column in the Second World War.* Translated by C. M. Geyl. Chicago: University of Chicago Press, 1956.

Deschner, Günther. *Reinhard Heydrich: A Biography.* New York: Stein and Day, 1981.

Deutsch, Harold C. *The Conspiracy against Hitler in the Twilight War.* Minneapolis: University of Minnesota Press, 1968.

De Zayas, Alfred M. *The Wehrmacht War Crimes Bureau, 1939–1945.* Lincoln: University of Nebraska Press, 1989.

Dicks, Henry V. *Licensed Mass Murder: A Socio-Psychological Study of Some SS Killers.* New York: Basic Books, 1972.

Diehl, James M. *Paramilitary Politics in Weimar Germany.* Bloomington: Indiana University Press, 1977.

Dimsdale, Joel E., ed. *Survivors, Victims, and Perpetrators: Essays on the Nazi Holocaust.* London: Taylor and Francis, 1980.

Dirks, Carl, and Karl-Heinz Janssen. *Der Krieg der Generäle: Hitler als Werkzeug der Wehrmacht.* Berlin: Propyläen, 1999.

Dollinger, Hans, ed. *Kain, Wo ist dein Bruder? Was der Mensch im Zweiten Weltkrieg erleiden musste—dokumentiert in Tagebüchern und Briefen.* Frankfurt/Main: List, 1992.

Dostert, Paul. "Die Luxemburger im Reserve-Polizei-Bataillon 101 und der Judenmord in Polen." *Hémecht* 52 Revue D'Histoire Luxembourgeoise (2000).

Dressen, Willi. "The Role of the Wehrmacht and the Police in the Annihilation of the Jews." *Yad Vashem Studies* 22 (1993).

Drobisch, Klaus. "Die Judenreferate des Geheimen Staatspolizeiamtes und des Sicherheitsdienstes der SS 1933 bis 1939." In *Jahrbuch für Antisemitismusforschung,* vol. 2, edited by Wolfgang Benz. Frankfurt/Main: Campus Verlag, 1993.

Eidenbenz, Mathias. *"Blut und Boden": Zu Funktion und Genese der Metaphern des Agrarismus und Biologismus in der nationalsozialistischen Bauernpropaganda R.W. Darrés.* Frankfurt/Main: Peter Lang, 1993.

Elble, Rolf. *Die Schlacht and der Bzura im September 1939 aus deutscher und polnischer Sicht.* Freiburg im Breisgau: Verlag Rombach, 1975.

Eyck, Erich. *A History of the Weimar Republic.* 2 vols. Translated by H. P. Hanson and R. G. L. Waite. New York: Wiley and Sons, 1962.

Fajkowski, Józef. *Wieś w Ogniu: Eksterminacja wsi Polskiej w Okresie Okupacji Hitlerowskiej.* Warsaw: Ludowa Spółdzielnia Wydawnicza, 1971.

Fattig, Richard C. "Reprisal: The German Army and the Execution of Hostages during the Second World War." Ph.D. dissertation, University of California, San Diego, 1980.

Fest, Joachim C. *Hitler.* Translated by Richard and Clara Winston. New York: Harcourt Brace Jovanovich, 1974.

———. *Plotting Hitler's Death: The Story of the German Resistance*. Translated by B. Little. New York: Henry Holt, 1996.

Fiedor, Karol. "The Attitude of German Right-Wing Organizations to Poland in the Years 1918–1933." *Polish Western Affairs* 14, no. 1 (1973).

Fiedor, Karol, Janusz Sobczak, and Wojciech Wrzesinski. "The Image of Poles in Germany and of the German in Poland in Inter-War Years and Its Role in Shaping the Relations between the Two States." *Polish Western Affairs* 19, no. 2 (1978).

Fischer, Conan. *Stormtroopers: A Social, Economic, and Ideological Analysis, 1929–1935*. London: George Allen and Unwin, 1983.

Fleming, Gerald. *Hitler and the Final Solution*. New York: Oxford University Press, 1986.

Förster, Jürgen. "Complicity or Entanglement? Wehrmacht, War, and Holocaust." In *The Holocaust and History: The Known, the Unknown, the Disputed, and the Reexamined,* edited by Michael Berenbaum and Abraham J. Peck. Bloomington: Indiana University Press, 1998.

———. "Das andere Gesicht des Krieges: Das 'Unternehmen Barbarossa' als Eroberungs- und Vernichtungskrieg." In *"Unternehmen Barbarossa": Zum historischen Ort der Deutsch Sowjetischen Beziehungen von 1933 bis Herbst 1941,* edited by Roland G. Förster. Munich: Oldenbourg, 1993.

———. "Das nationalsozialistische Herrschaftssystem und der Krieg gegen die Sowjetunion." In *Erobern und Vernichten: Der Krieg gegen die Sowjetunion, 1941–1945,* edited by Peter Jahn and Reinhard Rürup. Berlin: Argon, 1991.

———. "Die Sicherung des 'Lebensraumes.'" In Horst Boog et al., *Der Angriff auf die Sowjetunion*. Frankfurt/Main: Fischer Taschenbuch, 1991.

———. "Hitlers Entscheidung für den Krieg gegen die Sowjetunion." In Horst Boog et al., *Der Angriff auf die Sowjetunion*. Frankfurt/Main: Fischer Taschenbuch, 1991.

———. "Jewish Policies of the German Military, 1939–1942." In *The Shoah and the War,* edited by Asher Cohen, Yehoyakim Cochavi, and Yoav Gelber. New York: Peter Lang, 1992.

———. "Operation Barbarossa as a War of Conquest and Annihilation." In *Germany and the Second World War,* vol. 4, *The Attack on the Soviet Union,* edited by H. Boog et al., translated by E. Osers. Pp. 481–521. New York: Oxford University Press, 1998.

———. "The Relation between Operation BARBAROSSA as an Ideological War of Extermination and the Final Solution." In *The Final Solution:*

Origins and Implementation, edited by David Cesarani. London: Routledge, 1994.

———. "The Wehrmacht and the War of Extermination against the Soviet Union." *Yad Vashem Studies* 14 (Jerusalem 1981).

Fox, John P. "*Reichskristallnacht* 9 November 1938 and the *Ostjuden* Perspective to the Nazi Search for a 'Solution' to the Jewish Question." In *POLIN: A Journal of Polish-Jewish Studies*. Vol. 5. Oxford: Basil Blackwell: 1990.

Friedlander, Henry. *The Origins of Nazi Genocide: From Euthanasia to the Final Solution.* Chapel Hill: University of North Carolina Press, 1995.

Friedländer, Saul. *Nazi Germany and the Jews.* Vol. 1, *The Years of Persecution, 1933–1939.* New York: HarperCollins, 1997.

Frischauer, Willi. *Himmler.* New York: Belmont Books, 1962.

Fritz, Stephen G. *Frontsoldaten.* Lexington: University Press of Kentucky, 1995.

Galante, Pierre. *Operation Valkyrie: The German Generals Plot against Hitler.* Translated by M. Howson and C. Ryan. New York: Harper and Row, 1981.

Geiss, Imanuel. *Der polnische Grenzstreifen, 1914–1918: Ein Beitrag zur deutschen Kriegszielpolitik im Ersten Weltkrieg.* Lübeck: Matthiesen, 1960.

Gellately, Robert. *Backing Hitler: Consent and Coercion in Nazi Germany.* New York: Oxford University Press, 2001.

———. *The Gestapo and German Society: Enforcing Racial Policy, 1939–1945.* New York: Oxford University Press, 1990.

Gelles, Romuald. "Polish Issues in German Schoolbooks in the 1930s in the Evaluation of Polish Historians." *Polish Western Affairs* 16, no. 2 (1975).

Gerlach, Christian. *Kalkulierte Morde: Die deutsche Wirtschafts- und Vernichtungspolitik in Weissrussland, 1941 bis 1944.* Hamburg: HIS Verlagsges, 1999.

Gersdorf, Rudolf-Christoph Freiherr von. *Soldat im Untergang.* Frankfurt/Main: Ullstein, 1977.

Geschichtswerkstatt Marburg, ed. *"Ich musste selber etwas tun": Deserteure-Täter und Verfolgte im Zweiten Weltkrieg.* Marburg: Schüren, 2000.

Gessner, Klaus. "Geheime Feldpolizei—die Gestapo der Wehrmacht." In *Vernichtungskrieg: Verbrechen der Wehrmacht, 1941–1944,* edited by Hannes Heer and Klaus Naumann. Hamburg: HIS Verlagsges, 1995.

———. *Geheime Feldpolizei: Zur Funktion und Organisation des Geheimpolizeilichen Exekutivorgans der Faschistischen Wehrmacht.* Berlin: Militärverlag der Deutschen Demokratischen Republik, 1986.

Geyer, Michael. "The Crisis of Military Leadership in the 1930s." *Journal of Strategic Studies* 14 (December 1991).

——. "Das Stigma der Gewalt und das Problem der nationalen Identität in Deutschland." In *Von der Aufgabe der Freiheit: Politische Verantwortung und bürgerliche Gesellschaft in 19. und 20. Jahrhundert*, edited by Christian Jansen, Lutz Niethammer, and Bernd Weisbrod. Berlin: Akademie Verlag, 1995.

——. *Deutsche Rüstungspolitik, 1860–1980*. Frankfurt/Main: Suhrkamp, 1984.

——. "The Dynamics of Military Revisionism in the Interwar Years: Military Politics between Rearmament and Diplomacy. In *The German Military in the Age of Total War*, edited by Wilhelm Deist. Leamington Spa: Berg, 1985.

——. "Etudes in Political History: Reichswehr, NSDAP, and the Seizure of Power." In *The Nazi Machtergreifung*, edited by Peter Stachura. London: George Allen and Unwin, 1983.

——. "Restorative Elutes, German Society, and the Nazi Pursuit of War." In *Fascist Italy and Nazi Germany: Comparisons and Contrasts*, edited by Richard Bessel. New York: Cambridge University Press, 1996.

——. "The Stigma of Violence, Nationalism, and War in Twentieth-Century Germany." *German Studies Review* (Special issue, Winter 1992).

Gilbert, G. M. "The Mentality of the SS Murderous Robots." *Yad Vashem Studies* 5 (Jerusalem 1963).

Gill, Arnon. *Eine tragische Staatsgrenze: Geschichte der deutsch-polnischen Grenze von 1918–1945*. Frankfurt/Main: Peter Lang, 1997.

Giziowski, Richard. *The Enigma of General Blaskowitz*. London: Leo Cooper, 1997.

Glees, Anthony. "The 1944 Plotters and the War of Genocide." *Journal of Holocaust Education* 4, no. 1 (Summer 1995).

Golczewski, Frank. "Polen." In *Dimension des Völkermords: Die Zahl der jüdischen Opfer des Nationalsozialismus*, edited by W. Benz. Munich: Oldenbourg, 1991.

Goldhagen, Daniel J. *Hitler's Willing Executioners: Ordinary Germans and the Holocaust*. New York: Alfred Knopf, 1996.

Goshen, Seev. "Eichmann und die Nisko-Aktion im Oktober 1939: Eine Fallstudie zur NS-Judenpolitik in der letzten Etappe vor der 'Endlösung.'" *Vierteljahrshefte für Zeitgeschichte* 29, no. 1 (1981).

Gotschlich, Helga. *Reifezeugnis für den Krieg: Abituren des Jahrgangs 39 erinnern sich*. Berlin: Verlag der Nation, 1990.

Grabitz, Helge, Klaus Bästlein, and Johannes Tuchel, eds. *Die Normalität des Verbrechens: Bilanz und Perspektiven der Forschung zu den natio-nalsozialistischen Gewaltverbrechen.* Berlin: Edition Hentrich, 1994.

Graml, Hermann. "Die Wehrmacht im Dritten Reich." *Vierteljahrshefte für Zeitgeschichte* 45, no. 3 (July 1997).

Gumkowski, Janusz, and Kazimierz Leszczynski. *Poland under Nazi Oc-cupation.* Warsaw: Polonia, 1961.

Hachmeister, Lutz. *Der Gegnerforscher: Die Karriere des SS-Führers Franz Alfred Six.* Munich: C. H. Beck, 1998.

Hagen, William W. *Germans, Poles, and Jews: The Nationality Conflict in the Prussian East, 1772–1914.* Chicago: University of Chicago Press, 1980.

Hamburger Institut für Sozialforschung, ed. *Vernichtungskrieg: Verbrechen der Wehrmacht 1941 bis 1944, Ausstellungskatalog.* Hamburg: HIS Verlagsges, 1996.

Hamerow, Theodore S. *On the Road to the Wolf's Lair: German Resis-tance to Hitler.* Cambridge, MA: Belknap Press of Harvard University Press, 1997.

Hartmann, Christian. *Halder: Generalstabschef Hitlers, 1938–1942.* Paderborn: Schöningh, 1991.

Hartmann, Christian, and Sergei Slutsch. "Franz Halder und die Kriegsvorbereitungen im Frühjahr 1939: Eine Ansprache des General-stabschefs des Heeres." *Vierteljahrshefte für Zeitgeschichte* 45, no. 3 (July 1997).

Headland, Ronald. *Messages of Murder: A Study of the Reports of the Ein-satzgruppen of the Security Police and the Security Service.* East Ruther-ford, NJ: Fairleigh Dickinson University Press, 1992.

Heer, Hannes. "Killing Fields: Die Wehrmacht und der Holocaust." In *Ver-nichtungskrieg Verbrechen der Wehrmacht, 1941–1944,* edited by Hannes Heer and Klaus Naumann. Pp. 57–77. Hamburg: HIS Verlags-ges, 1995.

———. "Die Logik des Vernichtungskrieges: Wehrmacht und Partisa-nenkampf." In *Vernichtungskrieg. Verbrechen der Wehrmacht, 1941–1944,* edited by Hannes Heer and Klaus Naumann. Pp. 104–138. Hamburg: HIS Verlagsges, 1995.

Herbert, Ulrich. *Arbeit, Volkstum, Weltanschauung.* Frankfurt/Main: Fischer Verlag, 1995.

———. *Best: Biographische Studien über Radikalismus, Weltanschauung, und Vernunft, 1903–1989.* Bonn: J. H. W. Dietz Nachfolger, 1996.

Herbert, Ulrich, ed. *National Socialist Extermination Policies: Contempo-rary German Perspectives and Controversies.* New York: Berghahn Books, 2000.

Hermand, Jost. *Old Dreams of a New Reich: Volkish Utopias and National Socialism*. Translated by P. Levesque and S. Soldovieri. Bloomington: Indiana University Press, 1992.

Herwig, Holger H. *The First World War: Germany and Austria-Hungary, 1914–1918*. New York: St. Martin's Press, 1997.

Hilberg, Raul. *The Destruction of the European Jews*. Vol. 3. New York: Holmes and Meier, 1985.

———. *Perpetrators, Victims, Bystanders: The Jewish Catastrophe 1939–1945*. New York: HarperCollins, 1992.

Hildebrand, Klaus. *The Foreign Policy of the Third Reich*. Translated by A. Fothergill. Berkeley: University of California Press, 1973.

Hirschfeld, Gerhard, ed. *The Policies of Genocide: Jews and Soviet Prisoners of War in Nazi Germany*. London: Allen and Unwin, 1986.

Höhne, Heinz. *The Order of the Death's Head: The Story of Hitler's SS*. Translated by R. Barry. New York: Ballantine Books, 1971.

Hönsch, Jörg K. "Der Hitler-Stalin Pakt und Polen." In *Hitler-Stalin Pakt 1939: Das Ende Ostmitteleuropas?*, edited by Erwin Oberländer. Frankfurt/Main: Fischer Taschenbuch, 1989.

Horak, Stephan. *Poland and Her National Minorities, 1919–1939*. New York: Vantage Press, 1961.

Horne, John, and Alan Kramer. *German Atrocities 1914: A History of Denial*. New Haven, CT: Yale University Press, 2001.

———. "German 'Atrocities' and Franco-German Opinion, 1914: The Evidence of German Soldiers' Diaries." *Journal of Modern History* 66 (1994).

Jäckel, Eberhard, and Jürgen Rohwer, eds. *Der Mord an den Juden im Zweiten Weltkrieg: Entschlussbildung und Verwirklichung*. Stuttgart: Deutsche Verlags-Anstalt, 1985.

Jacobson, Hans-Adolf. *Nationalsozialistische Aussenpolitik, 1933–1938*. Frankfurt/Main: A. Metzner, 1968.

Jahn, Peter. "'Russenfurcht' und Antibolschewismus: Zur Entstehung und Wirkung von Feindbildern." In *Erobern und Vernichten: Der Krieg gegen die Sowjetunion, 1941–1945*, edited by Peter Jahn and Reinhard Rürup. Berlin: Argon, 1991.

Jansen, Christian, and Arno Weckbecker. *Der "Volksdeutsche Selbstschutz" in Polen 1939/40*. Munich: Oldenbourg, 1992.

Janssen, Karl-Heinz. "Vorwärts mit Gott für Deutschland!" In *Zeit-Punkte. Gehorsam bis zum Mord? Der verschwiegene Krieg der deutschen Wehrmacht–Fakten, Analysen, Debatte*, edited by Theo Sommer. Hamburg: Zeitverlag, 1995.

Janssen, Karl-Heinz, and Fritz Tobias. *Der Sturz der Generäle: Hitler und die Blomberg-Fritsch-Krise 1938*. Munich: C. H. Beck, 1994.

Jastrzębski, Włodzimierz. *Der Bromberger Blutsonntag: Legende und Wirklichkeit*. Poznań: Westinstitut, 1990.

Jersch-Wenzel, Stefi, ed. *Deutsche-Polen-Juden: Ihre Beziehungen von den Anfängen bis ins 20. Jahrhundert*. Berlin: Colloquium Verlag, 1987.

Johnson, Eric A. *Nazi Terror: The Gestapo, Jews, and Ordinary Germans*. New York: Basic Books, 1999.

Jonca, Karol. "The Expulsion of Polish Jews." In *POLIN: Studies in Polish Jewry*, vol. 8, edited by Antony Polonsky, Ezra Mendelsohn, and Jerzy Tomaszewski. London: Littman Library of Jewish Civilization, 1994.

Jones, Nigel H. *Hitler's Heralds: The Story of the Freikorps, 1918–1923*. New York: Dorset Press, 1987.

Joseph, Martin. "NS-Propaganda und Feldpost, Anspruch und Wirklichkeit." Bundesarchiv-Militärarchiv, Freiburg, 1987.

Katholischen Militärbischofsamt and Hans Jürgen Brandt, eds. *Priester in Uniform: Seelsorger, Ordensleute, und Theologen als Soldaten im Zweiten Weltkrieg*. Augsburg: Pattloch, 1994.

Kelman, Herbert C., and V. Lee Hamilton. *Crimes of Obedience: Towards a Social Psychology of Authority and Responsibility*. New Haven, CT: Yale University Press, 1989.

Kenkmann, Alfons, ed. *Villa Ten Hompel: Sitz der Ordnungspolizei im Dritten Reich*. Münster: Agenda Verlag, 1996.

Kenkmann, Alfons, and Christoph Spieker, eds. *Im Auftrag: Polizei, Verwaltung, und Verantwortung*. Essen: Klartext, 2001.

Kennedy, Robert M. *The German Campaign in Poland (1939)*. Washington, DC: Department of the Army, 1956.

Kershaw, Ian. *Hitler: 1936–1945 Nemesis*. New York: W. W. Norton, 2000.

———. *Hitler: 1889–1936 Hubris*. New York: W. W. Norton, 1998.

———. *The "Hitler Myth": Image and Reality in the Third Reich*. New York: Oxford University Press, 1987.

———. *Popular Opinion and Political Dissent in the Third Reich: Bavaria, 1933–1945*. New York: Oxford University Press, 1983.

Klee, Ernst, and Willi Dressen. *"Gott mit Uns": Der deutsche Vernichtungskrieg im Osten 1939–1945*. Frankfurt/Main: Fischer, 1989.

Klee, Ernst, Willi Dressen, and Volker Riess, eds. *"The Good Old Days": The Holocaust As Seen by Its Perpetrators and Bystanders*. Translated by D. Burnstone. New York: Free Press, 1991.

Klessmann, Christoph, and Wacław Długoborski. "Nationalsozialistische Bildungspolitik und polnische Hochschulen 1939–1945." *Geschichte und Gesellschaft* 23, no. 4 (1997).

Koonz, Claudia. "Eugenics, Gender, and Ethics in Nazi Germany: The Debate about Involuntary Sterilization, 1933–1936." In *Reevaluating the Third Reich,* edited by Thomas Childers and Jane Caplan. New York: Holmes and Meier, 1993.

Kopitzsch, Wolfgang. "Polizeieinheiten in Hamburg in der Weimarer Republik und im Dritten Reich." In *Die Deutsche Polizei und Ihre Geschichte,* edited by Peter Nitschke. Hilden: Verlag Deutsche Polizeiliteratur, 1996.

Kramer, Alan. "'Grueltaten' Zum Problem der deutschen Kriegsverbrechen in Belgien und Frankreich 1914." In *"Keiner fühlt sich hier als Mensch": Erlebnis und Wirkung des Ersten Weltkriegs,* edited by Gerhard Hirschfeld, Gerd Krumreich, and Irina Renz. Essen: Klartext, 1993.

Krausnick, Helmut. "Hitler und die Morde in Polen: Ein Beitrag zum Konflikt zwischen Heer und SS um die Verwaltung der besetzten Gebiete." *Vierteljahrshefte für Zeitgeschichte* 11: 2 (April 1963).

Krausnick, Helmut, and Martin Broszat. *Anatomy of the SS State.* Translated by R. Barry, M. Jackson, and D. Long. New York, Walker and Company, 1968.

Krausnick, Helmut, and Hans-Heinrich Wilhelm. *Die Truppe des Weltanschauungskrieges: Die Einsatzgruppen der Sicherheitspolizei und des SD, 1938–1942.* Stuttgart: Deutsche Verlags-Anstalt, 1981.

Kroener, Bernhard R. "Auf dem Weg zu einer 'nationalsozialistischen Volksarmee.'" In *Von Stalingrad zur Währungsreform,* edited by Martin Broszat, Klaus-Dietmar Henke, and Hans Woller. Munich: Oldenbourg, 1988.

———. "Die personellen Ressourcen des Dritten Reiches im Spannungsfeld zwischen Wehrmacht, Bürokratie und Kriegswirtschaft, 1939–1942." In *Organisation und Mobilisierung des Deutschen Machtbereichs. Erster Halbband: Kriegsverwaltung, Wirtschaft und Personnelle Ressourcen 1939–1941,* edited by Bernhard R. Kroener, Rolf-Dieter Müller, and Hans Umbreit. Stuttgart: Deutsche Verlags-Anstalt, 1988.

Krüger, Peter. "Hitlers Europapolitik." In *Der Nationalsozialismus: Studien zur Ideologie und Herrschaft,* edited by Wolfgang Benz, Hans Buchheim, and Hans Mommsen. Frankfurt/Main: Fischer Taschenbuch, 1994.

Kulka, Otto Dov. "'Public Opinion' in Nazi Germany and the 'Jewish Question.'" In *The Nazi Holocaust,* vol. 5, edited by Michael Marrus. Westport, CT: Meckler, 1989.

Kulski, Władyslaw. *Germany and Poland: From War to Peaceful Relations.* Syracuse, NY: Syracuse University Press, 1976.

Kutterman, David. "Those Who Said No: Germans Who Refused to Execute Civilians during World War II." *German Studies Review* 11, no. 2 (May 1988).

Kwiet, Konrad. "Auftakt zum Holocaust: Ein Polizeibataillon im Osteinsatz." In *Der Nationalsozialismus: Studien zur Ideologie und Herrschaft,* edited by Wolfgang Benz, Hans Buchheim, and Hans Mommsen. Frankfurt/Main: Fischer Taschenbuch, 1994.

———. "Erziehung zum Mord—Zwei Beispiele zur Kontinuität der deutschen 'Endlösung der Judenfrage.'" In *Geschichte und Emanzipation: Festschrift für Reinhard Rürup,* edited by Michael Grüttner, Rüdiger Hachtmann, and Heinz-Gerhard Haupt. Frankfurt/Main: Campus Verlag, 1999.

Latzel, Klaus. *Deutsche Soldaten–nationalsozialistischer Krieg? Kriegserlebnis-Kriegserfahrung, 1939–1945.* Paderborn: Schöningh, 1998.

———. "Tourismus und Gewalt: Kriegswahrnehmungen in Feldpostbriefen." In *Vernichtungskrieg. Verbrechen der Wehrmacht, 1941–1944,* edited by Hannes Heer and Klaus Naumann. Hamburg: HIS Verlagsges, 1995.

Levine, Herbert S. *Hitler's Free City: A History of the Nazi Party in Danzig, 1925–39.* Chicago: University of Chicago Press, 1973.

Lewis, Samuel J. *Forgotten Lessons: German Army Infantry Policy, 1918–1941.* New York: Praeger, 1985.

Lichtenstein, Heiner. *Himmlers grüne Helfer: Die Schutz- und Ordnungspolizei im "Dritten Reich."* Cologne: Bund Verlag, 1990.

Liddell Hart, B. H. *The Other Side of the Hill.* London: Pan Books, 1983.

Lifton, Robert Jay, and Eric Markusen. *The Genocidal Mentality: Nazi Holocaust and Nuclear Threat.* New York: Basic Books, 1990.

Liulevicius, Vejas Gabriel. *War Land on the Eastern Front: Culture, National Identity, and German Occupation in World War I.* New York: Cambridge University Press, 2000.

Löffler, Klara. *Aufgehoben: Soldatenbriefe aus dem Zweiten Weltkrieg. Eine Studie zur subjektiven Wirklichkeit des Krieges.* Bamberg: WVB, 1992.

Longerich, Peter. *Politik der Vernichtung: Eine Gesamtdarstellung der nationalsozialistischen Judenverfolgung.* Munich: Piper, 1998.

Longerich, Peter, ed. *Die Ermordung der europäischen Juden: Eine umfassende Dokumentation des Holocaust, 1941–1945.* Munich: Piper, 1989.

Lukas, Richard C. *The Forgotten Holocaust: The Poles under German Occupation, 1939–1944.* Lexington: University Press of Kentucky, 1986.

Madajczyk, Czesław. *Die Okkupationspolitik Nazideutschlands in Polen, 1939–1945*. Berlin: Akademie Verlag, 1987.

———. "Die Verantwortung der Wehrmacht für die Verbrechen während des Krieges mit Polen." In *Kriegsverbrechen im 20 Jahrhundert*, edited by Wolfram Wette and Gerd R. Ueberschär. Darmstadt: Primus, 2001.

Mallmann, Klaus-Michael. "Vom Fussvolk der 'Endlösung': Ordnungspolizei, Ostkrieg und Judenmord." *Tel Aviver Jahrbuch für deutsche Geschichte* 26 (1997).

Manoschek, Walter. "'Gehst mit Juden erschiessen?' Die Vernichtung der Juden in Serbien." In *Vernichtungskrieg: Verbrechen der Wehrmacht, 1941–1944*, edited by Hannes Heer and Klaus Naumann. Hamburg: HIS Verlagsges, 1995.

———. "Partisanenkrieg und Genozid. Die Wehrmacht in Serbien 1941." In *Die Wehrmacht im Rassenkrieg: Der Vernichtungskrieg hinter der Front*, edited by Walter Manoschek. Vienna: Picus, 1996.

———. *"Serbien ist Judenfrei!" Militärische Besatzungspolitik und Judenvernichtung in Serbien, 1941/42*. Munich: Oldenbourg, 1993.

Manoschek, Walter, and Hans Safrian. "717./117.ID. Eine Infanterie-Division auf dem Balkan." In *Vernichtungskrieg: Verbrechen der Wehrmacht, 1941–1944*, edited by Hannes Heer and Klaus Naumann. Hamburg: HIS Verlagsges, 1995.

Marczewski, Jerzy. "The Nazi Concept of *Drang nach Osten* and the Basic Premises of Occupation Policy in the 'Polish Question.'" *Polish Western Affairs* 8, no. 2 (1967).

Matthäus, Jürgen. "Ausbildungsziel Judenmord? Zum Stellenwert der 'weltanschaulichen Erziehung' von SS und Polizei im Rahmen der 'Endlösung.'" *Zeitschrift für Geschichtswissenschaft* 47, no. 8 (1999).

———. "German Judenpolitik in Lithuania during the First World War." In *Leo Baeck Institute Yearbook 1998*. Vol. 43. London: Secker and Warburg, 1998.

Mazower, Mark. *Inside Hitler's Greece: The Experience of Occupation, 1941–44*. New Haven, CT: Yale University Press, 1993.

McKale, Donald M. *Hitler's Shadow War: The Holocaust in World War II*. New York: Cooper Square Press, 2002.

McTaggart, Pat. "Poland '39." In *Hitler's Army: The Evolution and Structure of German Forces, 1933–1945*, edited by Command Magazine. Conshohocken, PA: Combined Books, 1996.

Megargee, Geoffrey P. *Inside Hitler's High Command*. Lawrence: University Press of Kansas, 2000.

———. "The Shadow of the Great War: Changes in the Aims and Means of

Warfare in Germany, 1919–1942." Paper presented at the annual conference of the Society for Military History, Calgary, Alberta, Canada, May 25, 2001.

Melzer, Emanuel. "Relations between Poland and Germany and Their Impact on the Jewish Problem in Poland (1935–1938)." *Yad Vashem Studies* 12 (1977).

Messenger, Charles. *Hitler's Gladiator: The Life and Times of Oberstgruppenführer and Panzergeneral-Oberst der Waffen-SS Sepp Dietrich.* London: Brassey's, 1988.

———. *The Last Prussian: A Biography of Field Marshal Gerd von Rundstedt, 1875–1953.* London: Brassey's, 1991.

Messerschmidt, Manfred. "Die Wehrmacht als tragende Säule des NS-Staates (1933–1939)." In *Die Wehrmacht im Rassenkrieg: Der Vernichtungskrieg hinter der Front,* edited by Walter Manoschek. Vienna: Picus, 1996.

———. *Die Wehrmacht im NS-Staat: Zeit der Indoktrination.* Hamburg: Decker, 1969.

———. "Foreign Policy and Preparation for War." In *Germany and the Second World War.* Vol. 1, *The Buildup of German Aggression,* edited by the Militärgeschichtliches Forschungsamt and translated by P. S. Falla, D. S. McMurry, E. Osers, and L. Wilmot. 5 vols. New York: Oxford University Press, 1990.

Messerschmidt, Manfred, and Fritz Wüllner. *Die Wehrmachtjustiz im Dienste des Nationalsozialismus: Zerstörung einer Legende.* Baden-Baden: Nomos Verlagsgesellschaft, 1987.

Michael, Berthold. *Schule und Erziehung im Griff des Totalitären Staates: Die Göttinger Schulen in der nationalsozialistischen Zeit von 1933 bis 1945.* Göttingen: Vandenhoeck and Ruprecht, 1994.

Michman, Dan. "'Judenräte' und 'Judenvereinigungen' unter nationalsozialistischer Herrschaft: Aufbau und Anwendung eines verwaltungsmässigen Konzepts." *Zeitschrift für Geschichtswissenschaft* 46, no. 4 (1998).

Mik, Ryszard. "Zbrodnie Wehrmachtu na Jeńcach Polskich w Rejonie Bitwy nad Bzura." In *Biuletyn Głównej Komisji Badania Zbrodni Hitlerowskich w Polsce.* Vol. 32. Warsaw: Wydawnictwo Prawnicze, 1987.

Militärgeschichtliches Forschungsamt, ed. *Germany and the Second World War.* Vol. 1, *The Buildup of German Aggression.* Translated by P. S. Falla, D. S. McMurry, E. Osers, and L. Wilmot. Oxford: Clarendon Press, 1990.

———. *Germany and the Second World War.* Vol. 2, *Germany's Initial Conquests in Europe.* Translated by D. S. McMurry, E. Osers, and P. S. Falla. Oxford: Clarendon Press, 1991.

Milton, Sybil. "The Expulsion of Polish Jews from Germany, October 1938 to July 1939: A Documentation." In *Leo Baeck Institute: Yearbook 1984*. Vol. 29. London: Secker and Warburg, 1984.

Mitcham, Samuel W., Jr., and Gene Mueller. *Hitler's Commanders: Officers of the Wehrmacht, the Luftwaffe, the Kriegsmarine, and the Waffen-SS*. New York: Cooper Square Press, 2000.

Mommsen, Hans. *The Rise and Fall of Weimar Democracy*. Translated by E. Forster and L. E. Jones. Chapel Hill: University of North Carolina Press, 1996.

———. *Von Weimar nach Auschwitz: Zur Geschichte Deutschlands in der Weltkriegsepoche*. Stuttgart: Deutsche Verlags-Anstalt, 1999.

Moritz, Erhard, and Wolfgang Kern. "Aggression und Terror: Zur Zusammenarbeit der faschistischen deutschen Wehrmacht mit den Einsatzgruppen der Sicherheitspolizei und des SD bei der Aggression gegen Polen." *Zeitschrift für Geschichtswissenschaft* 22 (1974).

Moser, Jonny. "Nisko: The First Experiment in Deportation." In *Simon Wiesenthal Center Annual*, vol. 2, edited by Henry Friedlander and Sybil Milton. White Plains, NY: Kraus International Publications, 1985.

Mosse, George L. *The Crisis of German Ideology: Intellectual Origins of the Third Reich*. New York: Schocken, 1964.

———. *Fallen Soldiers: Reshaping the Memory of the World Wars*. New York: Oxford University Press, 1990.

———. *Toward the Final Solution*. New York: H. Fertig, 1978.

Müller, Klaus-Jürgen. *Armee und Drittes Reich, 1933–1939: Darstellung und Dokumentation*. Paderborn: Schöningh, 1987.

———. *The Army, Politics, and Society in Germany, 1933–45*. New York: St. Martin's Press, 1987.

———. "The Brutalization of Warfare: Nazi Crimes and the Wehrmacht." In *Barbarossa: The Axis and the Allies*, edited by David Dilks and John Erickson. Edinburgh: Edinburgh University Press, 1994.

———. *Das Heer und Hitler: Armee und nationalsozialistisches Regime, 1933–1940*. Stuttgart: Deutsche Verlags-Anstalt, 1969.

———. "Zu Vorgeschichte und Inhalt der Rede Himmlers vor der Höheren Generalität am 13. März 1940 in Koblenz." *Vierteljahrshefte für Zeitgeschichte* 18, no. 1 (1970).

Müller, Rolf-Dieter. *Hitlers Ostkrieg und die deutsche Siedlungspolitik: Die Zusammenarbeit von Wehrmacht, Wirtschaft, und SS*. Frankfurt/Main: Fischer Taschenbuch, 1993.

Müller, Rolf-Dieter, and Hans-Erich Volkmann, eds. *Die Wehrmacht: Mythos und Realität*. Munich: Oldenbourg, 1999.

Mulligan, Timothy P. *The Politics of Illusion and Empire: German Occupation Policy in the Soviet Union, 1942–1943.* New York: Praeger, 1988.

Musial, Bogdan. *Deutsche Zivilverwaltung und Judenverfolgung im Generalgouvernement: Eine Fallstudie zum Distrikt Lublin, 1939–1944.* Wiesbaden: Harrassowitz, 1999.

Nachtwei, Winfried. "Ganz normale Männer: Die Verwicklung von Polizeibataillonen aus dem Rheinland und Westfalen in den nationalsozialistischen Vernichtungskrieg." In *Villa Ten Hompel: Sitz der Ordnungspolizei im Dritten Reich,* edited by Alfons Kenkmann. Münster: Agenda Verlag, 1996.

Nelson, Gail H. "The Molding of Personality: SS Indoctrination and Training Techniques." Master's thesis, University of Colorado at Boulder, 1966.

Neufeldt, Hans-Joachim, Jürgen Huck, and Georg Tessin, eds. *Zur Geschichte der Ordnungspolizei, 1936–1945.* Koblenz: Schriften des Bundesarchivs, 1957.

Neumann, Joachim. *Die 4. Panzerdivision, 1938–1943.* Bonn: Im Selbstvertrag des Verfassers, 1985.

Niewyk, Donald, and Francis Nicosia. *The Columbia Guide to The Holocaust.* New York: Columbia University Press, 2000.

Noakes, Jeremy. "Social Outcasts in the Third Reich." In *Life in the Third Reich,* edited by Richard Bessel. New York: Oxford University Press, 1987.

Oberländer, Erwin, ed. *Hitler-Stalin Pakt 1939: Das Ende Ostmitteleuropas?* Frankfurt/Main: Fischer Taschenbuch, 1989.

Ogorreck, Ralf. *Die Einsatzgruppen und die "Genesis der Endlösung."* Berlin: Metropol, 1996.

Okonski, Walter. *Wartime Poland, 1939–1945: A Select Annotated Bibliography of Books in English.* Westport, CT: Greenwood Press, 1997.

O'Neill, Robert J. *The German Army and the Nazi Party, 1933–39.* London: J. H. Heinemann, 1968.

Otto, Reinhard. *Wehrmacht, Gestapo und sowjetische Kriegsgefangene im deutschen Reichsgebiet 1941–42.* Munich: Oldenbourg, 1998.

Paget, Reginald T. *Manstein: His Campaigns and His Trial.* London: Collins, 1951.

Paul, Gerhard. *Ungehorsame Soldaten: Dissens, Verweigerung, und Widerstand deutscher Soldaten (1939–1945).* St. Ingbert: Röhrig Universitätsverlag, 1994.

Paul, Gerhard, and Norbert Haase, eds. *Die anderen Soldaten: Wehrkraftzersetzung, Gehorsamsverweigerung, und Fahnenflucht im Zweiten Weltkrieg.* Frankfurt/Main: Fischer Taschenbuch, 1995.

Paul, Gerhard, and Klaus-Michael Mallmann, eds. *Die Gestapo—Mythos und Realität*. Darmstadt: Wissenschaftliche Buchgesellschaft, 1995.

———. *Die Gestapo im Zweiten Weltkrieg: Heimatfront und besetztes Europa*. Darmstadt: Wissenschaftliche Buchgesellschaft, 2000.

Peukert, Detlev J. K. "The Genesis of the 'Final Solution' from the Spirit of Science." In *Reevaluating the Third Reich*, edited by Thomas Childers and Jane Caplan. New York: Holmes and Meier, 1993.

———. *Inside Nazi Germany: Conformity, Opposition, and Racism in Everyday Life*. New Haven, CT: Yale University Press, 1987.

Piekalkiewicz, Janusz. *Polenfeldzug*. Bergisch Gladbach: Gustav Lübbe Verlag, 1982.

Piotrowski, Tadeusz. *Poland's Holocaust: Ethnic Strife, Collaboration with Occupying Forces, and Genocide in the Second Republic, 1918–1947*. Jefferson, NC: McFarland, 1998.

Poeppel, Hans, Wilhelm-Karl Prinz von Preussen, and Karl-Guenther von Hase, eds. *Die Soldaten der Wehrmacht*. Munich: F. A. Herbig, 1998.

Pohl, Dieter. *Nationalsozialistische Judenverfolgung in Ostgalizien, 1941–1944: Organisation und Durchführung eines staatlichen Massenverbrechens*. Munich: Oldenbourg, 1997.

———. *Von der "Judenpolitik" zum Judenmord: Der Distrikt Lublin des Generalgouvernements, 1939–1944*. Frankfurt/Main: Peter Lang, 1993.

Pohl, Karl Heinrich. *Wehrmacht und Vernichtungspolitik: Militär im nationalsozialistischen System*. Göttingen: Vandenhoeck and Ruprecht, 1999.

Polonsky, Antony. "Polish Jewry." In *The Holocaust Encyclopedia*, edited by W. Laqueur. New Haven, CT: Yale University Press, 2001.

Rabenau, Friedrich von. *Seeckt, Aus seinem Leben, 1918–1936*. Leipzig: V. Hase and Koehler, 1940.

Rachfal, Antoni. "Eksterminacja Ludności Żydowskiej w Latach Wojny, 1939–1944 Na Terenie Obecnego Woj. Przemyskiego." In *Studia nad okupacją hitlerowską południowo-wschodniej częsci Polski*, edited by T. Kowalski. Rzeszów: Tow.Nauk w Rzeszowie, 1985.

Reitlinger, Gerlad. *The SS: Alibi of a Nation, 1922–1945*. New York: Da Capo Press, 1989.

Rhodes, Richard. *Masters of Death: The SS-Einsatzgruppen and the Invention of the Holocaust*. New York: Alfred A. Knopf, 2002.

Rich, Norman. "Hitler's Foreign Policy." In *Total War and Historical Change: Europe, 1914–1955*, edited by Arthur Marwick, Clive Emsley, and Wendy Simpson. Buckingham: Open University Press, 2001.

———. *Hitler's War Aims: Ideology, the Nazi State, and the Course of Expansion*. New York: W. W. Norton, 1973.

Richardson, Horst Fuchs, ed. and trans. *Sieg Heil! War Letters of Tank Gunner Karl Fuchs, 1937–1941.* Hamden, CT: Archon, 1987.

Riekhoff, Harald von. *German-Polish Relations, 1918–1933.* Baltimore: Johns Hopkins University Press, 1971.

———. "Revisionism vs. Reconciliation: Germany's Poland Policy during the Period of the Weimar Republic." Ph.D. dissertation, Yale University, 1965.

Rosen, Hans Freiherr von. *Dokumentation: Der Verschleppung der Deutschen aus Posen und Pommerellen in September 1939.* Berlin: Westkreuz, 1990.

Rossino, Alexander B. "Destructive Impulses: German Soldiers and the Conquest of Poland." *Holocaust and Genocide Studies* 11, no. 3 (Winter 1997).

———. "Eastern Europe through German Eyes: Soldiers' Photographs, 1939–1942." *History of Photography: Photography of the Holocaust* 23, no. 4 (Winter 1999).

———. "Nazi Anti-Jewish Policy during the Polish Campaign: The Case of the Einsatzgruppe von Woyrsch." *German Studies Review* 24, no. 1 (February 2001).

Runzheimer, Jürgen. "Die Grenzzwischenfälle am Abend vor dem deutschen Angriff auf Polen." In *Sommer 1939: Die Grossmächte und der Europäische Krieg,* edited by Wolfgang Benz and Hermann Graml. Stuttgart: Deutsche Verlags-Anstalt, 1979.

Rürup, Reinhard, ed. *Der Krieg gegen die Sowjetunion, 1941–1945: Eine Dokumentation.* Berlin: Argon, 1991.

Safrian, Hans. *Die Eichmann Männer.* Vienna: Europa Verlag, 1993.

Schenk, Dieter. *Hitler's Mann in Danzig: Albert Forster und die NS-Verbrechen in Danzig-Westpreussen.* Bonn: J. H. W. Dietz Nachfolger, 2000.

Schoenbaum, David. *Zabern 1913: Consensus Politics in Imperial Germany.* London: George Allen and Unwin, 1982.

Schörken, Rolf, "Jugendalltag im Dritten Reich—Die 'Normalität' in der Diktatur." In *Geschichte im Alltag—Alltag in der Geschichte,* edited by Klaus Bergmann and Rolf Schörken. Düsseldorf: Schwann, 1982.

Schramm, Gottfried. "Grundmuster deutscher Ostpolitik, 1918–1939." In *Zwei Wege nach Moskau: Vom Hitler-Stalin Pakt bis zum "Unternehmen Barbarossa,"* edited by Bernd Wegner. Munich: Piper, 1991.

Schroeder, Richard E. "The Hitler Youth as a Paramilitary Organization." Ph.D. dissertation, University of Chicago, 1975.

Schüddekopf, Carl. *Krieg: Erzählungen aus dem Schweigen Deutsche Soldaten über den Zweiten Weltkrieg.* Reinbek: Rohwolt Verlag, 1997.

Schulte, Theo J. *The German Army and Nazi Policies in Occupied Russia.* Oxford: Berg, 1989.

Schulze, Hagen. *Freikorps und Republik, 1918–1920.* Boppard am Rhein: Boldt, 1969.

Schumann, Wolfgang, and Ludwig Nestler, eds. *Europa unterm Haken-kreuz: Die faschistische Okkupationspolitik in Polen, 1939–1945.* Berlin: Deutscher Verlag der Wissenschaften, 1989.

Seaton, Albert. *The German Army, 1933–1945.* London: Sphere Books, 1983.

Seidler, Franz W. *Die Militärgerichtsbarkeit der Deutschen Wehrmacht, 1939–1945.* Schnellbach: Verlag S. Bublies, 1999.

Showalter, Dennis E. "'The East Gives Nothing Back': The Great War and the German Army in Russia." *Journal of the Historical Society* 2, no. 1 (Winter 2002).

Smelser, Ronald, and Enrico Syring, eds. *Die Militärelite des Dritten Reiches: 27 biographische Skizzen.* Berlin: Ullstein, 1995.

Spiess, Alfred, and Heiner Lichtenstein. *Das Unternehmen Tannenberg.* Wiesbaden: Limes-Verlag, 1979.

Stein, George H. *The Waffen SS: Hitler's Elite Guard at War, 1939–1945.* Ithaca, NY: Cornell University Press, 1966.

Steinbacher, Sybille. *"Musterstadt" Auschwitz: Germanisierungspolitik und Judenmord in Ostoberschlesien.* Munich: K. G. Saur, 2000.

Streim, Alfred. *Die Behandlung sowjetischer Kriegsgefangener im "Fall Barbarossa."* Heidelberg: Juristischer Verlag, 1981.

Streit, Christian. *Keine Kameraden. Die Wehrmacht und die sowjetischen Kriegsgefangenen, 1941–1945.* Stuttgart: Deutsche Verlags-Anstalt, 1978.

Sydnor, Charles W., Jr. *Soldiers of Destruction: The SS Death's Head Division, 1939–1945.* Rev. ed. Princeton, NJ: Princeton University Press, 1990.

———. "Theodor Eicke: Organisator der Konzentrationslager." In *Die SS: Elite unter dem Totenkopf 30 Lebensläufe,* edited by Ronald Smelser and Enrico Syring. Paderborn: Schöningh, 2000.

Szarota, Tomasz. "Poland and Poles in German Eyes during World War II." *Polish Western Affairs* 19, no. 2 (1978).

———. "Polen unter deutscher Besatzung, 1939–1941: Vergleichende Betrachtungen." In *Zwei Wege nach Moskau: Vom Hitler-Stalin Pakt bis zum "Unternehmen Barbarossa,"* edited by Bernd Wegner. Munich: Piper, 1991.

Szefer, Andrzej. "Zbrodnie Hitlerowskie na Górnym Śląsku we Wrzesniu

1939R." In *Biuletyn Głównej Komisji Badania Zbrodni Hitlerowskich w Polsce.* Vol. 32. Warsaw: Wydawnictwo Prawnicze, 1987.

Tessin, Georg. *Verbände und Truppen der deutschen Wehrmacht und Waffen-SS im Zweiten Weltkrieg, 1939–1945.* 16 vols. Osnabrück: Biblio Verlag, 1973.

———. *Waffen-SS und Ordnungspolizei im Kriegseinsatz, 1939–1945: Ein Überblick anhand der Feldpostübersicht.* Osnabrück: Biblio Verlag, 2000.

Thomas, Donald E., Jr. "Richard Walther Darré and the Doctrine of Blood and Soil." Master's thesis, University of Chicago, 1962.

Tooley, T. Hunt. *National Identity and Weimar Germany: Upper Silesia and the Eastern Border, 1918–1922.* Lincoln: University of Nebraska Press, 1997.

Trevor-Roper, Hugh R. "Hitlers Kriegsziele." *Vierteljahrshefte für Zeitgeschichte* 8, no. 2 (April 1960).

Ueberschär, Gerd R. "The Ideologically Motivated War of Annihilation in the East." In *Hitler's War in the East, 1941–1945: A Critical Assessment,* edited by Rolf-Dieter Müller and Gerd R. Ueberschär. Providence, RI: Berghahn, 1997.

———. "Militäropposition gegen Hitlers Kriegspolitik, 1939 bis 1941." In *Der Widerstand gegen den Nationalsozialismus,* edited by Jürgen Schmädeke and Peter Steinbach. Munich: Piper, 1986.

Ueberschär, Gerd R., ed. *NS-Verbrechen und der militärische Widerstand gegen Hitler.* Darmstadt: Primus, 2000.

Ulrich, Bernd. "Militärgeschichte von unten: Anmerkungen zu ihren Ursprüngen, Quellen, und Perspektiven im 20. Jahrhundert." *Geschichte und Gesellschaft* 22, no. 4 (October 1996).

Umbreit, Hans. *Der Militärbefehlshaber in Frankreich, 1940–1944.* Boppard am Rhein: H. Boldt, 1968.

———. *Deutsche Militärverwaltungen 1938/39: Die militärische Besetzung der Tschechoslowakei und Polens.* Stuttgart: Deutsche Verlags-Anstalt, 1977.

Uziel, Daniel. "Wehrmacht Propaganda Troops and the Jews." In *Yad Vashem Studies,* vol. 29, edited by David Silberklang. Jerusalem: Yad Vashem, 2001.

Vogel, Detlef. "Der Kriegsalltag im Spiegel von Feldpostbriefen (1939–1945)." In *Der Krieg des kleinen Mannes: Eine Militärgeschichte von unten,* edited by Wolfram Wette. Munich: Piper, 1992.

Wagner, Patrick. "Feindbild 'Berufsverbrecher': Die Kriminalpolizei im Übergang von der Weimarer Republik zum Nationalsozialismus." In

Zivilisation und Barbarei: Die widersprüchlichen Potentiale der Moderne, edited by Frank Bajohr, Werner Johe, and Uwe Lohalm. Hamburg: Christians, 1991.

Waite, Robert G. "'Judentum und Kriminalität': Rassistische Deutungen in kriminologischen Publikationen, 1933–1945." In *Rassismus, Faschismus, Antifaschismus,* edited by Manfred Weissbecker and Reinhard Kühnl. Cologne: PapyRossa Verlag, 2000.

Waite, Robert G. L. *Vanguard of Nazism: The Free Corps Movement in Postwar Germany, 1918–1923.* New York: W. W. Norton, 1952.

Waller, James E. "Perpetrators of the Holocaust: Divided and Unitary Self-Conceptions of Evildoing." *Holocaust and Genocide Studies* 10, no. 1 (Spring 1996).

Wegner, Bernd. *Hitlers Politische Soldaten: Die Waffen-SS, 1933–1945.* Paderborn: Schöningh, 1990.

Weinberg, Gerhard L. *The Foreign Policy of Hitler's Germany: Diplomatic Revolution in Europe, 1933–36.* Chicago: University of Chicago Press, 1970.

———. *The Foreign Policy of Hitler's Germany: Starting World War II, 1937–1939.* Chicago: University of Chicago Press, 1980.

———. *Germany, Hitler, and World War II: Essays in Modern German and World History.* New York: Cambridge University Press, 1995.

———. "Germany's War for World Conquest and the Extermination of the Jews." *Holocaust and Genocide Studies* 10, no. 2 (Fall 1996).

———. *A World at Arms: A Global History of World War II.* New York: Cambridge University Press, 1994.

Weingartner, James. "Joseph 'Sepp' Dietrich—Hitlers Volksgeneral." In *Die Militärelite des Dritten Reiches,* edited by Ronald Smelser and Enrico Syring. Berlin: Ullstein, 1995.

Weiss, John. *Ideology of Death: Why the Holocaust Happened in Germany.* Chicago: Ivan R. Dee, 1996.

Welch, Steven R. "'Harsh but Just?' German Military Justice in the Second World War: A Comparative Study of the Court-Martialing of German and U.S. Deserters." *German History* 17, no. 3 (1999).

Westermann, Edward B. "'Friend and Helper': German Uniformed Police Operations in Poland and the General Government, 1939–1941." *Journal of Military History* 58, no. 4 (October 1994).

———. "Himmler's Uniformed Police on the Eastern Front: The Reich's Secret Soldiers, 1941–1942." *War in History* 3, no. 3 (1996).

———. "'Ordinary Men' or 'Ideological Soldiers'? Police Battalion 310 in Russia, 1942." *German Studies Review* 21, no. 1 (February 1998).

Wette, Wolfram. "'Rassenfeind' Antisemitismus und Antislawismus in der Wehrmachtpropaganda." In *Die Wehrmacht im Rassenkrieg*, edited by Walter Manoschek. Vienna: Picus, 1996.

Wette, Wolfram, ed. *Deserteure der Wehrmacht: Feiglinge—Opfer—Hoffnungsträger?* Essen: Klartext, 1995.

———. *Manfred Messerschmidt: "Was Damals Recht war . . ." NS-Militär- und Strafjustiz im Vernichtungskrieg.* Essen: Klartext, 1996.

Wette, Wolfram, and Gerd R. Ueberschär, eds. *Kriegsverbrechen im 20. Jahrhundert.* Darmstadt: Primus, 2001.

Wieland, Lothar. *Belgien 1914: Die Frage des belgischen "Franktireurkrieges" und die deutsche öffentliche Meinung von 1914 bis 1936.* Frankfurt/Main: Peter Lang, 1984.

Wildt, Michael. "Before the 'Final Solution': The Judenpolitik of the SD, 1935–1938." In *Leo Baeck Institute Yearbook 1998.* Vol. 43. London: Secker and Warburg, 1998.

———. "Der Hamburger Gestapochef Bruno Streckenbach: Eine nationalsozialistische Karriere." In *Hamburg in der NS-Zeit,* edited by Frank Bajohr and Joachim Szodrzynski. Hamburg: Ergebnisse, 1995.

———. *Generation des Unbedingten: Das Führungskorps des Reichssicherheitshauptamtes.* Hamburg: Hamburger Edition, 2002.

———. "Gewalt gegen Juden in Deutschland 1933 bis 1939." *Werkstattgeschichte* 18, no. 6 (November 1997).

———. "Radikalisierung und Selbstradikalisierung 1939: Die Geburt des Reichsicherheitsamtes aus dem Geist des völkischen Massenmords." In *Die Gestapo im Zweiten Weltkrieg: Heimatfront und besetztes Europa,* edited by Gerhard Paul and Klaus-Michael Mallman. Darmstadt: Wissenschaftliche Buchgesellschaft, 2000.

———. "Violence against Jews in Germany, 1933–1939." In *Probing the Depths of German Antisemitism: German Society and the Persecution of the Jews, 1933–1941,* edited by David Bankier. New York: Berghahn, 2000.

Wildt, Michael, ed. *Die Judenpolitik des SD 1935 bis 1938: Eine Dokumentation.* Munich: Oldenbourg, 1995.

Wilhelm, Hans-Heinrich. *Die Einsatzgruppe A der Sicherheitspolizei und des SD 1941/42.* Frankfurt/Main: Peter Lang, 1996.

Winkler, Heinrich August. "Im Schatten von Versailles: Das deutsch-polnische Verhältnis während der Weimarer Republik." In *Deutsche und Polen: 100 Schlüsselbegriffe,* edited by Ewa Kobylińska, Andreas Lawaty, and Rüdiger Stephan. Munich: Piper, 1992.

Wippermann, Wolfgang. "Der 'Deutsche Drang nach Osten': Ideologie und Wirklichkeit eines politischen Schlagwortes." In *Impulse der Forschung*. Vol. 35. Darmstadt: Wissenschaftliche Buchgesellschaft, 1981.

——. *Der Ordenstaat als Ideologie: Das Bild des Deutschen Ordens in der deutschen Geschichtsschreibung und Publizistik*. Berlin: Colloquium Verlag, 1979.

Witter, Robert E. *Die deutsche Militärpolizei im Zweiten Weltkrieg*. Wölferscheim-Berstadt: Podzun-Pallas, 1995.

Zabierowski, Stanisław. "Zbrodnie Wehrmachtu W Południowo-Wschodniej Części Polski." In *Biuletyn Głównej Komisji Badania Zbrodni Hitlerowskich W Polsce*. Vol. 32. Warsaw: Wydawnictwo Prawnicze, 1987.

Zentrale Stelle der Landesjustizverwaltungen. "Einsatzgruppen in Polen: Einsatzgruppen der Sicherheitspolizei, Selbstschutz, und andere Formationen in der Zeit vom 1 September 1939 bis Frühjahr 1940." Vol. 1, Ludwigsburg, 10 June 1962.

——. "Einsatzgruppen in Polen: Einsatzgruppen der Sicherheitspolizei, Selbstschutz, und andere Formationen in der Zeit vom 1 September 1939 bis Frühjahr 1940." Vol. 2, Ludwigsburg, 20 May 1963.

Zorn, Gerda. *"Nach Ostland geht unser Ritt": Deutsche Eroberungspolitik und die Folgen. Das Beispiel Lodz*. Röderberg: Pahl-Rugenstein Verlag, 1988.

Zukier, Henri. "The 'Mindless Years'? A Reconsideration of the Psychological Dimensions of the Holocaust, 1938–1945." *Holocaust and Genocide Studies* 11, no. 2 (Fall 1997).

INDEX

Abwehr (Military
Counterintelligence), 10, 16,
22, 75, 82, 116
Aktion Schwedenhöhe. See
Bydgoszcz
Allenstein (Olsztyn), 46, 48
Anti-Semitism. *See* Jews, German
prejudice against
Armed Forces High Command. *See*
Oberkommando der Wehrmacht
Armies
Third, 48, 59, 103, 105, 108
Fourth, 44, 59, 62, 102
Eighth, 17, 43, 109–110, 126,
129, 154, 175
Tenth, 40, 129, 174
Fourteenth, 37, 75, 97, 99, 133,
175, 193
Army Corps
I Corps, 48, 130
II Corps, 46, 72
III Corps, 62, 66–67, 73
VIII Corps, 75–76, 91, 125
X Corps, 43, 169
XI Corps, 170
XIII Corps, 43, 109, 154,
161–165, 169, 175
XV Corps, 110
XVI Corps, 169
XVII Corps, 75
XVIII Corps, 97, 193
XIX Corps, 46
XXII Corps, 97
XXVI Corps, 105
Army Groups
North, 10, 43, 59, 125–126

South, 17, 43, 59, 76, 83, 110,
126
Army High Command. *See*
Oberkommando des
Heeres

Będzin, 75, 80, 90–91
Best, Werner
and atrocities, 84
and formation of
Einsatzgruppen, 12–13, 15, 21,
29–30, 53, 55–57, 228
and Operation TANNENBERG, 20,
22
Beutel, Lothar, 12, 15, 43–44, 53,
56, 60, 62, 67–69, 71,
101–103
Białystok, 102
Bischoff, Helmut, 44–45, 56,
60–61, 69–70, 229
Blaskowitz, Johannes, 43
and atrocities, 175
and the "Polish Question," 7
and XIII Army Corps, 154, 164
Block, Hans, 98–99
Block, Major General, 63
Blomberg, Werner von, 8
Bock, Fedor von, 13, 59, 125–126
Böhm-Bezing, Diether von, 133,
177
Böhm-Tettelbach, Alfred, 110–112,
114
Bolesławiec, 157–158
Both, Kuno Hans von, 27, 132
Braemer, Walter, 62, 67, 69, 71–73,
102, 120

Brandt, Georg, 75, 81, 91, 100, 119–120, 176
Brauchitsch, Walther von, 77
  and atrocities, 88, 117–118, 176–177
  and Hitler, 1, 27
  and invasion of Poland, 1
Briesen, Kurt von, 169
Brunner, Karl, 35–36, 53, 56, 77
Busch, Ernst, 75–77, 81, 91, 125
Bydgoszcz (Bromberg), 40, 46
  pacification of, 61–74, 229

Canaris, Wilhelm
  and atrocities, 21, 99, 116–117
  and cooperation with the SS, 57
Case White, 11, 17, 27
Chefs der Zivilverwaltung (CdZs) (chiefs of civil administration), 19–20, 72
Ciepielów, 182–184
Cochenhausen, Conrad von, 123, 154–155
Cyc ów, 134
Częstochowa, 25, 83, 124, 174

Dabrowa, 75
Daluege, Kurt, 14, 19–20, 120
Damzog, Ernst Paul, 12, 46, 53, 55–56, 103–104, 107
Danzig, 5, 194, 197, 199, 221
Darré, Richard Walter, 3–4
Death's Head Units. *See* SS *Totenkopfverbände*
Demarcation Line, 92, 94–95, 101–102, 108, 232
Der Stürmer, 210
Dietrich, Josef "Sepp," 157, 163–164
Discipline, 174–185, 232

East, German concept of, 206–208

Eastern Jews. *See Ostjuden*
East Upper Silesia, 38, 55, 74–82, 90, 100, 133, 204, 221
Eichman, Adolf, 94
Eicke, Theodor, 21, 110–111, 113
Einsatzgruppen (EGs) (operational groups)
  duties of, 17–18, 23, 228
  formation of, 10–13, 20, 29
  Einsatzgruppe I, 12, 20, 31–38, 75, 82, 90, 92, 97
  Einsatzgruppe II, 12, 38–41, 83–84, 90, 124
  Einsatzgruppe III, 12, 41–43
  Einsatzgruppe IV, 12, 17, 43–46, 60, 68, 70, 90, 101–103
  Einsatzgruppe V, 12, 46–48, 90, 103–104, 108
  Einsatzgruppe VI, 243n71
  Einsatzgruppe von Woyrsch (Special Purpose), 12–13, 48–52, 80–82, 90–92, 96–101
Einsatzkommandos (EKs) (subcommands), 11–12, 15, 17, 20, 23, 29, 36, 76, 85–86, 97, 228
  Einsatzkommando I/I, 32, 37, 76, 78, 96–97
  Einsatzkommando 2/I, 33, 37, 76
  Einsatzkommando 3/I, 34, 37, 76, 98
  Einsatzkommando 4/I, 35, 37, 76
  Einsatzkommando I/II, 39, 83
  Einsatzkommando 2/II, 40, 55
  Einsatzkommando I/III, 41, 43
  Einsatzkommando 2/III, 41–43
  Einsatzkommando I/IV, 44, 60, 67
  Einsatzkommando 2/IV, 45, 60, 62, 71

Einsatzkommando I/V, 46, 48, 55, 103–104
Einsatzkommando 2/V, 46, 48, 103–104
Enthusiasm for war, 197–202
Eppendorf, Lieutenant Colonel, 76
Erlebnisberichte (experience reports), 192–215

Falkenhorst, Nikolaus von, 48
Feldgendarmerie (military police), 83, 97, 117, 204
Feldpostbriefe (soldiers' letters), 192, 206
Fischer, Hans, 12, 15, 40–41, 54
Forster, Albert, 19–20, 72
France, 6–7
Freikorps (volunteer corps), 31, 35, 37, 39, 43, 49–51, 135, 221, 228
Freikorps Ebbinghaus, 75, 78–80, 82
Frontier Guards
  3d, 77, 81, 175–176
  12th, 126
  13th, 126–128
  14th, 126

Gablenz, Eccard Freiherr von, 64, 73
Gebirgsjägerdivisionen (Mountain Divisions)
  1st, 193
  2d, 193
  3d, 193
Gebirgsjägerregimente (Mountain Regiments)
  98th, 196, 201
  99th, 197, 210
  136th Rifle, 195, 202–203
  137th, 200
  137th Rifle, 202–203, 205

  138th, 201, 208
  140th Rifle, 210
Geheime Feldpolizei (GFP) (Secret Field Police), 18–19, 76, 83, 84, 105, 107, 117, 133, 204
Geist, Raymond, 4
Generalgouvernement, 96
Gerke, Ernst, 15, 44
Germanization, 3
Gestapo, 10, 15, 19, 36, 38–42, 44–45, 56, 76, 89, 230
Gienanth, Curt Ludwig Freiherr von, 126
Gliwice (Gleiwitz), 76, 81, 194
Globisch, Alois, 41
Goebbels, Joseph, 196
Göring, Hermann, xiii, 98
Goworowo, 105–108
Graefe, Heinz, 46–47, 54–56, 104
Great Britain, 6–7, 198–200
Groscurth, Helmuth
  and atrocities, 116
  and invasion of Poland, 8
Grudziądz (Graudenz), 102–103, 132
Guderian, Heinz, 46

Haase, General, 67
Hahn, Ludwig, 32–33, 54, 56, 76–79, 96, 229
Halder, Franz, 193
  and atrocities, 13, 116, 176
  and security preparations, 10, 21–22, 57
  and war with Poland, 6–7
Hammer, Walter, 45, 54, 56, 60–61, 71
Hasselberg, Alfred, 34, 54–56, 76, 98
Hellwig, Otto, 50–51, 53–56

Heydrich, Reinhard, xiii, 89
  and cooperation with the army,
    20–21
  and formation of
    Einsatzgruppen, 10, 13, 15,
    29–30, 53–57, 228
  and Operation TANNENBERG, 14,
    19–20, 56–57, 92, 94–96, 113,
    116–120, 228
Himmler, Heinrich, xiii, 49, 65–66,
    68, 77, 83–86, 89, 90, 94,
    107–109, 110, 113–115,
    117–118
Hingnoz, Major General, 96–97
Hitler, Adolf, 68, 77, 107, 198
  and decision for war, 1, 5, 9–10,
    194, 199
  and formation of
    Einsatzgruppen, 10, 14
  and ideological objectives, 2–5,
    9–10, 19, 26–27, 88–89,
    94–96, 116, 227–228
Hitlerjugend (Hitler Youth),
    217–219
Hoepner, Erich, 7
Hoth, Hermann, 110
Huppenkothen, Walter, 15, 22, 36

Infantry Divisions
  2d Motorized, 203
  3d, 60, 123, 125
  4th, 176
  7th, 97, 175
  8th, 75–76
  10th, 123, 154, 164–165, 168,
    204, 217, 219
  17th, 154–155, 158, 160,
    164–165
  19th, 122, 132, 170, 172
  20th Motorized, 46
  21st, 103, 132, 27
  24th, 171, 178
  28th, 75

30th, 169
31st, 175
44th, 75
45th, 75–76
46th, 144–152
50th, 60, 63
206th, 126, 132
208th, 126
228th, 103
239th, 75
252d, 177
Infantry Regiments
  13th, 198
  15th Motorized, 182–184, 199,
    214
  20th, 217–219
  21st, 161–162
  31st, 170–171
  41st, 123, 154, 166, 204, 217,
    219
  42d, 144–152
  48th, 210
  55th, 161
  59th, 132, 201
  85th, 166, 217, 219
  94th, 195
  95th, 162–163
  101st, 214
  121st, 63
  122d, 63
  151st, 198
  179th, 197, 199, 203, 205,
    209
  199th, 203, 208
  309th, 197–198, 201, 207

Jews
  German prejudice against,
    26–27, 174, 177–178, 192,
    208–214, 216, 231
  murder of, 157, 172–174,
    186–190, 232
Jost, Heinz, 16

Katowice, 75–80, 82, 90–91, 229
Keitel, Wilhelm, 108, 116–117
Kempf, Werner, 106–107
Kielce, 75, 83, 211
Kienitz, Werner, 75
Kluge, Günther von, 46
Knobelsdorff, Otto von, 77, 175
Knochen, Helmut, 11
Koch, Erich, 107
Konskie, 174, 186–190
Korück 580, 62, 102
Korück 581, 110
Kraków, 38, 75, 91–92, 94–95, 99, 126
Krichbaum, Wilhelm, 18
Kriminalpolizei (Kripo) (Criminal Police), 13, 15, 19, 36
Kroessinsee, 43, 45, 60
Kruttke, Fritz, 45
Küchler, Georg von, 48, 59, 103–104, 106–109

Lahousen, Erwin, 116
Langhäuser, Rudolf, 76, 83–86
Lebensraum, 2–5, 9, 89, 202
Leeb, Emil, 170
Liphardt, Fritz, 41–43, 54–56
List, Wilhelm, 37, 99–101, 120, 175, 193
Lithuania, 95
Loch, Herbert, 154, 164, 174
Łódź, 23–24, 43, 91, 154, 162, 164–166
Lölgen, Jakob, 233
Łowicz, 170–171
Lublin, 95–98
Lubliniec, 83–85
Lutomiersk, 171
Lviv (Lwów), 96

Mackensen, Eberhard von, 100
Manstein, Erich von, 9

Meisinger, Josef, 44, 60, 102
Metz, Hermann, 126
Military counterintelligence. *See Abwehr*
Military justice, 122, 129–130, 174–178
Military Police. *See Feldgendarmerie*
Mława, 103–104, 108
Mountain Divisions. *See Gebirgsjägerdivisionen*
Mountain Regiments. *See Gebirgsjägerregimente*
Muelverstedt, Police General, 62, 68–70
Müller, Bruno, 33, 54, 56, 76
Müller, Erich, 45, 54
Müller, Heinrich, 113

Nethe, Walther, 64–65
Neuling, Ferdinand, 75
Nonaggression pacts
Germany and Poland, 2–3
Germany and the Soviet Union, 12, 95
Nostitz, Paul, 110–114

Oberkommando der Wehrmacht (OKW) (Armed Forces High Command), 94, 110
and preparations for war, 11
Oberkommando des Heeres (OKH) (Army High Command)
and preparations for war, 8, 229–230
and relationship with SS, 13, 68, 84, 88, 94, 100, 108, 116–117, 121–122, 133–134, 230
Olbricht, Friedrich, 170
Operation TANNENBERG, 14, 19, 22, 61–74, 116, 228, 230, 234

Ordnungspolizei (Orpo) (Order
Police), 12–13, 49, 64, 70–71,
81, 90, 96, 99
Ostjuden (Eastern Jews), 88–89,
210, 216, 232
Ostrówek, 154–155
Oświęcim (Auschwitz), 75, 77, 80

Pancke, Günther, 110–111
Panzer Divisions
1st, 138–140
4th, 164, 169
5th, 75, 77
Petzel, Walter, 48, 130, 132
Pilsudski, Jozef, 3
Piotrków Trybunalski, 174
Police Battalion 6 (Motorized), 62,
68
Police Battalion 62, 49
Police Battalion 63, 49
Police Battalion 92, 49
Police Battalion 171, 49
Polish intelligentsia
orders for murder of, 13, 20–21,
68, 72, 77, 228, 234
reprisals against, 133–134
Polish people
attacks on ethnic Germans by,
62, 64, 73, 202–203
German prejudice against,
23–28, 177, 192, 197–198,
202–207, 215–216, 222–225,
231, 233
Polizeigruppe I (Police Group 1), 49
Poznań, 33, 43, 128, 132, 204,
221
Pragmatic violence, principle of,
142–143
Prisoners of war (POWs), 179–185
Propaganda
anti-Polish, 23–28, 62, 192–193,
196
anti-Semitic, 26–27, 210

Przemyśl, 96–97, 99–100, 210
Pułtusk, 102–103

Rasch, Emil Otto, 15, 49, 53–56,
81, 99–100
Rawa Mazowiecka, 172–173, 180
Reichenau, Walter von, 40,
109–110, 129
Reichskriegsgericht (Reich War
Court), 175–176
Reichssicherheitshauptamt (RSHA)
(Reich Security Main Office),
95
Reinhardt, Georg-Hans, 169
Reprisals, 121–143
in Bydgoszcz, 61–74, 229–230
in Częstochowa, 124, 144–152,
230
history of, 135–137
in Katowice, 78–80, 229–230
in Konskie, 186–190
in Rawa Mazowiecka, 172–174
Ribbentrop, Joachim von, 5, 95
Riefenstahl, Leni, 186, 190
Rollkommando (small unit), 98–99
Rosenberg, Alfred, 90
Rundstedt, Gerd von, 83–86
Rux, Karl-Heinz, 15, 39–40, 55

San River, 92, 94–96, 98–99, 101
Schaefer, Emanuel, 12, 38–39,
53–56, 83–84, 86
Scharpwinkel, Wilhelm, 41–43,
55–56
Schefe, Robert, 46–47, 54–56, 104
Schellenberg, Walter, 30
Schenckendorff, Max von,
126–129, 132
Schmer, Johann, 36–37, 53, 56
Schoene, Edmund, 60–61, 63
Schwantes, Günther, 170
Secret Field Police. *See Geheime
Feldpolizei*

Seeckt, Hans von, 6
Sens, Otto, 15, 20, 39–40, 53, 56, 83
Sicherheitsdienst (SD) (Security Service), 13, 15, 19, 21, 36, 38, 41, 44, 47–48, 53, 75
Sicherheitspolizei (Sipo) (Security Police), 13, 15, 19, 36, 42, 44, 48, 50, 53, 65–66, 76, 89, 102, 133
Sieradz, 161–162
Six, Franz, 10–11
Sonderfahndungslisten (wanted persons lists), 14–16, 60–61, 72, 78, 82, 99
Sorsche, Konrad, 63
Sosnowiec, 75, 80, 90, 93
SS *Leibstandarte* "Adolf Hitler," 109–110, 154, 157–159, 161, 163–165, 174–175
SS Panzer Division Kempf, 103, 105–106
SS *Standarte* "Germania," 75–77
SS *Totenkopfverbände* (SS Death's Head units), 20–21, 109–114
Stahlecker, Franz, 94
Stahlhelm (Steel Helmet) (right-wing organization), 32, 35, 42, 224
Stalin, Josef, 95
Stanek, Leo, 41
Strauss, Adolf, 46, 72
Streckenbach, Bruno, 12, 31–32, 53, 56, 75–76, 84, 92, 96–97
Sturmabteilung (SA) (storm troopers), 32, 34–35, 52, 89, 219–220, 225

Teilkommandos (TKs), 36, 46, 60–61, 63, 67, 78, 83
Tesmer, Hans, 11–12, 29–30, 55–57
Torzeniec, 154

Trummler, Hans, 48, 50–53, 55–56

Ulex, Wilhelm, 169

Vernichtungskrieg (war of annihilation), xiv–xv, 136, 191, 226–227, 235
Versailles Treaty, 7
Vilnius (Wilno), 95
Vogel, Kurt, 60–61, 67
Volksdeutsche (ethnic Germans), 20, 62, 64–65, 70, 134–135, 196–198, 207
and *Selbstschutz* (self-defense units), 135, 221

Wagner, Eduard, 77
and atrocities, 100, 116–118, 120
and cooperation with SS, 13–14, 20, 57, 94, 120
and war with Poland, 11, 17
Wanted persons lists. *See Sonderfahndungslisten*
Warlimont, Walter, 95
Warsaw, 24, 91, 102, 116
Wedel, Hasso von, 193
Wehrmachtpropagandaamt (Wehrmacht Propaganda Office), 193
Weichs, Maximilian Freiherr von, 154, 164
Wieruszów, 154, 157–158, 174
Włocławek, 110–114, 174
Wodrig, Albert, 105–106
Wolfstieg, Friedrich, 49, 81
Woyrsch, Udo von, 12, 48–49, 53, 55–56, 80–82, 90–91, 99–101, 119

Zentralstelle II P (Central Office II P in Poland), 10–11
Złoczew, 159–161